T0304138

ROUTLEDGE LIBRARY EDITIONS:
THE ECONOMICS AND BUSINESS OF
TECHNOLOGY

Volume 46

GROWTH POLICY IN THE AGE OF HIGH TECHNOLOGY

GROWTH POLICY IN THE AGE OF HIGH TECHNOLOGY
The Role of Regions and States

Edited by
JURGEN SCHMANDT AND ROBERT WILSON

LONDON AND NEW YORK

First published in 1990 by Unwin Hyman

This edition first published in 2018
by Routledge
2 Park Square, Milton Park, Abingdon, Oxon OX14 4RN

and by Routledge
711 Third Avenue, New York, NY 10017

Routledge is an imprint of the Taylor & Francis Group, an informa business

© 1990 J. Schmandt, R. Wilson and contributors

British Library Cataloguing in Publication Data
A catalogue record for this book is available from the British Library

ISBN: 978-1-138-50336-6 (Set)
ISBN: 978-1-351-06690-7 (Set) (ebk)
ISBN: 978-0-8153-5870-1 (Volume 46) (hbk)
ISBN: 978-1-351-12171-2 (Volume 46) (ebk)

Publisher's Note
The publisher has gone to great lengths to ensure the quality of this reprint but points out that some imperfections in the original copies may be apparent.

Disclaimer
The publisher has made every effort to trace copyright holders and would welcome correspondence from those they have been unable to trace.

GROWTH POLICY IN THE AGE OF HIGH TECHNOLOGY

The Role of Regions and States

EDITED BY

Jurgen Schmandt

Robert Wilson

Boston
UNWIN HYMAN
London Sydney Wellington

Unwin Hyman, Inc.,
8 Winchester Place, Winchester, Mass. 01890, USA

Published by the Academic Division of
Unwin Hyman Ltd,
15/17 Broadwick Street, London W1V 1FP, UK

Allen & Unwin (Australia) Ltd,
8 Napier Street, North Sydney, NSW 2060, Australia

Allen & Unwin (New Zealand) Ltd in association with the
Port Nicholson Press Ltd, Compusales Building,
75 Ghuznee Street, Wellington 1, New Zealand

First published in 1990

Library of Congress Cataloging in Publication Data

Growth policy in the age of high technology: the role of regions
and states / Jurgen Schmandt & Robert Wilson.
p.   cm.
Includes bibliographical references.
ISBN 0-04-445621-2
1. Technology and state—United States—States. 2. Regional
planning—United States. 3. High technology industries—United
States—Location. 4. United States—Economic conditions—Regional
disparities. I. Wilson, Robert Hines. II. Title.
T21.S34 1990

338.97306—dc20   89-24989
                                                     CIP

British Library Cataloguing in Publication Data

Growth policy in the age of high technology: the role of
regions and states.
1. United States. Regional economic development
I. Schmandt, Jurgen II. Wilson, Robert
330.973

ISBN 0-04-445621-2

Typeset in 10 on 11 point Melior Roman and
printed in Great Britain at the University Press, Cambridge

Contents

III STATE DEVELOPMENT STRATEGIES

13   University–industry R & D relationships   313

Irwin Feller

14   State government–university cooperation   344

Karen M. Paget

15   Creating and sustaining the U.S. technopolis   381

David V. Gibson & Raymond W. Smilor

IV CONCLUSIONS

List of tables

Notes on contributors

Rob Atkinson is a doctoral candidate in the Department of City and Regional Planning at the University of North Carolina, Chapel Hill. He received a master's degree in city and regional planning from the University of Oregon and has worked as a research associate for the National Association of State Development Agencies. His doctoral dissertation examines the process by which state technology innovation policy is made.

Richard Barke received a B.S. in physics from the Georgia Institute of Technology, and M.A. and Ph.D. degrees in political science from the University of Rochester. He has been employed as a geophysicist and as a transportation environmental planner. He has published articles, papers, and chapters on a range of science and technology policy issues, including hazardous waste regulation, technical standard-setting, transportation regulation, and state technology and economic development policy. Among his publications is *Science, technology, and public policy* (1986). Dr. Barke currently is an associate professor of political science in the School of Social Sciences at the Georgia Institute of Technology, where he teaches courses in science and technology policy, regulatory policy, research design, and American government. He is a co-founder of the Science and Technology Studies Section of the American Political Science Association.

Ed Bergman is director, Economic and Community Development Area of Specialization; professor and director, Institute for Economic Development, University of North Carolina at Chapel Hill. Dr. Bergman teaches courses in local economic development and industrial policy, labor market and employment planning, and planning theory. He directs a U.S.I.A.-funded faculty exchange program between the University of North Carolina at Chapel Hill and the Vienna University of Economics. Bergman consults with Southern Growth Policies Board, Southern Technology Council, and other public and private clients. He has also maintained an active research agenda with funding from numerous foundations (Ford, Kellogg, Aspen and Mary Reynolds Babcock), federal agencies (EDA, NSF, DOT, HUD, DOL) and various state programs. His publications and research focus on industrial restructuring among state and local economies, regional development potential across metropolitan and rural areas, and comparative U.S.–European development policy.

Marianne K. Clarke is a senior policy analyst in the Economics, Trade and Development Program of the National Governors' Association's Center for Policy Research. She is responsible for conducting research and providing technical assistance to states in the areas of science and technology policy, and economic and community development. She is the author of numerous reports including *Economic development policies and programs, The role of science and technology in economic competitiveness*, and *An introduction to the economic development planning process.* Ms. Clarke holds an M.P.A. in urban affairs from American University and a B.A. in sociology from Newton College of the Sacred Heart.

Irwin Feller is a professor of economics, director of the Institute for Policy Research and Evaluation; director, graduate program in policy analysis, the Pennsylvania State University. His research centers on the economics of technological change, diffusion of innovations in the public and private sector, intergovernmental science relationships, and university-industry relationships. His articles have been published in the *Journal of Policy Analysis and Management, Policy Sciences, Policy Studies Review,* and *Knowledge,* as well as other journals. He is the author of *Universities and state governments: a study in policy analysis* (1986). Dr. Feller has received research grants from the National Science Foundation, the U.S. Department of Agriculture, and the National Aeronautics and Space Administration. He has served as a consultant to the president's Office of Science and Technology Policy, National Science Foundation, U.S. Office of Education, Ford Foundation, National Governors' Association, National Conference of State legislatures, and others.

R. Scott Fosler is vice president and director of government studies for the Committee for Economic Development. He is editor of *The new economic role of American states* (Oxford University Press, 1988) and served as director for CED's policy statement, *Leadership for dynamic state economies.* He is a former member of the Montgomery (Maryland) County Council and served two terms as president of the Washington Metropolitan Area Council of Governments (COG). Mr. Fosler is a member of the National Academy of Public Administration and serves on the Board of Directors of the National Civic League and the Public Administration Service. He is a graduate of the Woodrow Wilson School of Public and International Affairs at Princeton University, and Dickinson College. Mr. Fosler has authored numerous publications on public policy and management, productivity, economic development, and public-private partnership.

David V. Gibson is an assistant professor in the Department of Management Science and Information Systems in the College and Graduate School of

Business at the University of Texas at Austin, and a research fellow in the IC2 Institute. He received a Ph.D. in sociology (organizational behavior and communication theory) from Stanford. Dr. Gibson's research and publications focus on the management of information systems, cross-cultural communication and management, and technology transfer.

Amy Glasmeier holds a Ph.D. from the University of California at Berkeley, Graduate Program in City and Regional Planning, and is an assistant professor in city and regional planning at the University of Texas at Austin. She has served as consultant to the Congressional Office of Technology Assessment on high-technology industries and regional development. Currently, in collaboration with Dr. Norman Glickman of Rutgers University, she is completing a major research project sponsored by the Economic Development Administration of the U.S. Department of Commerce. This work explores the regional development implications of foreign direct investment in America. Dr. Glasmeier was invited to be one of four organizing faculty members at the First Annual Conference of Urban Economics and Planning in Beijing, China. Her other current work includes a study of the rôle of distributors and merchants in regional development, the evolution of the world watch industry, and the U.S. Southern regional political economy.

W. Norton Grubb is an economist who has taught at the LBJ School of Public Affairs at the University of Texas at Austin and now teaches at the School of Education at the University of California at Berkeley. His major interests include the rôle of education in labor markets, vocational education, public policy issues in education and in other social programs for young children. He is a member of the board of directors of the Center for Research in Vocational Education at the University of California at Berkeley.

Timothy Lewington is a doctoral student in geography at Syracuse University. His research interests include economic development, technological change, and public policy.

Edward J. Malecki received his B.A. degree in international studies from Ohio State University in 1971 and his Ph.D. in Geography in 1975. He is presently professor of geography at the University of Florida, Gainesville. He was previously on the faculty at the University of Oklahoma, Norman, where he was also a Research Fellow in the Science and Public Policy Program. In 1982 he was a visiting researcher in the Centre for Urban and Regional Development Studies at the University of Newcastle-upon-Tyne, Newcastle, England. He has lectured in several countries, including Canada, West Germany, Sweden, and The Netherlands, and at the University of Glasgow, University of Sussex, University of Newcastle, Boston University, University of Iowa, University of Nebraska, and the University of Washington. He is co-author of *Energy from the West*, and is the author or co-author of four research reports, and author or co-author of over 60 book chapters and papers in such journals as: *Economic Geography, Research Policy, Journal of the American Planning Association, Regional Studies, Technology Review,* and *Technovation.* He is currently working on a book entitled *Regional economic development: a technological perspective.*

Ray Marshall is a former U.S. Secretary of Labor and current holder of the Audre and Bernard Rapoport Centennial Chair in Economics and Public Affairs, the University of Texas at Austin. He is the author or co-author of 25 books and monographs and approximately 100 articles in professional journals and chapters in books on such topics as economic policy, rural development, industrial relations, employment of minorities and women, the international migration of workers, agriculture, labor markets, trade unions, industrial policy and the impact of technology on employment. His current research interests include labor and economic policy; the competitiveness of American industry; technology, the economy and education; and the employment problems of women.

Karen M. Paget, director of the California Policy Seminar of the University of California, has had a wide range of political, administrative, and academic experience. She holds a doctorate in political science from the University of Colorado, and has taught there as well as at the Western Australian Institute of Technology. She was elected twice to the Boulder, Colorado City Council—serving also as Deputy Mayor during her second term—and worked as staff to the Colorado legislature. She was a Carter administration appointee to ACTION, the federal government's principal agency for volunteer service programs, where she managed the domestic program and a budget of $128 million. For four years she was executive director of the Youth Project, a public foundation in Washington, D.C. that supports social change organizations at local, regional, state, and national levels. Prior to coming to the Policy Seminar, she was a Fellow at the Institute of Politics in Harvard University's Kennedy School of Government.

John Rees is professor and head of the Geography Department at the University of North Carolina at Greensboro. He received his Ph.D. from the London School of Economics and has also taught at the University of Texas at Dallas and Syracuse University. Dr. Rees's research interests include economic development, industrial location and the impacts of public policy and technical change on regional growth in the United States. He has edited three books and written over 50 journal articles and book chapters on these topics. In addition to several research grants from the National Science Foundation, Dr. Rees has conducted studies for the Joint Economic Committee of Congress, the General Accounting Office, the Office of Technology Assessment, the Economic Development Administration and the U.S. Department of Housing and Urban Development.

Stuart A. Rosenfeld is the deputy director for the Southern Growth Policies Board and the director of the Southern Technology Council in Research Triangle Park, North Carolina. He has an Ed.D. in education planning, social policy, and administration from Harvard University, an M.S. in educational philosophy from the University of Wisconsin-Milwaukee, and a B.S. cum laude in chemical engineering from the University of Wisconsin-Madison. Dr. Rosenfeld worked for General Electric Company as an engineer and management scientist and later directed a private alternative school in Vermont. In 1976 he joined the National Institute of Education as a policy fellow and then as a senior associate. Dr. Rosenfeld has written extensively on education, economic development, and technology policy in periodicals, including *Education Week, Phi Delta Kappa, Progressive, VocEd, Economic Development Quarterly*, and *Forum on Applied Research and Public Policy* as well as producing numerous monographs for the U.S. Department of Education and the Southern Growth Policies Board. He has contributed chapters to many books and was principal author of *After the factories* and *Technology, the economy and vocational education*. Dr. Rosenfeld represented the United States in two international studies on education and local development for the Organization for Economic Cooperation and Development (OECD) in Paris.

Jurgen Schmandt is professor at the LBJ School of Public Affairs, the University of Texas at Austin, and director of the Center for Growth Studies, HARC. He has published books on nutrition policy, the acid rain dispute between Canada and the United States, and, most recently, on new state rôles in economic development, water management and telecommunications. His research has focused on the social and policy implications of science and technology. He is currently working on the regional impacts of global climate change. He was a member of the Governor's Science and Technology Council and a senior environmental fellow at the U.S. Environmental Protection Agency. He has previously served as associate director of Harvard University's Program on Technology and Society. At the Organization for Economic Cooperation and Development in Paris, he directed studies of member countries' science policies.

Raymond W. Smilor is executive director of the IC2 Institute and associate professor of management in the Graduate School of Business at The University of Texas at Austin. He is also chairman of the College on Innovation Management and Entrepreneurship of the Institute of Management Sciences. He has published widely, is a consultant to business and government, and lectures internationally.

Robert Wilson is associate professor at the LBJ School of Public Affairs, the University of Texas at Austin. He received his Ph.D. in city and regional planning from the University of Pennsylvania. Prior to coming to the LBJ

School in 1979, he taught three and one-half years in an urban and regional planning program at the Universidade Federal de Pernambuco in Brazil. Dr. Wilson served as assistant dean of the LBJ School from 1980 to 1983. His current research interests include community-based economic development, urban economic change in Texas, local economic development policy, state science and technology policy, changes in U.S. income distribution, and economic development in Brazil. Dr. Wilson has recently served as consultant to the Organization of American States in Recife, Pernambuco, Brazil. At the LBJ School, he teaches courses on quantitative methods, and seminars in urban and regional economics and state and local economic development policy.

I

The states as actors

1

Introduction: technology, regions, and states

JURGEN SCHMANDT & ROBERT WILSON

A MAJOR REVIVAL of state government has occurred during the last decade. In many policy areas states have seized the initiative to an extent not seen since the beginning of the century. This new activism on the part of state governments is particularly evident in the area of economic development which, in recent years, has become closely linked to technology policy. Some of the state efforts date from the end of the 1970s and early 1980s; many are more recent. Detailed knowledge about what works and what does not is still limited. This volume attempts to fill this gap.

The emergence of the states (or better, their re-emergence, as some of the following chapters will show) as promoters of economic development can be explained by profound changes in the national and global economy and by changes in state government itself. Among authors writing about the new direction of technological and economic change there is agreement that a major economic restructuring is underway. Robert Ayres, for example, views recent advances in science and technology, and their economic implications, as the next industrial revolution.[1] In Ayres's view two powerful technological trends are at work that lead to a radical restructuring of the economy. First, a systematic search for substitutes of limited resources and materials has gained high priority. No leading industrial power today remains self-sufficient in natural resources. The search for petroleum substitutes may seem less urgent than a decade ago, but new energy sources will be necessary to sustain future growth in the next century. Environmental threats further stimulate the search for safer materials and processes. Sustainable growth requires cleaner and safer raw materials. Thus, powerful incentives combine to make the search for new or improved materials a strong thrust of technological innovation now.

A second technological thrust is the result of advances in information processing and data transmission. The previously separate forces of computers and telecommunications are merging, and this results in vastly improved communications capabilities that make possible a radical transformation in manufacturing and the service industries. In manufacturing the change is from mass production of standardized commodities to batch production of advanced technological products. Information-intensive services are growing rapidly because they are needed for high value-added manufacturing.

The two trends have in common that basic scientific advances must precede new technological applications and the growth of new industries. Taken together, the science–technology connection has a profound impact on the spatial organization of the economy. Many manufacturing sectors have experienced declines in absolute levels of employment, due to the offshore location of traditional industries and the introduction of labor-saving technology. The economies of regions with large shares of traditional manufacturing firms have suffered. The spatial dynamics in manufacturing of advanced technological products, however, are different. Computer-assisted production techniques require proximity and interaction between research centers and production facilities. The rôle of research and development changes from a front-end activity to frequent interaction with all stages of the production process. Similarly, customers of high-tech products need access to specialized service and maintenance operations. While standardized industrial goods will continue to be manufactured in areas benefiting from low-cost labor, often found in Third World countries, complex technological products are manufactured in proximity to advanced research centers and large customers.

By using automated production techniques some traditional, standardized goods may again be produced domestically at competitive prices. Increasingly, a new international division of labor is emerging between offshore (standardized, large numbers) and domestic (batch, small numbers) production. Increased competition in foreign markets and the penetration of foreign investment in the United States have also played a significant rôle in the spatial restructuring of the U.S. economy. New state initiatives aimed at regional economic development need to be viewed in this context of a global industrial restructuring.

The new economic geography of the country poses serious analytical problems. In particular, what is the correct unit of analysis? Geographers inform us that there is no single correct way to "regionalize" an economy; rather the definition of region will vary depending on the subject under study. On one hand, we speak of different regional adaptations to economic restructuring. For example, the industrial heartland, which is a multistate region, has demonstrated relative declines in its share of national manufacturing employment. We know, however, that this region is not homogeneous, and various areas within this region have responded differently. Rural areas have been affected differently when compared to the cities. In addition, some industrial sectors in a region may be sensitive to forces outside the region to a much greater extent than other sectors. To take an extreme case, the financial sector in New York is relatively disconnected from the local economy, but rather attuned to other financial centers like London, Tokyo, and Los Angeles. Each of these instances can produce a different form of regionalization.

The search for the "correct" definition of an economic region is unending, but this need not obstruct our study. In this volume we are concerned with public policy at the state level. Region, therefore, will generally refer to the economy of a state or of some subarea of the state. We fully recognize that a state economy is not a satisfactory analytic category for economic geography, but we must be attuned to political geography and jurisdiction given our focus on policy. If a regional policy is not implemented by the federal government, state governments are the only general government available. Specialized regional governments, whether encompassing several states or parts of one state, have limited powers. States, at least in theory, have broad jurisdiction over taxes, spending, and legislation. The key question, however, is whether a state government has policy instruments sufficiently powerful to affect the level and growth rate of its economy. Alternatively, are economic forces originating outside the state at work that render state action ineffective? These questions are central to this book.

While recent technological and market changes have brought economic dislocation to many states, they also offer opportunities to those states that know how to capture them. For most of the post-World War

II period, state governments have deferred to the federal government for policy initiatives dealing with urban and regional economic distress. In the 1980s, however, state and city governments began to assume more active and independent rôles in policy concerning economic development, either to overcome difficulties or to build new capacities. As a matter of fact, both strategies are often pursued simultaneously.

The expanded rôle of state government in regional development is part of a larger trend of states beginning to play a more active rôle in a number of policy areas. A survey on state innovations was compiled in 1982 by the National Governors' Association. Governors and top staff in each state were asked to list the programs or management improvements installed by their administrations over the past two to four years (see Table 1.1). Fiscal/non-fiscal management was reported to be the most common area in which states initiated innovative programs and policies. Economic development, environment/energy, income/social services, criminal justice, and education were other areas of innovation. In examining yet another policy area, Scholz found that state regulatory efforts, which had been eclipsed by the rapid growth of federal regulation during the last 15 years, were regaining a more prominent rôle under the Reagan administration's regulatory reforms.[2] In more recent research we have examined innovative state policies in environmental permitting, water management, and telecommunications.[3] Most of these domestic policy areas, except

Table 1.1 State innovations, by policy area (43 states reporting).

Policy area	Total programs	Percent of total
Fiscal management	58	21
Non-fiscal management	54	20
Economic development	36	13
Environment/energy	26	10
Income/social services	26	10
Criminal justice	21	8
Education	19	7
Transportation	10	4
Health	9	3
Natural resources	8	3
Regulatory	4	1
Other	2	1
Total	271	100

Source: Compiled from a 1982 survey conducted by the National Governors' Association, the Council of State Planning Agencies, and the Governors' Center at Duke University, reported in Suzan K. Cheek, "Gubernatorial innovations," *State government,* **56**, 1983, 53–7.

for education, have been dominated by federal policy making since the New Deal period.

We now observe how one domestic policy area after another reverts to a more decentralized pattern of policy making and administration. Philosophically, renewed decentralization in the federal system was a central goal of Republican administrations, dating back to President Nixon. More recently, however, the desire to play a more active rôle in shaping their own future has led Democrats and Republicans alike to build more active and aggressive state initiatives. What started as devolution has become a regional grassroots movement toward more independent involvement on the part of the states.

In our studies of regional water, environmental, and telecommunications policies we also found that states are gradually becoming more competent in dealing with technically complex policy issues, such as environmental permitting, water management or nuclear waste management. Until recently, state personnel and agencies were rarely able to administer data- and research-intensive policies. Now this gap is beginning to be closed. At the same time, we found only limited evidence that state economic development policies take into account longer term resource, infrastructure and environmental concerns.

In economic development, on which we focus in this volume, we find an impressive range of state initiatives. Though substantial political support for these initiatives has built over the last few years, little so far is known about programatic success. A number of generalizations derived from the early round of initiatives, however, can be made.[4] (a) Many of the early efforts focused only on the so-called high-tech sectors, excluding any rôle for technological innovation in traditional sectors. (b) Most programs, even the university-based initiatives, were predominantly focused on business assistance, and excluded other state functions such as infrastructure provision and management of natural resources. (c) Great confidence was placed on the ability of universities to develop and fulfill a technology transfer function. (d) There were expectations of quick, if not immediate, results. (e) Much hope was placed on contributions to state objectives by the private sector, and new state funding remained limited.

State technology policy has evolved over the last few years. Expectations are now more realistic. Policy makers recognize that employment growth in advanced technology sectors will be limited, but employment opportunities generated by technological innovation in traditional manufacturing and services are substantial. In fact, the introduction of new production processes in several traditional industries is starting to blur the distinctions between traditional and advanced technology sectors; segments of the chemical and textile industries are using advanced technology, while some microelectronics industries are maturing quickly. Broadening the focus of state technology and economic policies to include traditional manufacturing and service industries has had the effect of broadening the base of political support for the policies. It also raises questions about the most effective strategies: broad-based structural measures, such as changes in taxation and educational improvements, or targeted programs for highly specific industries or subregions.

A recent feature of the evolution of state policy is the merging of economic development policy and technology policy. The principal state rôle in economic development in the past was industrial recruitment, that is attracting manufacturing firms to a state. The range of economic development programs has expanded substantially and those that deal with high-tech firms and technological innovation become a key focus for state technology policy itself, thus setting the stage for the merging of these two policy areas.

Though much of the technology-focused evolution of regional economic development policy has been widely acclaimed, there are at least two concerns that continue to be neglected. The new state policies largely neglect the question of equity. Seldom are the impacts of technology policy and technological innovation on low-income or disadvantaged workers and on distressed areas within the state's jurisdiction noted or studied. The second concern is that economic development policy has not been extended to longer term state responsibilities, such as infrastructure development and resource and environmental management.

The literature assessing state economic policy is not well developed. It is a relatively new policy field for state government and state action has been driven largely by political pressure for governments to respond quickly to serious economic problems rather than by convincing results of new policy research. In the rush to formulate policies and programs, the analytic foundations were frequently not examined. This volume seeks to contribute to this task. We attempt to improve the empirical and conceptual understanding of state economic policy by exploring four themes:

(a) Do states have instruments sufficiently powerful to influence growth?
(b) Of the range of instruments available, which are most commonly used and with what effectiveness?
(c) How well do the universities and other educational institutions

involved in improving general education and vocational training serve the economic development responsibilities being thrust upon them?

(d) Is state government responding creatively and responsibly to the new needs and opportunities in regional development? Or are there economic or political constraints on state action that prevent it from being a significant actor in regional growth?

The volume is organized in four parts. Part I examines the political and intergovernmental aspects of renewed policy activism of state government, especially in terms of development policy. Part II asks what contribution theory and empirical studies of technology and regional growth can make for assessing state actions aimed at influencing regional growth. Part III evaluates alternative action strategies. Part IV discusses the implications of state policy for institutional innovation and issues of governance.

In Part I, the rôle state government plays in technology and development policy is placed in a historical context. Jurgen Schmandt examines how technological innovation has affected governmental agendas and institutions over time. He argues that today's emerging technologies allow for increased political and governmental decentralization, unlike the heavily centralizing effect of technologies earlier in the century. Also, the rôle the state plays in planning and mobilizing resources may be more important than the traditional rôles in program implementation.

Robert Wilson provides an inventory of policy instruments available to state government and asks three questions. Are state governments using the full range of instruments in their development strategies? Are the available instruments sufficiently powerful to affect levels of economic activity in a state? What political, budgetary, and institutional constraints do states face as they move into the development policy arena?

While economic decline induced many states to adopt development policies and programs, states frequently do so without sound theoretical or empirical justifications. Can states correctly expect to recreate a Silicon Valley or Route 128 through policy instruments available to them? The chapters in Part II examine the forces producing regional economic change. Amy Glasmeier examines location patterns of advanced technology industries. Can these patterns be affected by state government through its various policy instruments? If states can influence location patterns, will these patterns at an intra-state level produce a spatial bias favoring metropolitan regions over rural areas?

It is generally accepted that advanced technology sectors can influence regions. It is less widely recognized that technological innovation in traditional manufacturing can be another effective means of promoting regional growth. Edward Malecki examines technological innovation and regional economic growth. He identifies the limits of using the spatial product cycle model for policy to promote regional growth and then identifies entrepreneurship as the potentially critical factor. This presents two problems: (a) university-led technology policy, in the form of a strong university research capability, is not a sufficient condition for regional growth; and (b) state policies may only have limited ability to affect entrepreneurship.

Edward M. Bergman studies the empirical patterns of technology-dependent growth and state policy initiatives in the Southeast of the United States. He analyzes in particular university research centers and transportation investment. He makes a distinction between two types of technology-dependent growth, one the result of new firm formation and the other the result of expansion of existing firms. Transportation investments and university research parks may be useful in promoting growth of one type but not the other. Since the research parks are the product of explicit state policy, his chapter provides a transition to examining state technology and development policies.

The discussion of state development strategies in Part III begins with a review of existing technology and development policies and programs. Marianne Clarke provides an overview of state science and technology initiatives, including identification of goals and objectives, categorization of programs and future directions. Commercialization of university-based R&D activities is an important dimension of state involvement, but little evaluation research on past efforts is available. She also notes that many states are debating the rôle of education, particularly higher education, in improving the economic health of a state.

R. Scott Fosler examines state business assistance programs. While many of these programs predate the recent state activism in economic development, it is interesting to note that the range of initiatives has expanded substantially and that technology policy and economic development policy have tended to merge. In many of the more recent efforts, innovative institutional arrangements have emerged, frequently with the participation of the private sector.

A criticism of long standing is that technology and development programs have not been adequately evaluated. Not only have performance measures not been embedded in the programs, but rarely are the effects of the programs studied. John Rees and Tim Lewington report on an important effort to rectify this situation. Over 100 companies that were potential clients of advanced technology centers specializing in microelectronics and computer-aided manufacturing were surveyed and their experiences documented. Though these results are preliminary in nature, they suggest that the original objectives of these centers are not being fully achieved, but that some unintentional benefits have accrued. Rees also discusses the methodological problems in evaluating these programs.

While education and training strategies were not important components of early technology and development initiatives, this has changed in recent years. The potential contribution to development is attracting much attention, and education reform has become a central strategy for the states. The National Commission on Excellence in Education, through its report, *A nation at risk*, has placed educational reform on the political agenda of many states. Education and training strategies as instruments for promoting development is an important theme in the reform movement.

Ray Marshall argues that to be effective, a state's elementary and secondary school policies must be related to a coherent economic development strategy. He examines, among others, these questions: (a) What are the main functions of education in the age of high technology? (b) How do a state's explicit or implicit development strategies affect its education policies? (c) What are the implications for education of internationalization, technological innovation, and demographic change? (d) Do the schools really make a difference or does most learning take place outside of (and in spite of) them?

Norton Grubb questions the prevailing wisdom that assumes vocational education and training are effective instruments for development policy. Grubb argues, through an analysis of the market effects of training, that employment growth may not occur even though businesses can benefit through reductions in training costs. The benefits of training programs that many people assume will occur may not. Reform of the system of vocational education and training would be complex, but this reform is required to ensure that the system responds to labor market demand. Part of the solution is the continual evaluation and monitoring of the demand for labor and better coordination among the many institutions that provide vocational education and training.

Stuart Rosenfeld and Robert D. Atkinson examine supply, demand and quality of the scientific and technical laborforce. They conclude that the quality and quantity of scientific and technical resources are more strongly related to geographic areas defined by commuting patterns or state boundaries than to regional geographic territories. While there are regional implications of human resources, the policies and programs that shape them have traditionally been enacted by the federal government, such as in the aftermath of the Sputnik crisis. Now that science and technology are perceived as contributing to economic development, state strategies are much more important, and states must address the needs of their colleges and universities or risk losing their technological competitiveness.

The remaining chapters on alternative strategies consider a set of initiatives that have universities as the major focus of attention. Public universities have been under great pressure to reinforce or expand their links with the private sector. A good deal of information is emerging on these initiatives and there are some surprising results. Irwin Feller examines the relationship between universities and industry in research and development through a technology transfer model. He discovers that the conventional wisdom explaining the reasons for participation of each party may be wrong. He suggests that, at best, this relation may continue but it will be a problematic relationship and, more importantly, it will not have a significant effect on industry and subsequent economic growth. There are other grounds for encouraging these relations, but economic growth is not likely to be one of the products.

The new demands being placed on universities include one for greater cooperation between public universities and state government. Karen Paget examines this demand and notes a shift from the traditional "public service" rôle of universities and professors to one based more upon research. Though, in principle, there should be grounds for extensive collaboration between a university research community and public policy makers, there are fundamental differences between the goals and purposes of universities and government. Based largely on the experience of California, Paget describes how the objectives of the current forms of university/state cooperation differ from those of the past and examines the problems with making the current form effective.

David V. Gibson and Raymond W. Smilor argue that new institutional alliances among business, government and academia are altering the strategy of economic development and diversification. While the emergence of these institutional partnerships has been widely noted, their chapter provides more detailed insight on the interaction among the partners and the specific rôles they tend to play. The authors present a conceptual framework encompassing seven components: university; large corporations; emerging companies; federal government; state government; local government; support groups.

In the concluding part of this book, Richard Barke reviews the chapters in this volume and places them in the context of the literature on recent changes in institutional and technical capacities of state government. Though some of the rôles identified below are those of traditional program implementation, many involve coordination, information provision and mobilization of other institutions. Given the initiatives of and demands on state government identified earlier in this volume, Barke assesses the ability of state governments to respond creatively in this new policy arena. He concludes:

> The most successful state economic development programs could be those in which control and influence become *futile* because of the inherent dynamism of the technological sector. We should expect to see a variety of policy instruments being developed and tested, in various combinations, as states continue to do what they have done so well for more than a century: to continue the experiments in the politics and economics of progress.

It will take the better part of the 1990s to find out whether this optimistic assessment of the new state rôle is justified.

Notes

1 R. U. Ayres, *The next industrial revolution: reviving industry through innovation* (Cambridge, Mass.: Ballinger, 1984).
2 J. T. Scholz, "State regulatory reform and federal regulation," *Policy Studies Review* **1**, November 1981, 347–60.
3 *Environmental permitting in Texas* (Austin: LBJ School of Public Affairs, University of Texas, 1986). J. Schmandt, E. T. Smerdon & J. Clarkson, *State water policies* (New York: Praeger, 1988). J. Schmandt, F. Williams & R. Wilson (eds.) *Telecommunications policy and economic development: the new state role* (New York: Praeger, 1989).
4 J. Schmandt & R. Wilson (eds), "State science and technology policies: an assessment," *Economic Development Quarterly* **2** May 1988, 124–37.

2

Regional rôles in the governance of the scientific state

JURGEN SCHMANDT

Introduction

SUCCESSFUL TECHNOLOGICAL change drives social and economic change. Karl Marx was one of the first to see this connection when he said: "The water mill gives you society with the feudal lord; the steam mill society with the industrial capitalist."[1] The insight expressed here had escaped earlier students of social change, but is fundamental to understanding the course of recent history. Yet Marx was mistaken in postulating a strict cause-and-effect relationship between technology and society. "Soft determinism," a term coined by William James, better describes the relationship. This concept suggests that technological change, once widely accepted, inevitably leads to social and economic change. Yet the exact form and nature of the social response to new technology varies considerably. "Soft determinism" leaves room for a social response that takes into account the history, institutions, and values of a given society. It allows for freedom and options in the ways different people adjust to technological change. There is no absolute freedom, however, because a social response that ignores new technological opportunities, or exploits them inefficiently, will exact the price of inferior standing, economic or otherwise, in the world community.

Since the times of Marx and James the pace of technological change has accelerated, and the impact on the economy has grown ever more important. To cope with the social impact of technological change, it has become customary to call on the government for help. In particular, when change touches upon the livelihood of many people, we expect government to ease the transition. Government has not always played this rôle. At the beginning of the Industrial Revolution, there was less governmental intervention in the economy than today, and what little intervention did occur was mostly the work of state or local governments, not the national government.

In this chapter I will examine the interplay between regional and national policy responses to technological change. My hypothesis is that, until recently, technological change provided strong incentives for shifting political power from the regional to the national level. Technology was a centralizing force—economically, socially, and politically. The current thrust of technological change may allow for a partial reversal of this trend, leading to more decentralization and a more balanced division of labor between regional and national policies.

I begin with a brief discussion of the state rôle in the American federal system; I then review the historical evidence. Regional initiatives in response to technological change dominated the first half of the 19th century. This regional focus gave way to national policies in the decades following the Civil War. At this time regional economies were integrated into one large national market. In response to rapid industrialization and urbanization the U.S. government, along with the governments of other industrial powers, faced two large new tasks: (a) How could the country reap the benefits of rapid industrial growth while at the same time retaining public control of an increasingly powerful industrial sector? (b) How could the government protect workers and their families from the risks associated with the new industrial environment? The policies that emerged in response to these tasks led to a decisive shift from regional to national decision making. Large centralized governments, increased national legislation, and nationwide policies became the norm. In the United States the trend toward centralization in government was further strengthened by the policy demands created by the Depression of the 1930s, World War II and the following Cold War, and the new environmental and resource concerns that began to surface in the 1960s. All of these developments required political will, organization, and resources at a scale that could not be mustered at the regional level.

The historical account is designed to provide a perspective for asking how the recent resurgence of the states will affect the century-old trend toward political centralization. The states, as we have witnessed over the course of the last decade, have initiated innovative policies in economic development, resource management, science and technology, education, welfare and social services, and related fields. There are several reasons for this shift. The states have acted partly because the federal government has actively sought to reduce its rôle. Conservative administrations have called for less government involvement at the federal level. In addition, the recognition is spreading that national solutions to regional or local problems are sometimes elusive or inefficient. There are also more positive reasons behind the new state activism. Many states have regained the confidence that they can make a difference in shaping their own future. Rather than wait for federal directives, they prefer to find their own solutions to new policy needs. This then is the central question for this chapter: If technology in the past has strengthened centralized policy making, are there reasons to believe that the current thrust of technological change will support regional action, at least in some policy areas?

The state rôle in the federal system

By "regional government" I mean the governments of the American states. There are other forms of regional government, such as regional compacts between states, or councils of governments (COGs) within states. These organizations are of fairly recent origin and have been created to address specific policy needs.[2] But none of these bodies is a general-purpose government, and none has been a constituent part of the American system of government. Therefore, I focus on state governments.

The balancing of political power between the states and the federal government was a central issue confronting the framers of the Constitution. When the Union was formed, the states were powerful, the federal government was not. The states, in the early history of the Union, acted in much the same way as they had during the Colonial period. The colonies, because of their great distance from the Crown, had long developed the habit of acting independently and in pursuit of their individual interests. The original 13 states continued in this tradition. The Constitution viewed them as *the* general government responsible for most aspects of domestic policy. Among the framers, Madison was most explicit on the need for a balanced political system: "Let it be tried," he wrote, "whether any middle ground can be taken, which will at once support a due supremacy of the national authority, and leave in force the local authorities so far as they can be subordinately useful." He foresaw that the ideal would be difficult to achieve: "It will be fortunate if the struggle [between the nation and the states] should end in a permanent equilibrium of powers."[3]

The Constitution enumerates specific powers as the exclusive domain of the federal government. In the economic realm, these include the authority to regulate foreign and interstate commerce. The interstate commerce clause (Article 1, Section 8) was later used extensively by the Congress to broaden the federal rôle in economic policy. Other provisions in the Constitution preserved the strong rôle of the states. They were to control business, labor, farming, trades, and the professions. Licenses and franchises were to be issued by the states. They were also responsible for the provision of education, welfare, health, highways, canals, and other public works. The Tenth Amendment codified the strong state rôle: "The powers not delegated to the United States by the constitution are reserved to the states respectively, or to the people." A few years after the Civil War, the Supreme Court reaffirmed the constitutional principle of shared powers between central and regional governments, and did so in the strongest possible terms: "The constitution, in all of its provisions, looks to an indestructible union, composed of indestructible states."[4]

Yet only a short time after this reaffirmation of a strong state rôle, the policy-making powers of the states began to decline. And this trend was constantly reinforced over the course of the next century. Madison and his followers would have been dismayed. The federalists would have objected to the loss of state power because the states could no longer act as a check on federal power. This was a serious change that, in their view, would have undermined the very foundations of the American system of governance. Later generations emphasized the variety and experimentation that state initiatives contributed, as in Justice Brandeis's concept of the states as laboratories of democracy. From this perspective the loss of state initiatives would have increased uniformity, reduced opportunities to learn from the experience of other states, and eliminated the possibility of building federal policy on the best state innovations. As we shall see, powerful forces explain the shift from regional to central government. "Modernization"—the massive structural changes in technology, economy, society, and the international order—required a strong national government. Yet in the process the country came close to disabling a workable federal system of governance.

Not long ago this was a reasonable prediction of the future of American federalism. In the mid-1960s, after having served a term as governor of North Carolina, Terry Sanford visited other states throughout the country. He wanted to see whether his experience at home—the inability of the state to cope with new policy demands—was a common occurrence. He found the states in crisis, incapable of dealing effectively with the important issues of the day.[5] At the height of the Depression a leading scholar of public administration in the United States had already come to a more radical conclusion: "I do not predict that the states will go, but affirm that they have gone... . [They have] gone because they were unable to deal even inefficiently with the imperative, the life and death tasks of the new national economy."[6]

What accounted for this decline? How had the traditionally strong state rôle become irrelevant to the policy issues that needed to be faced in the 1930s and 1960s, two periods that made unusually strong demands on government to resolve pressing social needs? And is the decline reversible? I shall argue that technological change played a key rôle in these developments. Thus, the following historical account will provide a base for answering three broad questions:

(a) Why has technological change advanced the emergence of centralized national and the decline of regional policy making?
(b) Do today's leading technologies offer the opportunity for less centralization in policy making?
(c) Would more decentralized policy making be feasible under current economic and social conditions?

In asking these questions I make the assumption that decentralized action, wherever appropriate for the task at hand, is preferable to centralized action. I hold this to be an important principle of democracy in general, and believe that it is even more fundamental to the functioning of a federally structured democracy. At the same time, the traditional arguments against localized democracy[7]—factionalism, narrowness, resistance to change, maintenance of regional inequities—remain valid and must be considered in searching for the right balance between federal and regional actions.

Early state promotion of economic development

Two chains of events come into play in asking how technology has influenced political centralization and decentralization. The first is the contribution of technological change to the development of the United States as a large common market and a world industrial power. The second deals with policies on the part of the states and the federal government aimed at promoting and regulating technology. Both stories have been told independently, but little attention has been given to the linkages between them.[8] In the brief sketch offered here I emphasize how closely the two themes are intertwined.

There are three stages to the story. In the first century after independence, promotion and regulation of technology played an important rôle at the state level. During the following century the federal rôle became dominant. At present, a more balanced division of labor between state and federal rôles seems to be emerging. But it is impossible to say whether this trend is temporary or will establish itself firmly.

At the time of independence the U.S. economy was mostly agrarian, and the country lagged behind Britain in the technologies of the Industrial Revolution—iron making, steam power, and the cotton industry. State initiatives involving technology were small compared with today's standards, but they were far from negligible. Several states supplied venture capital. In so doing, they sought to stimulate local business, increase land values, and improve the commercial and industrial prospects for the regional economy. Agriculture was a favorite target of state investments. Nine states subsidized silk production. Georgia maintained public warehouses for the grading and storing of tobacco.[9]

After independence the first domestic priority in the United States was improvement of the transportation system, and this task was initially addressed by the states. Several federal initiatives failed. State and federal governments shared the view that the shortage of capital made it necessary to assist public works. State governments rose to the task by letting contracts to private enterprises for surface as well as water transportation projects. With the use of private–public cooperation many turnpikes were built. Private companies did the construction work while state and local governments provided assistance for the acquisition of land and gave the right to charge a toll. However, it soon became obvious that competing local interests and rivalries limited the usefulness of this approach. Competition led to many economically questionable projects, and scarce resources were squandered.

To improve this situation, a federal program was proposed by Albert Gallatin, who served as secretary of the treasury under President Jefferson. In 1808 he submitted to the Senate an ambitious plan for building a system of federal roads and canals.[10] The estimated cost exceeded three years' worth of the entire federal budget. Both Madison and Monroe favored internal improvements. They concluded, however, that the Constitution did not warrant such large undertakings by the federal government. Following the war of 1812, another vision of bold federal action was advocated by John C. Calhoun, then a congressman from South Carolina: "Let us bind the republic together with a perfect system of roads and canals. Let us conquer space."[11] But only a few years later, Calhoun had changed his mind and became an ardent defender of states' rights.

That the federal government should play a limited rôle was also a widely held view during "the great internal improvements mania of the 1820s and 1830s."[12] President Jackson vetoed a congressional project proposing support for road construction in Kentucky. He did so for two reasons. The federal government, in his view, should not support a project that was located entirely within the confines of a single state. More important, he found it improper to mix the funds of the federal government with those of private citizens who would have subscribed stock in support of the project.[13] After Jackson's veto, Congress appropriated no funds for public improvements until after the Civil War.[14] For many years, therefore, only the states were willing and able to provide public funds for important public works.

Early in the 19th century canals were immensely popular as the most efficient means to advance the economy. The Erie Canal, completed in 1825, failed to attract federal aid and became entirely a New York State enterprise. De Witt Clinton, the political organizer of the Erie Canal project and Governor of New York when the canal was completed, concluded his 1816 memorial in support of the project with an admonition not to miss this great opportunity: "It remains for a free state to create a new era in history, and to erect a work more stupendous, more magnificent, and more beneficial than has hitherto been achieved by the human race."[15] The Erie Canal measured 363 miles, longer than any canal ever built in Europe. Throughout the country 4,000 miles of canals were constructed. More than two-thirds of the funds invested for canal projects between 1815 and 1860 were paid from public sources, mostly by state and local governments.

The State of Virginia went from support of isolated projects to a general policy designed to establish a system of mixed public–private enterprises. Based on a report of its committee on roads and internal navigation, in 1816 the Virginia legislature approved a public–private cooperative scheme for internal improvements. The state provided engineering expertise and partial funding. It also had minority representation on the company's board of directors. These arrangements were designed "to elicit private wealth for public improvement" while leaving initiative and direction in the hands of individuals and local leadership. The enterprise undertook a large number of improvements and came to an end only when the outbreak of the Civil War halted work on the Chesapeake and Ohio Railroad.[16]

By mid-century enthusiasm for regional improvements had shifted from the financing of roads and canals to the railroads. In the two decades before the Civil War state and local governments had paid for more than 25 per cent of total railroad capital stock. The federal government began to provide support for the railroads only later, when transcontinental lines were built. Fogel has written that the contribution of the railroads to economic growth in the 19th century was less than people assumed during the railroad era.[17] He bases his argument on the critical importance of other factors (capital, labor, technology) in building the economy of the 19th century. The question may be difficult to answer conclusively. However, while the railroad boom lasted, the utility of these state investments in the economy was rarely questioned. Only when a state-supported venture failed would critics speak up. Unfortunately, failure was not a rare outcome. In the late 1830s and 1840s numerous state-supported enterprises defaulted. Eventually, the high risk associated with railroad ventures caused the states to curtail their investments in railroads, canals, and other regional improvements.

There were additional reasons for a gradually declining state rôle. Public support of the railroad industry was no longer needed once the industry had matured. In the East, the new railroad companies did so well that they could manage without public funding. When railroad construction expanded westward beyond the more densely populated states, the state rôle was superseded by the federal government, which, after the Civil War, was more willing than in the past to make grants of capital as well as land.

In economic regulation, too, a strong state rôle gradually gave way to federal dominance. The right to incorporate had first been granted by the states to nonprofit enterprises, such as churches, libraries, and fire companies. Gradually other areas of economic life also came under state licensing or franchising authority. Business licensing became a primary source of state revenue, and many monopolies were enfranchised and protected from competition. In exchange for granting special rights to the corporations, the state protected the consumer from abuses of monopoly power. A Pennsylvania law of 1781 asserted that it was "the duty and interest of all governments to prevent frauds, and promote the interests of just and useful commerce."[18] But by 1840 public confidence in government regulation had been eroded: "Private capital was strong enough to demand successfully that the states significantly reduce their intervention in business matters."[19]

In summary, then, the 19th century was the high period of state activism. "Thousands of state laws and local ordinances provided subsidies, eased the path of incorporation, and regulated the activities of the turnpikes, land companies, canals, railroads, corporations and banks that were creating a new American economy."[20] The power of state governments to regulate business in order to protect the public interest was confirmed one last time by the Supreme Court in 1877. In *Munn* v. *Illinois* a Chicago warehouse firm had refused to apply for a state license under which its services and prices would have been controlled. The Court strongly upheld the state's right to regulate; it ruled that businesses affected "with a public interest" were not to be free of governmental control and that such control was rightly vested in the state.[21]

But in spite of this strong endorsement, the state rôle continued to decline. This was due, in part, to the behavior of the states themselves. Some states had begun to engage in activities designed to enrich themselves at the cost of other states. They had hit upon an ingenious expansion of their regulatory powers in order to make it attractive for businesses to incorporate in their territories. In 1888 New Jersey allowed its corporations to transact all their business outside the state, thus encouraging the creation of holding companies and mergers. Delaware followed with similar legislation a few years later. The state laws of general incorporation, which were passed in the 1870s and 1880s, encouraged the creation of powerful new corporate organizations, such as trusts and holding companies, with huge financial assets. It was now increasingly clear that only federal intervention could curb the power of the new industrial giants.

The federal policy response to the
Second Industrial Revolution

Federal economic regulation began to supersede state regulation with the passage of the Act to Regulate Commerce (1887), which also created the Interstate Commerce Commission—the first of many federal regulatory agencies to follow. The Sherman Antitrust Act was passed in 1890 in response to the inability of the states to control business concentration and monopolies.[22]

The new federal activism came in response to fundamental economic and demographic changes in the country. The settlement of the West, the mass production of consumer goods, and the growth of a nationwide railway network transformed regional economies into a large national market. Now the federal government was prepared to use its constitutional power under the interstate commerce clause in order to keep the economy free from the internal restrictions that the states imposed to protect their regional interests. Striking down such unwarranted regionalism was the thrust of a key Supreme Court decision that opened the door to federal economic regulation. This decision, which came only a decade after the reaffirmation of states' rights in *Munn v. Illinois*, essentially removed the states from their traditional key rôle in economic regulation. In *Wabash, St. Louis & Pacific Railway v. Illinois* the Court enjoined the state of Illinois from setting discriminatory railroad tariffs. Illinois, the Court argued, had interfered with commerce between the states by setting railroad rates that favored the regional economy: "It cannot be too strongly insisted upon that the right of continuous transportation from one end of the country to the other is essential in modern times." The Court made explicit reference to the commerce clause of the Constitution, which would be "feeble and almost useless" if states along transportation routes were allowed to regulate carriers and thereby obstruct commerce.[23]

As the new leading industries—steel, the railroads, internal combustion engine manufacture, and mass production of consumer goods—operated on a national scale, the scope of federal regulation expanded rapidly. The new forms of economic regulation that emerged from the 1880s through the New Deal period were essentially federal in nature. They covered a wide range of business activities—transportation, trade practices, industrial concentration, banking, the stock market, and other financial services. In the 1930s regulations affecting the social environment of industry were added, such as those governing working conditions, labor relations, and social welfare.

To understand the rôle played by technological change in the gradual movement toward increased centralization of U.S. policy making, it is useful to reflect more generally on the nature of technological change during the Industrial Revolution. We are used to reserve the term "industrial revolution" for the 18th century—the new technologies of coke and iron making, the steam engine, the factory system, mill towns, and the Poor Laws. But the process of technological change is continuous, and another, equally important, industrial revolution took place a century ago. This one shaped the industrial, social, and political environment in which we still live. In the current context it is particularly important to recognize that the policy tasks, organization, and administrative procedures of the U.S. government have been molded to a large extent by the response to the massive technological change that took place in the latter part of the 19th and the early part of this century. Because this experience has not yet fully receded into history, it serves well to illustrate the general pattern of change in modern industrial revolutions.

We always observe two opposing trends. On the one side we find the painful obsolescence of well-established industries and their workers; on the other, the emergence of new industries, which, starting from humble beginnings, soon become an important part of the national economy. This is the process of technological innovation that Schumpeter called "creative destruction."[24] Robert Ayres has labeled the changes of the late 19th century the "second industrial revolution," and his approach is useful for recognizing the strong centralizing forces that technology unleashed during this period.[25] The changes in technology that Ayres and others describe had a direct impact on governmental organization and policy making. In order to illustrate the worldwide effect of these events on the political scene, I include some observations comparing the U.S. experience with that of other industrialized nations.

The Second Industrial Revolution spans the century from 1860 to 1960. Five technologies determined the pace of industrial development during the latter part of the 19th century: the shift from iron to steel, the application of electricity as a source of power and lighting, the development of the internal combustion engine, the expansion of communications via telegraph and telephone, and the mass production of consumer goods. Combined with improved methods of financing and management, these technologies created industrial enterprises of previously unknown magnitude and power. They employed large numbers of workers and used large hierarchically structured organizations to administer their activities.

Britain had led the First Industrial Revolution. The United States and Germany led the Second. The two countries pursued different goals. The United States used technology to reduce its chronic labor shortage.[26] Germany sought substitutes for scarce natural resources. Both countries pioneered what turned out to be the most far-reaching innovation of the period—organized research. They grasped the economic potential of science and began to link scientific research to the production process. From small beginnings they developed new homes for research in universities, government, and industry. The new approach enhanced the rôle of engineering as the systematic refinement of products and processes. Technology began to be based on fundamental scientific advances. And the methods of engineering also became scientific. The chemical industry became the model of a science-dependent industry; it used advances in organic chemistry to develop and market synthetic dyes and fertilizers, and within a few decades it had established itself in a key position. The first research laboratories were established in the chemical and electrical industries. Freeman has called this step the most important social and economic change in modern industry.[27] The full power of scientific research as a source of new industries would not be felt until much later, but the foundations were laid at this time.

The new leading technologies encouraged economic, demographic, and political concentration and centralization. The factory system depended on the rapid movement of raw materials and finished goods. Centrally located harbors and railroad terminals provided advantageous locations for industrial facilities. The large number of workers needed by industry led to the rapid growth of cities. When urban congestion impaired working conditions and more flexible transport became available, inner-city centralization was replaced by metropolitan centralization. Automobile and truck transportation, combined with telephone communications, reduced the dependency of the consumer goods industry on centrally located railroad terminals and harbors. Manufacturing firms began to move from central cities to the suburbs, where cheaper land made it economical to build large one-story plants, ideally suited for assembly line production.[28]

In a political context, the Second Industrial Revolution posed two major challenges. First, government was called upon to find a balance between desirable economic growth and oppressive concentration of economic might in the hands of a few huge companies. The second problem was "the social question," as Marx had called it: the need to provide social services and security for the new masses of industrial workers and their families. This issue had not been resolved during the First Industrial Revolution, even though England had begun to address the problems of the new form of urban poverty with passage of the Poor Laws in the 1830s, which placed social welfare on the national policy agenda. For much of the 19th and 20th centuries the social and economic adjustments to industrial society provided powerful social dynamite, fueling the political debate and leading to violent confrontation among classes and parties. Different countries tried different solutions to the two questions of industrial control and social welfare, and out of the protracted political battles that were fought over these issues emerged the political systems that still dominate contemporary politics in the industrialized world.

At one extreme, the communist dream of doing away with private property and capitalism was translated into state capitalism in the Soviet Union and its followers. Central and Western Europe tried socialism as well as fascism. The socialist ideal for control of industrial power, kept alive until the 1960s, was to nationalize key sectors of industry and to give limited management rights to the workers. Social programs of various kinds, eventually unified under the label of the "welfare state," were designed to resolve the social question. Britain became the model for the modern welfare state when it implemented the social reforms designed by Lord Beveridge and supported by the Labour Party. Strong right-wing groups in Germany flirted with an antitechnology philosophy and the return to a simpler agrarian economy. But the pragmatists among them won the upper hand and joined the Nazi alliance with conservative industrialists and the army.

After World War II a policy consensus emerged in the West that was based on two main components: a managed or regulated market economy and an extensive social welfare system. Keynes and Beveridge were the two intellectual architects of this policy response that, at least for a short period during the 1950s and early 1960s, seemed to provide a satisfactory answer to the challenges brought by industrialization and urbanization.[29] Market regulation was based on the assumption that the economy would be less subject to dangerous depressions if the state used its financial and budgetary powers to guide the economy. In the arena of social policy the state accepted the rôle of using the wealth generated by industry to protect workers and their families against the risks of an industry-dependent life cycle—accidents at the workplace, sickness, disability, unemployment, retirement. Some countries went beyond these welfare goals and redistributed some of the accumulated wealth through taxation and subsidies.

The United States put in place an extensive system of business regulation that controlled entry, prices, safety, and other business practices. Regulation was entrusted to so-called independent (from the Congress and the executive branch) regulatory agencies, whose decisions were subject to detailed scrutiny by the courts. Initially, regulation applied only to those businesses that provided monopoly services (such as utility companies) or that were otherwise considered to require public control, such as financial institutions following the bank crash of 1929.[30] Later social and environmental concerns led to broad regulations affecting all sectors of the economy.[31]

Compared with the European practice, the American federal government was late in adopting national policies to provide social security to workers, the poor, and the sick. For a long time this task remained a state responsibility. Gradually, however, it became obvious that the states were unable to cope with the new demands placed upon them. Institutions, resources, and political support remained far behind the level of need that had been created by the change from an agrarian to an industrialized urban society. A few progressive states tried innovative solutions. For example, Wisconsin established the first workers' compensation and unemployment programs. Illinois pioneered a mothers' pension law. Several states passed minimum-wage laws long before the federal government enacted legislation in 1938.[32] But the number of progressive states was small. The failure of both state and federal governments to provide for social security contributed to the severity of the Depression. When the federal government, under President Roosevelt's leadership, finally introduced national social security programs, the states gladly conceded the lead rôle to Washington.

The new national policies were far from comprehensive, however, and the President himself believed that they would be needed only as temporary relief while the country recovered from the Depression. That the new policies were needed as a permanent response to structural economic changes was not yet recognized. Thus, the United States acted, in Wilensky's terms, as a "reluctant welfare state."[33] During the 1960s, when the Great Society programs renewed the attack on old and new forms of poverty, especially among racial minorities, many of the older Social Security programs were expanded and new features were added, such as health insurance for the elderly and the poor. But even then the national commitment remained smaller than in European countries under socialist governments.

Welfare policies, as well as the environmental programs of the 1960s and 1970s, were introduced at the federal level, and federal dollars provided the bulk of funding. But with few exceptions—the Social Security program being one—the federal government relied on the lower levels of government to administer the programs. In general this meant the states. In some instances, however, they were bypassed as implementing agents because they were not trusted to run the programs efficiently and to reach out for the intended target populations. Instead, the federal government contracted directly with local governments or private groups to provide services. Customarily, however, the states were given an important though subsidiary rôle as the administrative agent of the federal government. Under the widely used grants-in-aid procedure, policy is made in Washington—first by the Congress and then, to work out the regulatory and financial details, by an administrative agency of the federal government. Program funds are then channeled to the states, sometimes with the requirement that they provide matching funds. The states have to comply with federal program guidelines but retain considerable administrative discretion. Yet the basic policy decisions are no longer theirs, and state agencies and their employees working for these programs look toward Washington for new ideas and additional funds. This attitude among state employees makes it difficult to develop innovative state programs—a problem the states had to contend with when they began to reaffirm their own policy interests.[34]

The policies and institutions built by different nations in the attempt to deal with the policy challenges of the Second Industrial Revolution differ greatly. All of them, however, make use of highly centralized organizations and rely on the national government for direction and resource allocation.

The policy response to the Third Industrial Revolution: a more balanced system?

The Third Industrial Revolution began around 1960, using the technologies developed during World War II. It is far from having run its full course, so it is difficult to make definitive statements about its nature and impact. We do not yet have the kind of perfect vision that comes only from hindsight. Yet two strong technological thrusts are discernible, and one of these has the potential partially to reverse the trend toward centralization of the previous industrial revolution.

First, there is an intensive search for new materials and resources to supplement or substitute for limited natural resources. For the United States this reflects a fundamental change from its previous position as a resource-rich and labor-poor economy. Today the country is no longer self-sufficient in vitally important resources, and all other large industrial powers share this condition, often to an extreme degree. The search for petroleum substitutes may seem less urgent at present, but the long-term outlook requires sustained efforts to find economical and environmentally sound energy sources. Beyond substitution of currently used materials there is the broader search for new materials with desirable properties and potential for industrial applications, which provides a strong incentive for intensive research and development efforts. The increased use of reinforced plastics in automobile production, for example, would yield lighter cars as well as cheaper re-tooling for model changes.

The second technological thrust gives this period its unique characteristic. Advances in information processing and telecommunications technologies have led to a merger of these two technologies. This makes possible another round of radical changes in the economy. The implications for the traditional workforce are already severe. But opportunities for new jobs exist as well. As a result, the location of "old" and "new" industries is changing.

The leading sectors of the Second Industrial Revolution, with their emphasis on standardized manufactured commodities, matured some time ago to the point that they could be exported to the Third World. The production technologies that were dominant during this period have been packaged and standardized, and transferred to countries with lower labor costs, longer work hours, and the urgent desire to enter the industrial age. Many of the aging industries of Europe and the United States have lost their competitive edge in this environment. The receiving countries, on the other hand, have made good use of this opportunity for economic takeoff.[35]

In the current round of change, as in previous ones, there are losers and winners. The process is painful for those associated with the ailing sectors of the economy. From their perspective it is natural to call for protection of their old position. But only the new technologies make it possible to reach a new stage in economic growth. The shift from manufacturing to service jobs is significant in this context. Like yesterday's change from a mainly agricultural to an industrial workforce, "today's shift into service industries is being driven by forces that will appear irresistible with hindsight."[36]

The new workforce in rich countries will follow the model already emerging in the United States: less than 5 percent in agriculture, less than 20 percent in manufacturing, and 75 percent in the service economy. The latter term encompasses many activities and needs to be divided into more meaningful employment categories. Those at the heart of an advanced economy provide health care, education, research, administration, transport, and finance. Half of today's services are not performed directly for people but are related to production.[37] Producer services—research and development, planning, management, financing, marketing, legal, and accounting services—create opportunities for added value in more refined and

advanced products. They make possible a new kind of manufacturing.

Manufacturing has changed from the mass production of standardized products to flexible batch production of advanced technological
products.[38] The new products and the techniques used for their production undergo continuous technological innovation. New technologies,
particularly those based on microprocessors, will optimize control
and offer increased flexibility. Advances in flexible manufacturing
systems (FMS) are more valuable to batch manufacturers with frequent
modifications in machinery requirements than to mass producers of
standard parts with infrequent design changes.[39] FMS offer flexibility
with rapid setup and small production runs. Computer integrated
manufacturing (CIM) carries this approach even further by gathering,
tracking, processing, and routing information that links purchasing
and distribution, marketing, and financial data with design, engineering, and manufacturing data. For customized products it can be an
important source of competitiveness and flexibility.[40] Use of the new
manufacturing techniques will decrease labor costs, while the costs
of equipment, materials, distribution, and energy will increase.[41] The
rôle of organized research becomes ever more important under these
conditions. Research, instead of a front-end input, interacts with the
production process on a continuous basis.

The new manufacturing environment has important implications
for economic decentralization. Brooks and Guile see opportunities
for reversing the trend of the last three decades, which favored the
global homogenization of markets and the transnational integration of
production. The new technologies "appear to be giving a competitive
advantage to more localized production and distribution. For example,
the relative importance of close interaction between producers and
users seems to be growing as products become more complex and
customized."[42] The advantages of localized production include a
variety of factors: effective product design, prompt maintenance and
service, frequent consultation services to customers. The increasing use
of just-in-time inventories further enhances the advantage of colocation
of suppliers and distributors with manufacturing.[43]

This trend toward localized production will not reverse the advantages of centralized production. Instead, a new division of labor is
emerging between standardized production, which remains highly centralized, and customized production, which is increasingly localized.
Some product and service markets will be globally organized, driven
by ever increasing economies of scale. Other markets are fragmenting
and differentiating. As Brooks and Guile note, "New manufacturing and

service delivery technologies, new methods of work organization, and a new importance of local market responsiveness all can decrease the significance of scale economies and favor decentralized production."[44]

The policy response to the Third Industrial Revolution is still in its early stages. There is much concern about international competitiveness and enhanced economic productivity. Science and technology policies are gradually coming to be recognized as important policy areas. But no dominant concept as forceful as the welfare state of the Second Industrial Revolution has yet emerged. The policies of the welfare state—a managed market economy, a social security net, and a plurality of power centers (such as unions, industrial associations, and interest groups)—will remain, but they will have to be reconciled with the new economic realities. Policies that begin this adjustment are starting to emerge but are often opposed by the interests associated with the old industrial order.

The central rôle played by science as a gateway to technology is an important part of the new policy. This is evident in the two policy challenges that have become clearly visible. On the one hand, the power of many of the new technologies—nuclear, biotechnology, materials science, microelectronics—is so large that these new forms of technological risk require new forms of regulation. The new classes of environmental and health risks are often long-term in their effects, difficult to detect, perhaps irreversible beyond a certain point. Regulation, in response, has become much more complex, expensive, slow, and dependent on detailed scientific research to understand its nature and seriousness.[45] Without research the very nature of the risks would be unknown. Risk assessment and management are giving rise to new government policies, agencies, and procedures. These innovations in policy are best made at the national level. A related task is also best left to national decision making. A proper balance between, on the one hand, protection from risks by regulating industrial products and processes and, on the other hand, encouragement of free enterprise and innovation needs to be found. The careful balancing of environmental, health, resource, and economic policies is a major policy challenge for the future.

The second new policy task opens up opportunities for more aggressive regional policy rôles. Several of the key ingredients that determine success in the changed economic environment of the new industrial revolution are better served by regional than federal policies. First, there is the need for a first-class educational system. However, to have such a system macro-managed from a central national agency may be less desirable than allowing state governments to focus on this task. The states have historically been in charge of education and today spend the largest part of their budgets in this area. Second is the need for improved and updated infrastructure facilities—transportation, energy, and communications. Transportation, for many states, is the second largest budgetary item. Third, the states can play a vital rôle in creating a favorable business climate. This is a task that must be responsive to regional and local conditions.

There is evidence that the regions are beginning to respond to the new challenges. For a number of years they have been active in promoting regional economic development. Many are concerned about the quality of their educational systems. In the future, they will need to give more attention to the underlying conditions for growth: infrastructure, human services, protection of the physical environment, and assessment of future resource needs. To attack these tasks they will need to think and act in longer time frames and recognize connections between economic and social issues. The magnitude of the social and economic upheaval created by the Second Industrial Revolution overwhelmed the states. Using the greater flexibility and diversity offered by today's technologies, they may have the opportunity to reverse, in areas that are important to their future, the past trend toward political centralization. They can work with the people and institutions in their regions to help build the economy and the social institutions needed for success in the Third Industrial Revolution.

The significance of the new state rôle

A number of important changes have occurred at the state level. Many of the new policy tasks have a technical component; an ability to address the technical side of issues with competence is an important indicator of strengthened state capacities. I shall first review general changes in state governments and then discuss their capacity for handling technically complex policy issues.

The political climate of state government has shifted from passive reliance on Washington to a more active desire to shape the region's future. There are signs of new confidence that the states have the capacity to act as agents for change. Reforms in state government organization and procedures have been documented in a detailed study by the Advisory Commission on Intergovernmental Relations, which took an in-depth look at state government capabilities. The Commission found that states have made progress in reforming their leadership, institutions, and administrative procedures.[46] The reform efforts have led to modernized state constitutions, improved legislative procedures, an increased capacity of governors to lead and manage, better agency organization and management, and more efficient judicial systems. State governments have become more open in their operations through such mechanisms as open meeting laws, televised coverage of legislative sessions, greater participation in primary elections, and increased opportunities for citizen participation in regulatory proceedings.[47] Studies of the governorship and of individuals seeking this highest state office find better prepared, often less partisan chief executives.[48] McKay has found a remarkable increase in the professional outlook and capabilities of state officials.[49] Dye found a strong relationship between policy innovation in the states and increased professionalism.[50] While increasing professionalism benefits state operations, it also makes successful state officials attractive targets for headhunters from the federal government, nonprofit organizations, and industry. A recent study has documented how an innovative state program lost its leading staff before it could be fully tested and refined.[51]

In a survey conducted in 1982 by the National Governors' Association the areas of fiscal and nonfiscal management were listed by governors and key staff as the most promising for state innovations. Economic development followed, with large numbers of new program initiatives reported by administrators. Environment/energy and income/social services came third.[52] Our own study of state high-tech initiatives found a significant change from administrative to cooperative approaches. Instead of creating new state agencies and budgets, state governments emphasized cooperation among government, universities, industries, and—at times—labor.[53] This approach has two immediate effects. It allows states to take action without committing significant public funds, thus making possible speedy action. On the questionable side, new initiatives may be underfunded from the outset, thus reducing their potential for success. The cooperative approach recognizes the need for working jointly with research institutions and industries. Only by bringing together these various groups is it possible to integrate research and development, business incentives, entrepreneurship, education, training, and financial assistance, all of which are part of a comprehensive development strategy.

On the negative side our study found that many state initiatives were narrowly focused and tended to expect short-term results. There was no linkage between economic development strategies and resource, infrastructure, and environmental needs. The mechanisms for long-term and comprehensive policy development do not exist. The same weakness exists at the federal level, and success in developing comprehensive policy initiatives will be slow in coming at either level of government.

At the same time, a study of state initiatives in water management, an important area for long-term development needs, showed a promising level of new thinking, experimentation, and institutional innovation. We found that state water policies have undergone major changes in recent years. In the past, flood control and the provision of a dependable water supply dominated public policy. Large water development projects were often necessary to reach these goals, and the federal government took the lead in providing the expertise and financing. Now environmental concerns and water quality are judged to be most critical, and the nature of the debate has changed from building new water projects to managing existing resources more efficiently.

Case studies of water policy in six states found rapidly increasing recognition of the importance of water for the overall development of the state. Often some crisis has been necessary before states took the initiative and devised new policies. We found a number of significant institutional changes, policy innovations, and new funding mechanisms. The case of water management is particularly interesting because the federal government is no longer providing the leadership and financing needed to solve many of the current problems. And even if federal resource constraints were less severe, the need to design policies around regional conditions is increasingly recognized. The case of groundwater policy is illustrative. Arizona, one of the states included in the study, has enacted legislation to phase out, over the course of several decades, its practice of overdrafting. Only time will tell whether the 40-year timetable for eliminating overdrafting is acceptable. Already, however, an important spinoff has resulted. After organizing the passage of the appropriate legislation for Arizona, Governor Babbitt took the lead in developing guidelines for federal groundwater policy, providing a new example of the rôle of the states as national laboratories.[54]

State initiatives in environmental policy show improvements in technical and managerial capability but, in general, also reveal little desire to take bold action. Examining state innovations in integrated environmental management, Rabe found that state policy makers "have devoted enormous attention to securing more functional management" of the various parts making up the environmental policy system.[55] He documents how several states used the permitting system, which allows industries to operate under the various environmental statutes, as a vehicle for comprehensive environmental management. But a study of permitting in Texas found less promising results. Agencies still exhibited the behavior of subordinate players in a centralized policy system, fearful of overstepping federal directives and lacking the technical sophistication needed to deal with intermedia migration of toxic pollutants.[56] At the same time, the federal government recognizes the limits of centralized decisions. The US Environmental Protection Agency's first comprehensive study of the air toxics problem in the United States provided evidence for the local and regional nature of many pollutants.[57] In response, the EPA began an experiment under which it provided technical assistance to the states for regulating locally or regionally significant instances of pollution that were not sufficiently widespread to warrant national regulation. The experiment differed from previous federal–state cooperative programs in one important respect: the federal agency agreed to abide by regulatory decisions that the states would reach after careful assessment of the risk involved. In the past, states have been reluctant to participate in intergovernmental programs because they would often see their conclusions overruled by the federal government.[58]

New policy initiatives by state governments are also underway in other policy areas that have long been dominated by the federal government. The list of examples is long: telecommunications, science and technology, resource development, drought management, welfare reform, park management, space applications, and others. The immediate task is carefully to document and evaluate these experiments. With this information in hand it will then become possible to form a judgment on the significance and long-term prospects of the new state rôles.

But even now it is possible to draw four main conclusions:

(a) State governments are more active and innovative in their policy initiatives than at any time since the Depression.

(b) They are experimenting with a wide variety of activities aimed at improving the economy and wellbeing in the region by increased support of education, science, and advanced technology.

(c) As a rule, states do not initiate large and costly programs. Instead, they act as facilitators for new initiatives, bringing other institutions into play, and attempting to work with them in close partnerships.

(d) The technical competence and the quality of professional staffs in state agencies are improving; so is the quality of elected officials.

(e) States have recognized the close connections between economic performance on the one hand, and education, training, and research on the other. Yet there is little evidence, so far, that longer term policy needs and linkages between different policy areas are sufficiently considered in policy development. Economic, environmental, and resource policies will need to be more closely integrated.

(f) The new state initiatives make it necessary for federal and state officials to re-examine the traditional division of labor between the two levels of government.

The available evidence, while incomplete in regard to final outcomes, is significant for two reasons. (a) The states are again assuming their constitutional rôle. As a result, the continuous search for balance between federal and state rôles takes place between more equal partners, not one all-powerful federal and many weak state governments acting as the administrative agents of the federal master. (b) The resurgence of the states is the more significant because many of the new complex policy tasks that come to the forefront of the political agenda in advanced industrial societies no longer seem to elude them. I have elsewhere used the term "scientific state" to argue that the rôle of science—and through it, technology—in the policy process has become so important that it leads to broad changes in policy tasks, institutions, and procedures.[59] The new evidence suggests that the states now build the capacity and show the political will actively to participate in the governance of the scientific state.

Notes

1 K. Marx, *The poverty of philosophy*, in *Werke*, K. Marx & F. Engels, vol. 4 (Berlin: Akademie, 1959), p. 130.
2 Council of State Governments, *Interstate compacts and agencies* (Lexington, Ken., 1983).
3 Quoted in M. Derthick, "American federalism: Madison's middle ground in the 1980s," *Public Administration Review* **47**, 1987, 66. The two citations are from different works by Madison.
4 *Texas v. White, 7 Wallace 700* (1869).
5 T. Sanford, *Storm over the states* (New York: McGraw-Hill, 1967).
6 L. H. Gulick, "Reorganization of the State," *Civil Engineering*, August 1933, 421.
7 A. Hamilton, J. Madison & J. Jay, *The Federalist* **1**, 1901 (New York and London: Dunne) 62–70.
8 An excellent account of how technological change shaped the American economy is N. Rosenberg, *Technology and American economic growth* (Armonk, New York: M. E. Sharpe, 1972). The history of policy making at the state level is less well covered in the literature. The evolution of intergovernmental relations is a partial substitute, but authors tend to focus mainly on the federal rôle and do not give equal attention to innovative state policies. For a recent review of the literature

see T. J. Anton, "Intergovernmental change in the United States: an assessment of the literature," in Public sector performance ed. T. C. Miller (Baltimore: Johns Hopkins University Press, 1984), pp. 15–64. For a reader on the topic see D. S. Wright (ed.), Federalism and intergovernmental relations (Washington, D.C.: American Society for Public Administration, 1984).

9   E. F. Morrisson, "State and local efforts to encourage economic growth through innovation: an historical perspective," in Technological innovation: strategies for a new partnership, ed. D. O. Gray, T. Solomon, & W. Hetzner, (Amsterdam: North Holland, 1986), pp. 57–68.

10   A. Gallatin, A plan for national action: report on roads and canals, 1808. Reprinted in The government and the economy, 1783–1861, ed. C. Goodrich, (Indianapolis: Bobbs-Merrill, 1967), pp. 3–42.

11   Quoted in M. Keller, "State power needn't be resurrected because it never died," Governing, October 1988, 54.

12   J. R. T. Hughes, The governmental habit: economic controls from colonial times to the present (New York: Basic Books, 1977), p. 70. See in particular the chapter "The new system and internal communications," pp. 67–77.

13   Goodrich, The government and the economy, p. 43.

14   Ibid., p. 44.

15   De Witt Clinton, "Erie Canal Memorial," reprinted in Goodrich, The government and the economy, p. 93.

16   Goodrich, The government and the economy, p. 58.

17   R. W. Fogel, Railroads and American economic growth (Baltimore: Johns Hopkins University Press, 1964).

18   Hughes, The governmental habit, p. 80.

19   D. Vogel, "Why businessmen distrust their state: the political consciousness of American corporate executives," British Journal of Political Science 8, 1978, 56.

20   Keller, "State power needn't be resurrected," p. 54.

21   Hughes, The governmental habit, p. 4.

22   Ibid., p. 74.

23   Cited in ibid., p. 5.

24   J. Schumpeter, Capitalism, socialism and democracy (New York: Harper & Row, 1942).

25   R. U. Ayres, The next industrial revolution: reviving industry through innovation (Cambridge, Mass.: Ballinger, 1984), Chs. 4–6. Writing from a Marxist point of view, J. Kuczynki distinguishes among the Great Industrial Revolution, the electrotechnical, and the scientific-technical revolution. See his Vier Revolutionen der Produktivkraefte: Theorie und Vergleiche (Berlin: Akademie, 1975).

26   This view is widely held by historians but has been challenged by economists. According to Rosenberg, "this disagreement between the theorists and the economic historians remains unresolved." See N. Rosenberg, Inside the black box: technology and economics (Cambridge: Cambridge University Press, 1982), p. 15.

27   C. Freeman, The economics of industrial innovation (Cambridge, Mass.: MIT Press, 1982), p. 7. This book contains a detailed case study of the rôle of science in the chemical industry.

28   J. Schmandt, "The urban crisis: a note about its technological and political context," in Social innovation in the city, ed. R. S. Rosenbloom & R. Marris (Cambridge, Mass.: Harvard University Program on Technology and Society, 1969), p. 12.

29   An excellent analysis of the connections between the economic and social policies designed by Keynes and Beveridge is R. Mishra, The welfare state in crisis: social thought and social change (New York: St. Martin's Press, 1984).

30   J. Q. Wilson (ed.), The politics of regulation (New York: Basic Books, 1982).

31 J. Schmandt, "Regulation and science," *Science, Technology and Human Values* **9**, Winter 1984, 51–62.

32 J. Leiby, *A history of social welfare and social work in the United States* (New York: Columbia University Press, 1978), Chs. 9 & 10.

33 H. L. Wilensky & C. N. Lebeaux, *Industrial society and social welfare* (New York: Free Press, 1965).

34 D. S. Wright, "Intergovernmental relations: an analytical overview," *Annals of the American Academy of Political and Social Science* **416**, 1974, 1–16.

35 See Ayres, *The next industrial revolution*, Chs. 5 & 6.

36 "They also serve," *Economist*, August 22, 1987, 16.

37 See the section, "The growth of consumer services," in *Rethinking urban policy: urban development in an advanced economy*, ed. R. Hanson (Washington, D.C.: National Academy Press, 1985), pp. 21–2.

38 Ayres, *The next industrial revolution*, p. 182.

39 Manufacturing Studies Board, National Academy of Engineering, *Toward a new era in U.S. manufacturing: the need for a national vision* (Washington, D.C.: National Academy Press, 1986), p. 31.

40 Ibid., pp. 35–6.

41 Ibid., p. 7.

42 "Overview," in *Technology and global industry: companies and nations in the world economy*, ed. B. R. Guile and H. Brooks (Washington, D.C.: National Academy Press, 1987), p. 4.

43 Ibid., p. 5.

44 Ibid., p. 7.

45 Schmandt, "Regulation and science," pp. 23–38.

46 Advisory Commission on Intergovernmental Relations, *The question of state government capability* (Washington, D.C., Advisory Commission 1985), p. 363.

47 Ibid.

48 T. F. Beyle & L. Muchmore, *Being governor: views from the office* (Durham, N.C.: University of North Carolina Press, 1983); L. Sabato, *Goodbye to good-time Charlie: the American governorship transformed*, 2nd. edn. (Washington, D.C.: Congressional Quarterly Press, 1983).

49 D. H. McKay, "Fiscal federalism: professionalism and the transformation of American state government," *Public Administration* **60**, Spring 1982, 10–22.

50 T. R. Dye, *Policy analysis* (University, Al.: University of Alabama Press, 1976).

51 J. Aisenberg, J. A. Marone & H. M. Sapolsky, "The call to Rome: obstacles to state innovation," *Public Administration Review* **47**, March/April 1987, 135–42.

52 S. K. Cheek, "Gubernatorial innovations," *State Government* **56**, 1983, 53–7.

53 J. Schmandt and R. Wilson, (eds.), *Promoting high-technology industry* (Boulder: Westview Press, 1987).

54 J. Schmandt, E. Smerdon & J. Clarkson, *Innovative state water policies* (New York: Praeger, 1988).

55 B. G. Rabe, *Fragmentation and integration in state environmental management* (Washington, D.C.: The Conservation Foundation, 1986), p. 160.

56 J. E. Katz and J. Schmandt (eds.), *Environmental permitting in Texas* (Austin: Lyndon B. Johnson School of Public Affairs, University of Texas, 1986).

57 U.S. Environmental Protection Agency, *The air toxics problem in the United States: an analysis of cancer risks* (Washington, D.C., 1984).

58 Science Applications International Corporation, "EPA's Acrylonitrile state/local referral project: an evaluation of the program and implications for current air toxics policy," review draft, 1987 (mimeographed).

59 J. Schmandt & J. E. Katz, "The scientific state: a theory with hypotheses," *Science, Technology, and Human Values* **11**, Winter 1986, 40–52.

3

Structural economic change and the powers of state government: the viability of regional development strategies

ROBERT WILSON

Introduction

EVEN AS "FREE MARKETERS" and supply-siders dominated national economic policy making during the Reagan Adminstration, state governments became more interventionist. While lacking the range of policy instruments available to the federal government, Democratic- and Republican-led state governments alike are experimenting with initiatives and programs to promote development in their states. They are doing so, for the most part, with little help and certainly little encouragement from Washington.

The emergence of greater state government activity in economic affairs mirrors expanded state activism in a number of other policy areas and marks a historical shift in intergovernmental relations. In the early part of this century, state governments were innovators in public policy, especially in social policy. During the 1930s, the policy initiative shifted to the federal government. In the late 1970s and especially 1980s, a shift is again noted, and in many domestic policy areas state governments have seized the initiative.[1] This is certainly the case in economic development policy.

While state activism in economic development must be seen in the context of broader changes in intergovernmental relations, a number of economic forces have contributed to this specific rôle. The U.S. and world economies are in the midst of a new industrial revolution, to use the Schumpeterian imagery. The revolution is being led by advances in microelectronics, telecommunications, materials science, and forthcoming advances in the application of biotechnology. The most salient impact of this industrial revolution in the United States is the relative decline of traditional manufacturing sectors, the emergence of a number of so-called advanced technology sectors, and the growth of producer services, such as finance, legal, accounting, marketing, engineering, and information processing services. These basic changes in economic structure, referred to here as structural change, became evident at least a decade ago in the United States and have been observed in the industrialized European economies.

The environment created by structural change or economic diversification can be usefully contrasted with that produced by normal business cycles. Business cycles produce swings in industrial capacity utilization and unemployment. Keynesian-inspired public policy attempts to smooth the swings, to stimulate the economy during downturns, and to constrain the economy in upswings. In addition to the various macroeconomic and monetary policies for stimulating a weak economy, temporary work programs may also be advised. Since the timing and severity of business cycles varies among regions, a federally administered countercyclical program is difficult—at least politically—to administer. While state governments cannot influence downturns through monetary policy, expenditure policies could have a countercyclical objective.[2]

But the problem currently before state governments is not simply one of business cycles and temporary underutilization of capacity and laborforce in the state. The structure of state economies is changing; even in periods of economic growth, unemployment may remain high and much industrial capacity remains unused. Even when recapitalization in traditional industries is occurring, such as in textiles in North Carolina, former levels of employment in these industries will not be reached. On the other hand, a new set of industrial and service sectors is developing with location factors differing from those for traditional manufacturing. This has caused a substantial spatial reallocation of investment and people.

The activism of state governments in economic development is directly linked to the way in which structural change has played itself out spatially in the U.S. economy. At the end of the 1970s, the effect of this change was especially severe in the states of the industrial heartland. Rising unemployment and deteriorating financial conditions of state and local governments became part of the policy agenda of industrial states. States in the South attempted not only to acquire an increasing share of decentralizing traditional manufacturing, but also to capture a share of the new advanced technology sectors. State government in the West, particularly in California, had additional concerns resulting from competition from the highly productive economies in the Pacific Rim.

The spatial impact of structural change varied among regions and cities, and it continues to present policy dilemmas for the federal government. Policies designed to accelerate structural change in the U.S. economy, in order to compete more effectively in the international arena, are likely to have substantially different effects in various regions. The representatives of the "losing regions" are likely to oppose such policies and favor adjustment policies that would ease the transition for the disadvantaged areas.[3] State governments, on the other hand, may be better at identifying local problems and designing strategies for these problems than is the federal government.

The principal purposes of this chapter are to identify the means by which state government affects the economy of the state and to determine the potential effectiveness of these means in a period of structural change. Do states have the capabilities, in terms of powers and resources, to affect significantly their economies? Or do other factors, such as the existing levels of the factors of production, federal macroeconomic policy, and the forces of structural change and international competition, predominate and diminish the effectiveness of state actions? If state actions can be effective, which of the wide range of activities are most important? Can "beggar thy neighbor" policies be avoided by state government or is one state's gain another state's loss?

This chapter will first look briefly to history to identify instances where state action has been important, if not decisive, in economic development. Then the contemporary rôle of state government will be examined. This will be done by reviewing the principal functions of state governments that can affect the economy of a state. These functions include fiscal policy, regulation, infrastructure provision, and economic development programs. The final section will conclude by assessing the potential of current state strategies to promote development given the forces of structural change.

State government and economic development: an historical note

Even a brief look at the historical record produces many examples of actions taken by state governments to promote economic development. Some examples even predate the U.S. Constitution.[4] States have always invested in the provision of economic infrastructure, sometimes with a dramatic economic benefit, as in the construction of the Erie Canal.[5] Produce and commodities from the Mississippi and Ohio river basin had previously passed through the port of New Orleans. The canal changed forever the pattern of commerce and allowed New York to project its commercial presence throughout the Great Lakes area.[6] State governments also participated in the enormous expansion of the railroad system during the last century.[7] Even though there are many examples of investments by state governments that proved ineffective, in some instances state governments were instrumental in promoting development through infrastructure investment.

State governments have made enormous contributions in public education, and these had subsequent effects on the economies of states. The Morrill Land Grant Act, though federal legislation, led to the formation of state colleges and universities.[8] In addition, state governments have participated in the agricultural extension services that have contributed to the high standing of U.S. agriculture in the world economy.[9]

Transportation investments, support of education, and technology transfer are actions that affect levels of economic activity indirectly; they usually affect the productivity of existing factors of production but are not themselves commodities and, consequently, are somewhat removed from the marketplace. Another form of state action of long standing, more directly linked to the marketplace, is industrial recruitment. In 1936 the Mississippi state government created the Balance Agriculture with Industry (BAWI) program with the objective of attracting manufacturing investment to the state to diversify its economy.[10] The instruments of the program included advertising, tax abatement, and tax-exempt financing of buildings for industrial firms locating in the state. Following World War II, many states pursued industrial recruitment strategies.

The historical record shows that state governments have consciously and explicitly undertaken actions to promote a state's economy. Some of these actions were indeed effective. The question we examine shortly is whether a state can be systematic and deliberate in its economic development policies. First, we need to review the range of state functions and how each can affect a state's economy.

Traditional state government functions

Though the U.S. Constitution defined a federalist system with a fairly clear delineation of responsibilities between the federal and state governments, this system has evolved substantially during the last two centuries. In virtually all policy areas, powers are now shared by the federal and state governments. Even so, it is still possible to identify policy areas related to economic development in which state governments have a major rôle. After examining expenditure patterns of state government, we will examine these policy areas. And finally we will identify the relevant federal economic development efforts.

State expenditure patterns

Though the rôle of the public sector in the U.S. economy is less significant than that found in other industrialized economies, it is nevertheless quite substantial (see Table 3.1). In 1984 total government expenditures represented around 34 percent of gross national product, and expenditures of state and local governments represented about 10 percent of gross national product. In 1985 state government expenditures in capital outlays amounted to $30.6 billion or 19.5 percent of total government capital outlays.[11]

Fiscal conditions of state government have been volatile during the last decade.[12] Slow economic growth during the 1970s and early 1980s, the legacy of the citizen tax revolt movement, and the cutbacks in federal aid have placed fiscal stress on state governments. In recent years, fiscal conditions in many states have substantially improved though the future remains uncertain for all states.

What interests us, though, is not just total expenditures but also expenditures for specific functions and other activities that may have important implications for the economy within a state. For example, state governments invest heavily in infrastructure and in the development of human capital; they perform a variety of regulatory functions that affect the business environment and also establish the statutory environment and powers of local governments. The principal objective of these functions is not necessarily to promote economic development. Even so, each affects a state's economy, and a broad-based economic strategy would need to consider these functions in addition to programs that have an explicit economic development objective.

Expenditures by state governments during 1984–5 are disaggregated by function in Table 3.2. In Table 3.3, the share of expenditures by level of

Table 3.1 Government expenditures share of gross national product, selected years (in %).

	Government expenditures as a percentage of GNP*		
Year	Total	Federal	State and local
1950	21.3	14.3	7.0
1960	26.9	18.3	8.5
1970	31.6	20.6	11.0
1980	33.0	22.9	10.1
1981	33.3	23.3	10.0
1982	35.5	24.9	10.6
1983	35.3	24.8	10.5
1984	34.3	24.0	10.3

*Expenditures on income and product account. They are on an accrual basis, include trust account transactions with the public, and exclude capital transactions that do not represent current production, etc.

Source: Tax Foundation, Incorporated, *Facts and figures on government finance*, 23rd edn (Washington, D.C.: Tax Foundation, Incorporated, 1986), Table A31.

government for selected economic development functions is presented. These tables show that state governments play a very significant rôle in funding education and highway systems. In most of the other categories, the state rôle is less important than that of local governments or the federal government, but frequently responsibilities are shared.[13]

Slow economic growth and limited increases in productivity during the 1970s placed revenue constraints on governments. Investment in infrastructure, particularly maintenance, suffered[14] as did support of public education. There has recently been public reaction to these perceived deficits, especially at the level of state government; many states have embarked on educational reform, with increases in spending for public education and for research and development in universities, and in more efficient planning of infrastructure investments.[15] A frequent justification for increased expenditures is that they will improve the competitiveness of economic activities in the state.

Tax policy

State tax policy has received much attention in discussions of state economic development policy. The search for revenues to fund development programs during a period of fiscal stress has, in part, caused the examination of tax policy. Furthermore, tax policy itself may be an

Table 3.2 State government expenditures by function, 1984–5 (in %).

Function		Percentage
Education services:		33.0
Education	32.9	
Libraries	0.1	
Social services and income maintenance:		25.0
Public welfare	17.2	
Hospitals	4.1	
Health	3.0	
Social insurance administration	0.7	
Transportation:		9.1
Highways	8.5	
Air transportation (airports)	0.2	
Other transportation	0.6	
Public safety:		3.7
Police protection	0.9	
Correction	2.3	
Protective inspection and regulation	0.6	
Environment and housing:		2.8
Natural resources	1.7	
Parks and recreation	0.5	
Housing and community development	0.4	
Sewerage	0.2	
Government administration:		2.8
Interest on general debt		3.8
General expenditure, n.e.c.:		7.7
Other		12.9
Total		100.0

Source: Bureau of the Census, U.S. Department of Commerce, *Governmental finances in 1984–85*, GF85, no. 5 (Washington, D.C.: Government Printing Office, December 1986), Table 9.

instrument of economic development policy. Though the share of state and local taxation that falls initially on businesses has declined during recent decades, differentials among states still exist and interstate tax competition is intense.[16] There are two principal analytic questions: do state tax rates affect rates of growth, and can targeted tax incentives be effective instruments for attracting industrial investment to a state?[17]

Though these questions are currently receiving much attention, they certainly are not new.[18] Nor are they easy to answer. There are quite complex methodological issues to be assessed; past patterns of regional economic growth have been ruptured by structural change and during the last five years many states have modified their taxation policy. Several years ago, when the Sunbelt–Snowbelt paradigm was popular, high tax rates and excessive welfare benefits of states in the traditional industrial

Table 3.3 Expenditures by level of government for selected economic development related functions, 1984–5 (in %).

Function	All governments	Federal government	State governments	Local governments
Education:	100.0	6.4	26.1	67.5
Higher education	100.0	(NA)	84.6	15.4
Elementary and secondary education	100.0	(2)	.8	99.2
Transportation:				
Highways	100.0	1.8	59.2	38.9
Air transportation (airports)	100.0	47.7	6.6	45.7
Parking facilities	100.0	—	—	100.0
Water transport and terminals	100.0	55.5	15.9	28.6
Transit subsidies	100.0	—	47.6	52.4
Utility expenditure:				
Water supply	100.0	—	.5	99.5
Electric power	100.0	—	8.1	91.9
Gas supply	100.0	—	—	100.0
Transit	100.0	—	23.4	76.6
Sewerage	100.0	—	2.7	97.3

Source: Bureau of the Census, *Government finances in 1984–85*, Table 10.

heartland were perceived to be significant factors in the deterioration of these economies. For these reasons, some states reduced tax burdens.[19] While such reductions may play some rôle in economic recovery, other more powerful factors are also at work in states such as Massachusetts.[20]

The literature on the effect of state taxation on economic growth is extensive and surprisingly inclusive.[21] Principal findings are that state differentials in tax rates, though significant, probably do not have much effect on rates of economic growth. State taxes are just one of many costs incurred by firms and for many firms other factors, such as availability of labor and labor costs, are much more important. In addition, high state taxes may lower the costs of some factors of production through the provision of high-quality services, such as education or infrastructure. The methodological problems, while still substantial, are being addressed. Improved definitions of state tax rates[22] and sector-specific studies[23] suggest that further econometric research is warranted.

State tax incentive programs for industrial recruitment have also received a good deal of attention. There are several relevant questions. Do these programs effectively attract industrial firms? Is the cost:benefit ratio of the programs less than one? Do the programs significantly affect the rate of economic growth? Given that these types of programs have existed for decades and that most states operate or have operated these programs, the answer to the first question, at least for the political and legislative environment, is almost certainly yes. Whether the state benefits from these programs is not altogether certain. The forgone revenues of the tax incentive programs represent a cost to state government, and the additional tax revenue generated by the industrial firms attracted to the state may or may not exceed the state's tax expenditure.

The empirical evidence supporting tax incentive programs is weak.[24] At the same time, it is almost certain that these programs will not have a perceptible impact on the rate of economic growth in the state, simply because they affect a small number of firms. Some argue that tax incentives targeted to firms in advanced technology sectors or for research and development might have a significant impact, but this has yet to be demonstrated empirically. Tax incentive programs, in addition, are criticized on the grounds of equity by firms not benefiting from them and by taxpayers who suffer the tax expenditures. These programs are also strongly criticized for placing states in competition in a zero-sum game. To conclude, tax incentive programs appear to have at best a marginal effect on a state's economy and may, in fact, not be cost-effective.

State development programs

The increasing involvement of state governments in economic development is amply documented by the proliferation of state economic development plans and programs. Most states have adopted programs for the expressed purpose of promoting economic development. The decision to consider these programs only after discussing traditional state functions that affect economic development was intentional. In terms of state expenditures, *explicit* economic development programs absorb a growing but still small proportion of state budgets. The National Association of State Development Agencies reported that the average budgets of state development agencies increased from $7 million in 1984 to $17.5 million in 1986.[25] A growing number of programs are funded through bonds and, consequently, are not fully reflected in state budgets. In addition, a few states invest heavily; in Illinois and Pennsylvania the state development agency had budgets of $187 million and $180 million respectively.[26] Even so, the level of expenditures for states is relatively low and it is important to note this for two reasons: first, it may represent the lack of real political commitment by state governments, and second, it certainly means that the policy instruments requiring high levels of expenditures are not likely to be implemented.

Given the wide range of programs of economic development adopted by state governments, the challenge resulting from lack of substantial state funding has fostered the identification of new, innovative policy instruments, frequently with the participation of the private sector. A more cynical view might explain the wide range of instruments as the product of desperation and lack of conceptual basis for state government action or of intense political pressure being brought to bear on governments in severely depressed states to "do something." In any event, the range of state efforts is impressive.[27]

There are programs designed to affect virtually all costs of production, with the intent of either improving the productivity of various factors of production or reducing costs. These programs can be grouped in the following manner:

(a) capital-loan programs, venture and seed capital programs;
(b) labor-education and training programs;
(c) technical assistance—technology transfer, marketing;
(d) land and facilities—industrial parks;
(e) tax incentives—investment tax credits, tax abatements.

In addition, some programs are not directed at specific factors of production but rather at product and firm life cycles, including industrial incubation and technological innovation programs, and at demand generation through export promotion[28] and procurement policies.

Structural economic change has affected state industrial recruitment, particularly in terms of the orientation of the programs. Many state programs are now directed toward the rapidly growing, advanced technology sectors and are concerned with the process of new product generation and research and development. The proliferation of university–industry research centers is an example of this concern. Another effect has been an increasing and significant emphasis on technological innovation in traditional industries. It is now broadly accepted, and reflected in state policy, that technology policy can make a significant contribution to increasing productivity and competitiveness in traditional industries, even though these industries may not employ as many workers as in the past.[29]

The methodology for evaluating these programs is not well developed. The outcome measures are frequently uncertain or at least hard to identify.[30] While employment generation may appear to be an obvious measure of performance for many programs, frequently it is difficult if not impossible to attribute a "new job" to a particular program; the job may have been created without the program, or, more commonly, the program may have made some contribution—but not a decisive one. Even when a sufficient number of "new jobs" can be attributed to a program to deem it successful, it is unlikely that these jobs will have a discernible effect on the rates of economic growth in the state. This is the same problem of evaluation described above for tax incentive programs.

Regulation

State governments undertake a broad range of regulatory activities that clearly affect businesses and individuals. Though state actions are constrained by the interstate commerce clause of the U.S. Constitution, which gives to the federal government the power to regulate interstate commerce, states have substantial authority to regulate economic activities within their boundaries. In this section an attempt is made to categorize the various types of state regulation by functional area (see Tables 3.4 & 3.5) and to provide a brief description of the objective of the regulations and their effect on the economy of a state. Finally, an assessment is made of the potential rôle that regulation, or deregulation, might play in a state's economic development strategy.

The states began fully to exercise their regulatory authority during the second half of the last century. A principal motivating factor was the fear, particularly in western states, of large corporations in the railroad and banking industries that placed rural interests and small business interests at a severe disadvantage.[31] At the turn of the century states became involved in utility regulation.[32] However, the argument for the need to combat economic abuse was not the only reason for increased state activity.[33] Intense competition resulted in some support from business and industrial interests for the regulation of markets. Regulation in the oil industry during much of this century was frequently advocated by "independent" oil producers who wanted stability in the price of oil.[34]

Deregulation and regulatory reform have been very much part of the national agenda for the last decade, especially in the fields of transportation and communication.[35] The arguments supporting this change have rested largely on grounds of economic efficiency; regulation affects the price of goods and thus creates price distortions and results in inefficiencies. Though the deregulation trend has certainly affected economic activities throughout the country, the influence of this trend on state-level regulation has been principally in terms of regulatory reform rather than deregulation.

Table 3.4 Categories of state regulatory activities.

Economic regulation:
  –Financial institutions – regulation of state chartered banks, insurance companies, etc.
  –Public utilities, especially setting of rates and bond rating of the companies.
  –Natural resource regulation – extraction of resources.
  –Transportation-regulation intrastate trucking.
Social or "horizontal" regulation:
  –Health, safety, environmental, consumer, labor laws.

Source: Leigh Boske (ed.), *Regulation in Texas: its impact, process and institutions,* Policy Research Project no. 76 (Austin: LBJ School of Public Affairs, University of Texas, 1986).

Table 3.5 State regulatory instruments.

Economic controls-pricing
Information disclosure
Licensing
Mandatory standards – product standards, environmental, health
Penalties
Economic incentives

Source: L. Boske (ed.), *Regulation in Texas: its impact, process and institutions,* Policy Research Project no. 76 (Austin: LBJ School of Public Affairs, University of Texas, 1986).

The potential rôle of state regulation in economic development strategy depends on the ability of a state, through its regulatory activities, to create a competitive advantage over other states, and thus attract investment or create the conditions by which new wealth can be generated from resources internal to the state. Since the nature and purpose of state regulation varies substantially among the areas of regulation—for example, the purpose of utility regulation is very different than that of financial regulation—we proceed by considering a number of cases.

The first case to be examined is regulation of electric utility companies. If utility regulation is to be used as an instrument of economic growth, the regulatory objective would be to keep the price of energy for commercial and industrial uses within the state, lower than the price in other states. There are two problems with this regulatory strategy. Though regulation of utility companies—justified because they are natural monopolies—was first established to curb abuse by utility companies, the regulatory process must also ensure the economic vitality of the companies. Pursuit of the economic development goal, through low energy prices, may well result in insufficient investment in the utility companies and, subsequently, decline in bond prices and higher costs of capital. In the long run, energy prices may have to rise, thus defeating the objective of maintaining low energy prices.

Another instance of potential conflicts arises in environmental regulation. This example is further complicated by the fact that the federal government, not state governments, sets minimum environmental standards, though states can adopt stricter standards. Since environmental regulation places additional costs on firms, one might assume that the economic development strategy of the state would be not to impose stricter standards, since such action would place the state at a competitive disadvantage *vis-à-vis* other states. While a state cannot gain an advantage in this context, it can avoid incurring disadvantages. This argument might be appropriate when considering pollution-intense industries, but it is likely to be inconsequential for most firms. Firms and industries that place high value on quality-of-life factors may be attracted to those states that protect their natural environment through enacting higher than minimum standards. Furthermore, at a political level, the population of a state may place a higher priority on environmental quality than on economic growth. In sum, a state has limited ability to use its environmental regulatory capacity to promote economic development through acquiring advantages over other states.

There are, however, examples where direct governmental intervention in the economy through regulation has promoted growth. In response to a series of hurricanes on the Gulf Coast in the 1960s, the State of Texas passed the Catastrophe Property Insurance Pool Act of 1971. The Act established the Catastrophe Property Insurance Pool Association (CPIPA) for issuing wind and hail insurance policies and all companies underwriting wind and hail damage in the state are required to be members. Members are required to pay premiums to the CPIPA, and these are used to cover claims; state government assumes losses in excess of $100 million dollars. Before the Act was passed, insurance for construction along the Gulf Coast was either unavailable or prohibitively expensive. The tremendous construction boom that occurred on the Coast in the late 1970s and 1980s is in part attributable to this Act. The Act represents a clear intervention of government into the marketplace, but one that was successful in inducing economic growth. State governments do have considerable power to require cooperation among businesses and firms to overcome such market failures, particularly in the financial sector, but these powers are rarely exercised.

Two principal points can be drawn from this discussion of the potential effect of state regulation on economic development. First, the ability to adapt regulatory action to promote economic development is frequently constrained by the purpose of the particular regulatory action and by the institutions that have developed around the regulatory process. The regulated industry has frequently been strengthened by the regulatory process, and the industry may be weakened when the objecttive of regulation is reformulated as one of economic growth. Furthermore, the regulatory process has frequently become an institutional setting for resolving conflict among the various interested parties. Pressures are already being brought to bear, particularly by consumer groups, to "keep prices low." The political system has developed these regulatory mechanisms over many years, and it is very unlikely that the imposition of an economic development goal can be effectively imposed on them.

A second observation to be made is that regulatory activities may exist that unduly restrict economic development. Though state professional licensing may serve some legitimate and useful purposes, it does restrict entry into the market and consequently reduces competition. State regulatory activities, in addition, have accumulated over decades, and as the economy and society evolve it is only to be expected that some forms of regulatory activities may no longer be necessary. For example, many of the populist constraints on banking dating from the early part of the century seem less needed and, in any event, have been dropped. When constraints are removed, however, rarely will there be no losers. If regulation is viewed as a means to resolve conflict, it is obvious that regulation itself creates winners and losers and deregulation does the same, even when economic development occurs. In any event, it is unlikely that the objective of economic development will be, or even should be, a decisive factor in regulatory decision making.

The rôle of state government in the regulation of telecommunications is a special case for several reasons. The traditional rôle of telephone regulation that states shared with the Federal Communications Commission is being dramatically transformed. The federal government has supported the divestiture of AT&T resulting from the 1982 consent decree of federal district court Judge Harold Greene, which largely eliminated the federal regulatory presence. A number of regulatory issues have subsequently been thrust upon states.[36] In addition, the nature of communications infrastructure in the U.S. economy has been transformed by the ever increasing integration of communications and computer technology. Telecommunications infrastructure, vital to the growth of producer services but also providing the possibility of technological innovation in traditional industries and services, has been the most important type of infrastructure of the emerging economy. A nation or state that does not acquire a sufficient level and quality of telecommunication services will certainly be at a competitive disadvantage.

As we have seen, state governments have long played important rôles in securing adequate infrastructure. Telecommunications presents a unique challenge for two reasons. The traditional regulatory rôle in telecommunications, based on the need to regulate a natural monopoly, the telephone company, involved a fairly stable industry with little technological innovation. For the last decade and for the foreseeable future, this is not the case. Advances in technology, such as satellites, microwave transmission, and fiber optics, have eroded the natural monopoly base of the local exchange companies. This has been recognized in the political and regulatory arena, and deregulation of many telecommunications services has occurred. Even so, state governments face a number of difficult questions. While deregulation will certainly lead to increased competition, will this necessarily lead to economic development? In the deregulated environment the continuation of universal service, a long-standing pillar of government regulation of telephone service, is not guaranteed. While low-income residential users are at greatest risk, the telecommunications needs of small businesses may not be attended to in the competitive environment. State governments are just now attempting to wrestle with these complex questions. Innovative states may well find solutions and take action that places them at an advantage over other states.

Labor laws

State governments promulgate a variety of measures that affect workers. The two types of action relevant for discussion are right-to-work laws and social wage programs, such as unemployment insurance. Differences among states are determined by decisions of state governments to adopt, or not, right-to-work laws and by levels of the social wage. To be explored here is the potential of these actions as instruments for economic development. For example, some argue that by adopting a right-to-work law and maintaining a low social wage, a state will lower the price of labor within its borders and therefore attract investment.

The Taft-Hartley Act of 1947, which drew upon the interstate commerce clause of the U.S. Constitution to justify federal labor laws, delegated to states the power to establish "union shop" agreements as legal pacts. Under the union shop agreement, all employees are required to join the union if the local unit wins an election. State laws prohibiting such agreements are known as right-to-work laws. Ostensibly, such legislation makes it illegal for a company to require or prohibit union membership as a condition of employment. In practice, such laws are seldom used to guarantee the right of union members to jobs with nonunion employers. Rather, they keep unions from influencing hiring practices by allowing companies to hire nonunion workers. As of late 1987, 22 states had right-to-work laws.

Much research has been conducted on the effect of right-to-work laws on wages, unionization, and economic development.[37] Though levels of unionization are relatively low in right-to-work states, it is difficult to attribute this to the law itself rather than to predominating cultural attitudes which produce both the right-to-work law and low levels of unionization. The evidence concerning the effect of industrial location patterns of right-to-work laws is also unclear. It appears that there may have been a positive effect in the 1950s, but once location adjustments were made by firms, any remaining potential effect from further change in the 1980s is unlikely.

Similar attitudes appear to be at work in determining levels of the social wage. The social wage encompasses such initiatives as unemployment insurance, workers' compensation, and welfare programs. These programs were pioneered by the states in the early years of the 20th century; only later did they become part of the federal mandate. Levels of the social wage vary drastically from state to state: states with high levels of unionization tend also to have high social wages; right-to-work states tend to have low social wages. In 1980 the maximum unemployment benefit available to a Massachusetts worker was more than twice that available to the unemployed in Georgia and Alabama. Similarly, California, Connecticut, and Michigan offered very high levels of welfare assistance compared with Alabama, Georgia, the Carolinas, or Arizona.[38]

States that provide low levels of benefits to workers and their families can tax business and industry at lower rates. Conventional location theory argues that low tax rates may attract new firms and lead to economic development. Examples for the 1980s appear to contradict that argument. Throughout the decade, Massachusetts and California, two states that led in all categories of the social wage, also led in economic development. Massachusetts' recovery was so vigorous that its minuscule unemployment rates rendered its excellent unemployment benefits unimportant in terms of interstate differentials.

Nevertheless, it is unlikely that either labor laws or the social wage can become a flexible tool for use by state policy makers. While many southern states experienced significant growth after they passed right-to-work laws, much of the postwar industrialization in the South can be attributed to relatively low existing real wage levels. Various historical reasons account for this, and it is unlikely that right-to-work laws had any significant effect on this pattern. Additionally, much of the industrial growth in the South occurred in nationally slow growing sectors. These sectors were decentralizing from the industrial heartland, attracted to the South by the availability of low-wage, low-skill labor.[39]

We also know that the rapidly growing advanced technology sectors are subject to location factors somewhat different from those of traditional industry. At one end, the R&D activities are attracted to centers with highly skilled workers; wage levels are virtually unimportant. At the manufacturing end, the search is often for low-wage areas, particularly where it is hoped to use women in the manufacturing process. When these trends are coupled with recapitalization and slow employment growth in traditional manufacturing and higher rates of growth in various services sectors, the ability of states to influence rates of economic growth through labor laws seems very limited. Similarly, neither raising nor lowering the social wage seems likely to provide much control over economic growth, at least in the short term.[40]

Intergovernmental relations

Intergovernmental relations are important to the issue of state economic development policy for two reasons. There are a number of federal programs which promote economic development, and state governments have a rôle in administering some of these. In addition, the evolving system of intergovernmental finance is placing new pressures on state government, and these may limit states' ability to pursue economic development initiatives.

It was argued above that the policy initiative in economic development had passed from the federal government to state governments. While this is true in terms of policy innovation, the funding of economic development programs by the federal government is considerably greater than that provided by state governments (see Table 3.6).[41] This differential is even larger when one notes that a significant portion of state expenditures represents a federal tax expenditure resulting from the deductibility of most state taxes. Many of the programs, such as the Economic Development Administration, Small Business Administration, Department of Housing and Urban Development, and the Department of Labor, have existed for many years.[42] Though the Reagan Adminstration generally attempted to reduce, if not eliminate, these programs, they continue to receive substantial funding from Congress. It appears that the Bush adminstration will cease attempts to reduce funding, but at the same time significant increases are not likely.

Table 3.6 Funding for economic development programs by state and local governments, in fiscal year 1983 (in $ million).

Type	State programs	Federal programs Federal administered	State administered
Direct expenditures[1]	280.0	18,260.2	8,604.0
Major expenditure functions:			
Small business assistance[2]	5.4	1,152.0	61.0
Training, employment, and other labor services	121.4	1,892.0	4,002.0
Research and development[3]	67.4	13,936.0	18.0
International trade promotion	36.0	608.0	0.0
Direct loans	114.8	2,872.6	0.0
Loan guarantees	23.2	12,095.9	0.0
Venture capital corporations	9.7	—	—

Notes:
[1] Excluding promotions for agriculture and energy.
[2] Includes only grants, not state technical assistance to small businesses.
[3] Civilian research and development.
Source: Congressional Budget Office, U.S. Congress, *The federal role in state industrial development programs* (Washington, D.C.: Government Printing Office, July 1984), p. 4.

State administration of federal economic development programs occurs, but infrequently. The principal cases are the Job Training Partnership Act (JTPA) and the Small Cities Community Development Block Grant (CDBG). The decentralization of federal programs has been a goal of Reagan's New Federalism, but with these two exceptions, little more than coordination of state and federal efforts occurs, usually through the provision of information, by state government, about federal programs to relevant constituents in the state.

The second relevant aspect of intergovernmental relations in the U.S. federalist system involves fiscal relations. During the last two decades state and local governments have become increasingly dependent on financial transfers from the federal government.[43] Local governments, in particular, are sensitive to cutbacks or limited growth in federal spending. Increasing pressure is being brought to bear on state governments to increase aid to cities or expand the use of state credit, especially for capital investments. In fact, state governments are becoming more important actors in the intergovernmental fiscal system.[44]

In addition to the fiscal responsibility of state governments toward local governments, local governments themselves are largely defined by state law; that is the powers of local government are derived from state laws. Local governments are also becoming involved in local development policies. Their ability to act is determined by enabling legislation and this varies among states. States, therefore, can mobilize resources of local governments in economic development through empowering these governments to undertake various actions.

Functions of state government and economic development: a summary

To bring this section to a close, a matrix of state activities which affect economic development has been developed (see Table 3.7). Two categories structure the matrix: (a) funding requirements, and (b) principal policy objective. The funding requirement is important for several reasons. First, state government funding of activities principally concerned with promoting economic development is relatively small, though state investments in infrastructure may be substantial. Yet there are other state activities with large budgets that indirectly affect state economies. The second dimension attempts to distinguish between activities with either an explicit or a direct effect (or both) on a state economy and those activities which have a potentially significant effect but whose principal objectives are not economic development.

Though many state functions can affect levels of economic activity within a state, the ability of states to use these functions as instruments to create a competitive advantage over other states is limited. The limitations are of three types. Traditional state functions emerged for various historical reasons, and the objectives of each of these functions have evolved. A single function can have several objectives, but to reformulate these objectives or add the objective of promoting economic development may, in fact, be inconsistent with other objectives,

Table 3.7 State activities affecting economic development: policy objectives and funding requirements.

	Funding	
	Own source revenue	No expenditures
Policy objective:		
Explicit economic development objective or effect	1 Economic development agencies 2 Infrastructure investments 3 Tax incentives	1 State administration of federal programs (JTPA, CDBG) 2 Regulation 3 Institutional mobilization
No explicit economic development objective	1 Education 2 Aid to cities 3 Fiscal policy 4 Procurement	1 State-derived powers of local governments 2 Labor laws

as we noted in the discussion of state regulation. In addition, many of the economic development policy instruments derived from these state activities are weak instruments in that other economic factors may dominate the impact of the instrument, as with tax incentives. The third limitation is financial. Though some states currently have a strong fiscal standing, long-term fiscal pressures make it unlikely that economic development programs will become major budget items.

On the other hand, state government can serve useful development functions in two areas. Some aspects of traditional functions can easily be reformulated or modified to incorporate existing objectives as well as to support development. Telecommunications infrastructure, in particular, is increasingly important, and the state rôle in securing the provision of this is not yet well established. In addition, state government can contribute to the development process by assuming responsibility for information generation and dissemination, whether in terms of research or export promotion, and of mobilization of resources. State government can provide the forum for identifying existing economic strengths and weaknesses and for formulating strategies for development. This very process itself mobilizes public and private resources.

State economic development policy: what is new and what is effective

Though state government is in a period of innovation and experimentation in economic development policy, this general concern of state government is not new. Examples of state action predate the Constitution, and a state rôle has continued to the present. In the post-World War II period states have played an important rôle in infrastructure provision, pursued industrial recruitment, and adopted countercyclical policies.

Before the recent upsurge in state activism, the principal explicit strategy that states pursued for economic development was industrial recruitment through state economic agencies and utility companies. Tax incentives and training subsidies were the principal policy instruments. States with relatively low levels of industrial activity competed for firms decentralizing from the industrial heartland. For these incentives to work, taxes and labor costs had to be important costs of production to the firms. The very success of this form of industrial recruitment reinforced the low-wage economy of these states and kept the level of public expenditures low. The effectiveness of this type of policy instrument, intended to make the state the low-cost site for a particular firm, places the state in competition with other states in a zero-sum game.

Although there is nothing wrong, in principle, with direct competition among states in industrial recruitment, the long-term effectiveness of this strategy for individual states is questionable and certainly does little to improve the national economy. The firms likely to be attracted by tax incentives, restrictive labor laws, or lax environmental standards are not ones likely to be leaders in the new economy.

Structural change has greatly complicated industrial recruitment strategies and has caused a change in the types of firm being targeted. For the rapid growth firms, tax concessions are relatively unimportant. In addition, structural change has focused attention on research, new products, innovative production technology, new firms, and foreign investment. Again, traditional incentives are not particularly important in these types of innovative activity.

It is the challenge presented by structural change that has produced the rapid growth in initiatives by state governments in science and technology.[45] The economic geography of the country is evolving, and many states are attempting to position themselves for the future. As the economic transition works itself out, there is a clear merging of state policies for economic development and for science and techno-logy. Industrial recruitment is frequently targeted to so-called high-tech firms, research-related facilities, and foreign investment with presum-ably advanced processes of production. States are investigating a wide range of activities well beyond the traditional tax-based incentives to compete in this new environment.

The human capital needs of the Information Age, with workers making increasingly frequent job and even occupation changes, are paramount. This generates very important implications for the public education system and for training programs, particularly for minorities and other disadvantaged groups. Many states are fully aware of these trends and are pursuing educational reform. State governments can clearly play a decisive rôle in meeting the human capital needs of the new economy. It is important to note that some states are already well positioned in this regard. While a state may, for a period, attract workers educated in some other state and thus avoid some education expenditures, this is no solution for the long term.

Judging by the historical record, state governments do not seem to be exercising their full potential in the area of infrastructure provision. While the immediate past problems of inadequate maintenance are being remedied, states do not seem to be thinking comprehensively about the infrastructure needs of the future, as did New York when it built the Erie Canal. This lack of activity and uncertainty about policy objectives is particularly evident in the area of telecommunications. The current rôle assumed by states is that of telephone industry regulation, and this rôle differs considerably from one which develops a policy to meet future telecommunication needs in the state.

While structural change is focusing attention on new industrial sectors and on research and development, it has also led to the very rapid growth of producer services, which consist of financial, managerial, and technical services rendered to businesses. The emerging economy has a great need for these services, and the economic structure and vitality of major metropolitan areas are becoming determined by them. The contribution that state policy can make to the development of these services is unclear. Even so, it is important to note that these sectors are a very significant feature of the economic landscape and policies have not been developed that support or nurture them.

Actions of state governments affect economies within states in many ways. There were instances in the past where state action had a decisive effect on the growth potential of a state. In most of these examples, the action involved the development of resources within a state rather than the attraction of resources from outside the state. The actions were not directed at a particular firm or set of firms but rather realized their effect through increasing the productivity of factors of production within the state. The current economic transition provides an opportune moment for states to act, as new patterns of development emerge. Although states may not have the resources for bold new actions, certain traditional functions should be reformulated and made consistent with the needs of the new economic reality. States already have center stage in discussions of development strategy. The proliferation of programs mobilizes resources, private and public, at fairly low expense. While these strategies and programs may not themselves have a decisive effect on economic development, they contribute toward creating an innovative and experimental environment that may well produce long-term effects in a state.

Notes

The author wishes to acknowledge helpful comments from Lynn Anderson, David Warner, Richard Barke, and Norton Grubb on an earlier version of this chapter. This chapter also received valuable support from the Elspeth Rostow Centennial Fellowship.

1   J. Herbers, "The new federalism: unplanned, innovative and here to stay," *Governing*, October 1987, 28–37.
2   While this policy may have some merit, empirical work has found that either states cannot maintain the integrity of the policy or do not have access to sufficient funding to make an impact. See R. Bahl, *Financing state and local government in the 1980s*

(New York: Oxford University Press, 1984), pp. 19–21, for a brief discussion of the literature.

3   N. Glickman & R. Wilson, "National context for urban policy" in *Local economies in transition*, ed. E. Bergman (Chapel Hill: Duke University Press, 1985), pp. 15–35.

4   E. E. Smead, *Governmental promotion and regulation of business* (New York: Appleton-Century-Crofts, 1969), pp. 3–9.

5   State governments were major investors in the rapid expansion of canals in the 18th century. State governments in New York, Pennsylvania, Ohio, Indiana, Illinois, and Virginia accounted for about 60 per cent of the investment in canals between 1815 through 1860. See H. H. Seagal, "Cycles of canal construction," in *Canals and American economic development*, ed. C. Goodrich (New York: Columbia University Press, 1961), pp. 213–15; see also C. Goodrich, *Government promotion of American canals and railroads, 1800–1890* (New York: Columbia University Press, 1960) p. 287.

6   H. H. Seagal, "Canals and economic development," in *Canals and economic development*, Goodrich, pp. 216–48; A. Watkins & D. Perry, "Regional change and the impact of uneven urban development," in *The rise of the Sunbelt cities*, ed. D. Perry & A. Watkins (Beverly Hills: Sage Publications, 1977), pp. 15–54.

7   Smead, *Governmental promotion and regulation of business*, pp. 201–2.

8   P. Wolf, *Land in America: its value, use and control* (New York: Pantheon, 1981), pp. 66–7.

9   T. W. Schultz, *Economic crisis in world agriculture* (Ann Arbor: University of Michigan Press, 1965), pp. 70–5; H. C. Knoblauch, "State agricultural experimental stations: a history of research policy and procedures," U.S. Department of Agriculture Miscellaneous Papers 904 (Washington, D.C.: Government Printing Office, 1962).

10   N. R. Pierce & J. Hagstrom, *The book of America: inside 50 states today* (New York: Norton, 1983), p. 468.

11   U.S. Department of Commerce, Bureau of the Census, *Governmental finances in 1984–1985*, GF85, no. 5 (Washington, D.C.: Government Printing Office, December 1986), Table 2.

12   S. D. Gold, "State fiscal conditions," Legislative Finance Paper no. 55 (Denver: National Conference of State Legislators, June 1987).

13   Tables 3.2 and 3.3 present expenditures and not source of funds. Intergovernmental transfers are important for several categories of expenditures. The consideration of intergovernmental transfer provides further evidence of the sharing of responsibilities among the various levels of government. See Bahl, *Financing state and local government*.

14   Bahl, *Financing state and local governments*, pp. 77–80.

15   See R. Devoy and H. Wise, *The Capitol budget* (Washington, D.C.: Council of State Planning Agencies, 1979).

16   S. D. Gold, "Taxation of business by American state and local governments," Legislative Finance Paper no. 53 (Denver: National Conference of State Legislatures, March 1986), p. 5.

17   There are a few recent examples of states making tax concessions to firms that are threatening to relocate outside the state. One example is Nebraska's concession to Con-Agra.

18   Advisory Commission on Intergovernmental Relations, State-local taxation and industrial location (Washington, D.C.: Advisory Commission on Intergovernmental Relations, April 1967).

19   M. K. Clarke, *Revitalizing states' economies: a review of state economic development policies and programs* (Washington, D.C.: National Governors' Association, 1986), p. 18.

20   R. F. Ferguson & H. Ladd, "Massachusetts," in *The new economic role of American states: strategies in a competitive world economy*, ed. R. Scott Fosler (New York: Oxford Univeristy Press, 1988), pp. 21–87.

21 Surveys of the literature can be found in M. Wasylenko, "Business climate, industry and employment growth: a review of the evidence," Occasional Paper no. 98 (Syracuse, N.Y.: Maxwell School of Citizenship and Public Affairs, Syracuse University, October 1985), and M. Kieschnick, *Taxes and growth: business incentives and economic development* (Washington, D.C.: Council of State Planning Agencies, 1981).

22 See W. C. Wheaton, "Interstate differences in the level of business taxation," *National Tax Journal* **36**, March 1983, 83–94.

23 R. J. Newman, "Industry migration and growth in the South," *Review of Economics and Statistics* **65**, February 1983, 76–86; and M. Wasylenko & T. McGuire, "Jobs and taxes: the effects of business climate on state employment growth rates," *National Tax Journal* **39**, December 1985, 497–512.

24 See Kieschnick, *Taxes and growth*, Ch. 4.

25 National Association of State Development Agencies, *1986 state development agency expenditure and salary survey* (Washington, D.C.: National Association of State Development Agencies, 1986). Not all economic development programs of a state are implemented by a state's development agency, so these figures underestimate total state expenditures for economic development.

26 Ibid., Summary Table.

27 A number of inventories of state economic development programs have been developed. J. Schmandt and R. Wilson (eds.), *Promoting high technology industries: initiatives and policies of state governments* (Boulder: Westview Press, 1987); Clarke, *Revitalizing state economies*; National Association of State Development Agencies, *Directory of incentives for business investment and development in the United States* (Washington, D.C.: The Urban Institute, 1983); C. Watkins, "Programs for innovative technology research in state strategies for economic development" (Washington, D.C.: National Governors' Association, December 1985).

28 D. E. Pilcer, *The states and international trade: new roles in export development* (Denver: National Conference of State Legislators, 1985).

29 Clarke, *Revitalizing state economies*, pp. 14–15.

30 Ibid., pp. 101–6.

31 For a discussion of the development of regulation in the railroad industry see Smead, *Governmental promotion and regulation of business*, pp. 202–6.

32 Ibid., pp. 438–9.

33 M. D. Reagan, *Regulation: the politics of policy* (Boston: Little, Brown, 1987), pp. 20–2.

34 Smead, *Governmental promotion and regulation of business*, pp. 412–17.

35 Reagan, *Regulation: the politics of policy*, Ch. 4.

36 R. M. Entman, *Issues in telecommunications regulation and competition: early policy perspectives from the states* (Cambridge, Mass.: Program on Information Resources Policy, 1985).

37 W. J. Moore & R. J. Newman, "The effects of right-to-work laws: a review of the literature," *Industrial and Labor Relations Review*, July 1985, 571–85.

38 B. Bluestone and B. Harrison, *Capital and communities: the causes and consequences of private disinvestment* (Washington, D.C.: The Progressive Alliance, 1980), pp. 180–5.

39 J. Rees, "Regional industrial shifts in the U.S. and the internal generation of manufacturing in growth centers of the Southwest," in *Interregional movements and regional growth*, ed. W. Wheaton (Washington, D.C.: The Urban Institute, 1979).

40 It should be remembered that the social wage may change for reasons unrelated to economic development.

41 There is considerable disagreement on the real level of expenditures by state government. These data must be obtained from individual states, and there is substantial variation among the states in terms of budgeting systems and definitions.

In addition, many state activities may be off-budget, such as capital programs capitalized through bonds.

42 For an inventory of federal programs see Northeast-Midwest Institute, *The 1983 guide to government resources for economic development* (Washington, D.C.: Northeast-Midwest Institute, 1982).

43 Bahl, *Financing state and local government*, pp. 8–17.

44 Ibid., pp. 197–9; Gold, "State fiscal conditions," pp. 20–4.

45 J. Schmandt and R. Wilson, "State science and technology policies: an assessment," *Economic Development Quarterly* **2**, 2 (1988) pp. 124–37.

II
Theory and evidence

4

High-tech policy, high-tech realities: the spatial distribution of high-tech industry in America[1]

AMY GLASMEIER

Introduction

STATE GOVERNMENT OFFICIALS are actively pursuing high-tech development[1] strategies to both boost employment levels and increase states' potentials for creating new industrial innovations. Programs range from the grand to the mundane. Recent plums in the competition for high-tech industry include the publicly sponsored super-collider/superconducting high-energy physics accelerator and Sematech—a technological enterprise consortium (the U.S. semiconductor industry's most recent response to Japan's current fundamental manufacturing advantage).

That competition for high technology is intense, and perceived rewards are great, may explain why so many states have redirected economic development policy to attract it. At last count, in the summer of 1988, at least 45 states had some type of high-tech development program. A desired outcome of these programs is to alter the existing distribution of high-tech industry in favor of particular states and localities (Clarke 1986; Glasmeier 1988).

Given established spatial tendencies of high-tech industry in the U.S., it is appropriate to question the efficacy of these programs. Can state economic development policy—which generally focuses on the short term—actually influence the spatial distribution of high-tech industries?[2] Or are there long-standing forces which would be difficult to affect significantly? Furthermore, is the advent of high-tech industrial growth a deviation from or a reinforcement of the long-standing patterns of uneven regional growth and development between rural and urban areas?

This chapter examines the spatial distribution of high-tech industrial development during the 1970s and early 1980s (a period of rapid high-technology growth). Policy concerns are addressed through a systematic analysis of high-tech employment and industrial location behavior.

The chapter begins by providing a broad overview of manufacturing location in the U.S. since the 1950s and discusses recent literature on high-tech industry location. Distribution of high-tech jobs over the 1972–82 period is examined as broad census regions are disaggregated to show that manufacturing states are still important centers for high-tech industry.

Continuing with a discussion of high-technology distribution, the chapter points out that despite some decentralization over the study period, few states boast large numbers of high-tech jobs. Not only is high-tech industry growth more prevalent in states with histories of manufacturing, high technology is also basically a big-city phenomenon. Again, while some decentralization is evident, new establishment formation is heavily represented in large urban agglomerations. This suggests that current state policies will reinforce existing urban concentrations of high-tech jobs rather than redirect current locational tendencies.

From this discussion, the chapter shifts focus from what is more generally known about high-tech industrial location tendencies to less known realities of high-tech industry in America's rural areas.[3] Here the story turns particularly grim. Despite significant manufacturing decentralization during the 1970s, little high-tech industry has moved into America's rural areas. Instead, assembly has moved offshore, and R&D and technical production has further concentrated in existing high-tech centers.

Armed with these facts, state policy makers can begin to formulate policies that balance the desire to attract high technology with the need for broad-based policies which address long-standing problems of individuals and communities which will otherwise be left out of the race for high technology. Thus the policy implications of the spatial distribution of high-tech industry conclude the chapter.

The spatial location of manufacturing in America

Spatial location of manufacturing industries in the United States has undergone significant change over the last 30 years. Prior to 1960, states in the Midwest (Ohio, Illinois, Wisconsin, Indiana, Michigan) and in the Northeast (Pennsylvania, New York, New Jersey, Massachusetts, Connecticut) accounted for 64 per cent of national manufacturing employment (Perloff, Wingo, Lampard and Muth 1960). But since 1960, major shifts have occurred. Currently, western and southern states harbor almost 50 percent of the nation's total manufacturing employment (Markusen 1988).

Manufacturing decentralization occurred not only between regions, but also within regions, from metropolitan to non-metropolitan (rural) areas (Lonsdale and Seyler 1979). Between 1962 and 1978, rural and nonmetropolitan areas gained 1.8 million jobs, as opposed to metropolitan growth of only 1.4 million.

Not only was manufacturing job growth in rural areas higher than in cities, rural areas also actually increased their share of total national manufacturing employment. Between 1962 and 1978, rural and nonmetropolitan areas' share of national manufacturing employment rose from 23.5 to 28.8 per cent (Haren and Holling 1979).

In addition to employment increases in traditionally rural, resource-based industries (e.g. timber and chemicals), rural areas also gained jobs in furniture, electronics, fabricated metal products, and textiles. The much-heralded rural renaissance of the 1960s and early 1970s is, therefore, largely attributable to rural gains in mature industry manufacturing employment. And while rural job gains during this period were substantial, new jobs did not substantially differ from the previously dominant low-wage and economically less significant manufacturing employment already present.

Explanations for shifts in manufacturing

A number of theories have been proposed to account for the spatial shift of U.S. manufacturing employment. One explanation links employment filtering and the product cycle model of industrial development (Erickson 1978).[4] This model offers observations to help explain manufacturing decentralization. For example, the model points out that as industries mature, the location of their employment changes over time.

The product cycle model follows three stages—innovation, growth, and maturation. Across all three stages, demand-led growth of industrial output drives the industry through successive states of technological development—from unstandardized single-unit output that is heavily dependent on highly skilled labor to capital-intensive standardized mass production employing low-skilled workers. Dependence on skilled labor in the early stage of the model serves to concentrate production in "industrial agglomerations" (Rees 1979; Norton and Rees 1979; Markusen, Hall and Glasmeier 1986).

As production becomes more standardized, hence routinized, increases in scale of output decrease the per-unit transaction cost of acquiring inputs, and locational flexibility of production increases. The product cycle model predicts spatial clustering in the early stage of a product's life, and spatial decentralization as it reaches mass production and maturity. As an industry matures over time, the organizational structure of firms also changes from single- to multi-unit branch plants. These production facilities are often spun off to low-cost locations.

Thus manufacturing employment shifts away from traditional industrial centers and from metro to nonmetro areas as mature phases of production seek low-cost manufacturing sites. And certainly, in the case of rural industrialization, most growth in manufacturing jobs occurred in mature industries (Bloomquist 1987).

The spatial division of labor

While the product cycle model is valuable for explaining the spatial decentralization of manufacturing, it underestimates the importance of other strategic factors which shape the spatial distribution of industry. In particular, the model overlooks the constraint that firms face when production requires a technical labor force. It also fails to recognize that one solution to this problem includes creating a spatial division of labor. This is particularly important in the case of high-tech industries because on the basis of this dimension, we can begin to explain the contemporary spatial location of high-tech industries in the United States.

Most authors suggest that the spatial division of labor evolves as firms seek locations with profitable supplies of appropriate labor. Historically, location decisions of single-unit firms were constrained by transportation costs, access to markets and labor, and rigid, mechanically integrated methods of production (Storper 1982). But in recent years, firms' locational choices have increased dramatically due to changes in corporate organization from single to multi-establishment firms (Hymer 1979). Telecommunications advances assist in decentralization by allowing real-time communication between far-flung production operations. Transportation developments such as air freight have further decreased shipping time and costs. Finally, the application of microelectronics to manufacturing processes makes production capacities more flexible, hence, more divisible.

Locational choices of high-tech firms are, however, constrained by the need for different types of labor. In the design stage, firms employ high proportions of technically trained engineers and technicians. As a product becomes stable and production standardizes, engineers and technicians become less important, and other types of labor, particularly production-oriented, take over. This dependence on different types of labor means that firms producing high-tech products face both choices and constraints in selecting production locations.

Firms can and do operate vertically integrated production facilities with technical, production, and assembly workers in one location. But increasingly, employers choose to separate technical from non-technical workers, and some product characteristics may encourage or impede spatial segregation.

For example, Clark argues that differences in bargaining power among workers encourage separation of technical and nontechnical employees (1981). Employers have the option of moving technical activities outside core industrial areas to restrict skilled workers' inter-firm mobility. But anecdotal evidence suggests this is dysfunctional because employers also find it difficult to attract highly trained workers to remote locations. On the other hand, unskilled production workers can ill afford to be choosy. Thus employers are more apt to decentralize low-skilled production activities to rural outlands.

The nature of products and production technologies can also influence the feasibility of a spatial division of labor (thus regulating decentralization). Case studies of the semiconductor industry indicate that although firms maintain technical activities in core industry centers, production work is often spun off to satellite centers, and assembly work is shifted to low-wage, low-skilled locations (Saxenian 1981; Storper 1982; Massey 1984). The resulting pattern is highly automated production primarily shifting to the Sunbelt, beyond core centers of technical activity (Sayer 1985; Glasmeier 1986a).

High-tech industry location

The literature on the location of high-tech industries in the U.S. has expanded rapidly over the last five years (Glasmeier, Hall and Markusen 1983; Armington, Harris and Odle 1983; Malecki 1985; Malecki 1986). But although numerous studies exist, it is difficult to make generalizations about high-tech industry location because authors have addressed varying levels of spatial aggregation, worked with different time periods, and utilized numerous databases. Nevertheless, even without a common framework, a review of available work reveals several significant patterns.

With few exceptions, high-tech industries grow in places which have existing bases of business support services. Thus while one might argue that, prior to 1950, Silicon Valley was a fruit orchard, in fact, this benchmark industrial cluster is a subregion of the Greater Bay area. Capital, business services, social infrastructure, and, importantly, markets, were all available within a 30-mile radius.

Defense spending constitutes another important factor in high-tech industry's location. Since World War II, high levels of defense spending have been key to the development of science-based industry. The Department of Defense served dually as a major source of R&D funding, and the market for resulting high-tech products. Areas that were awarded high levels of defense spending also gained large numbers of high-tech jobs.

High-tech industries are also attracted to places with existing technical workforces. New high-tech firm formation has been highest in these areas. In the early years, high-tech industries created their own labor market by hiring engineers from universities across the nation. Over time, as high technology took root and began to form agglomerations, principal sources of technical labor were strengthened.

High-tech industries have created their own spatial division of labor (Glasmeier 1986b). Because few states have high numbers of engineers and engineering technicians, a large portion of high-tech development occurring outside the primary technical centers consists of branch plants. Little product-related R&D occurs in these outlying facilities, although process R&D has been important in a number of places (e.g. Austin, Texas). Overall, regions which received branch plants have experienced low levels of new high-tech firm formation. Thus while branch plants have produced significant numbers of direct jobs, there has been relatively little innovation resulting in new products which form the basis for an integrated high-tech agglomeration.

Thus a pattern of contemporary high-tech industry location emerges. High-tech industries are likely to be found in states with traditions of innovative manufacturing, and within major metropolitan areas where business services and other urban amenities are ample. The sizes of both a state's industrial base and individual metropolitan areas are key factors in explaining concentrations of high-tech employment. And locations experiencing rapid increases in new firm formation are those with pools of technically trained labor. Thus states and cities with high-tech manufacturing bases (including corporate headquarters and R&D labs) have the highest rates of new firm formation. These findings suggest that the composition of high-tech industries is quite different across locations. Some places are clearly centers of research and development and advanced manufacturing. Others have gained highly automated production. Still others have received the more mundane, least technical, and most labor-intensive aspects of high-tech industries.

Decentralization of manufacturing in the United States has long produced shifts in jobs both across regions and between metropolitan and nonmetropolitan areas. Explanations for this development focus on product maturation which leads firms to shift production to low-cost locations. In high-technology industries, the division of labor facilitates such decentralization. High-tech products can be segmented; firms locate technical activities in core regions, but move production to other regions where appropriate pools of labor can be found.

Recognition that the spatial division of labor is an important factor in high-tech industry location is the ingredient most often missing from policy discussions. Consequently, our understanding (or misunderstanding) of the spatial inclinations of these industries tends to be unidimensional. In fact, high-tech employment location also reflects long-standing tendencies in the distribution of population and economic activity. While shifts in high-tech employment are clearly discernible at a regional level, employment distribution is still greatly influenced by past patterns of industrial development.

Clearly states that are primarily recipients of mature phases of manufacturing employment cannot expect to compete equally for all phases of high-tech employment. Firms in the early stages of innovation are attracted to existing concentrations of technical activities. And there are structural constraints on states' abilities to create new industrial seedbeds.

Where high-tech jobs are

Like the population and industry as a whole, high-tech industries have been broadly decentralizing since the early 1970s (Table 4.1). The southern and western regions have apparently been gaining high-tech employment at the expense of northeastern and midwestern states (Table 4.2).

From 1972 to 1982, distribution of high-tech jobs became more evenly divided among regions. Starting in the early 1970s, the Northeast and Midwest together accounted for a majority of high-tech jobs. Over the ten-year period, the South emerged as the dominant high-tech region followed by the Northeast with 26 percent, the Midwest with 25.2 percent, and the West with 22.6 percent of high-tech employment.

While this shift in high-tech job shares modestly favored the South, western states actually gained the largest number of new high-tech jobs created during the 1972–82 period (Table 4.3). And whereas new job growth in the South occurred over the earlier five-year period, rapid high-tech expansion in the West occurred more recently.

In spite of the South's rapid job gains and considerable increase in absolute numbers of high-tech jobs in 1982, the region's manufacturing

Table 4.1 Regional population change, absolute shares, 1980, 1970, 1960.

Region	1980	1970	1960
Northeast	21.69	24.13	24.91
Midwest	25.99	27.84	28.79
South	33.28	30.97	30.66
West	19.06	17.14	15.64

Source: U.S. Bureau of the Census, *State and metropolitan data book* (Washington, D.C.: U.S. Government Printing Office, 1986).

Table 4.2 Proportion of high-tech employment in four census regions, 1972, 1977, 1982.

Region	1972—Percentage of nation	1977—Percentage of nation	1982—Percentage of nation
Northeast	29.72	27.79	25.95
Midwest	31.03	29.97	25.21
South	22.63	24.23	26.25
West	16.63	18.00	22.59

Source: U.S. Bureau of the Census, *Census of manufacturers, plant location tape* (Washington, D.C.: U.S. Government Printing Office, 1986).

Table 4.3 Absolute difference of regional high-tech job change, 1972–82.

Region	Absolute difference 1972–82
Northeast	151,975
Midwest	53,058
South	479,639
West	537,054

Source: U.S. Bureau of the Census, *Census of manufacturers, plant location tape* (Washington, D.C.: U.S. Government Printing Office, 1986).

base is still dominated by non-high-tech manufacturing industries (Glickman and Glasmeier 1989). Only the Northeast and West exceeded the national average (29 percent) of high-tech jobs (Table 4.4). The Midwest and South both lagged behind with, respectively, 26 and 25 percent of all regional manufacturing employment in high-tech industries.

These theoretical insights present conflicting signals to policy makers. On the one hand, few centers of technical skill exist, therefore indiscriminate attempts to foster new innovation are likely to fail. On the other hand, if most states receive only production employment, how can they turn this to their benefit? Currently, state policy efforts ignore important distinctions between technical and nontechnical functions of high-tech industry (and their differing supportive contexts). By emphasizing characteristics thought to attract technical aspects of high-tech industry, states compete — often imitating each others' policies. Yet few can realistically achieve their goals because regardless of success in attracting high technology, there is pressure to maintain a pro-business, low-cost image to compete for other forms of manufacturing. Thus the real issue is whether states can simultaneously promote and pay for the glamorous regional attributes thought necessary to attract the technical elements of high technology while

Table 4.4 Percentage of high-tech to total manufacturing in four Census regions, 1981.

Region	% high-tech jobs
Northeast	30
Midwest	26
South	25
West	41
Nation	29

Source: U.S. Bureau of the Census, *Census of manufacturers, plant location tape* (Washington, D.C.: U.S. Government Printing Office, 1986).

maintaining low wages and low taxes. Massachusetts, New York, and Florida recognize this inherent contradiction and have implemented multifaceted programs supporting labor skills improvement along with research and development.

The Sunbelt's strategy of low wages and a union-free environment is attractive to those aspects of high-tech manufacturing most sensitive to labor cost differentials. But can these factors alter the existing distribution of high-tech industry technical functions? Probably not. Because it is the engineering and new product development aspects of high-tech industry that states most desire, policy makers must address the inherent contradictions in economic development policies designed to attract both the low and the high ends of high-tech industry.

Growth of high-tech jobs in U.S. Census divisions

At an aggregate level, high-tech employment decentralized toward the southern and western regions. Yet more disaggregated analysis indicates that only a few states within each region enjoyed significant levels of high-tech employment (Table 4.5). The following section

Table 4.5   High-tech job shares by Census division, 1972, 1977, 1982.

Census division	Census division employment 1972	Census division employment 1977	Census division employment 1982	Census division employment as a percentage of the nation 1972	Census division employment as a percentage of the nation 1977	Census division employment as a percentage of the nation 1982
New England	402,356	439,298	517,161	9.19	9.23	9.23
Middle Atlantic	899,101	883,439	936,271	20.53	18.56	16.71
East North Central	1,081,026	1,107,121	1,049,330	24.68	23.26	18.73
West North Central	277,898	319,745	362,652	6.35	6.72	6.47
South Atlantic	447,595	507,714	653,123	10.22	10.67	11.66
East South Central	190,200	211,922	239,976	4.34	4.45	4.28
West South Central	353,151	433,952	577,486	8.06	9.12	10.31
Mountain	117,867	145,536	251,509	2.69	3.06	4.49
Pacific	610,582	711,563	1,013,995	13.94	14.95	18.10

Source: U.S. Bureau of the Census, *Census of manufactures, plant location tape* (Washington, D.C.: U.S. Government Printing Office, 1986).

examines high-tech employment by states within census divisions. Because constituent states have historically shared common economic elements, census divisions are convenient units of analysis. For example, states in the West South Central division possess major economic components in oil and agriculture. And while we can expect some decentralization due to national trends, industrial filtering has often occurred among states which shared a common industrial history (e.g. within the Midwest, many states have received auto parts and assembly plants spun out of the Michigan auto complex). Studies of spatial filtering have shown that rural midwestern manufacturing plants are headquartered in the major cities within the surrounding region (Erickson 1978). Therefore, we would expect the filtering process associated with industrial decentralization to be evident among states in a census division.

New England states

High-tech growth in New England states ranged from the phenomenal (Maine increased by 83 percent, New Hampshire by 89 percent) to the unremarkable (Rhode Island and Vermont grew much less dramatically). Except for Connecticut, which trailed the national average for both the earlier and later periods, the region's remaining states grew at rates above the national average for high-tech job change over the entire ten-year period. Yet high-tech employment growth was concentrated in Massachusetts. For every job created in any of the peripheral states, Massachusetts added two.[5]

Middle Atlantic states

High-tech employment in the Middle Atlantic region failed to grow at the national rate over the ten-year period. Weak employment growth accompanied reconcentration of employment shares in New York and New Jersey at the expense of Pennsylvania (which actually declined). Of the modest 37,100 new jobs created over the ten-year period, 57 percent occurred in New Jersey, with the remainder in New York. Much of New Jersey's growth was tied to the state's large chemical complex.

East North Central states

With the exception of Michigan, East North Central states lost considerable numbers of jobs during the 1972–82 period. To the extent that there were shifts in states' shares of regional employment, Michigan's gains were experienced as modest losses by other states.

West North Central states

Unlike their midwestern sister, states in the West North Central division experienced healthy gains in both high-tech plants and employment over the ten-year period. Except in Iowa and Missouri, job gains were at or above the national average. As with other regions, employment shares remained concentrated over the period studied. Minnesota emerged as the dominant state in the region. In contrast, Missouri lost ground, falling from first to second place in regional employment shares.

South Atlantic states

Rapid job growth in the South Atlantic region accompanied a process of consolidation of high-tech employment shares in Florida, North Carolina, and to a lesser extent, Georgia. Other states (Maryland, Virginia, South Carolina and Delaware) lost modest shares of the region's total high-tech base over the same period. Florida, with the region's largest employment base, also experienced the greatest share of net job gains (33 percent), followed by North Carolina, Georgia, South Carolina, and Maryland.

South East Central states

The South East Central region experienced some high-tech employment decentralization. In terms of job change, Alabama gained 38 percent of new high-tech jobs, followed by Tennessee, Kentucky, and Mississippi. Over the ten-year period, only Alabama and Mississippi grew above the national rate for high-tech job change.

West South Central states

The West South Central division exhibited one of the greatest levels of high-tech employment concentration. Between 1972 and 1982, Texas' share of high-tech employment increased from 67 to 69 percent. Louisiana and Arkansas saw their shares drop modestly over the same period.

Texas' employment gains dwarfed those of all surrounding states—with job increases six times that of the region's next most populous state, Oklahoma. In absolute terms, Texas gained seven out of ten new jobs created in the region over the ten-year period.

Mountain states

Mountain states demonstrated a reversal in which the dominant state, Colorado, lost shares while Arizona gained slightly more of the region's net new jobs. Arizona accounted for 35 percent of high-tech jobs, followed by Colorado with 30 percent, and Utah with 13 percent. Except for Wyoming, the remaining seven states posted percentage gains at least triple the national average.

Pacific states

States in the Pacific division reflected the most extreme pattern of employment and plant concentration. Ninety percent of the region's high-tech employment was concentrated in California. Additionally, California had ten times as many jobs as the next largest state, Washington. California also experienced ninety percent of total jobs gains, i.e. nine out of ten jobs created in the region over the ten-year period were in California.

Key states continue gains

This analysis shows that high-tech job growth is much more variegated than most analyses suggest. While in some regions high-tech jobs appeared to be decentralizing, the majority of states in these substate regions experienced growth rates below that of the dominant state. Therefore, rapid growth appeared to concentrate rather than spread high-tech jobs among states.

Of critical importance for policy, rapid growth of high-tech industries has not promoted the significant intra-regional decentralization that some researchers reported for earlier periods (Markusen et al., 1986). For decentralization to be apparent, one would expect much more rapid rates of high-technology growth in peripheral states adjacent to urban industrial cores. In fact, the reverse appears to be true. Few states gained large numbers of high-tech jobs and plants. States that began the period with a majority of high-tech jobs maintained and, in some instances, improved their positions over other states and regions. We don't dispute that peripheral areas gained high-tech jobs, but analysis does not reveal major changes occurring during a period of rapid growth within these industries.

Finally, the notion that high-tech job shifts occur across regions is analytically insignificant given the varied experiences of different regions and the fact that concentrations of high-tech jobs and plants have been remarkably stable over the last 10 to 20 years.

Concentrations of high-tech industry

State-level high-tech jobs and plants

That the Northeast and Midwest boast significant numbers of high-tech jobs indicates that a history of manufacturing can be an asset for high-tech development. A region's success with high-tech industries is tied in part to its economic history. Those that enjoyed earlier eras of innovation clearly have an advantage in further rounds of industrial growth (e.g. New England and the West North Central states). Thus it is hardly surprising that absolute distribution of high-tech employment is also intimately tied to the historic concentration of industry among particular U.S. regions.

States with the largest concentrations of high-tech jobs were located in traditional manufacturing regions. Ten of the fourteen states with the largest concentrations of total high-tech plants and employment were located in the Northeast, Middle Atlantic and Great Lakes regions (Table 4.6). In 1982 these 14 states were collectively responsible for 73 percent of total high-tech employment.

The spatial concentration of high-tech employment was even more powerfully manifest in the proportions of both total and manufacturing employment accounted for by these states. Collectively, while comprising three-quarters of all high-tech employment, these 14 states also contained 68 percent of all manufacturing employment and 64 percent of all nonagricultural jobs. Thus the importance of traditional manufacturing states as centers of high-tech employment cannot be disputed.

Proportional measures of high-tech employment

That long-standing centers of manufacturing exhibited large numbers of high-tech jobs simply reflects the influence of place size on the composition of industry. But how important is high-tech industry to the economic base of manufacturing states? By examining the proportion of a state's manufacturing base comprising high-tech industries, we see an indication of the changing regional distribution of high-tech manufacturing jobs.

Comparing 1982 levels of high-tech jobs to total manufacturing employment revealed that 21 states have a high-tech base exceeding the national average of 29 percent. Based on this measure, state rankings varied considerably. Seven states (Texas, Connecticut, California, Massachusetts, New Jersey, Illinois, and Florida) exhibited large numbers of absolute jobs as well as having a manufacturing base specializing in high-tech industry. The residual states with a specialization in high-tech jobs were primarily southern and western.

How do we interpret these findings? Manufacturing in the industrial heartland is clearly of mixed vintage. In a number of important cases, states which have established bases of innovative industries (Connecticut, Massachusetts, and Illinois) maintained a substantial high-tech job base. The success of southern and western states in attracting or spawning innovative industries is more likely tied to federal investments in postwar defense spending, the space program, and even federal policies mandating the decentralization of military production away from the coasts.

This measure provides the first indication of changes occurring in manufacturing employment distribution in the United States. While states in the Northeast and Midwest had large numbers of high-tech

Table 4.6 Estimated employment in high-tech industry, 1982.

States	1982 High-tech employment[a]	Percentage of total national manufacturing[b]	Percentage of total national employment[b]
California	907,512	11	11
Texas	400,276	6	7
Wyoming	366,761	7	8
Illinois	327,096	6	5
Pennsylvania	312,280	6	5
Ohio	284,773	6	5
New Jersey	257,230	4	3
Massachusetts	241,295	3	3
Florida	174,265	2	4
Michigan	173,011	5	4
Connecticut	172,790	2	2
Indiana	138,885	3	2
Wisconsin	125,566	3	2
North Carolina	123,844	4	3
Percentage of national total	73%	68%	64%

Sources: Employment estimates of high-tech jobs in (a) U.S. Bureau of the Census, *Census of manufactures, plant location tape,* and (b) U.S. Bureau of the Census, *State and metropolitan data book* (Washington, D.C.: U.S. Government Printing Office, 1986).

jobs, other locations with a more recent history of manufacturing have also been the recipients of high-tech job growth. An important caveat: the high ratio of high-tech manufacturing in many smaller states with no history of manufacturing was often due to the *absence* of employment in other manufacturing industries. Thus although the tendency is to predict from this observed employment that a location will be capable of spawning innovation, really it is difficult to evaluate the significance of such findings based on the proportional measure of high-tech to manufacturing jobs alone.

Certainly, growth in high technology is cause for some optimism. But these aggregate data do not describe the *type* of high-tech activity occurring in each location. As noted earlier, the concentration of high-tech employment based on absolute job shares closely matched the spatial division of labor (Glasmeier 1986a). States with higher proportions of engineers and technicians and lower proportions of production workers in high-tech industries also tended to have large numbers of high-tech jobs and manufacturing histories. In contrast, many states which experienced rapid increases in high-tech jobs were not new centers of innovation, but rather were technical centers of production employment.

If this new source of employment indeed reflects the growth and maturation phases of high-tech job change, it is questionable whether states should treat this component of high-tech industry differently from general manufacturing. Nor should expectations about the effect of such manufacturing on the structure of a local economy necessarily include the creation of industrial innovation centers. While it is true that numerous states experienced large percentage increases in new high-tech jobs during the 1972–82 period, with the exception of California, most states began with a small manufacturing base and in no way rivaled the primacy of the few existing cores of high technology. Put most simply, long-standing centers continued to dominate the high-tech landscape.

Can states change high-tech industry location?

The persistent concentration of high-tech jobs in particular areas raises serious questions about the potential of state policies to modify the spatial pattern of technology-based employment. How should we evaluate the success of these programs? Since states with the greatest existing base of high-tech industry (i.e., those needing assistance least) will have the resources to invest the most, it will be difficult to separate the impact of high-tech programs from that of states' existing advantages. Independent of state policies, established centers of high technology will simply benefit most from the spatial division of labor in high technology because they are likely to harbor the technical elements of these industries. In peripheral areas where resources are more limited, high-tech programs and development efforts may only marginally adjust a state's relative share of high technology.

The metropolitan concentration of high-tech industry

High technology: a big-city phenomenon

General manufacturing has slowly decentralized since World War II. In 1969, 82 percent of the nation's manufacturing employment was already concentrated in metropolitan areas. By 1982, major cities still captured 80 percent of manufacturing jobs. High-tech jobs are even more concentrated in cities. In 1972, a total of 87 percent of high-tech jobs and 89 percent of plants were concentrated in cities over 250,000 in population. By 1982, high-tech employment and plants showed only a negligible propensity to decentralize (86 percent of high-tech jobs and 87 percent of all plants were still found in cities with over 250,000 inhabitants). Key sectors—computers, semiconductors, electronic components, and communications equipment—were even more spatially concentrated. Over the same ten-year period, these industries became increasingly concentrated in large cities. In 1972, 86 percent of jobs and 89 percent of plants were in metropolitan areas with populations over 250,000. By 1982, although plant concentration declined somewhat, the metropolitan share of these high-tech jobs increased to 95 percent. The most dynamic sectors of high technology, therefore, gravitate toward cities where both skilled and unskilled labor are abundant.

Metropolitan manufacturing and high-tech industry

Despite these statistics, it has become fashionable to assume that high-tech industries avoid large cities with established histories of manufacturing. In fact, the distribution of high-tech jobs shows that metropolitan areas of over one million in population remain the primary locations for most high-tech employment.

Of 300 cities, 28 accounted for 50 percent of all U.S. high-tech employment (Table 4.7). With few exceptions (e.g., the Wichita, Kansas; Rochester, New York; and Bridgeport, Connecticut SMSAs),

Table 4.7 Proportionate share of 1982 high-tech employment and national laborforce.

SMSA	Share of 1982 national laborforce (%)	Share of national high-tech employment (%)
Los Angeles, CA	5.08	6.05
Chicago, IL	3.90	4.17
San Jose, CA	1.05	3.78
Boston, MA	2.63	3.20
Philadelphia, PA	3.19	2.47
Anaheim, CA	1.33	3.32
Houston, TX	2.28	2.21
Dallas, TX	1.60	2.11
Newark, NJ	1.19	1.76
Nassau-Suffolk, NY	1.26	1.61
New York, NY	5.33	1.58
Detroit, MI	2.17	1.53
Minneapolis, MN	1.54	1.48
San Diego, CA	0.90	1.30
Cleveland, OH	1.67	1.23
Hartford, CT	0.67	1.23
Milwaukee, IL	0.68	1.16
Bridgeport, CT	0.59	1.13
St. Louis, MO	1.42	1.13
Phoenix, AZ	0.89	1.00
San Francisco, CA	1.24	0.98
Rochester, NY	0.58	0.96
Denver, CO	1.07	0.90
Wichita, KS	0.29	0.85
Pittsburgh, PA	1.23	0.80
Seattle, WA	0.94	0.80
Cincinnati, OH	0.83	0.79
Baltimore, MD	1.13	0.76
Total share:		50.29

Source: U.S. Bureau of the Census, *Census of manufactures, plant location tape* (Washington, D.C.: U.S. Government Printing Office, 1986).

all have populations exceeding one million and rank among the top 40 metropolitan areas based on absolute population size (Bureau of the Census 1986). Although high-tech industry is attracted to newly growing areas, traditional manufacturing centers boast considerable numbers of high-tech jobs.

While much has been made of the declining ability of manufacturing cities to maintain high-tech jobs, large cities' shares of high-tech employment changed little from 1972 to 1982 (although some shifting among cities is evident) (Table 4.8). Thus while there has been

Table 4.8 Share of national high-tech employment, 1972, 1977, 1982.

SMSA	1972	1977	1982
Los Angeles, CA	6.45	5.87	6.05
Chicago, IL	5.78	5.36	4.17
San Jose, CA	1.69	2.23	3.78
Boston, MA	2.94	3.00	3.20
Philadelphia, PA	3.32	2.88	2.47
Anaheim, CA	1.42	1.95	3.32
Houston, TX	1.43	1.71	2.21
Dallas, TX	1.73	1.84	2.11
Newark, NJ	2.05	1.93	1.76
Nassau-Suffolk, NY	1.38	1.39	1.61
New York, NY	2.05	1.70	1.58
Detroit, MI	1.89	1.83	1.53
Minneapolis, MN	1.45	1.44	1.48
San Diego, CA	0.86	1.15	1.30
Cleveland, OH	1.70	1.39	1.23
Hartford, CT	1.49	1.32	1.23
Milwaukee, IL	1.61	1.46	1.16
Bridgeport, CT	1.32	1.22	1.13
St. Louis, MO	1.34	1.27	1.13
Phoenix, AZ	0.65	0.77	1.00
San Francisco, CA	0.93	0.99	0.98
Rochester, NY	1.09	1.10	0.96
Denver, CO	0.68	0.75	0.90
Wichita, KS	0.79	0.77	0.85
Pittsburgh, PA	1.13	1.03	0.80
Seattle, WA	0.78	0.71	0.80
Cincinnati, OH	0.89	0.85	0.79
Baltimore, MD	0.82	0.67	0.76
Total share:	49.66	48.58	50.29

Source: U.S. Bureau of the Census, *Census of manufactures, plant location tape* (Washington, D.C.: U.S. Government Printing Office, 1986).

some geographic spreading of high-tech jobs, they remain remarkably concentrated in a few large metropolitan areas.

High-tech manufacturing centers[6]

Analyzing the distribution of high-tech jobs across the USA's regions requires measures which capture both the importance of high-tech job levels and the composition of this employment. We first examine those cities whose manufacturing base consists of 50 percent or more of high-tech jobs.

In 1982 high-tech manufacturing employment made up 50 percent or more of all manufacturing in 51 of 305 metropolitan areas (Table 4.9). In this group of predominantly southern and western metropolitan areas, one of every two manufacturing jobs was in high-tech

Table 4.9 Cities in which high-tech employment comprises 50% or more of total manufacturing, 1982.

SMSA	Population (1000s)	% high-tech employment
Reno, NV	212	99
Melbourne, FL	329	99
Huntsville, AL	210	92
Oxnard, CA	584	91
Tucson, AZ	595	89
Wichita, KS	428	88
Colorado Springs, CO	349	86
Lake Charles, LA	175	84
Hagerstown, MD	112	83
Fort Collins, CO	166	82
Victoria, TX	74	81
Greeley, CO	132	80
Albuquerque, NM	449	80
Midland, TX	114	77
Portsmouth, ME	206	77
San Jose, CA	1,371	77
Galveston, TX	215	76
Lakeland, FL	355	69
Wilmington, DE	540	68
Casper, WY	75	68
Lubbock, TX	219	68
Santa Barbara, CA	323	67
Sherman-Dennison, TX	95	67
Fort Walton, FL	128	66
Baton Rouge, LA	538	66
Bloomington, IL	122	66
Boise City, ID	189	65
San Diego, CA	2,063	65
Enid, OK	65	63
Odessa, TX	144	62
Savannah, GA	232	62
Charleston, NC	267	61
Daytona Beach, FL	300	61
Richmond-Petersburg, VA	761	59
Abilene, TX	123	58
Richland, WA	149	57
Beaumont, TX	392	56
Anaheim, CA	2,075	56
Binghampton, NY	264	55
Austin, TX	645	55
Fort Lauderdale, FL	1,093	54
Rockford, IL	279	54
Springfield, IL	190	54
Nassau-Suffolk, NY	2,653	53
Phoenix, AZ	1,714	52
Lima, OH	152	52
Asheville, NC	166	51
Johnson City, WV	442	51
Charlotte, NC	1,031	51
Longview, TX	168	50
Orlando, FL	824	50

Source: U.S. Bureau of the Census, *Census of manufactures, plant location tape* (Washington, D.C.: U.S. Government Printing Office, 1986).

production. A number of features distinguished these places from both traditional centers of manufacturing and fast-growing metropolitan areas.

The distinct clusters of metropolitan areas in this group include: a) seven dominant cores of more than one million in population—Anaheim, California; Fort Lauderdale, Florida; Phoenix, Arizona; San Diego, California; Charlotte, North Carolina; and San Jose, California; b) technical branch plant locations with more than 500,000 in population—including Austin, Texas; Orlando, Florida; Santa Barbara, California; and Tucson, Arizona; and c) many smaller metropolitan areas with fewer than 500,000 inhabitants—Charleston, West Virginia; Colorado Springs, Colorado; Huntsville, Alabama; and Melbourne, Florida.

Sunbelt high-tech jobs appear most significantly in some of the region's largest cities. This concentration is partly due to the information-intensive nature of these industries and their need for high levels of manufacturing and business services. And given the long-standing rôle these nodal centers play in the evolution and dissemination of industrial innovations, the presence of high-tech industries is not surprising.

Rural development and high-tech industry

Rural America falls behind

Historically, rural areas had some possibility of competing for the least technical aspects of manufacturing. However, given the tendency toward globalization of production, this source of employment and economic growth is now in question. And unlike previous generations of industrialization, high-tech industries have largely eluded the less technically adept and sparsely populated areas of the United States.

A central theme of this chapter has been the uneven distribution of high-tech industries. In considering state high-tech development strategies, it is important to recognize that there are distributional consequences of policies, particularly for places outside urban America. Less developed areas of the country have neither the infrastructure nor the pre-existing industrial base necessary to compete for jobs in high-tech industries. As this section suggests, national growth of high-tech jobs has not contributed significantly to rural economic development.

Tracking the rural renaissance

The 1960s and 1970s were important decades for rural America. After years of decline in both population and jobs, rural communities began growing again. A portion of this growth was due to rising prices for agricultural commodities and energy resources. But manufacturing growth was also significant during this period. Rural communities actually gained more new manufacturing jobs than their metropolitan counterparts.

Unfortunately, rural America's revival was short-lived. Recent studies of manufacturing location indicate the flow of jobs to rural areas (if not completely over) has slowed dramatically. And since 1980, manufacturing jobs have been increasing in metropolitan areas at higher rates than in rural communities (Garnick 1985).

The composition of rural manufacturing has contributed to this reversal. Since the mid-1970s, traditional rural industries which are particularly vulnerable to international competition (e.g. textiles, apparel, timber, and chemicals) have experienced serious employment declines. Firms are pressed to either automate or shift production to lower cost locations in order to remain competitive.

During a decade of rapid growth, rural areas gained few high-tech jobs. While nationwide, high-tech industries experienced a growth rate of 29 percent, rural high-tech jobs increased by only 24 percent. Had rural high-tech industries grown at the national rate, they would have created an additional 23,000 jobs.

Not only has the rate of growth in rural areas been less than the national average, the composition of this employment consists largely of slow-growing industries. For example, of 33 industries with more than 20 percent employment in rural areas, 16 lost jobs between 1972 and 1982, and another 10 grew at substantially lower rates than the high-tech industry average. Most rural high-tech industries also have occupational profiles which are decidedly low-skill. This is particularly true in the South where technical workers made up only one-third as much of the labor force as they did in urban areas. While high-tech jobs have grown in rural areas, they are reinforcing, not altering, the existing occupational structure.

The microelectronics, computers, and communications complex (MCC)

Unlike previous sections, in which industries were classified by broad definitions, here we analyze four discrete industries—computers, semiconductors, electronic components, and communications equipment (MCC). Over the study period these industries were tremendous job generators; one of every two new high-tech jobs was part of the MCC complex. Nevertheless, by examining them, the limits to rural high technology are even more apparent.

In 1982 rural counties in the United States had 67,000 jobs in the microelectronics, computers and communications industries. This represents roughly 5 percent of all jobs in these industries. Growth rates of MCC industries in rural counties lagged behind national industry growth rates. And although the four industries accounted for 22 percent of all high-tech jobs nationally, they made up only 5 percent of all rural high-tech employment.

MCC industry jobs in rural areas were concentrated within a few states. Pennsylvania, New York, Minnesota, and Virginia embraced 35 percent of all rural jobs in the four industries. Mirroring previous generations of industry, high-tech firms have shifted from high-wage cities to rural areas of the Northeast and Midwest.

Jobs in the microelectronics, computer and communications industries were tied to metropolitan areas. Sixty-six percent of this employment was in counties adjacent to metropolitan areas, a significant portion of which is within commuting distance of major metropolitan areas. Truly rural areas had minuscule amounts of employment in the microelectronics-computer industries. Clearly these less competitive areas have not benefited from the electronics and computer revolution.

Are MCC industries simply too technical for America's rural communities? This question is open to debate. Some 100,000 semiconductor assembly jobs are in U.S. plants in Southeast Asia (Scott and Angel 1987). One could argue that these low-wage, low-skill assembly jobs are no different from those found in rural areas of the U.S. However, we know anecdotally the principal reasoning behind U.S. firms' shifting these jobs to developing countries. U.S. trade policy encouraged exportation of labor-intensive assembly jobs. Under the 806 and 807 in-bond programs, corporations are able to re-import parts processed in low-cost locations while paying tariffs only on the value added in assembly. This encourages job shifts to cheap labor locations. Additionally, the culture and politics of newly industrializing countries attract offshore assembly. Employees in Asia work longer hours for less pay and are largely prohibited from organizing to improve their working conditions. Over time, these countries developed specializations in electronics assembly which encouraged firms to expand assembly outside the U.S.[7] But regardless of why firms shifted assembly to the Third World, America's lowest wage regions can no longer compete—even for the least technical, most labor-intensive aspects of modern manufacturing.

Policy implications of high-tech industry location

States are taking the lead in encouraging high-tech industry development. Given that states experience the immediate effects of industrial change, this is not surprising. It is also true that state-level politicians are often held accountable by their constituents for the health of their state economies.

That high-tech industries appear to follow changes in the distribution of population and jobs suggests state programs should embrace a more long-term view of economic development. But there is still an inclination for states to react to promises of more immediate payoffs. For example, communities jump at the chance to attract a branch plant. While in the short term this may seem sensible, frequently the incentives used to woo firms are costly and may preclude investments in programs which have payoffs only in the longer term. If states really want to alter their comparative advantage, programs must be planned within a more realistic time frame. As evidence, consider California, much-touted as a model of the nation's high-tech success. State government deserves some credit for the economy's resiliency and innovativeness because it has maintained its commitment to investment in public infrastructure over many decades. For example, California recognizes there are no quick recipes for state-sponsored high-tech development. The state has been making strategic investments in such areas as education since the turn of the century.

Thus in establishing high-tech economic development policies, it is important that states review three major influences which shaped the current distribution of high-tech industries. While there are no doubt many others, this discussion will focus on three particularly significant factors—defense spending, investment in education, and the presence or absence of a pre-existing industrial base.

Defense spending

For many communities, the roots of high-tech development can be traced to postwar era defense and space programs. Colorado Springs, Colorado; Melbourne-Titusville, Florida; northern Virginia;

and Tucson, Arizona, owe much of their high-technology fortunes to federal defense and aerospace spending. Even places such as Los Angeles, California and Boston, Massachusetts, have benefited greatly from research and development funding over the last 40 years.

But there is no predetermined development outcome of defense spending. Many communities (such as Albuquerque, New Mexico, and Oakridge, Tennessee) with defense and weapons labs have experienced minimal commercial spinoffs from this activity. In fact, defense establishments are notorious for being islands of R&D with little or no connection to the local economy. So should states chase defense dollars as part of high-technology development strategies? Probably not. Defense spending decisions are political (therefore unstable), and communities must remain wary that today's pet Pentagon project could be eliminated in tomorrow's Congressional vote. But neither should states ignore the defense high-technology connection. Alabama and New Mexico, while experiencing the highs and lows of the defense-dependent roller coaster, have certainly benefited from local defense spending.

Investment in education

There appears to be an irrefutable connection between education, the creation of a skilled labor supply, and a resulting environment conducive to new firm formation. However, the long-term commitment necessary to create a successful educational system eludes most states. Political leaders' allegiance to the goal of excellence in education is notoriously short-lived. Even in the best circumstances, building a world-class university system or other high-quality state education programs is fraught with problems.

Funding for education is a function of a state economy's health. Educational reforms are often derailed by unforeseen changes in the economy which cause states to abandon new programs. For example, recent declines in the price of oil have forced Texas and Louisiana to scale back programs with expectations of greatly improved educational systems. Thus it is difficult for major universities in these regions to continue to attract the best graduate students and world-renowned professors.

The importance of investing in education as a means of creating a lively state economy is clear. The ideal composition of such investments is less clear. That is, on what should university systems focus their funding and expansion efforts? Further research is needed to determine how resources should be allocated. The current fixation with high technology finds states reordering budget priorities and redirecting funding almost solely toward engineering and physical sciences. But the success of both public and private educational systems in California and Massachusetts has greatly depended on extensive commitments to higher education in *all* fields, including both the social and physical sciences.

Industrial base

This analysis shows a positive connection between an existing industrial base and the possibility of future high-tech industry growth. Admittedly, several states in the traditional industrial heartland lost high-tech jobs over the period studied. However, a few states, such as Connecticut, Michigan, and Illinois, still have large numbers. The number of new high-tech manufacturing plants in Michigan (even as job growth remains stable) suggests that long-standing centers of industrial innovation are still capable of spawning new enterprises (even if they can no longer maintain the more labor-intensive aspects).

The connection between industrial structure and the growth of high-tech industries is far from straightforward. In New England there appears to be an important relationship between new industry formation and a pre-existing industrial skill base. For states with no history of manufacturing, high-tech development takes the form of branch plants of high-tech corporations.

There is debate surrounding the long-term implications of externally owned high-tech enterprises. Some evidence suggests branch plant locations are not developing an import-substituting economy but instead embrace relatively autonomous plants that produce mainly standardized high-tech products (Glasmeier 1986b, 1987; Goldstein and Malazia 1985). Few spinoffs occur, and linkages are mostly long distance in nature.

Fifty years of branch plant development has produced surprisingly limited additional industrialization in many parts of the South. While the industries have changed, the region remains low-skilled, and firms locate plants there to take advantage of a low-wage, pliant labor force. With the notable exception of a few major cities, high technology in the South mirrors past eras of industrialization.

A recurring concern is the impact that state high-tech development policy will have on nonurban communities. High-tech industrial policy focuses on new, admittedly pressing, local and state economic problems. Yet programs avoid more familiar and enduring concerns about uneven economic development (including urban poverty, inequitable income distribution, and access to adequate economic livelihood). Existing high-tech policy is poised to repeat past mistakes that will further contribute to uneven economic development. Specifically, there is an apparent, but unintentional, urban bias in state policies that exclude rural and less developed parts of individual states.

Moreover, resulting inequities of existing high-tech policy and programs may have much more severe impacts on rural areas. For example, technological biases such as the existing priority on new product development should be replaced by an emphasis on process developments. The latter could help make existing rural manufacturing industries more competitive. Some states (North Carolina and Arkansas) have begun reorienting policy in this direction.

Another important factor limiting rural areas' ability to compete is the intimate connection between the "know-how" needed to garner current aspects of high-tech manufacturing and an ability to participate in future rounds of high-tech development. Rural areas may suffer disproportionately as their populations are increasingly locked out of future jobs because they lack experience with existing technological innovations.

State policy should embrace evaluation criteria which chart the distribution of program benefits. Beneficiaries should include not only the businesses for which states design most programs, but also members and groups within the society which traditionally find it difficult to penetrate the more advanced aspects of today's economy. While "competitiveness" heads the list of national political phraseology, we must not forget the long-standing problems of economically disadvantaged groups within the U.S. economy — including those lacking skills or living in less populous areas. Their problems do not disappear as attention shifts away from them. State policy makers must therefore add these issues to the complete lexicon of problems facing our advanced industrial society.

Notes

Support for research was provided by the Rural Economic Policy Project, a collaborative project of the Ford Foundation and Aspen and Wye Institutes, Washington, D.C.

1 Over the last four years, some degree of consensus has emerged regarding the definition of "high-tech" industry. The difficulties of defining high-tech

industries have been documented elsewhere, and I will not review them here
(Vinson & Harrington 1979, 1983; Glasmeier *et al.* 1983; Riche *et al.* 1983;
Malecki 1984).

To summarize the argument, however, and provide a benchmark for this
chapter, we define high-tech industries as those industries with greater than
the national average of engineers, engineering technicians, computer scientists,
mathematicians, and life scientists including chemists and geologists. The
definition is based on 1982 Department of Labor data from the national industry
occupational matrix. This data base provides detailed occupational profiles for
three-digit industry groups. According to this definition, 28 three-digit industries
are identified as producing high-tech products. The industries discussed in this
chapter are strictly manufacturing because of limitations associated with other
data sources.

As most researchers in urban and regional economic development will admit,
this working definition is not without flaws. The definition concentrates on
industries producing high-tech products. Thus it does not account for the
economic benefits of using high-tech production processes.

Ideally a definition of high technology should be based on firm-level data.
Otherwise it is possible to identify plants which produce a product called
"high-tech" that represent mature aspects of production. However, data do
not exist to selectively delineate locally-based high-tech plants with technical
operations. Recognizing these limitations, researchers have settled on a working
definition of high technology based on the human capital component of the
labor process. This study conforms with such a definition.

The data used here are from the *U.S. Census of manufactures.* The data
include industry and plant counts for all four-digit manufacturing industries
for all U.S. counties. The time period studied spans three census periods –
1972, 1977 and 1982. Readers should note that the end point of the data
series was a year of serious economic recession. Although in 1982 high-tech
industries generally gained jobs, the definition of high technology masks peculiar
sectoral experiences. More current data could significantly improve this analysis.
Unfortunately, limitations of the census precluded this option.

2   See Feller 1984 for a critical review of state high-tech development programs.
3   The definition of "rural" used in this study was developed by Calvin Beale of
    the U.S. Department of Agriculture. The definition is based on population and
    commuting patterns. Using this standard, U.S. counties are designated "urban"
    and "rural" based on nine population categories.

    There are six rural categories. Three identify counties adjacent to metropolitan
    areas which have urban populations of 20,000 to 50,000; urban populations of
    20,000 or fewer; and those which are completely rural. The remaining three
    have similar population groupings, but are not adjacent to metropolitan areas.
    For the purposes of this chapter, except where otherwise specified, "rural" is
    an aggregate of the six types of counties designated by the above definition.

4   Employment filtering refers to the process whereby, as manufacturing processes
    become mature and stable, other cost considerations such as land and labor
    become important facets of location decision-making. Consequently, companies
    filter employment and select locations that reduce land and labor costs.

5   High-tech jobs are concentrated within key metropolitan areas of individual
    states. Massachusetts is not an exception.

6   The cities in this group all had location quotients greater than one.

7   This is particularly true of the 806 and 807 in-bond program, which allows
    U.S. firms to ship components to offshore locations where they are assembled
    by cheap labor. These assembled goods are then re-imported into the U.S.
    Tariffs on these products reflect only the value of the wages paid to workers
    and not the market value of the final assembled product.

Bibliography

Armington, C., C. Harris & M. Odle 1983. *Formation and growth in high-tech businesses: a regional assessment.* (Washington, D.C.: Brookings Institution, Micro Data Project).

Bloomquist, L. 1987. "Performance of the rural manufacturing sector," in *Rural economic development in the 1980s: preparing for the future.* (Washington, D.C.: U.S. Department of Agriculture, Economic Research Service), pp. 3.1–3.31.

Bluestone, B. & B. Harrison 1983. *The deindustrialization of America.* (New York: Basic Books).

Clark, G. 1981. "The employment relation and the spatial division of labor: a hypothesis," *Annals of the Association of American Geographers,* 412–24.

Clarke, M. K. 1986. *Revitalizing state economies, a review of state development policies and programs.* (Washington, D.C.: Center for Policy Research and Analysis, National Governors' Association).

Cohen, R. 1977. "Multinational corporations, international finance and the Sunbelt," in *The rise of the Sunbelt cities,* ed. D. Perry & A. Watkins, Urban Affairs Annual Reviews, 14:211-26.

Erickson, R. 1978. "The industrial filtering process," *Earth and Minerals Science Bulletin,* Pennsylvania State University, University Park, PA.

Feller, I. 1984. "Political and administrative aspects of state high-technology programs," *Policy Studies Review,* 3, 460–66.

Garnick, W. 1985. "Patterns of growth in metropolitan and nonmetropolitan areas: an update," *Survey of Current Business,* May, 33–8.

Glasmeier, A. 1986a. "The structure of locations and the role of high-tech industries in U.S. regional development." Unpublished dissertation.

Glasmeier, A. 1986b. "High tech and the regional division of labor," *Industrial Relations* 25, 197–211.

Glasmeier, A. 1988. "Bypassing America's outlands: rural America and high technology." Final Report to the Aspen Institute, Rural Economic Policy Program, Ford Foundation, Washington, D.C.

Glasmeier, A., P. Hall & A. Markusen 1983. *Defining high-technology industries.* Working Paper 407 (Berkeley: Institute of Urban and Regional Development, University of California).

Glickman, N. & A. Glasmeier 1989. "The international economy and the 'new' American South," *Deindustrialization and regional economic transformation,* Rodwin, L. & H. Sazanami et al. (Boston: Unwin Hyman).

Goldstein, H. & E. Malizia 1985. "Microelectronics and economic development in North Carolina," in *High hopes for high tech: microelectronics in North Carolina,* ed., Dale Wittington (Chapel Hill: University of North Carolina Press), pp. 256–95.

Hansen, N. 1980. "Dualism, capital-labor ratios and the regions of the U.S.: a comment," *Journal of Regional Science* 20, 401–3.

Haren, C. C. & R. W. Holling 1979. "Industrial development in non-metropolitan America: a locational perspective," in *Non-metropolitan industrialization,* ed. R. E. Lonsdale & H. L. Seyler. (New York: Wiley), pp. 13-46.

Hymer, S. 1979. "The multinational corporation and the spatial division of labor," in *The multinational corporation: a radical critique,* ed. R. Cohen (Cambridge, Mass.: Harvard University Press) pp. 140–207.

Lonsdale, R. E. & H. L. Seyler 1979. *Non-metropolitan industrialization.* (New York: Wiley).

Malecki, E. J. 1985. "Industrial location and corporate organization in high technology industries," *Economic Geography.* 61, 345–69.

Malecki E. J. 1986. "Linkages in high technology industries: a Florida case study," *Environment and Planning A* 18, 1477–98.

Malecki, E. J. 1987. "Regional economic development and state science policy." Paper presented at the National Science Foundation PRA Workshop, An Agenda for State Science Policy Research, Washington, D.C., September 1987.

Markusen, A. & V. Carlson 1988. "Bowing out, bidding down and betting on the basics: midwestern responses to deindustrialization in the 1980s." Unpublished paper, Center for Urban Affairs and Policy Research, Northwestern University.

Markusen, A., P. Hall, & A. Glasmeier 1986. *High-tech America: the what, how, where and why of the sunrise industries.* (London: Allen and Unwin).

Massey, D. 1984. *Spatial divisions of labor: social structures and the geography of production.* (New York: Macmillian).

Norton, R. D. & J. Rees 1979. "The product cycle model and the spatial decentralization of American manufacturing," *Regional Studies* **13**, 141–51.

Perloff, H., E. Dunn, E. Lampard, & R. Muth 1960. *Regional resources and economic growth.* (Lincoln, Nebraska: University of Nebraska Press).

Perry, D. and A. Watkins (eds.) 1977. *The rise of the Sunbelt cities.* Urban Affairs Annual Reviews **14**, 211–26.

Rees, J. 1979. "Technical change and regional shifts in American manufacturing," *Professional Geographer* **31**, 45–54.

Riche, R., D. Hecker & J. Burgan 1984. "High technology today and tomorrow: a small slice of the employment pie," *Monthly Labor Review* **107**, 50–8.

Saxenian, A. 1981. *Silicon chips and spatial structure: the semiconductor industry organization in Santa Clara, California.* (Berkeley: University of California Press).

Sayer, A. 1985. "Industry and space: a sympathetic critique," *Environment and Planning D, Society and Space* **3**, 3–29.

Scott, A. & D. P. Angel 1987. "The U.S. semiconductor industry: a locational analysis," *Environment and Planning D* **19**, 875–912.

Storper, M. 1982. *The spatial division of labor: technology, the labor process and the location of industries.* Unpublished Ph.D. dissertation (Berkeley: Department of Geography, University of California).

Storper, M. & R. Walker 1983. "The spatial division of labor: labor and the location of industries," in *Sunbelt-Snowbelt: urban development and regional restructuring,* ed. W. Tabb & L. Sawyer. (London: Oxford University Press), 19–47.

U.S. Bureau of the Census 1986. *Census of Manufacturers, plant location tape.* (Washington, D.C.: U.S. Government Printing Office).

U.S. Bureau of the Census 1986. *State and Metropolitan databook* (Washington, D.C.: U.S. Government Printing Office).

U.S. Department of Labor 1982. *Industrial occupation matrix* (Washington, D.C.: U.S. Government Printing Office).

5

Technological innovation and paths to regional economic growth

EDWARD J. MALECKI

IN AN AGE OF high technology, it is easy to lose sight of the multifaceted influence of technological innovation on local, regional, and national economies. Although much interest lately has centered on high-tech industries, high technology represents only a small, albeit an important, part of technology's rôle.[1] Product and process technology pervade modern economic life and affect regions in subtle as well as in direct ways. Most importantly, entrepreneurship is the fundamental avenue by which technological change enters the economy and provides new jobs and economic growth.[2] This chapter systematically reviews the theoretical and empirical work on technological innovation and deals with the major stages of activity within technological change, including research and development (basic research, applied research, and development), innovation, diffusion of innovations and technology transfer, and new firm formation in regional growth. Although the focus of the chapter is not on policy, it will suggest avenues by which public policies can influence the process of technical change. The intention is to emphasize the diverse ways in which technology refashions regional economies and the critical rôle of entrepreneurship in the passage from innovation to regional economic change.

The complexity of technological change

Technological change is a complex process—a "black box"—whose workings are only partially understood.[3] The same is true in a regional context.[4] Feller has identified four distinct types of technological change that can impact the location of economic activity:

(a) Technological change that is site specific and enhances the competitiveness of a region's resources, especially raw materials.

(b) Technological change that, by reducing production costs (process innovation), increases the market for the product and thus permits the exploitation of economies of scale. A geographical redistribution of output in an industry will result.

(c) Technological change that provides the basis for a new, "footloose" industry (product innovation).

(d) Technological change that is equally applicable to all firms within a regionally dispersed industry, where the subsequent location of that industry's output will depend upon the rate of adoption of the new technology by firms within each region.[5]

Types (a), (b), and (d) are all types of process innovation, and this is the typical concept of technical change on which economic models have dwelt. By means of technology embodied in capital equipment, whereby newer "vintages" of capital stock embody newer technology, process innovations raise the productivity of firms that have developed or adopted such new technology. Regional economic research indicates that this is indeed the case.[6] Regions in which "best practice" technology operates will have a competitive advantage over other regions.[7]

By contrast, Feller's type (c) includes new-product, demand-creating innovations of the sort at which firms' R&D efforts are largely aimed.[8] Both product and process innovation necessitate adjustments in an economy and among economies.[9] To a great extent, new product innovations are the greatest source of new jobs, since this type of innovation allows the creation of new firms and new industries to provide the new products. Computers, electronics, and biotechnology are prominent current examples of the job-creating effects of product innovation. Successive generations of innovations have permitted new firms to enter these industries and have created jobs in old firms.

Innovations that originate in a region do not always benefit that region's economy. There is no simple one-way causality between science and technology and regional economic development; instead there are strong mutually supportive relationships according to a study by the National Academy of Sciences (NAS) and the National Academy of Engineering (NAE); research by Buswell and by Malecki has reinforced this view.[10] The development of regional research and development and scientific complexes takes long periods of time, and economic effects such as the generation of new local industry are highly unpredictable. Part of the unpredictability concerns the degree of local linkages or purchases by high-tech firms. As the NAS/NAE study suggested, local purchasing varies, as do the characteristics of firms encompassed under the designation of high technology.[11] Consequently, the benefits of science and technology—jobs, new firms, and increased production—do not necessarily remain in that region. The principal route by which the economic benefits stay within a region is new firm formation, and entrepreneurship is characteristically a local phenomenon.[12]

The importance of entrepreneurship is increasingly acknowledged, but its relationships to technological innovation are not yet clear, particularly in a regional context. The conclusions of the Office of Technology Assessment report suggest the links which are present: "The most important conditions for 'home grown' [high-technology development] are the technological infrastructure and entrepreneurial network that encourage the creation of indigenous high-technology firms and support their survival."[13]

Discussions of *regional* growth and regional policies are difficult, because the real world does not allow regions to be isolated, especially in the context of science and technology. Even nations are unable to contain knowledge and the fruits of research and development within their borders. As Nelson puts it: "Technological knowledge and capability are international rather than national."[14] They certainly are not regional or local; "techno-regionalism" is even less likely to be a successful strategy than "techno-nationalism."[15] Regional fortunes are dependent on the activities of the firms operating within them, on the level and types of federal activities, on the strength of their regional institutions, such as universities, and on the nature of the regional culture regarding education, investment, and entrepreneurship. These create a complex dynamic that does not allow simple models to hold. Just as simple models of the innovation process are appealing but misleading,[16] conventional wisdom about regional change is also overly simplistic.[17] Moreover, entrepreneurship is a local phenomenon, not transferable from place to place, and is dependent upon the economic structure as well as the attitudes and culture of the region.[18]

The "linear model" of innovation provides the conventional wisdom that underlies most science-based economic development policies (Fig. 5.1). This model suggests that the sequence from research to product and process development to production to marketing is the standard or predominant path of innovation in firms and national economies.[19] In a regional context, the sequence would suggest that where research and development take place, production will also take place, generating jobs and economic growth. The policy implications are also clear. It is commonly assumed that if the level of research and development is increased, there will be a corresponding increase in technological innovation, so that government science and industrial policy must include measures aimed at achieving an appropriate balance between basic and applied research. Since it is basic research from which innovation ultimately flows, basic research is a necessary object of policy.[20]

Kline and Rosenberg elaborate on the linear model's shortcomings, stressing instead the diversity of activities that make up the innovation process, the variation across industry lines, and the apparent disorderliness of the innovation process in reality.[21] The numerous loops of feedback must take place as solutions must be found to production problems, as new products are sought to solve a customer's needs, and as learning and process innovation occur during production (Fig. 5.2). In order for a firm to succeed in innovation, it must have not only an R&D capability, but also production engineering skills and a network of information about competitors and other sources of technology and product ideas. This multifaceted view of innovation contrasts with most prevailing approaches, including one of the most

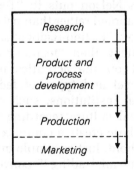

Figure 5.1 The linear model of innovation.

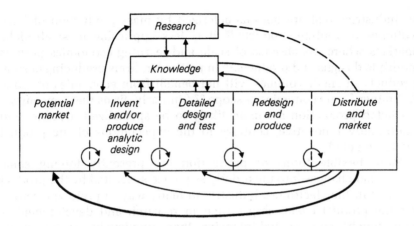

Figure 5.2 The linear model of innovation and feedback loops in technological change. Adapted from S. J. Kline & N. Rosenberg, "An overview of innovation," in *The positive sum strategy*, R. Landau & N. Rosenberg (eds.) (Washington, D.C.: National Academy Press, 1986), p. 290.

common models for relating innovation to corporate activities, the product cycle model.

The impact of the product cycle on regional development

Perhaps the dominant model in recent years for understanding the nature of technological change and regional economic development is the product cycle model and its corollaries, the profit cycle, the innovation cycle, and the manufacturing process cycle.[22] This model makes use of differences in skill levels and wage rates among regions to suggest regional specialization of economic activity over at least the medium run. In the innovation phase, firms require skilled labor, such as scientists and engineers, for refinements and improvements. The standardization or mature phase, by contrast, is characterized by shifts of production to low-cost, and especially low-wage, locations.

Despite its comparable linear form, the advantages of the model are several: it emphasizes the labor as well as the capital needs of firms related to products at different phases; it emphasizes the ebb and flow of innovative activity observed in many industries; and it emphasizes that the location of economic activity varies with the type of activity undertaken.[23] Criticisms have multiplied as the product cycle model has seen wider use.[24] De Bresson and Lampel and Sabel and colleagues focus on the inapplicability of the model to industries that are not characterized by mass production of large volumes of routine products.[25] It is less applicable to small-niche markets where the absence of scale and learning economies permits multiple designs and products.[26] In particular, firms producing custom products in small volumes will not benefit from economies of scale, but rather from economies of scope.[27] Similarly, firms that concentrate on *batch* production are more likely to be specialized, flexible, and continually innovative, contrary to the expectations of the product cycle model.[28]

More flexible forms of production are presently forcing some additional changes into the orderly sequence suggested by the product cycle.[29] In the electronics industry, in many ways a prototype setting for the product cycle, chip design in research and development is now much more capital-intensive than previously, as expensive equipment is needed to create the intricate products that are often of a semi-custom nature. This capital intensity renders labor a less important consideration for the firm even at the production stage.[30] In other industries as well, flexible systems have reduced the appeal of low-wage labor pools in favor of concentrations of different functions that contribute to production.[31]

The overall impact of this form of technological and organizational change is to make industry concentrate in areas where specialized firms and skilled labor are abundant, and where unforeseen changes could also be accommodated. In fact, Kaplinsky sees the trend in automation to be very different from that of the past 25 years, when peripheral areas and Third World countries were able to benefit from industrialization.[32] In the future, little production will disperse in the manner of the recent experience. As Jaikumar puts it, "Flexible automation shifts the arena of competition from manufacturing to engineering."[33]

The linear model and paths to growth

As the preceding section on the product cycle illustrates, elements of the linear model remain appropriate for understanding the dynamic nature of technology within economic activity. This section discusses in turn each of the components of the linear model, with the aim of showing the possible direct paths to regional growth and development. Clearly, the route will typically be more circuitous and indirect, because of the feedback loops which in fact are present. However, it is valuable none the less to assess the potential impact of each component. Figure 5.3 illustrates the stages of innovation, the policies suggested for each stage in order to bring about economic growth, and the constraints posed by addressing stages individually.

Basic research

The origin of technological innovation in the linear model of technology is basic research, whether prompted by market pull or by the accumulation of scientific knowledge. Basic research is primarily the purview of universities, although some is conducted at research institutes and at the central laboratories of large firms. The feedback loops within the innovation process,[34] and the frequent and intermittent need for new scientific knowledge, have led many researchers to focus on the links between industry and academic institutions. These links are also used as a justification for increasing local or state R&D funding: the expectation is that firms will form these links within the area, and

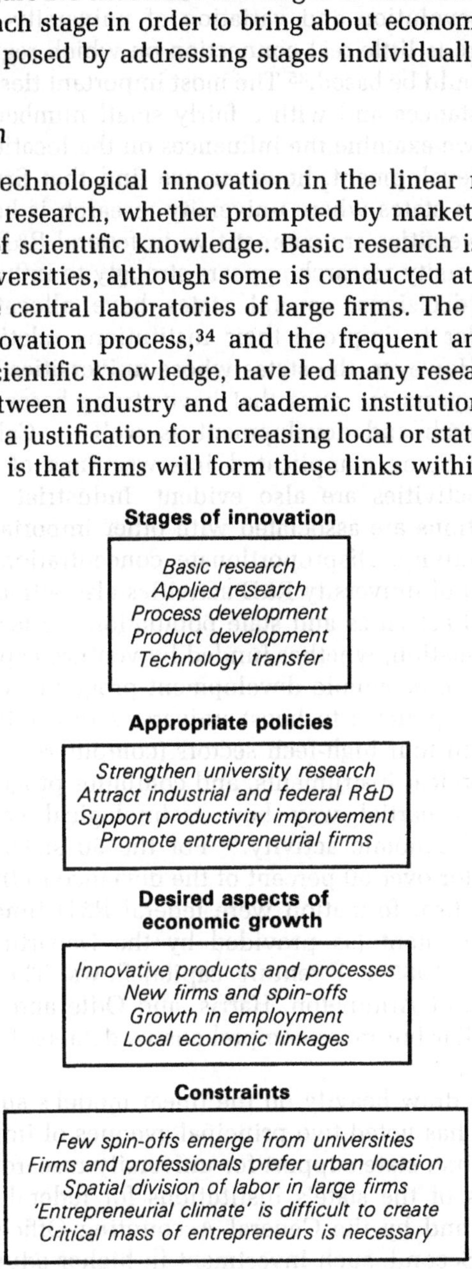

Stages of innovation

> *Basic research*
> *Applied research*
> *Process development*
> *Product development*
> *Technology transfer*

Appropriate policies

> *Strengthen university research*
> *Attract industrial and federal R&D*
> *Support productivity improvement*
> *Promote entrepreneurial firms*

Desired aspects of economic growth

> *Innovative products and processes*
> *New firms and spin-offs*
> *Growth in employment*
> *Local economic linkages*

Constraints

> *Few spin-offs emerge from universities*
> *Firms and professionals prefer urban location*
> *Spatial division of labor in large firms*
> *'Entrepreneurial climate' is difficult to create*
> *Critical mass of entrepreneurs is necessary*

Figure 5.3 Paths to economic growth suggested by the linear model of innovation.

innovations and production will take place locally as well. Howells, reviewing the evolution and variation of university–industry links, shows that there is little real connection on which regional economic development could be based.[35] The most important ties are often made across long distances and with a fairly small number of prestigious institutions. If we examine the influences on the location of industrial research and development, however, we find that firms locate their R&D facilities in states where university research is being conducted and where universities are competitive in federal R&D programs.[36]

Because university research appears strongly to influence industrial R&D location decisions, several states have allocated substantial funding in order to improve their institutions relative to those in other states.[37] However, the states whose universities have improved most in recent years are ones that have strong bases in federal and industrial research and development as well — California, Texas, and Virginia.[38] Some complicated interweavings of economic and technological activities are also evident. Industrial and university R&D concentrations are associated with other important components of economic activity. Disproportionate concentrations of large-firm laboratories and of university R&D activities also attract venture capital; federal R&D activities and state population are less influential.[39]

New firm formation, whether funded by venture capital or not, is a major objective of economic development programs and an outcome envisioned from policies to boost university research. Data on new firm formation in four high-tech sectors (computers, semiconductors, medical and surgical instruments, and computer programming) allow us to see in a partial way how technological capability translates into new economic activity.[40] For the 50 states, the variables that accounted for over 50 percent of the deviance in the geographical pattern of new firm formation were federal R&D funds to industry, high-tech employment (as provided by the Department of Labor), and cumulative (1969–83) venture capital flows. These findings are similar to those of Armington, Harris, and Odle and of Harris, who had used a similar but more comprehensive data set for metropolitan areas.[41]

State policies draw heavily on the linear model's support for basic research. Texas has noted two principal avenues of impact from such investment.[42] First, state support for university research increases the competitiveness of the state's institutions for federal grants. Recent work by Drew and by the General Accounting Office supports this relationship.[43] Second, such investment in higher education helps in the competition for industry currently taking place among a group of large or growing states, including Arizona, Massachusetts, California, Illinois, and Michigan.

University research is by itself not a certain path to economic growth. Universities have not been prominent sources of spinoffs, despite the examples of MIT and Stanford which are so frequently cited and used to justify policies to upgrade state institutions.[44] Cooper has consistently made the case that firms, and not universities or government facilities, tend to be the "incubator organizations" of entrepreneurs.[45] The desired economic effect of new firms and jobs related to university research depends, then, on circumstances that influence entrepreneurship. The improvement of local universities can, in addition to improving research itself, have the side-effect of improving the "intellectual climate" or "intellectual atmosphere" of an area. This, in turn, improves the perceived quality of life by enhancing the "ambience" and reputation of a place as high-tech.[46] These characteristics can enhance entrepreneurship in that such areas will be more attractive to entrepreneurially inclined professionals.

Applied research

Applied research is the customary entry point of industrial firms into the innovation process, since they typically undertake relatively little fundamental or basic research. At the level of applied research, however, the capabilities of many firms match or exceed that of many universities and research institutes. Potential products are already envisioned although considerable research—more focused in nature than in basic research—might still be necessary.

The biotechnology industry illustrates well the place of applied research in the technological innovation process. As Kenney's analysis makes clear, biotechnology has followed rather closely the linear sequence from university-based scientific research through to the marketing of innovative products.[47] The example of biotechnology also exemplifies the entry of large firms into the innovation process. Firms primarily, but not only, from the pharmaceutical industry have attempted both to influence the direction of research and to draw upon the entrepreneurial energies of small firms and university scientists through equity investments, joint ventures, and contracts with university researchers. As commercial products become available, both small and large firms are likely to have a part in the expanding market.[48] To a large degree, the location of applied research is a puzzle, governed by the location choices of scientists and engineers and of large firms and their R&D laboratories. These

choices tend to favor large urban areas, a point to which we will
return below.

Product development

Product development is the last major stage in the linear model of
innovation, and is that toward which the bulk of industrial R&D
activity is oriented. Product development and refinement customarily
occur within product-line laboratories of large firms, rather than in
central research facilities.[49] Interaction and "coupling" with marketing
and with manufacturing become critical as product design, production
engineering, and market acceptance must all be assessed and incorporated into decision making. These tasks recur intermittently throughout
a product's "life," and perhaps more within firms which specialize
and innovate as part of their routine activity.[50] More typically in
the product cycle pattern, product development peaks early in
the commercial life of a product, whereupon process innovation
begins to take precedence as the firm prepares for large-volume
production.[51]

The locational pattern is still dependent on the locational decisions
of firms for their R&D facilities, for the work of product development
and its overlaps with other corporate functions are still highly reliant
on professional and technical workers. The locational concentration
of research and development in established regions reinforces the
regional economic growth of those areas, such as California and
Massachusetts, where universities, industrial R&D activity, and federal
R&D contracts are plentiful.

Process development

Regional economic competitiveness is a product of the ability of firms
to operate at the *best-practice* level in their industry.[52] Production
technology (machinery, equipment, management practices) ranges
from the best currently known and available to the worst. The spectrum
from best-practice to worst-practice technology is largely a function of
the age or vintage of capital equipment employed. Newer vintages will
incorporate or embody newer concepts, techniques, and knowledge
which tend to give an advantage to firms—and regions—where newer
technology is employed.[53]

The level of technology in a region, however, goes beyond considerations of machinery and plant design. It encompasses the stock of
knowledge within a firm or region concerning both what is being

made and how things are made. Technically progressive firms obtain knowledge from customers and suppliers as well as generate it internally. For a region, links to outside information networks and a high level of technical skill define a level of best-practice that in many respects is cultural and which goes well beyond what is encompassed by research and development.[54]

The diffusion of process innovation and the resulting distribution of best-practice (and older) technologies is a critical determinant of regional economic competitiveness. To a large extent, however, it remains somewhat a mystery as to why investment in new technologies varies from region to region. The simple and attractive finding, that the largest firms adopt earliest, has numerous proponents and supporters.[55] This finding is often used to justify the linear model of innovation, since it is large firms which also carry out most of the R&D activity in any industry. For regions, the implication again is often that research and development lead to general economic competitiveness.

The complex view of innovation thrusts some complications into this argument. Gold, Rosenberg, and others have noted that innovations—especially process innovations—do not remain constant during their diffusion.[56] Rather, in large part because most process innovations are the product innovations developed by supplier firms, improvements and modifications alter the characteristics of the innovation over time. Adoption may lag because of the expectation, based on past experience, that newer and better innovations will come along in the near future.[57]

A number of other factors contribute to delays in adoption and, again, regional variations are present. Adaptation and implementation within each adopting firm can greatly affect the rate of adoption of new technologies.[58] Perhaps even more important are access to information and channels of supply for the innovation[59]—factors which vary markedly from place to place.[60] Information may be withheld or proprietary to an innovator, or it may be slow to accumulate as firms adopt and gain experience with new technology. The slowness of diffusion is often noted, and is part of the reason why equilibrium rarely characterizes economic change.[61] These institutional factors provide elements of a more realistic model of the diffusion of technological innovation, even if they are much more complex than what we have relied on in the past.[62]

One of the key pieces to the diffusion of innovations in industry is simply the organizational structure of large firms. As Oakey, Thwaites, and Nash have shown for Great Britain,[63] process innovations are implemented earliest in branch plants of large, multilocational firms. If the process is still under development, it is likely to remain in the South East, where most R&D activity in the firms takes place; once it is readied for standardized, large-volume production, peripheral locations are more likely. A similar regional division of labor is evident in U.S. high-tech industries.[64]

The diffusion of product innovations

The diffusion of product innovations is perhaps somewhat different. In British research, product innovations were "adopted" earliest (i.e., produced) mainly in plants where research and development were conducted. In general, this can be thought of as typical of the pattern expected in the product/innovation cycle as the product moves from the innovation phase to the growth phase where volume production is the priority. The combination of product and process innovation at this point relies on interaction between R&D activity and production within the firm.[65] The implications of this pattern for regional development are clear. Technological capability for new product research and development remains concentrated in some regions, where early production and associated new employment also take place.[66] Process innovations, which usually result in employment declines as new capital equipment reduces the demand for labor, are nevertheless related to product innovations. Ettlie and Rubenstein show that product innovations, especially radical ones, usually require substantial process changes as well.[67] It is large firms, although not the very largest, which tend to dominate in the introduction of radical product innovation.

The interaction between product and process innovation reinforces the organizing concept of *best-practice*. Johne demonstrates that firms which are active at product innovation tend to demand innovative components from their suppliers, thus reinforcing the concept of the "user as innovator" put forward by von Hippel.[68] Firms which are abreast of one dimension of technology (e.g., *machine technology*) tend to be competent in *procedural* or *organizational technology* as well.[69] *Knowledge technology* integrates these dimensions within a firm and provides for the observed feedback which weakens the linear model of innovation. The amalgam of technology provides the impetus for coupling or integration of different corporate functions which is widely viewed as a critical element of the R&D strategy of firms. Knowledge as conceived here also enhances the ability of firms to utilize profitably strategies for technology acquisition from outside the firm, through licensing, joint ventures, equity participation in other firms, and outright acquisition of innovative firms.[70]

The biotechnology example discussed earlier illustrates how large firms, which must tend a broad portfolio of products and technologies, seek out such technological opportunities. Graham stresses that firms which acquire technology from outside must have substantial in-house R&D activity, and it must be broader-based in order to integrate internal and external technology.[71] In essence, firms—and regions—follow technological trajectories which build on existing strengths and which have difficulty dealing with new paradigms.[72]

The integration between corporate R&D activity and other information- and innovation-related functions typically has a geographical impact: research and development take place at or near corporate headquarters, in order to communicate with corporate marketing, financial, and strategy functions. As discussed above, R&D activity also is found at a small number of production locations, particularly where production technology is being worked on. The regional economic impact is to reinforce the level of knowledge and information at headquarters, sites and at a few manufacturing sites where R&D activity takes place.

Technology transfer

Technology transfer is a term used to describe the diffusion of the complex bundle of knowledge which surrounds a level and type of technology. At one level, all innovation diffusion is a type of technology transfer, but it can also be seen as a broader process. Technology transfer takes place within firms, through training sessions and experience; it is an integral purpose of technical education at universities and other levels of education; it takes place among firms as information diffuses and as specific knowledge is passed on to suppliers and customers. Firms transfer technology internally as they attempt to incorporate new products, processes, and organizational forms. Inter-firm technology transfer tends to occur more slowly and in a less organized fashion, as information leaks out or is transferred by means of employees who formerly worked with other firms.[73]

Interest in technology transfer has been greatest on the international scale, where the gap between global best-practice and local technology is greatest. The issue is largely outside the scope of this chapter, but is comprehensively reviewed by Contractor and Sagafi-Nejad.[74]

The relationship between large and small firms seems significant for technology transfer within regions, and is dependent on the industrial structure of the region and its effect on information flow. Allen, Hyman, and Pinckney have shown that the transfer of technology to small firms is nearly always accomplished through informal channels.[75] Sweeney also believes that much of a region's technological capability can be attributed to the degree to which large firms openly share elements of their knowledge (generic technology) with the small firms in the vicinity.[76] He maintains that less technology is transferred in the context of large firms and branch plants, for which there is typically little interaction in the surrounding region.

The regional context of technological innovation

We can usefully translate a recent summary of international competitiveness into the regional context:

> The . . . competitiveness of a [regional] economy is built on the competitiveness of the firms which operate within, and export from, its boundaries, and is, to a large extent, an expression of the will to compete and the dynamism of firms, their capacity to invest, to innovate both as a consequence of their own R&D and of successful appropriation of external technologies; but [t]he competitiveness of a [regional] economy is also more than the simple outcome of the collective or "average" competitiveness of its firms; there are many ways in which the features and performance of a [regional] economy viewed as an *entity* with characteristics of its own, will affect, in turn, the competitiveness of firms.[77]

The structural features of a region and a regional economy illustrate the gaps which exist among regions in spite of superficial similarities.[78] To a large extent, the structural deficiencies of peripheral regions, such as little local control, innovation, or inter-firm linkages, have led to proposals for local development based on entrepreneurship.[79] Policy proposals focus on the information gaps which are present in peripheral areas, because knowledge of the scientific and industrial state-of-the-art is critical for the identification of potential innovations and entrepreneurial opportunities.[80]

On the whole, the rôle of government policy may be limited. The main impetus in high-tech and science-based development will come from the private sector—from researchers, entrepreneurs, and venture capitalists. At the same time, very little is known about how to influence innovation and entrepreneurship; and there is little track record to date on the initiatives implemented thus far.[81]

What we know about technology and regional development

Despite numerous policy efforts to disperse new technology and innovative economic activities, they display a persistent tendency toward agglomeration and concentration.[82] Given our current understanding of nonroutine economic activities such as research and development, there appear to be sound reasons for this agglomeration. The information-intensive nature of technological activities and the resultant need for face-to-face communication favor those places that offer conditions for "regional creativity."[83] These conditions focus on three main elements: (a) the presence of abundant professional and technical labor; (b) urban agglomeration, or large city size, where cultural activity and communication are excellent; and (c) conditions that promote synergy or instability.[84] Oakey places even greater stress on agglomeration economies as a necessary condition for regional high-tech development.[85] A major advantage of large urban agglomerations is that contact potential is greatest there, where the quality of information is high and the costs of obtaining it are relatively low. Information links in peripheral regions are also mainly to such large information centers.[86]

More than agglomeration alone is necessary for regional development. Sweeney stresses instead elements of regional structure,[87] such as firm size and plant status, and indicators of regional innovative capability and entrepreneurial vitality.[88] Regions dominated by large firms and by branch production plants are unlikely to have the level of information and of R&D activity, and knowledge of the state-of-the-art needed to spawn new firms. Even outside high-tech sectors these aspects of technological capability are essential if regional growth is to ensue. Even in branch plants, product research and development and production of new products generally have positive employment effects, in contrast to process research and development, which tends to result in reduced employment.[89]

An additional regional variable, related to agglomeration, which has gained prominence in the context of high-tech industries, is the professional laborforce, especially the attraction and retention of mobile technical workers.[90] Labor has traditionally been undifferentiated in regional economic research except perhaps by cost, whereas now it

is recognized that quite a distinct labor market operates for professional and technical workers from that for production employees.[91]
The availability of technical and professional workers is related to
technological agglomeration in a complex way.[92] The mobility of
these workers and their access to information about employment in
a large number of possible locations make it particularly difficult to
foresee any reduction in their tendency to agglomerate in space. For
the workers themselves, large urban regions maximize their alternative
employment opportunities within the range of daily commuting
distance. In order to increase the likelihood of obtaining a sufficient
number of professional workers, firms in turn also locate in large cities.
Large urban regions have larger bundles of amenities which add to
their attraction to professional workers who are able to choose from
among a set of alternative locations. Labor markets are not constant,
and they respond to policy initiatives in education and training.[93]

A consequence of the agglomeration tendencies discussed thus far
is that new firm formation also tends to be higher in areas where
professional workers are concentrated. These may be large urban
regions (and nearly always the suburban or fringe areas of such
regions), or they may be small towns in attractive settings, but
they tend to be within reach of major airports and other essential
urban amenities.[94] The high rate of new firm formation reflects the
information networks of professional and technical workers and their
ability to identify sources of funding (such as seed capital and venture
capital) for the establishment of new firms. The "spinoff" process,
frequently identified as a consequence of technical change in a
regional context, is merely one dimension of the general process
of entrepreneurship which takes place in facilitating (usually urban)
environments. The formation of new firms in high-tech sectors is
more dependent, relative to that of firms in other sectors, on the
agglomeration of technical workers and on city size generally.[95]

Innovation and entrepreneurship

The linear model of technological innovation and its policy implications have caused regional technology policies to rely on innovative
firms, large and small. Large firms cannot be ignored, for they perform
the bulk of industrial R&D activity, both internal and government-
funded. Firms with 10,000 or more employees, for example, have
consistently accounted for over 80 percent of all U.S. industrial
R&D activity for the past several years. However, as stressed earlier,
these large firms choose locations which maximize opportunities for

information, communication, and acquisition of technical labor. Thus, large cities are the preferred locations.

At the same time, small firms, especially new firms, are of interest. They are assumed to be innovative, perhaps because of the allure of the product cycle model, which suggests that small firms will grow into large employers. Also embedded in the reasoning is the long-standing observation that innovation, especially more radical, "leap-frog" innovation, is more likely to originate in small firms where older products and technologies are less entrenched than in large organizations.[96] The regional industrial mix is a factor which influences the degree to which new firms are likely to be founded in any particular place. New firms are not equally likely to arise in all industries. Instead, they respond to the relative barriers to entry across sectors, and to the general level of opportunities presented in various technologies and markets.[97]

Just as not all research and development leads to successful innovations, not all research and development generates new spinoff firms. The state of the local industry's technology must be sufficiently unstandardized, preferably with multiple market niches, and the barriers to entry by new firms must be low.[98] Even so, it would seem that the European experience with branch plants and with public sector R&D activity in peripheral regions has led to very low levels of entrepreneurship.[99]

From a regional perspective, the sectoral variation shows itself through the industrial mix and the propensity for new firms to arise in sectors already found in the area.[100] This cumulative tendency is perhaps particularly important in technology-based sectors.[101] However, industry mix alone does not account for the observed geographical variations in new firm formation; the relative size of establishments may play a greater rôle.[102] Entrepreneurship and economic growth, then, depend on variations in innovation among firms and industries, and on the mix of firm sizes in a place.

As mentioned above, it is often asserted that small firms are more innovative than large firms, a point which is used to justify policies to cultivate and assist small firms. However, innovation is even more difficult to monitor than is new firm formation—not all innovations are patented or registered, unlike new firms. The research available suggests that small firms may not always be innovative; the variation depends largely on location. Low levels of innovativeness and of new firm formation are common in peripheral areas, compared to areas on the fringe of major urban regions.[103] The concentration of R&D activity, which agglomerates in core areas and is biased against peripheral regions, helps to keep regional levels of R&D and of technological capability low, as they are in the southeastern and West North Central states in the U.S.

Inadequate levels of regional innovative capability constrain the ability of a region to spawn innovative entrepreneurs, especially in comparison to densely populated regions and those in the vicinity of large urban centers. In the context of small, peripheral regions, innovative development is "too good to be true."[104] The human capital of such regions is limited and too mobile, i.e., many of the talented people will simply leave. Unless a local economy meets some fairly large threshold size, its base of potential entrepreneurs—and the likelihood that as a group they will be able to advance successive rounds of innovations as the product cycle progresses—will be inadequate to compete with other regions.[105]

Social characteristics are also at work in entrepreneurship. New firm formation rates tend to be lowest in rural areas, where education levels are low, in sharp contrast to regions with high formation rates, where "good" entrepreneurs and the numbers of in-migrants with high educations and salaries are abundant. Even more important for economic growth than differences in firm formation may be the tendency for some regions to have a greater proportion of successful, rapidly growing small firms. Again, social and occupational influences appear to be most significant in reinforcing existing spatial contrasts.[106] How do such regional variations come about? Successful entrepreneurs may simply be more prepared for starting a business: they have more starting capital, are more oriented to markets outside the local region, and have a larger number of clients.[107] Perhaps most important is the fact that some regions have a history of entrepreneurship, accumulated over a long period, from which rôle models and experiences are made available to potential entrepreneurs through local information networks.[108] Overall, there is a strong tendency for entrepreneurship to be strongest precisely in those regions which need it least, suggesting that to rely on new and small firms will not eliminate regional economic differentials.

The "entrepreneurial climate" of a region, which may be a particularly critical variable influencing entrepreneurship, relies almost entirely on a well-connected network of informal and formal investors, previous entrepreneurs, and an aura of nonroutine, innovative activity.[109] The entrepreneurial climate and other ingredients "essential" to the "environment for entrepreneurship"[110] underscore once again the thesis that the regional conditions which foster high rates of entrepreneurship are local attributes.

In large urban areas a sufficient number of potential entrepreneurs is present, as well as the other "environmental" factors that encourage entrepreneurship. In a pioneering work, Shapero studied technical company formation in relatively small American counties over a 28-year period.[111] The variables most highly correlated with firm formation tended to be those related to city size and agglomeration, such as manufacturing employment, educational expenditures, and income. Not all large cities are equally well-endowed in the complex interweaving of influences on economic growth. Thompson and Thompson have shown that large cities vary in their mix of occupations and corporate functions as well as in their entrepreneurial activity.[112] Within a region, the interrelatedness of (a) the functions of firms and their innovative activities, (b) the inter-firm flow of information, and (c) the entrepreneurial history and climate interact to bring about and bolster economic growth and development. To create this interaction or synergy is perhaps the most daunting challenge for policy formation.

Some implications for state policy[113]

Recently there have been a number of attempts to create or generate innovativeness in peripheral areas or regions.[114] In each case, success has seemed to elude peripheral regions for reasons that, in light of the arguments made in this chapter, are somewhat easily identified. A prominent shortcoming of peripheral regions seems to be the relative scarcity of R&D activity carried out there. Existing concentrations of R&D activity attract additional R&D activity, reinforcing the pool of professional and technical workers—and potential entrepreneurs. Entrepreneurs can emerge outside the context of technological innovation, but some elements in common with innovation must be present. Information, contact networks, and technical progressiveness are standard in areas where entrepreneurship is common. Simple and short-term solutions are not likely to work in a situation where contacts and progressiveness either are, or are not, part of the local culture.[115] In general, policies that provide information are preferable to those that rely on subsidies.[116]

Policies cannot create entrepreneurs

Entrepreneurship is largely a product of the local industrial firm and plant mix and the socioeconomic environment created by the local population. Consequently, it can respond over time to the results of industrial recruitment efforts. Attempts to lure the R&D activities of large firms, for example, will have a greater beneficial effect than the attraction of routine production.[117] Such a strategy is not guaranteed to spark spinoffs, however, even in the long run. Some places with considerable research and development have not been able to generate new firms in significant numbers, as evidence from Britain, France, and North Carolina shows.[118] Other policy tools, such as incubators, science parks, and venture capital pools, will not create entrepreneurs;[119] they might, however, encourage potential entrepreneurs to stay in the area rather than to seek more favorable local conditions elsewhere.[120]

It is clear that the location factors which predominate in high-tech industries and in the majority of innovation-oriented regional policies are broader than those common in previous generations of economic development policies. The critical importance of information and instability in the process of technological change itself brings this about. However, recent attempts to bring about more widespread growth are perhaps not very different from earlier growth center policies.[121] The most ambitious example of deliberate high-tech development is the Technopolis Concept in Japan, a plan to build a network of 19 regional high-tech cities linked to Tokyo by bullet trains.[122] Tsukuba Science City, planned during the 1960s and now the home of two universities and 50 national research institutes, is a prototype for the scheme. The criteria used by the Ministry of International Trade and Industry (MITI) to select the locations include a typical set of urban attributes: proximity to a "mother city" of at least 150,000 inhabitants to provide urban services; proximity to an airport or bullet train station; an integrated complex of industrial, academic, and residential areas; and a pleasant living environment. The provincial technopolises are unlikely to reduce significantly the allure and advantages of Tokyo within Japan for research and development and other key corporate activities.

The inability of policies to bring about entrepreneurship rests on the fact that networks of entrepreneurs and investors will not emerge from policy initiatives alone. In fact, they are based on personal contacts and thus rely largely on commonalities of social and occupational status. This critical element of a place's entrepreneurial environment is perhaps the least amenable to any public policy.[123] Policies have also shown little ability to speed up the process of technology-based regional development. It can take 20 or 30 years or more for a high-tech region to generate new firms (e.g., Ottawa in Canada and Silicon Glen in Scotland).

Policies will not substitute for a critical mass

Small high-tech regions find it more difficult to attract professional workers than do large urban areas. The labor market for professional workers and the constraint they impose on firm location are inadequately understood, even though high-tech policies critically depend on them.[124] The synergy of amenities, accessibility, and agglomeration factors found in large urban regions cannot really be substituted for in smaller regions.[125] Norris suggests that multistate regional policies would improve technology-based entrepreneurship in the Midwest by creating "a critical mass that no single state can achieve alone."[126] The suggestion has not yet really been tried, but it would seem to encompass regions too large to affect local environments for entrepreneurship.[127]

The implication is that there may be relatively little that policies as typically viewed can do to alter the situation.[128] Some possibility exists that a small region can become a technological complex, or that a declining city can revitalize itself around new technologies. More often, the choice must be among large, already rather prosperous urban regions.[129] The promotion of entrepreneurship on a regional basis, as has been tried notably in the Federal Republic of Germany, is too recent to be considered a long-term success. Increasingly, entrepreneurship and the locational preferences of mobile professional workers are seen to influence regional and technological policies.

Policies can have indirect benefits

Universities have not been prominent sources of spinoffs, as discussed earlier. Instead, universities provide a necessary resource to an area—technical personnel—as well as a pool of well-educated, potential entrepreneurs.[130] In the American context, and perhaps elsewhere as well, policies to improve local universities can also have the side-effect of improving the "intellectual climate" of the area, in addition to improving research itself. This improves the perceived quality of life by enhancing the "ambience" and reputation of a place as high-tech. In addition, the variety of university facilities and programs may well be combined in the perceptions of professional workers into an intangible image of an "intellectual atmosphere" which differs from the more rigorous examination of university research capabilities conducted by companies.

The recent boom in high-tech policies provides a focus for regional advantages not unlike the growth pole policies of a decade or two ago. The creation and evolution of North Carolina's Research Triangle as a focal point for high technology shows that, with some effort and a cognizance of the varying potential of places within a state, changes can be brought about. Unfortunately, political considerations can dilute scarce funding by designating too large a number of foci, or by selecting places that are inappropriate for high technology given the demands of firms and their workers. It is less clear that policies can facilitate the entrepreneurial climate in a significant way, although recent research suggests that this too has occurred, especially in the two most prominent high-tech regions, California and Massachusetts.[131] It is impossible to tell whether the cumulative advantages of those states are merely reinforcing growth dynamics already well established.[132]

The recent focus on high technology and entrepreneurship has had some positive effects on state and local policy. It has prompted a more long-term perspective about economic development; it has demonstrated the connection between universities and the economy; and it has shown the significant advantages to be gained from investments in human capital, especially through education. Even if implemented only partially and half-heartedly, such policies can have these effects.

Economic change does not take place in the same way, and policies will not be equally appropriate, in all places. Locally specific attributes, shortcomings, and histories all play a part in defining the future potential of a regional economy.[133] Finally, much of the variation found in entrepreneurship is a direct product of labor market processes. To a large extent, the professional labor market for high-tech workers, for example, determines that only some places will be R&D or high-tech locations.

Conclusions

Technology is fixed neither in time nor space. Scientific advances made in one location, whether in a university or a corporate laboratory, are typically shifted to other locations where further development takes place, and to yet other locations as commercial products enter into production. The aggregate economic impacts are thus dispersed to, and divided among, several locations. With large corporations, this internal process of technology transfer may have few benefits for any region. The same is true of most inter-firm technology transfer via licensing and other arrangements. In the end, corporate strategies and decisions regarding the location of activities determine which areas benefit from science and technology.

It is the spinoff process which is more commonly thought of as the route of local technology transfer and economic growth. Indeed, new ideas largely enter the economy through the identification of opportunities by entrepreneurs. The local nature of entrepreneurship poses great challenges, but it is just such a process that was the basis of the California and Massachusetts successes which other state science and technology policies are trying to emulate. The process of entrepreneurship may be a much more important one to regional and local economies than the process of technological change.

Notes

1   Definitions of high technology are many and varied. For discussions, see E. J. Malecki, "High technology and local economic development," *Journal of the American Planning Association* **50**, 1984, 262–9; E. J. Malecki, "Industrial location and corporate organization in high technology industries," *Economic Geography* **61**, 1985, 345–69; and A. Markusen, P. Hall & A. Glasmeier, *High tech America: the what, how, why, and where of the sunrise industries* (Boston: Allen & Unwin, 1986).

2   Definitions again vary, but I take the Schumpeterian position that entrepreneurship incorporates an element of innovation and that not all new business development is entrepreneurship. C. A. Kent, "The rediscovery of the entrepreneur," in *The environment for entrepreneurship*, ed. C. A. Kent (Lexington, Mass.: Lexington Books, 1984), pp. 1–19; J. Schumpeter, *The theory of economic development* (Cambridge, Mass.: Harvard University Press, 1934). The most frequently started businesses in the United States are imitative, often franchised, service establishments, such as eating and drinking places and retail shops, few of which are very innovative (D. L. Birch, "The truth about start-ups," *Inc.* **10**, January 1988, 14–15).

3   R. Gilpin, *Technology, economic growth, and international competitiveness*, prepared for the Joint Economic Committee, U.S. Congress (Washington, D.C.: U.S. Government Printing Office, 1975); N. Rosenberg, *Inside the black box: technology and economics* (Cambridge: Cambridge University Press, 1982).

4   M. Gertler, "Capital, technology, and industry dynamics in regional development," *Urban Geography* **8**, 1987, 251–63; E. J. Malecki & P. Varaiya, "Innovation and changes in regional structure," in *Regional economics*, vol. 1 of *Handbook of regional and urban economics*, ed. P. Nijkamp (Amsterdam: North-Holland, 1986), pp. 629–45.

5   I. Feller, "Invention, diffusion, and industrial location," in *Locational dynamics of manufacturing activity*, ed. L. Collins & D. F. Walker (New York: Wiley, 1975), pp. 83–107.

6   P. Varaiya & M. Wiseman, "Investment and employment in manufacturing in U.S. metropolitan areas 1960–1976," *Regional Science and Urban Economics* **11**, 1981, 431–69.

7 R. B. Le Heron, "Best-practice technology, technical leadership, and regional economic development," *Environment and Planning* **5**, 1973, 735–49.

8 F. M. Scherer, "Inter-industry technology flows in the United States," *Research Policy* **11**, 1982, 227–45.

9 S. Kuznets, "Innovations and adjustments in economic growth," *Swedish Journal of Economics* **74**, 1972, 431–51.

10 National Academy of Sciences/National Academy of Engineering, *The impact of science and technology on regional economic development* (Washington, D.C.: National Academy of Sciences, 1969); R. J. Buswell, "Research and development and regional development: a review," in *Technological change and regional development*, ed. A. Gillespie (London: Pion, 1983), pp. 9–22; E. J. Malecki, "Federal R&D spending in the United States of America: some impacts on metropolitan economies," *Regional Studies* **16**, 1982, 19–35.

11 M. J. Hagey & E. J. Malecki, "Linkages in high technology industries: a Florida case study," *Environment and Planning A* **18**, 1986, 1477–98.

12 G. P. Sweeney, *Innovation, entrepreneurs, and regional development* (New York: St. Martin's Press, 1987).

13 Office of Technology Assessment, *Technology, innovation, and regional economic development* (Washington, D.C.: U.S. Government Printing Office, 1984), p. 7. The elements of this regional technological infrastructure cited include: applied research and product development activities at nearby universities, federal laboratories, and existing firms; informal communication networks that provide access to information and technology transfer from those R&D activities; scientific and technical laborforce, including skilled craftsmen, newly trained engineers, and experienced professionals (who also represent a pool of potential entrepreneurs); a network of experts and advisors (often augmented by university faculties) specializing in hardware, software, business development, and venture capital; a network of job shoppers and other suppliers of specialized components, subassemblies, and accessories; and proximity to complementary and competitive enterprises, as well as distributors and customers.

14 R. R. Nelson, *High-tech policies: a five-nation comparison* (Washington, D.C.: American Enterprise Institute, 1984), p. 75.

15 R. B. Reich, "The rise of techno-nationalism," *Atlantic* **259**, May 1987, 63–9.

16 S. J. Kline & N. Rosenberg, "An overview of innovation," in *The positive sum strategy*, ed. R. Landau & N. Rosenberg (Washington, D.C.: National Academy Press, 1986), pp. 275–305.

17 Buswell, "Research and development and regional development"; Malecki & Varaiya, "Innovation and changes in regional structure."

18 Sweeney, *Innovation, entrepreneurs, and regional development.*

19 Buswell, "Research and development and regional development"; Kline & Rosenberg, "An overview of innovation"; J. Ronayne *Science in government* (London: Edward Arnold, 1984).

20 Ronayne, *Science in government*, pp. 64–5.

21 Kline & Rosenberg, "An overview of innovation."

22 R. Vernon, "International investment and international trade in the product cycle," *Quarterly Journal of Economics* **80**, 1966, 190–207; G. Krumme & R. Hayter, "Implications of corporate strategies and product cycle adjustments for regional employment changes," in *Locational dynamics of manufacturing activity*, ed. L. Collins & D. F. Walker (New York: Wiley, 1975); A. R. Markusen, *Product cycles, oligopoly, and regional development* (Cambridge, Mass.: MIT Press, 1985); S. F. Seninger, "Employment cycles and process innovation in regional economic change," *Journal of Regional Science* **25**, 1985, 259–72; L. Suarez–Villa, "Industrial export enclaves and manufacturing change," *Papers of the Regional Science Association* **54**, 1984, 89–111; M. D. Thomas, "Growth pole theory, technological change, and regional economic growth," *Papers of the Regional Science Association* **34**, 1975, 3–25.

23 J. M. Utterback, "The dynamics of product and process innovation in industry," in *Technological innovation for a dynamic economy*, ed. C. T. Hill & J. M. Utterback (New York: Pergamon, 1979), pp. 40–65.

24 M. J. Taylor, "The product cycle model: a critique," *Environment and Planning A* **18**, 1986, 751–61.

25 C. De Bresson & J. Lampel, "Beyond the life cycle: organizational and technological design. I: An alternative perspective," *Journal of Product Innovation Management* **2**, 1985, 170–87; C. F. Sabel, G. Herrigel, R. Kazis & R. Deeg, "How to keep mature industries innovative," *Technology Review* **90**, April 1987, 27–35.

26 D. J. Teece, "Profiting from technological innovation: implications for integration, collaboration, licensing, and public policy," *Research Policy* **15**, 1986, 285–305.

27 J. D. Goldhar, "In the factory of the future, innovation is productivity," *Research Management* **29**, 1986, 26–31.

28 De Bresson & Lampel, "Beyond the life cycle"; Sabel et al., "How to keep mature industries innovative."

29 R. U. Ayres & W. A. Steger, "Rejuvenating the life cycle concept," *Journal of Business Strategy* **6**, 1985, 66–76; Goldhar, "In the factory of the future."

30 E. Schoenberger, "Competition, competitive strategy, and industrial change: the case of electronic components," *Economic Geography* **62**, 1986, 321–33.

31 E. Schoenberger, "Technological and organizational change in automobile production: spatial implications," *Regional Studies* **21**, 1987, 199–214; M. Storper & S. Christopherson, "Flexible specialization and regional industrial agglomeration: the case of the U.S. motion picture industry," *Annals of the Association of American Geographers* **77**, 1987, 104–17.

32 R. Kaplinsky, *Automation: the technology and society* (London: Longman, 1984).

33 R. Jaikumar, "Postindustrial manufacturing," *Harvard Business Review* **64**, 1986, 69–76.

34 Kline & Rosenberg, "An overview of innovation."

35 J. Howells, "Industry–academic links in research and innovation: a national and regional development perspective," *Regional Studies* **20**, 1986, 472–6.

36 E. J. Malecki, "Dimensions of R&D location in the United States," *Research Policy* **9**, 1980, 2–22; E. J. Malecki, "Public sector research and development and regional economic performance in the United States," in *The regional economic impact of technological change*, ed. A. T. Thwaites & R. P. Oakey (London: Frances Pinter, 1985), pp. 115–31.

37 J. Schmandt & R. Wilson (eds.), *Promoting high-technology industry: initiatives and policies for state governments* (Boulder: Westview Press, 1987).

38 General Accounting Office, *University funding: patterns of distribution of federal research funds to universities* (Washington, D.C.: U.S. General Accounting Office, 1987), pp. 14–17.

39 E. J. Malecki, "Regional economic development and state science policy." Paper presented at the National Science Foundation PRA workshop, An Agenda for State Science Policy Research, Washington, D.C., September 1987.

40 Ibid.; Malecki, "Industrial location and corporate organization."

41 C. Armington, C. Harris & M. Odle, "Formation and growth in high-technology firms: a regional assessment," in Office of Technology Assessment, *Technology, innovation, and regional economic development*; C. S. Harris, "Establishing high-technology enterprises in metropolitan areas," in *Local economies in transition*, ed. E. M. Bergman (Durham, N.C.: Duke University Press, 1986), pp. 165–84.

42 E. Devereux et al., *Economic growth and investment in higher education* (Austin: Bureau of Business Research, University of Texas, 1987).

43 D. E. Drew, *Strengthening academic science* (New York: Praeger, 1985); General Accounting Office, *University funding*.

44 E. M. Rogers, "The role of the research university in the spin-off of high-technology companies," *Technovation* **4**, 1986, 169–81.
45 A. C. Cooper, "Technical entrepreneurship: what do we know?" *R&D Management* **3**, 1973, 59–64; A. C. Cooper, "The role of incubator organizations in the founding of growth-oriented firms," *Journal of Business Venturing* **1**, 1985, 75–86; A. C. Cooper, "Entrepreneurship and high technology," in *The art and science of entrepreneurship*, ed. D. L. Sexton & R. W. Smilor (Cambridge, Mass.: Ballinger, 1986), pp. 153–68.
46 Devereux et al., *Economic growth and investment in higher education*; C. S. Galbraith, "High-technology location and development: the case of Orange County," *California Management Review* **28**, 1985, 98–109.
47 M. Kenney, "Schumpeterian innovation and entrepreneurs in capitalism: a case study of the U.S. biotechnology industry," *Research Policy* **15**, 1986, 21–31.
48 Ibid.
49 L. W. Steele, *Innovation in big business* (New York: Elsevier, 1975).
50 Sabel et al., "How to keep mature industries innovative."
51 Utterback, "The dynamics of product and process innovation in industry."
52 Le Heron, "Best-practice technology."
53 Varaiya & Wiseman, "Investment and employment in manufacturing."
54 E. A. Brugger & B. Stuckey, "Regional economic structure and innovative behaviour in Switzerland," *Regional Studies* **21**, 1987, 241–54; Sweeney, *Innovation, entrepreneurs, and regional development*.
55 E. Mansfield, J. Rapoport, A. Romeo, S. Wagner & F. Husic, *The production and application of new industrial technology* (New York: W. W. Norton, 1977); R. P. Oakey, A. T. Thwaites & P. A. Nash, "The regional distribution of innovative manufacturing establishments in Britain," *Regional Studies* **14**, 1980, 235–53; J. Rees, R. Briggs & R. Oakey, "The adoption of new technology in the American machinery industry," *Regional Studies* **18**, 1984, 489–504; F. A. Rossini & A. L. Porter, "Who's using computers in industrial R&D – and for what?" *Research Management* **29**, 1986, 39–44.
56 B. Gold, "On the adoption of technological innovations in industry: super-ficial models and complex decision processes," *Omega* **8**, 1980, 505–16; N. Rosenberg, "On technological expectations," *Economic Journal* **86**, 1976, 523–35.
57 Rosenberg, "On technological expectations."
58 S. D. Fawkes & J. K. Jacques, "Problems of adoption and adaptation of energy-conserving innovations in U.K. beverage and dairy industries," *Research Policy* **16**, 1987, 1–15; C. A. Voss, "The need for a field of study of implementation of innovations," *Journal of Product Innovation Management* **2**, 1985, 266–71.
59 C. Ganz, "Linkages between knowledge, diffusion, and utilization," *Knowledge: Creation, Diffusion, Utilization* **1**, 1980, 591–612.
60 L. A. Brown, *Innovation diffusion: a new perspective* (New York: Methuen, 1981); Sweeney, *Innovation, entrepreneurs, and regional development*.
61 R. R. Nelson, "Research on productivity growth and productivity differences: dead ends and new departures," *Journal of Economic Literature* **19**, 1981, 1029–64; L. Soete & R. Turner, "Technology diffusion and the rate of technical change," *Economic Journal* **94**, 1984, 612–23.
62 C. Abraham & G. Hayward, "Understanding discontinuance: towards a more realistic model of technological innovation and industrial adoption in Britain," *Technovation* 2, 1984, 209–31.
63 Oakey, Thwaites, & Nash, "The regional distribution of innovative manufac-turing establishments in Britain"; R. P. Oakey, A. T. Thwaites & P. A. Nash, "Technological change and regional development: some evidence on regional variations in product and process innovation," *Environment and Planning A* **14**, 1982, 1073–86.

64 A. Glasmeier, "High tech industries and the regional division of labor," *Industrial Relations* **25**, 1986, 197–211; Malecki, "Industrial location and corporate organization."

65 Utterback, "The dynamics of product and process innovation in industry"; E. J. Malecki, "Product cycles, innovation cycles, and regional economical change," *Technological Forecasting and Social Change* **19**, 1981, 291–306.

66 R. Schmenner, *Making business location decisions* (Englewood Cliffs, N.J.: Préntice-Hall, 1982); A. T. Thwaites, "The employment implications of technological change," in *Technological change and regional development*, ed. A. Gillespie (London: Pion, 1983), pp. 36–53.

67 J. E. Ettlie & A. H. Rubenstein, "Firm size and product innovation," *Journal of Product Innovation Management* **4**, 1987, 89–108.

68 F. A. Johne, "The adoption of new technology in manufacturing firms," in *Advances in business marketing*, ed. A. G. Woodside (Greenwich, Conn.: JAI Press, 1986), vol. 1, pp. 141–62; E. von Hippel, "A customer active paradigm for industrial product idea generation," in *Industrial innovation*, ed. M. J. Baker (London: Macmillan, 1979), pp. 82–110.

69 P. Shrivastana & W. E. Souder, "The strategic management of technological innovations: a review and a model," *Journal of Management Studies* **24**, 1987, 25–41.

70 J. Friar & M. Horwitch, "The emergence of technology strategy: a new dimension of strategic management," in *Technology in the modern corporation: a strategic perspective* (New York: Pergamon, 1986), pp. 50–85.

71 M. B. W. Graham, "Corporate research and development: the latest transformation," in *Technology in the modern corporation: a strategic perspective* (New York: Pergamon, 1986), pp. 86–102.

72 G. Dosi, "Technological paradigms and technological trajectories: a suggested interpretation of the determinants and directions of technical change," *Research Policy* **11**, 1982, 147–62; R. R. Nelson & S. G. Winter, *An evolutionary theory of economic change* (Cambridge, Mass.: Harvard University Press, 1982).

73 E. M. Rogers, "Information exchange and technological innovation," in *The transfer and utilization of technical knowledge*, ed. D. Sahal (Lexington, Mass.: Lexington Books, 1982), pp. 105–123.

74 F. J. Contractor & T. Sagafi-Nejad, "International technology transfer: major issues and policy responses," in *International business knowledge*, ed. W. A. Dymsza & R. G. Vambery (New York: Praeger, 1987), pp. 515–37.

75 T. J. Allen, D. B. Hyman & D. L. Pinckney, "Transferring technology to the small manufacturing firm: a study of technology transfer in three countries," *Research Policy* **12**, 1983, 199–211.

76 Sweeney, *Innovation, entrepreneurs, and regional development*.

77 F. Chesnais, "Science, technology, and competitiveness," *Science Technology Industry Review* **1**, 1986, 91.

78 W. B. Stohr, "Structural characteristics of peripheral areas: the relevance of the stock-in-trade variables of regional science," *Papers of the Regional Science Association* **49**, 1982, 71–84.

79 W. J. Coffey & M. Polèse, "Local development: conceptual bases and policy implications," *Regional Studies* **19**, 1985, 85–93.

80 Ibid.; Sweeney, *Innovation, entrepreneurs, and regional development*.

81 R. Vaughan & R. Pollard, "State and federal policies for high-technology development," in *Technology, regions, and policy*, ed. J. Rees (Totowa, N.J.: Rowman & Littlefield, 1986), pp. 268–81.

82 N. Clark, "Science, technology, and regional economic development," *Research Policy* **1**, 1972, 296–319; E. J. Malecki, "Science, technology, and regional economic development: review and prospects," *Research Policy* **10**, 1981, 312–34; Malecki, "High technology and local economic development."

83   A. E. Andersson, "Creativity and regional development," *Papers of the Regional Science Association* **56**, 1985, 5–20.

84   W. B. Stohr, "Regional innovation complexes," *Papers of the Regional Science Association* **59**, 1986, 29–44.

85   R. P. Oakey, *High technology small firms* (New York: St. Martin's Press, 1984).

86   Sweeney, *Innovation, entrepreneurs, and regional development*.

87   Ibid.

88   Brugger & Stuckey, "Regional economic structure and innovative behaviour in Switzerland"; Stohr, "Structural characteristics of peripheral areas."

89   A. T. Thwaites, "Some evidence of regional variations in the introduction and diffusion of industrial products and processes within British manufacturing industry," *Regional Studies* **16**, 1982, 371–81; Thwaites, "The employment implications of technological change."

90   D. Keeble & T. Kelly, "New firms and high-technology industry in the United Kingdom: the case of computer electronics," in *New firms and regional development in Europe*, ed. D. Keeble & E. Wever (London: Croom Helm, 1986), pp. 184–202.

91   P. M. Flynn, *Facilitating technological change: the human resource challenge* (Cambridge, Mass.: Ballinger, 1988); P. Hall & A. R. Markusen, *Silicon landscapes* (Boston: Allen & Unwin, 1985).

92   E. J. Malecki, "The R&D location decision of the firm and 'Creative' Regions," *Technovation* **6**, 1987, 205–22.

93   Flynn, *Facilitating technological change*.

94   Keeble & Wever, *New firms and regional development in Europe*.

95   Armington, Harris & Odle, "Formation and growth in high-technology firms."

96   R. Rothwell & W. Zegveld, *Innovation and the small and medium-sized firm* (Hingham, Mass.: Kluwer Nijhoff, 1982); G. P. Sweeney, "Innovation is entrepreneur-led," in *Innovation policies: an international perspective* (London: Frances Pinter, 1985), pp. 80–113.

97   R. R. Nelson, "Incentives for entrepreneurship and supporting institutions," in *Economic incentives*, ed. B. Balassa & H. Giersch (New York: St. Martin's Press, 1986), pp. 173–87.

98   L. Bollinger, K. Hope & J. M. Utterback, "A review of literature and hypotheses on new technology-based firms," *Research Policy* **12**, 1983, 1–14; D. A. Garvin, "Spin-offs and the new firm formation process," *California Management Review* **25**, 1983, 3–20.

99   P. Cooke, "Regional innovation policy: problems and strategies in Britain and France," *Environment and Planning C, Government and Policy* **3**, 1985, 253–67; Sweeney, *Innovation, entrepreneurs, and regional development*.

100 P. S. Johnson & D. G. Cathcart, "New manufacturing firms and regional development: some evidence from the northern region," *Regional Studies* **13**, 1979, 269–80; Sweeney, "Innovation is entrepreneur-led"; E. Wever, "New firm formation in the Netherlands," in *New firms and regional development in Europe*, Keeble & Wever, pp. 54–74.

101 Bollinger, Hope & Utterback, "A review of literature and hypotheses"; Garvin, "Spin-offs and the new firm formation process"; Malecki, "Industrial location and corporate organization."

102 M. E. Beesley & R. T. Hamilton, "Births and deaths of manufacturing firms in the Scottish regions," *Regional Studies* **20**, 1986, 281–8; Sweeney, *Innovation, entrepreneurs, and regional development*.

103 Keeble & Wever, *New firms and regional development in Europe*; F. Meyer-Krahmer, "Innovation behaviour and regional indigenous potential," *Regional Studies* **19**, 1985, 523–34.

104 F. Martin, "L'entrepreneurship et la développement local: une evaluation," *Canadian Journal of Regional Science* **9**, 1986, 17.

105 Ibid.

106 Keeble & Wever, *New firms and regional development in Europe*; C. M. Mason, "The geography of 'successful' small firms in the United Kingdom," *Environment and Planning A* **17**, 1985, 1499–513.

107 H. M. Miller, E. E. Brown & T. J. Center, "Southern Appalachian handicrafts industry: implications for regional economic development," *Review of Regional Studies* **16** (3), 1986, 50–8; Wever, "New firm formation in the Netherlands."

108 A. Shapero, *An action program for entrepreneurship*. Report prepared for the Ozarks Regional Commission (Austin, Texas: Multi-Disciplinary Research, 1971); Sweeney, *Innovation, entrepreneurs, and regional development*.

109 J. M. L. Gruenstein, "Targeting high tech in the Delaware Valley," *Business Review* (Federal Reserve Bank of Philadelphia), May–June, 1984, 3–14; R. Miller & M. Cote, "Growing the next Silicon Valley," *Harvard Business Review* **63**, 1985, 114–23; A. Shapero, "The entrepreneurial event," in *The environment for entrepreneurship*, Kent, pp. 21–40.

110 A. V. Bruno & T. T. Tyebjee, "The environment for entrepreneurship," in *Encyclopedia of entrepreneurship* (Englewood Cliffs, N.J.: Prentice-Hall, 1982), pp. 288–307.

111 Shapero, *An action program for entrepreneurship*.

112 W. R. Thompson & P. R. Thompson, "National industries and local occupational strengths: the cross-hairs of targeting," *Urban Studies* **24**, 1987, 547–60.

113 Much of this discussion is taken from E. J. Malecki & P. Nijkamp, "Technology and regional development: some thoughts on policy," *Environment and Planning C: Government and Policy* **6**, 1988, 383–99.

114 Schmandt and Wilson, *Promoting high-technology industry*.

115 Sweeney, *Innovation, entrepreneurs, and regional development*.

116 E. F. Morrison, "State and local efforts to encourage economic growth through innovation: an historical perspective," in *Technological innovation – strategies for a new partnership*, ed. D. O. Gray, T. Solomon & W. Hetzner (Amsterdam: North-Holland, 1986), pp. 57–68.

117 "Technical branch plants," where both R&D and standardized production take place, are an increasingly common type of corporate facility in high-tech industries (Markusen, Hall & Glasmeier, *High technology America*). Their contribution to local economic growth hinges upon the local environment for entrepreneurship.

118 Cooke, "Regional innovation policy"; D. Whittington, "Microelectronics policy in North Carolina: an introduction," in *High hopes for high tech*, ed. D. Whittington (Chapel Hill: University of North Carolina Press, 1985), pp. 3–31.

119 J. Britton & M. Gertler, "Locational perspectives on policies for innovation," in *Competitiveness through technology*, ed. J. Dermer (Lexington, Mass.: Lexington Books, 1986), pp. 159–75.

120 D. N. Allen & V. Levine, *Nurturing advanced technology enterprises* (New York: Praeger, 1986).

121 Oakey, *High technology small firms*.

122 S. Tatsuno, *The technopolis strategy* (New York: Prentice Hall, 1986).

123 Committee for Economic Development, *Leadership for dynamic state economies* (New York: Committee for Economic Development, 1986); R. Miller & M. Cote, *Growing the next Silicon Valley: a guide for successful regional planning* (Lexington, Mass.: Lexington Books, 1987).

124 Malecki, "The R&D location decision."

125 Andersson, "Creativity and regional development"; Martin, "L'entrepreneurship et la developpment local"; Miller & Cote, *Growing the next Silicon Valley*.

126 W. C. Norris, "Cooperative R&D: a regional strategy," *Issues in Science and Technology* **1**, 1985, 98.

127 Organization for Economic Cooperation and Development, *New roles for cities and towns: local initiatives for employment creation* (Paris: Organization for Economic Cooperation and Development, 1987); Sweeney, *Innovation, entrepreneurs, and regional development*.

128 J. B. Goddard & A. T. Thwaites, "New technology and regional development policy," in *Technological change, employment and spatial dynamics*, ed. P. Nijkamp (Berlin: Springer, 1986), pp. 91–114.

129 C. Pottier, "The adaptation of regional industrial structures to technical changes," *Papers of the Regional Science Association* **58**, 1985, 59–72.

130 Keeble & Kelly, "New firms and high-technology industry in the United Kingdom"; N. S. Segal, "Universities and technological entrepreneurship in Britain: some implications of the Cambridge phenomenon," *Technovation* **4**, 1986, 189–204.

131 Committee for Economic Development, *Leadership for dynamic state economies*.

132 Malecki & Varaiya, "Innovation and changes in regional structure."

133 A. Kirby, "Nine fallacies of local economic change," *Urban Affairs Quarterly* **21**, 1985, 207–20; Sweeney, *Innovation, entrepreneurs, and regional development*.

6

State innovation policies and regional restructuring of technologically dependent industry

EDWARD M. BERGMAN

Introduction

POLICY MAKERS ARE understandably eager to implement the numerous individual approaches to technological upgrading of regional economies that come to their attention. However, the suitability of available policy instruments—both novel and traditional—is seldom examined much in advance of their wholesale application to a new class of problems. Evidence has been assembled here to provide a better descriptive account of the relationship between two traditional policy instruments of state policy—higher education and transportation—and their usefulness in promoting technologically dependent industry (TDI). This analysis relies upon evidence of change from 1977 to 1984 at the county level in 13 southern states. Three classifications of industrial activity thought to be dependent upon technological advance are available for each county. Counties are further coded by the varying degrees of access they enjoy to the state's principal transportation system and by an indicator of whether they host a university-based science/technology park.

It is always useful, even essential, to examine evidence of effects that state policies are intended to produce early enough to make necessary policy modifications or to alter expectations accordingly. There has been very little opportunity to evaluate evidence of policy effects on what is called here technologically dependent industry ("TDI" here, but more frequently and less precisely called "high-tech"). Part of the difficulty hinges on the weaknesses and lags of reported data, another part on definitional disagreements about technology, while still other difficulties stem from an elusiveness about the beneficial effects one ought logically to seek (and evaluate) in technology policy.

This chapter begins by reviewing three definitions of TDI used in policy research and their relationship to economic restructuring. The effects on TDI expected from traditional state policies for higher education and transportation are posed as significant in pursuing technology objectives. An exploratory investigation of TDI restructuring and these traditional state policies is conducted for all southern metropolitan region counties using data for 1977 and 1984. The concluding section identifies early opportunities for fine-tuning and refocusing these important policy elements.

Technologically dependent industry and restructuring

This analysis is based on the assumption that most of the difficulties mentioned above have receded sufficiently in importance to allow an early glimpse of relationships between state policy and TDI. That is, an emerging consensus emphasizes that beneficial effects of TDI (innovation, productivity gains, broad sectoral modernization, and upgrading) are more closely associated with industrial restructuring than with simple job or income growth, although long-term growth prospects also depend upon favorable restructuring of industry. Further, regional TDI data of sufficient detail measured across a full business cycle, are now available to detect these early and important effects. Finally, one can examine alternative definitions of TDI without fear of being locked into a single, inappropriate version of this key industrial sector. That is, technology dependence might result from the disproportional importance of technological innovation to a group of industries as compared with their lesser dependence on resource inputs, manual labor, or capital-intensive production.[1] The group of industries sensitive to technological innovation can be quite fluid over time: some may shift to lesser dependence as innovative alterations run their course during industrial restructuring phases, while other industries become more dependent on innovation to remain competitive with domestic and foreign producers. This "churning" of industrial membership in and out of innovative stages is what state policy is often intended to produce—or at least not inhibit—because of its overall upgrading effects on industrial development.

The absence of reliable "innovation markers" that would accurately indicate which, in fact, are TDIs has spawned several industrial technology proxies. This analysis examines alternative definitions of TDI that rely upon various technology proxies. Either individually or in combination, these proxies focus on corporate expenditures for research and development or on relative concentrations of technologically significant occupations. Perhaps the most systematic review of TDI definitions now in use is provided by the Office of Technology Assessment.[2] Without rehearsing here all the classification details, the following points are sufficiently pertinent to this study to bear mention. First, the occupational skill criterion was applied to the BLS occupational employment matrix. It yields a TDI definition that stresses technology used in the production process; employed 12.5 million workers in 1980 (13.6 percent total employment); and grew annually at a rate of 2.3 percent in the 1972–82 decade. Second, the research and development expenditure criterion was applied to the U.S. input–output matrix. It yields a TDI definition that stresses a firm's overall reliance on technological inputs; employed 2.5 million workers in 1980 (2.8 percent total employment); and grew annually at a rate of 2.7 percent in the 1972–82 decade. Both BLS and the Brookings group combined selected aspects of occupational composition and R&D expenditure criteria which, after netting out several questionable industrial sectors from each, yielded combined TDI definitions. This procedure defined technology-dependent industries that covered a comprehensive, tighter set of input and production technologies; employed 6.2 (BLS) and 6.7 (Brookings) million workers in 1980 (6.2 per cent and 6.8 per cent of total employment, respectively); and grew at average annual rates of 3.4 per cent (BLS) and 4.9 per cent (Brookings) during the 1970s.

Together, these definitions allow one to investigate which types of TDI are responding to various policy interventions. For example, the occupational definition includes far more workers, particularly those who are involved in some technological aspect of production processes; this implies a rather generous view of TDI, and it probably

includes numerous sectors that more strongly reflect capital intensi-
fication of production and policies that specifically promote capital
investment. This sector is not dependent upon or expected to be found
with much frequency in university research parks; accordingly, we
will not include it in subsequent analyses. On the other hand, the
R&D expenditure definition is far more restrictive in size and closer
to university research in technological function. Since this sector is by
definition more actively engaged with technology at the pre-production
phase, one might logically expect one of two distinctive development
patterns. The first features internal growth, entrepreneurship, venture
capital, and so forth which would "spin off" growth of this sector in
the form of new firms. The second focuses more on corporate research
centers, industrial laboratories, and federal installations that locate
(or relocate) in settings most congenial to their high-skill personnel.
Finally, the "blended" definition is more stringently defined than
either of its progenitors, but these mixed-criterion industries may be
quite heterogeneous from place to place and reveal less generalizable
influence due to the application of state policies.

One recent study[3] relied upon the Brookings data and TDI definition
to examine the comparative influence of metropolitan economic
variables on formation of TDI establishments in a sample of 35
Metropolitan Statistical Areas (MSAs). Results confirmed that, among
sample MSAs (all of which contained threshold, or greater, levels of
TDI in 1976), formation of all new TDI establishments between 1976
and 1980 was heavily dependent upon previous concentrations of
high-tech industry in the base year. Of particular interest are the
additional findings that skilled labor availability was more important
for predicting formation of TDI *branch plant enterprises*, but that prior
concentration of such industry proved more important in the formation
of *small or independent TDI establishments*. Harris's study provides
a good starting point, but it does not reveal enough about TDI's rôle
in economic restructuring or the influence of state policy. First, the
1976–80 study period coincides with a recovery phase of the national
economy when establishment formations are high in most industries;
as Howland shows for electronic component industries, employment
growth due to new establishment formations is actually negative
over a full business cycle phase of restructuring and becomes barely
positive only during a recovery phase.[4] Despite the widespread view
of most experts who argue the importance of small firm formation
and entrepreneurship in TDI,[5] recent evidence shows how limited its
direct effects can be on an area's base employment. Given the fact
that an exceptionally high fraction of TDI employment (88 percent)

is found in multi-establishment corporations,[6] one would fully expect Howland's finding that overall employment growth rates are due more to net expansion than to net formation.[7] Second, the restructuring potential of TDI ought to be measured as directly as possible: change in industry activity as a share of total area activity. Simple employment growth rates or firm formation rates are inherently self-referencing and at best imply some limited direct growth effect on a regional economy. Finally, TDI restructuring should now be assessed in terms of factors that reflect state policy or other known factors. The following sections provide additional evidence along precisely these lines.

Traditional state policy and TDI

The long-standing advantage of federal states as innovative policy laboratories is a key assumption that underlies this volume. Other chapters examine the range of policy experiments (or policy diffusion and adoption) across our 50 state laboratories. Considerable effort is now spent by states in designing or adopting a wide array of new technology policy initiatives.[8] This is entirely expected and indirectly encouraged within the U.S. federal system, which Schmandt and others argue is an honored rôle of the states.[9]

State policies for technology and industrial innovation are quite novel because they place state (and local) government in wholly unfamiliar territory: directly stimulating the innovative/technological phase of capitalist development. While states have never been particularly averse to the stimulation of commerce and industry, the bulk of such efforts was generally aimed at assisting transitions from agricultural to mass manufacturing (Mississippi's BAWI) and for broad, generic technological upgrading (transport, communication, energy production, etc.). One recent volume devotes a chapter to state-level economic development for the 1980s; it chronicles the history, basis, and current forms of state intervention, yet remains wholly silent about technology policy or the strategic rôle of TDI in a state's economic development.[10]

Still, some traditional state policies intended originally for economic development or other public objectives may, if refocused slightly, be of critical importance to TDI.[11] Two candidates fall cleanly into this category: public university policies and transportation system policies.

Thompson makes a general case for the considerable policy significance of these categories: "Those who allocate state funds for higher education and transportation have more control over the population settlement pattern of the state for decades to come than they know or perhaps want to know."[12] Plosila further identifies their facilitating importance for technological development by suggesting that "states are responsible for many of the functions essential to private sector/higher education interaction, e.g., from financing the construction of roads, bridges, and higher education facilities to investing in incubators and research parks."[13] Each of these two policy categories is of further regional importance precisely because each is spatially anchored in its implementation and, perhaps, also in its principal effects.

Public university policies

Public university systems have become important policy actors in their state's technology policy initiatives. Campus resources now openly favor departments and schools of physics, chemistry, biology, medicine, computer science, and business with new laboratories, additional faculty, and expanded research dollars. These increases are partly necessitated by rising enrollment demands and by the need to graduate more scientifically and technologically sophisticated professionals. But they are partly driven by the university's research function in the area of technological application. Universities are now expected as a matter of public policy to supply society with needed doses of "techne" at precisely the moment in their history when traditional responsibility for nurturing classical scholarship and the life of the mind is also found wanting.[14]

University preoccupations with independently established research agenda, full and timely publishing of findings, and freedom of inquiry have softened considerably as public universities rush to match their private counterparts' long-standing success in attracting applied research funds from corporate sources.

Although several models are available, the most visible university and state policy initiative is a science/research park. As a recent Urban Land Institute report makes clear,[15] there are many possible factors that might account for the enthusiastic response of universities. Chief among them are the anticipated benefits enjoyed by the universities and surrounding communities that host successful research parks, such as Research Triangle Park in North Carolina.

There are many previously successful instances of economic development in specific districts, zones, parks, or corridors where public and private investment are brought together. But in efforts to target specific state development initiatives,[16] only recently have university campuses constituted the spatial and strategic locus of state policy initiatives. A state university system remains a traditional policy instrument which, through its instructional degree programs, supplies a state's (and the nation's) need for scientists, engineers, and other trained personnel. Steinnes reviews the logic and empirical evidence in selected midwestern states (Iowa, Minnesota, North Dakota, South Dakota, Wisconsin) of the growing influence that colleges and universities, particularly those with small business support centers, may have on the local growth of broad industrial sectors (retail, services, and manufacturing).[17] University research activity is now thought to drive the technological restructuring of its regional economy and industrial base, although others are less certain that the fruits of research output and technological innovation invariably favor a university's home region.[18]

Whether its effects on the local economy are principally ecological (university facilities, community ambience, cultural events, and so forth that help attract similarly trained scientists to congenial corporate work settings) or functional (university research programs and degree programs that supply scarce knowledge or skill to technologically dependent industry) remains open to debate.[18] Premus elicited responses from industry managers who provided some partial answers: reasons for locating near universities appear to be based more upon ecological than functional grounds.[20] The preponderance of ecological factors may reflect relatively early "prefunctional" stages of involvement among the public universities, most of which are comparative latecomers to this policy rôle. Work in progress concerning regional development effects of university research parks by Luger and Goldstein will doubtless help settle this debate.[21] Early fruit of their work is a listing of 128 university research parks identified by 1987, about one-third of which are located in 36 counties spread across a 13-state region of the South.[22] Heavy reliance on university systems by southern states to foster research parks is to be entirely expected in a region whose ratio of expenditure per capita on university to elementary and secondary school systems exceeds the U.S. norm, where relatively fewer first-rank private research universities are available to sponsor such parks, and where state policy makers have more aggressively used incentives of every sort to support a broad range of industrial investment.[23] Since the South remains the nation's newest industrial region, yet is thought to lag behind the others in its overall level of technological advance, one might usefully investigate the early-round effects of these parks on

TDI in the South. Accordingly, our sample of southern states and their regional components provides an excellent empirical base for this analysis.

Transportation system policies

Transportation system policies are long-standing measures used by states to foster economic activity of nearly every sort. From the earliest farm-to-market roads to the most heavily traveled interstate highway corridors, transportation access remains vital to industrial development even among foreign investors.[24] And with the eclipse of federal road-building programs, state transportation policy emerges as a factor of growing importance. Wheat has amply demonstrated the overall growth effects of transportation, including interstate highway and air transport, while others have studied the regional effects of airports.[25] The relationships between TDI and transportation policy are more subtle, however. While goods-carrying capacity and worker commutation remain important to all types of industry, it appears that the transportation system must also adequately connect county components of a region to its air service for TDI to thrive.[26] Rosenfeld, Bergman, and Rubin examined 1977–82 growth contributed by new technology industry in counties adjacent to metropolitan areas in the South.[27] They discovered considerably greater growth (+9 percent) in metropolitan region counties connected to interstate highways (and, by inference, to the metropolitan airport) than in counties without such connections (−1 percent loss). The "internodal" nature of air transportation (i.e., the highway connection between industrial sites and airports) is quite subtle; this may in part be why one consultant concluded, understandably but unjustifiably, that "industry was attracted to [the growth site] because of good ground transportation facilities rather than because of the airport . . . airports have much less influence on [specific site] industrial location decisions than do other transportation systems."[28] The internodal connections are best understood in terms of transportation policies that affect "landside capacity" of airports.

Although transportation is crucially important for technology centers and innovative industries, the "airside capacity" of airports (i.e., terminal to aircraft capacity) remains out of the policy orbit of states and increasingly outside the federal policy domain since its deregulation in the early 1980s.[29] Airport authorities and major airlines now shape much airside capacity and share responsibility for landside capacity with various levels of local, state, and federal government.[30] Landside capacity generally includes all facilities and systems necessary to allow the internodal transfer of goods and passengers from airport property to the surrounding region by means of its surface transportation system. It is precisely at this point that state transportation policy becomes important: interchanges, exit and entry lanes, expressway extensions, and other components that service airports must generally fit within the state's transportation system plan and its capital allocation program. The importance of this policy is illustrated by the hotly contested allocation of resources in North Carolina for highway–airport connectors in locations other than Raleigh-Durham, the airport serving Research Triangle Park, the state's leading technology complex.[31] State control of highway transportation policy has lost none of its importance for TDI, and more attention may be expected in the future to focus on "bottleneck" transportation issues involving airport access.

The beneficial effects of TDI being connected with air transportation should be revealed through statistically defined relationships as well. This analysis will rely upon two measures of transportation policy to detect their influence on TDI expansion in local economies. First, an ordinal measure of comparative access to the current system of interstate highways will be used to detect internodal connections with the regional airport. Second, active transportation programs to complete partially developed systems (i.e., construction work-in-progress disruptions) could in fact deter TDI and other industrial sectors that are heavily dependent on operating, functional transportation. The work of Braggs and of Lichter and Fugitt indicates the likelihood of stronger, permanent growth effects well after the completion of interstate system segments.[32] Changes in 1977 and 1984 levels of highway and public works construction employment will be used to construct a proxy for completed transportation systems.

Other restructuring factors

At a very general thematic level, a consensus about "restructuring" has rapidly taken shape. This view places emphasis on the volatility, scope, and logic of alterations to nearly every connection within our systems of industrial production as well as between it and many other spheres of human activity. Elements of restructuring are widely agreed to be bound up in our efforts (West and East, capitalist and socialist alike) to apply technology in the design, production, and use of material output and to the institutional and social arrangements that are most congenial to that application. Accordingly, regional economies which are experiencing comparatively high degrees of overall industrial restructuring are those in which one might also logically expect to find conditions favorable for TDI. Restructuring will be indicated by the total amount of absolute (or gross) change in employment level of all industries produced over a full business cycle per 1,000 workers. Regions with higher degrees of gross change per 1,000 workers (i.e., overall restructuring) should provide more favorable niches for TDI.

Enterprise factors (e.g., entrepreneurial vs. corporate enterprise initiatives) are perhaps the second most significant set of considerations. While large corporations and firms with multiple location facilities dominate TDI sectors, the restructuring of production technologies and new product options should present further entrepreneurial opportunities for footloose corporate personnel and others. As Harris discovered, entrepreneurial formations of TDI seem to depend in part on previous TDI concentrations in a region.[33] Osborne is further correct in arguing that

> the task of building local capacity and mobilizing local actors is critical ... No amount of new roads, sewers, plants, convention centers or even businesses financed by government [will become self-sustaining], unless local actors become entrepreneurial themselves. Hundreds of southern towns that have recruited large manufacturing plants can testify to this fact.[34]

Entrepreneurial formations are widely thought to be dependent on the availability of local venture capital, supporting services, and agglomeration economies. However, in regional economies dominated by branches of large corporations, the very requirements for entrepreneurial startups (capital, overhead services, scale) are internalized by the dominant corporate establishments rather than openly available in the regional economy. Accordingly, we are able to judge whether overall TDI effects in a local economy stem primarily from activities of large corporate units or small enterprise formations by using two proxies. First, if proprietors (the smallest class of establishment) are able to expand in local economies with TDI expansion, we can infer entrepreneurial effects. However, if TDI expands inversely to proprietor growth, then corporate expansion is the better inference. Second, if a broad class of business services thought essential for successful entrepreneurial formations expands with TDI, we have another level of inferential support for entrepreneurial-driven TDI. The converse, of course, implies an internally supplied group of corporate branches that drive TDI.

Study methods and evidence

This exploration of the policy factors responsible for expansion of TDI shares several characteristics with other inquiries. First, it remains an exploratory policy analysis. The uncertainty surrounding how to measure TDI, the competing models of how or indeed whether the fruits of university-based research become integrated in a host region's industrial complex, and the exceptional variety of initiatives within a single class of policy (e.g., the scale, character, and synchronization of university linkages to TDI) present major difficulties in specifying a structural model. We must be content with testing and selecting a limited but plausible specification that reveals the permissive or enabling qualities of policies rather than attempting at this stage a confirmation of their "causal" influence. Second, although there are sufficient university parks to study them as a sample, they are so small a percentage of all southern metropolitan counties that their variance cannot be expected to explain much of the TDI variance measured in all counties. That is, TDI is generally present in all metropolitan region counties and expands or declines for many reasons that can be quite unsystematic or unique. Together, these features make it unlikely that the limited set of exploratory variables employed here will account for high proportions of TDI variance. Finally, we remain modest about our analytic intentions and expectations: the evidence is only now beginning to trickle in about an explosively wide range of policy initiatives. It will surprise no one to learn that state technology and innovation policies often emerge at different times and for quite different reasons.[35] Accordingly, even preliminary findings that reveal reasonably coherent relations between policies and likely effects are of considerable value.

Regression models will be used to fit policy and other independent variables in equations that account for employment change between 1977 and 1984 for various definitions of TDI. The dates were selected to coincide with approximately equal positions on the most recent business cycle. Change in TDI employment is standardized by the base year employment of the local economy. This formulation avoids difficulties associated with a simple growth rate (i.e., widely varying or zero base year employment), and it measures directly TDI's restructuring effect on its host economy. The units of observation are metropolitan region counties. The data for all but the policy variables were calculated from standard secondary data sources. ZIP codes of university parks were supplied by Luger and Goldstein,[36] and interstate highway access was drawn from a previous study.[37]

Influence of transportation and university parks on TDI

The exploratory policy models used here reveal some systematic relationships for all three definitions of TDI:

(a)   A comparatively small amount of variance in TDI restructuring is explained (about 10 per cent).
(b)   County access to completed transportation systems is a highly significant, positive predictor of TDI restructuring.
(c)   High degrees of overall industrial restructuring in counties is a highly significant, positive predictor of TDI restructuring.

This common set of findings applies to all definitions of TDI: the BLS research and development expenditure definition, BLS composite definition, and Brookings Institution composite definition. The effect of transportation access on TDI restructuring is interpreted as the result of two independent variables. Sheer access to the interstate highway system (and internodal landside access to air transportation) is a powerful but not wholly decisive transportation influence. It also appears that reduced levels of public works construction between 1977 and 1984, signaling completion of basic highway and other infrastructure improvements, are important preconditions to TDI restructuring. The combined effects appear quite consistent with other studies that demonstrate the influence of transportation on development, particularly completed systems and those connected with airports. Thus, state transportation system policy retains its long-term importance for the amount and location of TDI as well as other industries, and it probably deserves serious reconsideration as an element of state technology policy.

What about university parks? The general findings summarized above mentioned no systematic relationship to TDI. That is, the presence of a university research park did not show significantly consistent effects on the three definitions of TDI. Perhaps one should not expect to account for much variance in TDI restructuring across the South's 748 metropolitan region counties when only 34 of them host university research parks and the bulk of unattributed spinoff effects on TDI could easily spread to other metropolitan or surrounding counties.[38] Or perhaps the fact that many of these parks were established in the early 1980s reduces the possibility of any detectable effects with 1977 and 1984 data. In short, it may still be too early for even an exploratory analysis of this type.

However, a closer look at the pattern of findings in Table 6.1 reveals some tantalizing evidence about the type of TDI drawn by these university research parks. The BLS R&D definition of TDI barely misses positive significance at the .10 level with university research parks but is inversely (and significantly) responsive to growth of employment in small business proprietorships. Together, these relationships suggest that university research parks in the South either host or induce nearby growth of TDI that does not depend upon—indeed is inversely related to—evidence of favorable small business conditions that would favor entrepreneurial efforts. TDI restructuring near these parks is therefore likely to affect large established firms or firms that are corporate in organization and to be conducted in manufacturing industries with high levels of R&D expenditure on early-stage research and development or product innovation. These inferences gain further support from the remaining findings in Table 6.1: neither of the "blended" definitions (i.e., the BLS or Brookings composite TDI definition), which include sectors with higher percentages of small firms, is significantly dependent upon the presence of university research parks. Nor was their growth found to be inversely related to the supportive conditions for entrepreneurial R&D activity.[39] We may infer, then, that university research parks are the sites where R&D-intensive industry tended to concentrate.

Taken as a whole, the findings underscore some cautions of those who argue that "the research park model is also questionable ... Without mechanisms to stimulate technology transfer and the formation of new companies, research parks may become little more than attractive settings for corporate research departments."[40] The availability in southern states of extensive public university systems and a history of active industry recruiting, whatever its level of technology, appear to have produced a new variety of corporate incentive: university research parks. These may prove only temporarily advantageous unless other basic improvements are also forthcoming. As one observer warns, "You cannot fake it with a snappy name, a couple of buildings, and a nearby university of middling or less renown."[41] Even with a world-famous university nearby to anchor technologically driven development, regional development is heavily dependent upon technology transfer, small business formation, and innovative entrepreneurship.[42]

Table 6.1 Three models of TDI restructuring.[1]

Mean value	TDI definitions						
	BLS R&D .0067		BLS composite .0211		Brookings composite .0217		
Metro region counties (N) RSQUARE (ADJ)	748 .1004	(.093)	748 .1004	(.093)	748 .0973	(.090)	
Area restructuring (77–84)[2]	0.039	(.0001)	0.044	(.0001)	0.044	(.0001)	Significant and consistent for all TDI definitions
Transportation access (1984)[3]	0.008	(.0178)	0.014	(.0084)	0.013	(.0188)	Significant only for BLS R&D defined TDI
Increased construction (77–84)[4]	−0.294	(.0001)	−0.390	(.0002)	−0.380	(.0003)	
University research park (1986)[5]	0.0125	(.1052)	0.010	(.4308)	0.012	(.3170)	
Increased proprietors (77–84)[6]	−0.0452	(.0379)	−0.015	(.6610)	−0.014	(.6892)	
Increased producer services (77–84)[7]	−0.0385	(.0108)	0.032	(.1810)	−0.298	(.2154)	
INTERCEPT	−0.0181	(.0001)	−0.019	(.0014)	−0.018	(.0024)	

Notes:

[1] $(\text{TDI}_{84} - \text{TDI}_7)$/total employment$_{77}$

[2] $\sum_{i=1}^{i3} |I^i_{84} - I^i_{77}|$/total employment$_{77}$

[3] Transportation access:
No access to interstate system = 0
Near 1 route, interstate system = 1
Near 2+ routes, interstate system = 2
On 1 route, interstate system = 3
On 1 & near 1 route, interstate system = 4
On 2+ routes, interstate system = 5

[4] $(\text{SIC } 1600_{84} - \text{SIC } 1600_7)$/Total employment$_{77}$

[5] One or more university research parks = 1
No university research parks = 0

[6] $(\text{Props}_{84} - \text{Props}_7)$/Total employment$_{77}$

[7] $(\text{Producer SVS}_{84} - \text{Producer SVS}_7)$/Total employment$_{77}$

Conclusions

This chapter's exploratory analysis of two traditional state policies indicates their generally beneficial effects on TDI restructuring, but it also exposes their somewhat limited and conditional influence. State transportation policies have the potential to become even more important agents of TDI promotion, particularly those that fine-tune the internodal connections between airport landside and interstate highway system access in particular regions. Fine-tuning of regional capacity is also of importance for university-based research and innovation policy. Certainly, better efforts are needed to support entrepreneurial spinoffs, encourage more producer services for small business development, and generally encourage skilled engineers and scientists to apply their innovative talents in local organizations other than universities and corporations.[43] And other university-based initiatives such as the matching grant, research institute, or academic department models[44] to stimulate technological innovation may yield better fits with regional capacity than a generic university research park. But even if university research parks remain the state strategy of choice, their design and functioning could better reflect the uniquely regional position of local TDI along the technology transfer continuum and along local universities' basic-to-applied research continuum.[45]

This may be precisely the time for state policy makers to reassess their state's technology objectives and the rôle that universities are expected to play. As Schmitt puts it:

> The question to ask people from aspiring high-tech areas is not "why don't you lead the world in the most glamorous industries," but rather "why aren't you developing the strengths that you have?" That means making use of a university. But do not expect to turn it into an MIT or Stanford overnight, even with federal funds. Instead, develop the particular strength it already has—a technology related to a local industry or university, or a department built around an outstanding educator or researcher.[46]

Some preliminary answers are available from this study's principal findings. First, few if any southern university parks are set in local economies where entrepreneurship is likely to introduce basic innovations. In the absence of a thriving entrepreneurial community, commercial spinoffs by academic (or corporate) scientists and engineers are highly unlikely. Therefore, state policies that provide incentives for basic and applied research and that expect the nearby research park to serve automatically as a hospitable incubator are likely to be frustrated. It is extremely difficult to establish suddenly and by policy fiat an entrepreneurial culture in local economies that have been dominated by large universities and corporate installations; these large units seldom rely upon or stimulate the development of producer services for small enterprises. Moreover, it is often the very *absence* of entrepreneurial opportunity near research parks and the intercorporate raiding of skilled scientists and engineers in original centers that are initially responsible for corporations' decision to locate certain of their facilities in southern R&D parks. Protecting a corporation's scarce human resources is best served by selecting desirable living environments with weak employment alternatives.

At some point, however, the successful expansion of university research parks consisting solely of autonomous corporate facilities might generate enough new establishment growth to stimulate both producer services and a viable entrepreneurial culture. Exceptionally rapid development of such a culture recently in the Research Triangle region of North Carolina may in fact be partially responsible for the unexpected halt in new corporate locations in Research Triangle Park.[47] But until an entrepreneurial setting is firmly established, southern university research parks may need to build on other strengths. Precisely how innovations might be disseminated regionally from university R&D activities conducted under corporate auspices is a policy task of some significance.

Our second principal finding suggests a different strength. Because university research parks are more closely associated with TDI, which invests heavily in basic research and development, policy makers should try to build on this particular strength. Given the South's heritage of labor-intensive, late-product-cycle industries, the importance of university research parks in contributing to upgrading the region's traditional industrial base is unquestioned. A recent in-depth study of successful factory modernization in the rural South identifies two particularly relevant tasks: dissemination of new process technology information to smaller, independent firms; and investment in research and development directed toward heavily concentrated, traditional industries.[48] This need is dramatized by Atkinson's finding that southern technology policy already focuses more on advanced manufacturing than that of other regions and that relatively less policy emphasis is placed on technology diffusion as compared with university research centers.[49] As is the case in technologically sensitive transportation policy, there would appear to be ample room for maneuver in fine-tuning policies for southern university research parks.

Finally, the fine-tuning of state technology policies appears to depend heavily upon the regional setting to which policy applies most directly. Osborne is certainly correct to argue that "state governments are most successful when they take time to thoroughly analyze the regional economy before acting."[50] The wisdom that supports state policies as experiments in our federal laboratories of democracy applies equally well to regions. Just as effective federal policy is difficult to design at great distance from the everyday world it hopes to affect, that distance can be further reduced and policies made even more effective by linking state and regional technology policies. It is probably closer to the truth for one to consider all components of our broad federalist system as a fully equipped laboratory of democratic policy making. If so, then states are in the position to define their rôle as permanent intermediaries by effective brokerage with their national and regional policy partners.

Notes

1 Variants of this distinction have been incorporated into studies of economic and industrial restructuring at the international, national, and regional levels. *Economic survey of Europe in 1981* (New York: United Nations, 1982); R. Z. Lawrence, *Can America compete?* (Washington, D.C.: Brookings Institution, 1984); R. W. Gilmer & A. G. Pulsipher, "Cyclical and structural change in southern manufacturing: recent evidence from the Tennessee Valley," *Growth and Change* **17**, No 4, October 1986, 61–70.
2 U.S. Congress, Office of Technology Assessment, *Technology, innovation, and regional economic development* (Washington, D.C.: U.S. Government Printing Office, 1984), Ch. 2.
3 C. S. Harris, "Establishing high-technology enterprises in metropolitan areas," in *Local economies in transition*, ed. E. M. Bergman (Durham, N.C.: Duke University Press, 1986).
4 M. Howland, "Cyclical startups and closures in key industries of America's cities and suburbs," in *Local economies in transition*, Bergman, p. 119.
5 See E. J. Malecki, "Technological innovation and paths to regional economic growth," in this volume.
6 U.S. Congress, Office of Technology Assessment, *Technology, innovation, and regional economic development*, p. 121.
7 Howland, "Cyclical startups and closures," pp. 117–21.
8 R. Atkinson, "State technology development programs: a review," *Economic Development Review*, Spring 1988, 29–33.
9 D. Osborne, *Economic competitiveness: the states take the lead* (Washington, D.C.: Economic Policy Institute, 1987), p. 69.
10 P. H. Wer, "Economic development" in *The practice of state and regional planning*, ed. F. S. So, I. Hand & B. McDowell (Washington, D.C.: The International City Managers Association, 1986).
11 In reviewing factors behind successful technology development policies, Osborne argues that even the state level is not sufficiently decentralized to be effective.

He contends that "government should create comprehensive but decentralized development institutions. Economic development is a local process. Yet most state bureaucracies are not well equipped to respond to the varied needs of thousands of businesses. The best solution is a network of decentralized intermediary organizations. These organizations use state resources and carry out state objectives, but they have the flexibility to respond to a wide variety of specific, local problems" (Osborne, *Economic competitiveness*).

12 W. R. Thompson, "Policy-based analysis for local economic development," *Economic Development Quarterly* **1**, August 1987, 206.

13 W. H. Plosila, "State technical development programs," *Forum for Applied Research and Public Policy* **2**, Summer 1987, 35.

14 A. Bloom, *The closing of the American mind* (New York: Basic Books, 1986).

15 Osborne, *Economic competitiveness*.

16 R. L. Levitt (ed.), *Research parks and other ventures: the university/real estate connection* (Washington, D.C.: Urban Land Institute, 1985).

17 D. N. Steinnes, "On understanding and evaluating the university's evolving economic development policy," *Economic Development Quarterly* **1**, August 1987, 214–25.

18 S. P. Dresch & K. Pele, "Knowledge centers, technological development, innovation and regional economic growth," Working Paper 86-103 (Houghton, MI: MTU School of Business and Engineering Adminstration, 1986).

19 A. J. Scott and M. Storper, "High technology industry and regional development: a theoretical critique and reconstruction," *International Social Science Journal* **39**, 1987, 214–32; Malecki, this volume.

20 R. Premus, *Location of high technology firms and regional economic development*, Serial 94–670 (Washington, D.C.: U.S. Government Printing Office, 1982).

21 M. I. Luger & H. A. Goldstein, "Business parks and economic development" (proposal submitted to Ford Foundation, Chapel Hill: Department of City and Regional Planning, University of North Carolina, 1986).

22 Omitted from consideration are many existing state policies whose occasionally beleaguered advocates or agencies recognize the potent justification for program maintenance that TDI offers. To the degree that such programs assume the mantle of technology's fashionable status, states serve also as "policy couturiers" by refitting old policies in the latest style.

23 See R. Wilson, "Structural economic change and the powers of state government: the viability of regional development strategies," in this volume.

24 N. J. Glickman & D. P. Woodward, *Regional patterns of manufacturing: foreign direct investment in the United States* (Austin: LBJ School of Public Affairs, University of Texas, 1987).

25 L. F. Wheat, *The effect of airline service on manufacturing growth in cities below 40,000 population* (Washington, D.C.: Economic Development Administration, 1970); L. F. Wheat, *Urban growth in the nonmetropolitan South* (Lexington, Mass.: Lexington Books, 1976).

26 E. M. Bright, "Secondary impacts of airports: an assessment of planning procedures," *Transportation Quarterly* **36**, January 1982, 75–98; F. P. Kukla, "The impact of Genesee County Airport on Genesee County," in *Transportation research record 1025* (Washington, D.C.: National Research Council, 1984), pp. 1–6; J. A. Helmuth, *The economic impact of the Rochester Monroe County Airport on the local economy* (Albany: New York State Department of Transportation, 1981); D. McLeod, R. D. Sandler, E. T. Denham & J. Blair, "Economic impact of general aviation in Florida: suggested method of analysis," in *Transportation research record 958* (Washington, D.C.: National Research Council, 1984), pp. 20–3.

27 S. Rosenfeld, E. Bergman & S. Rubin, *After the factories* (Research Triangle Park, N.C.: Southern Growth Policies Board, 1985), p. 46.

28 National Council for Urban Economic Development, *Transportation and urban economic development* (Washington, D.C.: U.S. Department of Transportation, 1982), p. 64.
29 Y. Chan, "Aviation legislation and infrastructure: policy implementations," in *Transportation research record 958* (Washington, D.C.: National Research Council/Academy of Sciences, 1984).
30 M. Clark (ed.), *Airport landside capacity*, Special Report 159 (Washington, D.C.: National Research Council/Academy of Sciences, 1975).
31 N. Herndon, "RDU roads on short end of funds for major airports," *Raleigh News and Observer*, October 23, 1987, 1, 8.
32 A. Braggs, "Interstate highway system and development in nonmetropolitan areas," in *Transportation research record 812* (Washington, D.C.: National Academy of Sciences, 1982); D. T. Lichter and G. V. Fugitt, "Demographic response to transportation innovation: the case of the interstate highway," *Social Forces* **59**, December 1980, 492–512.
33 Harris, "Establishing high-technology enterprises."
34 Osborne, *Economic competitiveness*, p. 68.
35 Atkinson, "State technology development programs."
36 Luger & Goldstein, "Business parks and economic development."
37 Rosenfeld, et al., *After the factories*.
38 See note 18 above.
39 Rosenfeld extracted *Monthly Labor Review* data, which indicate that southern states are far more likely to host TDI based on production technology occupations than R&D expenditures. Thus, this form of advanced technology industry is evidently not located in southern counties with university research parks. S. Rosenfeld, "Southern strategies for economic development," *Forum for Applied Research and Public Policy* **2**, Summer 1987, 52.
40 Osborne, *Economic competitiveness*, p. 60.
41 R. W. Schmitt, "Excellence and inequality in research and development," *Forum for Applied Research and Public Policy* **2**, Summer 1987, 62.
42 Saxenian, in examining the limited success of Cambridge University and British technology policy, observes, "tenants of the Cambridge Science Park complain repeatedly that there is not interaction – social or technical – among firms there. This absence is critical. With little to integrate economic activity, the result is a disarticulated collection of small enterprises and services. While successes may emerge, the regional environment does not support innovation and high-tech growth." A. Saxenian, "The Cheshire cat's grin: innovation and regional development in England," *Technology Review* **91**, February–March 1988, 74.
43 Malecki, "Technological innovation and paths to regional economic growth."
44 Osborne, *Economic competitiveness*, p. 60.
45 See I. Feller, "University–industry R&D relationships," in this volume.
46 Schmitt, "Excellence and inequality," p. 63.
47 Concern about expanded entrepreneurial competition for high-skill employees was clearly expressed by a Research Triangle official who cited tenant objections in dismissing the prospect of converting unsold sites to small firm consortia or infant industry incubators. Comments by R. F. Leake, former executive director of Research Triangle Foundation, at Institute for Research in Social Science, University of North Carolina, November 1987.
48 S. Rosenfeld, E. Malizia & M. Dugan, *Reviving the rural factory* (Research Triangle Park, N.C.: Southern Technologies Council, Southern Growth Policies Board, 1988).
49 Atkinson, "State technology development programs."
50 Osborne, *Economic competitiveness*, p. 68.

III

State development strategies

7

Recent state initiatives: an overview of state science and technology policies and programs

MARIANNE K. CLARKE

IN 1985, THE National Governors' Association conducted a study of the 50 state economic development programs.[1] One of the major findings of that study was that states were placing increasing emphasis on the development of technology and technology-based businesses as a critical element of state development policy. Subsequent research by the National Governors' Association and others[2] reveals that states are continuing to pursue policies aimed at strengthening the technological base of their economies.

Although state activities to promote the development and application of science and technology and the formation of technology-based businesses have been widely documented, questions remain regarding the level of state commitment to these efforts. For example, how significant are state investments in research and development? Are states likely to maintain and/or increase their involvement in science and technology policy? How widespread are state technology development programs? Is it really only a handful of states that are

pursuing comprehensive strategies? What are the objectives of state
science and technology policy? How successful have the states been
in achieving their objectives?

This chapter argues that state science and technology efforts are
becoming more widespread and that states are indeed making long-
term, and in some cases substantial, commitments to the promotion
of science and technology. Although initial efforts are underway to
assess the effectiveness of these initiatives, however, few evaluative
data are currently available.

The first section provides information on the level of state commitment to science and technology programs based upon information
on the structure, staffing, and budget of state technology agencies. It
includes information from a recently completed survey on the structure
and function of state science and technology offices conducted by the
National Governors' Association in conjunction with the Society of
Research Administrators.[3] The second section discusses the objectives
of state technology policies and the rôle of these policies in technology
development. This is followed by a general description of state science
and technology initiatives. The chapter concludes with a discussion
of assessment strategies and future directions of state science and
technology policies and programs.

State science and technology policies

State support for the development of science and technology has
waxed and waned over the years. In the 1960s, the U.S. Department of
Commerce provided grants to improve the states' capacity to promote
technology transfer. The program, known as the State Technical
Services (STS) program, operated between 1965 and 1969. Many
states at this time created science and technology commissions and
foundations and appointed science advisors. Several states used
program funds to establish industrial extension services. Of the
programs established by the states under STS, the majority were
discontinued once federal funds were no longer available. The
notable exceptions are New York State's Science and Technology
Foundation and the Pennsylvania Technical Assistance Program
(PENNTAP), which are still in operation. In 1977 Congress authorized
the National Science Foundation (NSF) to spend up to $2.5 million
to support states that would "study" the possible use of science and
technology to meet their "needs." Subsequently, NSF created the
State Science, Engineering, and Technology (SSET) program, which

provided funding to both governors and state legislatures. Under the first phase of the program, grants of up to $25,000 were made available to each state executive and legislative branch for the development of a state plan. While the program was initiated with the expectation that federal funds would be available to implement the recommendations in the plans, the follow-up funding never materialized.[4]

During the late 1970s, a number of states began pursuing policies designed to attract high-tech companies to locate in their state. The economic health of areas with strong bases of high-tech firms, such as Silicon Valley in California, Route 128 in Massachusetts, and Research Triangle Park in North Carolina, led other states to seek to create the conditions which had supported the development and growth of technology-based businesses in these regions.

The recent growth of state science and technology programs, however, began in earnest in the early 1980s when states started broadening their economic development efforts to include the development of technology and technology-based businesses. Largely in response to the economic recession of 1981–82, states both increased their involvement in economic development and broadened their programs to include assisting existing businesses and promoting the growth of new businesses in addition to attracting businesses from out of state.[5] Often efforts to promote the creation and growth of new firms focused on technology-based businesses.

This new state activism in the area of economic development occurred even while the federal government was decreasing its support for such activities. So, while earlier state programs were developed in response to federal initiatives, state policies to support the development and application of new technology originated at the state level.

An indicator of the extent to which states have adopted and are implementing science and technology policies is the recent increase in the number of state agencies established to administer science and technology policies and programs. A survey conducted by the National Governors' Association found that 31 states currently maintain science and technology offices. In many, if not most, of the remaining states, there are specific programs aimed at supporting the development of science and technology resources, but these efforts are administered by a variety of offices, including economic development agencies, departments of higher education, and state universities. Of the states with science and technology offices, only three were established prior to 1982 (see Table 7.1).

For the most part, the science and technology offices have small staffs ranging from 1 to 19 professional employees. There are also

Table 7.1 Science and technology offices.

State	Name of office	Year established
AR	Arkansas Science and Technology Authority	1983
FL	Florida High Technology and Industry Council	1984
HI	Science and Technology Program, Department of Business and Economic Development	1965
ID	Division of Science and Technology	1987
IL	Governor's Commission on Science and Technology	1983
IN	Corporation for Science and Technology	1982
IA	Research and Development Office, Department of Economic Development	
KS	Kansas Technology Enterprise Corporation	1987*
KY	Office of Business and Technology	1985
ME	Maine Science and Technology Board	1985
MA	Centers of Excellence Corporation	1985
MI	Michigan Strategic Fund	
MN	Governor's Office of Science and Technology	1983
MO	Corporation for Science and Technology	1983
MT	Montana Science and Technology Alliance, Montana Department of Commerce	1985
NE	Nebraska Research and Development Authority	1987
NJ	New Jersey Commission on Science and Technology	1985
NM	New Mexico Science and Technology Commission	1983
NY	New York State Science and Technology Foundation	1963
NC	North Carolina Board of Science and Technology	1963
OH	Division of Technological Innovation, Ohio Department of Development	
OK	Oklahoma Center for the Advancement of Science and Technology	1987
PA	Office of Technology Development, Pennsylvania Department of Commerce	1983
RI	Rhode Island Partnership for Science and Technology	1985
SC	South Carolina Research Authority	1983
SD	Office of Enterprise Initiation, Governor's Office of Economic Development	1987
TN	High Technology Development, Department of Economic and Community Development	1982
TX	Technology Business Development Division, Texas Engineering Experiment Station, Texas A&M University	1986
UT	Utah Technology Finance Corporation	
VA	Center for Innovative Technology	
WY	Wyoming Science, Technology and Energy Authority	1987

*Replaced Kansas Advanced Technology Commission, established in 1983.

wide differences in operating budgets. Of the 21 offices that reported operating budgets, 13 had budgets of less than $500,000, one had a budget between $500,000 and $1 million, four had budgets between $1 million and $2 million, and three had budgets in excess of $10 million.

Goals and objectives of state science and technology policies

An examination of the legislation establishing these offices shows that the primary goal of state science and technology efforts is economic development, i.e., they are expected to contribute to the development of a healthy, diversified economy, an economy that will provide high-wage jobs for state residents.

There are three primary ways in which state science and technology policies are expected to result in economic gains for the state. The first is by creating a research base that will attract both talent and industry to the state. Centers of excellence and advanced technology centers, for example, are designed to become world-class centers performing research in a specific technological area. State investment in such centers is predicated on the belief that the presence of such a center will attract leading researchers and subsequently private businesses seeking access to both research findings and research facilities and equipment. In addition, such centers are usually university-affiliated and private firms are expected to be drawn to them as they seek access to students and faculty.

In this case, investment in research and development is being used in a traditional economic development strategy, i.e., to attract outside firms to locate in the state, although the incentives being offered differ. Whereas low wage rates and tax abatements may have been attractive to a company locating a manufacturing facility, a technology-based business is more likely to be drawn to an area with a high quality education system and a highly skilled workforce. State investments have, therefore, changed to reflect these differences.

In addition to establishing world-class research centers, states are pursuing this objective by attracting federal research facilities. This strategy is evidenced in the competition for the National Science Foundation's Engineering Research Centers, as well as centers established under the Department of Defense's University Research Initiative, among others. The competition for such federal investment is perhaps most clearly seen in the current contest for the Superconducting Supercollider. Here, individual states have pledged millions of dollars in an effort to have this facility located in their state, with the expectation that such a facility will attract sufficient private investment to more than offset any initial commitment of state resources.

While the attraction of people and businesses to a state is one goal of state science and technology policy, another goal is to encourage the establishment and growth of new technology-based businesses. During the 1980s, based on the research of Birch and others regarding the rôle of new and small businesses in job creation,[6] state development policy began to emphasize the development of "homegrown" or indigenous businesses. Such efforts have focused heavily on technology-based businesses.

State efforts to encourage the growth of new firms focus on creating a more entrepreneurial climate. To achieve such a climate, states have encouraged closer ties between universities and industry, sought to change university policies with regard to patent and intellectual property rights, and provided both financial and nonfinancial assistance to the technological innovator or entrepreneur. It is expected that such efforts will result in a larger number of successful business startups than might otherwise have occurred without the state-supported assistance.

The third goal of state science and technology policy is to support the state's existing economic base. Recognizing that every state cannot expect to become home to an entirely new industry, a number of states have focused their science and technology investments on specific technological areas with applications in traditional industries, particularly in the manufacturing sector. In addition to supporting research in these targeted technologies, states have undertaken initiatives to provide information to local firms on new technological applications and to encourage and support the adoption of new processes and the introduction of new products by individual firms.

The choice of which goal to emphasize depends on the strengths, weaknesses, and composition of the state economy. Those states heavily dependent on traditional manufacturing sectors such as Michigan, for example, have adopted strategies aimed at introducing advanced technology into the states' existing businesses. Other states meanwhile have emphasized promoting the creation of new firms or the attraction of technology-based enterprises. A review of current state strategies shows that as state efforts have expanded, they have become more comprehensive, adopting programs to address each of these goals.

While the primary goal of state science and technology policy is economic development, it is also clear that state science and technology policies address a variety of subsidiary goals: improving the quality of science and engineering education, improving the quality and skills of the local laborforce, and building closer ties among government, education, and industry.

While it is clear that states have initiated a variety of policies and programs designed to influence the level, direction, and/or speed of technological innovation, the question remains as to how much influence state policy can exert over the factors that influence the process of technological innovation.

State policies in support of technology development are based on the belief that there are three primary areas that affect the ability of a particular geographic area to support the development and application of new technology. The first is the underlying infrastructure of support for science and technology, i.e., the educational and research resources needed to support scientists and researchers and to train future scientists and engineers. The second factor is the level and quality of investment in research and development. The third factor, which will affect a region's ability to capitalize on research discoveries, is the availability of services and resources needed by entrepreneurs and innovators to commercialize research findings. This includes both access to the resources needed to establish new companies and to introduce new products and processes into existing businesses. The state rôle in promoting the development and application of new technology varies depending on which of these three areas is being addressed.

With regard to the need for a science and technology infrastructure, states play a critical and direct rôle. In addition to supporting those institutions of higher education where most university research and development takes place, state governments directly influence the quality of elementary and secondary education and employment and training that is essential for the development of human resources in scientific and technological disciplines. Thus states have a rôle to play in creating and maintaining a high-quality educational system.

The state rôle in supporting research and development is less direct. U.S. investment in research and development has been credited with making the United States the world leader in advancing knowledge in areas of science and technology. U.S. spending on research and development in 1987 is estimated to be \$125.2 billion. Roughly half of these funds are provided by the private sector, with the federal government providing the majority of the remaining half. States and other sources provide approximately 3 percent of the total. Given that, even with significant investment on the part of the states, state investment in research and development will continue to account for only a very small percentage of total expenditures, how can states expect to influence the level or direction of investment in research and development?

An analysis of state R&D programs shows that states are using their investments in research and development in an effort to change the way performers of research, primarily universities, and users of research, private firms, relate to one another.

A recent study that solicited the opinions of business leaders, university officials, and senior state government officials on the rôle of science and technology in economic competitiveness[7] identified three ways in which the nature of research is changing. First, research is becoming more complex and more capital-, instrument-, and computer-intensive. Second, research is becoming increasingly interdisciplinary in nature. Third, the line between basic and applied research is blurring, thus creating a need for greater interaction between basic research and technology development. One response to these changes has been the creation of new institutional relationships between businesses and universities. State governments have played an important rôle in facilitating these new industry/university partnerships.

The final area that affects the ability of a region to support the development of new technology is the presence of resources needed to support commercialization. The rôle of the state in promoting commercialization usually involves providing both financial and nonfinancial support services to the technological innovator or entrepreneur. State approaches differ, however, with some states emphasizing a broker rôle (i.e., putting entrepreneurs in touch with various sources of technical expertise and resources), and others providing direct services. Here once again, however, states are seeking to change the behavior of individuals and businesses, encouraging them to market new products and to adopt new technological processes.

State initiatives

State activities to promote science and technology cover a wide range of initiatives from investing in research and development to providing seed capital for new, technology-based firms and business and management assistance for technological entrepreneurs.

Over the past several years a number of studies have sought to categorize state technology policies and programs. Categorization is difficult due to the variation in programs from state to state. The categories used here build upon the work of Watkins and of Clarke.[8] State activities have been divided into three major categories: investment in education; support for research and development; and commercialization assistance.

Investment in education

The presence of a strong research and education system is a prerequisite of the development of a technology-based economy. As a result, state technology policies usually include initiatives to improve the quality of the state's educational system. Particular emphasis has been placed on improving mathematics, science, and engineering education at the university level. These efforts have focused primarily on improving facilities and equipment and upgrading the quality of faculty and students. In addition, states have established training programs for technicians and initiated policies to improve mathematics and science education at the K–12 level.

INVESTMENT IN FACILITIES AND EQUIPMENT

For many states, investment in the state's university system is the first step in seeking to develop a strong technology sector. Such investments are usually targeted for facilities and equipment, reflecting the widespread agreement on the need to modernize deteriorating and obsolete research facilities at universities and colleges.

Two major recent reports, the White House Policy Council (Bromley-Packard) report on the health of U.S. universities and a report published by the Government/University/Industry Research Roundtable of the National Research Council, documented this need, with the latter estimating that unmet demand for new facilities construction and renovation of research facilities will range from $4 billion to $20 billion in the next 10 to 20 years.

Similarly, the National Governors' Association survey on the relationship between science and technology and economic competitiveness revealed that over two-thirds of the business, university, and government respondents believe that access to state-of-the-art research and development equipment and facilities was having a critical impact on the competitiveness of the U.S. economy. The academic dean at one western college reported, "We haven't, with the exception of computers, replaced a single major piece of equipment since the college was completed ten years ago." Other university officials agreed on the need for investment in facilities and equipment.

To respond to this need, states have increased their investments in new capital facilities at state colleges and universities and have established matching grant programs to fund the acquisition of new equipment. For example, in November 1984 New Jersey voters passed a $90 million Jobs, Science, and Technology Bond issue. Approximately half of these funds were used to upgrade technical and engineering facilities at the state's universities and community colleges.

In 1985 Oregon passed a lottery bill requiring that the proceeds be dedicated to economic development. Of the total amount projected to be raised, 50 percent was earmarked for higher education. Out of $44 million, $23 million was designated for capital construction projects at Oregon's major universities.

Other states have established matching grant programs to encourage businesses to contribute state-of-the-art equipment to colleges and universities. Pennsylvania's Ben Franklin Partnership, for example, operates an engineering equipment matching grant program. This $3 million program awards grants to universities on a matching basis to purchase or upgrade engineering equipment.

A common component of many state development efforts has been the development of university-based research centers, often referred to as centers of excellence or advanced technology centers. In some instances, the state contribution to such centers has been used primarily to fund physical facilities to house a research effort. Michigan, for example, provided $12 million to construct a $17.3 million facility for its Industrial Technology Institute (ITI). ITI is an independent, nonprofit research center established by the state to develop advanced automated manufacturing technologies and to foster their implementation in the private sector. An additional $5.3 million was raised from private sources.

UPGRADING FACULTY AND STUDENTS

In addition to seeking to improve the condition of facilities and equipment, states have also undertaken programs designed to upgrade both the quality of the faculty and students in scientific areas by providing fellowships and establishing endowed chairs. Louisiana, for example, has created an Educational Quality Trust Fund with the proceeds from the resolution of a state–federal oil revenue dispute. A portion of this fund has been earmarked for the enhancement of higher education and the promotion of economic development within the state. The Louisiana Board of Regents administers the program, which funds endowed chairs, a graduate fellows program, a competitive equipment grants program, and a research and development grant program.

The newly established Oklahoma Center for the Advancement of Science and Technology is in the process of establishing a Most Eminent Scholars program, which will provide funding to institutions of higher education, nonprofit research foundations, and private enterprises to help these organizations raise funds in research areas where they have achieved recognition. The program will also provide funding on a matching basis for endowed chairs and research equipment.

It is difficult, if not impossible, to measure the impact of these expenditures on the quality of a state's university system. In addition, some would argue that while such expenditures may be worthwhile from an educational perspective, they are not likely to result in lasting economic development benefits. To date, however, little evidence is available to measure the effect of educational investments on a state's economy.

TRAINING TECHNICIANS AND OTHER TECHNICAL WORKERS

In addition to investing in higher education, states have also been active in providing additional training and retraining for technicians. In South Carolina the state directed six technical colleges to develop education expertise in specific scientific areas. The targeted technologies and the location of the programs were based on both the strengths of the school and the state's economic development plan. At Piedmont Technical College a two-year associate degree program in automated technology has been established. The program is expected to become a prototype for associate degree programs in robotics. The Robotics Resource Center at the college also conducts plant-specific, on-the-job industry training and retraining.[9]

IMPROVING SCIENCE AND MATHEMATICS EDUCATION

In addition to these technical education programs, efforts to improve science and mathematics education at the K–12 level figure prominently in state educational reform initiatives. States have raised standards, expanded the number of mathematics and science courses required of students, increased the amount of time devoted to mathematics and science, established more rigorous graduation requirements, and inserted computer literacy into the curriculum. In addition, some states have established special science and mathematics high schools, scholarships for students to pursue mathematics and science undergraduate degrees, and recruitment programs for science and mathematics teachers.

In Pennsylvania, for example, a Governor's School for the Sciences has been established at Carnegie-Mellon University. The goals of the School are to identify and encourage students who show exceptional promise as potential scientists and engineers to continue their efforts in a technical discipline; to develop a new, advanced-level curriculum that will aid these students in expanding their capabilities and interests; and to foster and reward excellence and creativity among secondary school students by identifying and including them in a unique experience. The School also seeks to encourage women and minority students to consider scientific careers and assists local school districts in upgrading their science programs and in increasing the quality and diversity of their offerings.

Supporting research and development

State support for research and development is a fairly recent phenomenon. While state governments have long provided core funding for state colleges and universities, states are now providing direct support earmarked for specific research and development at both public and private institutions.

The predominant mechanisms used to support research and development are matching grant programs and the creation of university-based technology research centers, sometimes referred to as centers of excellence and/or advanced technology centers.

RESEARCH AND DEVELOPMENT GRANT PROGRAMS

As of 1986, 29 states reported providing research grants.[10] The vast majority of these programs provide funding for applied research and development, although a few states also fund basic research. While there is no clear line distinguishing basic from applied research, most state programs are aimed at funding projects with near-term prospects for commercialization. Many of the grant programs also target key technological areas of importance to the state's economy. Often the research is conducted jointly by a university and a business sponsor with the business providing matching funds.

Another characteristic of research grant programs is that the awards are usually made on a competitive basis by some type of public/private board whose members include representatives of universities, private businesses, and the state. Applications are normally evaluated on their economic potential, technical merit, and private-sector support. The program may operate under the auspices of a private, nonprofit corporation, an independent public agency, or the state development agency.

The Arkansas Science and Technology Authority, for example, provides funding for both basic and applied research conducted at Arkansas colleges and universities. In the applied research program, industry or business cosponsors provide at least 50 percent of each project's costs, with the Authority providing the remainder. Cosponsors are eligible for state income tax credits for their contributions.

The Missouri Research Assistance Act (MRAA), enacted in 1982, provides funding for cooperative research projects undertaken by Missouri universities and businesses. The Act created two funds: the Higher Education Research Fund and the Higher Education Applied Projects Fund. The former funds basic research conducted at the University of Missouri, St. Louis University, and Washington University. The latter funds applied research at all public and private higher education institutions in Missouri, with the exception of the University of Missouri.

The MRAA was amended in 1986 to make participation more attractive to small businesses. The new legislation provides a 2:1 match of state to private-sector funding when the participating firm is a small business. Normally, the match is one state dollar for every two private dollars.

While many state research grant programs provide funds primarily for university-based research, the Pennsylvania Small Business Research Seed Grant Program provides direct grants of up to $35,000 to small firms undertaking research in selected areas. Firms with fewer than 250 employees are eligible to participate in the program, although preference is given to firms with fewer than 50 employees. Funding for this program increased from $660,000 in 1985–6 to $1 million in 1986–7.

TECHNOLOGY RESEARCH CENTERS

Technology research centers, which are usually university-based, are vehicles for conducting research in a specific technological area. Usually the state identifies those areas in which the university system has expertise and/or which are particularly pertinent to the state's major industries. A research center is established to focus on these technologies, and the state serves as a catalyst to bring together the resources of the private sector and university.

Technology research centers can be designed to achieve national leadership in a specific area of technology — thereby attracting researchers and industry to the state — to help solve the technological problems of existing industries or to try to encourage the creation of new firms in an emerging area of technology. Technology research centers have played a critical rôle in the technology development strategies of the states of Pennsylvania, Ohio, New York, and New Jersey, among others. For the most part, these programs have been funded at higher levels than research grant programs.

Pennsylvania's Ben Franklin Partnership program was established in 1983 to create and retain jobs, to improve productivity, and to diversify Pennsylvania's economy. Its largest program is the Challenge Grant Program, which established four advanced technology centers. Each center is a consortium of the private sector, labor, research universities, other higher education institutions, and economic development groups. The centers, which are organized as nonprofit organizations attached to a university, conduct joint R&D projects, sponsor education and training activities, and provide entrepreneurial assistance services.

The program is overseen by the Ben Franklin Partnership Board, which includes representatives from the private sector, small business, education, labor, and the state legislature. Between 1983, when the program was established, and 1986, $76.6 million in state funds have been matched by moore than $281 million in private funding.[11]

New Jersey has established seven advanced technology centers in the following areas: biotechnology and medicine, hazardous and toxic substance management, industrial ceramics, computer aids for industrial productivity, advanced food technology, advanced scientific computing, and plastics recycling. Plans are underway to establish an eighth center for biomolecular research in the agricultural and natural sciences. The funding for the centers is managed by the New Jersey Commission on Science and Technology, which contributes $2 million to $3 million a year per center for operating expenses. More than 100 member corporations pay annual fees ranging from $15,000 to $50,000. The centers operate in conjunction with one or more universities and involve substantial support from industry.

New York's Centers for Advanced Technology (CATs) are cooperative centers for research and development formed by a partnership among universities, private industry, and government. As in New

Jersey, each center focuses on a specific area of science and technology. The CATs receive partial funding from the New York State Science and Technology Foundation. These funds, which are matched by the private sector, are used for research and development, educational programs, dissemination of information, equipment and support for faculty, research staff, and graduate students working in areas of advanced technology with potential industrial application.

Thus far, state investments in research and development and state efforts to encourage industry/university partnerships have been met with enthusiasm on the part of both universities and businesses. States proudly point to the level of private matching funds contributed to these efforts as a measure of success. Without further study, however, it is difficult to measure the impact of these investments.

Two questions which have been raised regarding collaborative research, for example, are whether U.S. firms are truly committed to collaborative research and whether these joint ventures are producing commercial outcomes. For states, an additional question is whether a state can capture the benefits of its investment in research and development. State concern that these investments reap economic development benefits have led them to undertake additional activities designed to encourage the commercialization of results of research and development.

Commercialization assistance

State governments have developed a range of programs designed to speed the application of new technology to the marketplace. These include both financial and nonfinancial assistance for entrepreneurs and small business owners and efforts to provide these same entrepreneurs and business owners with access to research resources, particularly at universities. In addition, a number of states have undertaken efforts aimed at introducing new technological products and processes into the state's existing industries.

FACILITATING INFORMATION EXCHANGE

The ever increasing pace of technological change presents a challenge for policy makers: how to facilitate the diffusion of new knowledge and technology to the widest possible audience. Public policies to encourage such diffusion, often referred to as technology transfer programs, are not new. The agricultural extension service, for example, dates back to the early 1900s.

One of the primary ways in which the public sector can seek to accelerate diffusion is by facilitating the flow of information from researchers to potential users. States have, in fact, set up programs to link businesses with information and expertise on technological issues. Often such programs are designed to provide small businesses with access to the resources of the state's university system. Examples of state initiatives in this area include:

(a) Virginia's Commonwealth Technology Information Service (CTIS). This is a database (currently under development) which is designed to improve the access of business to the state's technology services. It will include information on faculty interests and qualifications, government and industry research personnel, research facilities, and equipment available in Virginia.

(b) The Michigan Technology Transfer Program. This is designed to simplify the access of business to the technical information and expertise within Michigan's state universities. Five centers have been established at the participating universities. Each center is staffed by full-time technology transfer agents who serve as advocates for the firms. The centers are linked by a Computer Information Network, which enables them to identify sources of expertise at any of the participating universities.

(c) Ohio's Innovation Exchange Network (TIE-IN). This is a statewide interactive database that includes information on faculty research activities throughout the state, venture opportunities, and patent information.

(d) Illinois Resource Network. This is a statewide electronic directory that can provide names, campus addresses, and educational background of 6,000 university faculty members. Through a key word or phrase, the network can help identify specialized consultants.

ASSISTING BUSINESSES AND ENTREPRENEURS

States have developed a variety of programs to aid existing firms seeking to introduce a new product or adopt a new process and to encourage new spinoffs from research findings. Most of these programs include an information dissemination component, but many go beyond the information function to provide in-depth counseling and technical assistance.

One mechanism to provide such assistance is through an industrial extension service. At least ten states currently operate industrial extension services, although the actual services provided vary greatly from state to state. In Missouri the Business and Industrial Extension Service of the University of Missouri in Columbia uses off-campus specialists to identify the educational or research needs of small firms and then to serve as a liaison for the company with campus resources.

The Michigan Technology Deployment Service (TDS) was established in 1985 to assist companies that are considering adoption of new, computer-based manufacturing tools and methods. TDS operates with a small central staff and several field representatives and training associates located across Michigan. The TDS field representatives are experienced managers and engineers with strong backgrounds in private industry. TDS training associates are senior staff at Michigan community colleges who have broad experience in designing customized training programs for manufacturing clients.

Maryland operates regional technology extension offices in conjunction with the Engineering Research Center at the University of Maryland. Offices are staffed by industrially experienced engineers who respond to companies requesting individual technical advice and problem solving.

Other states have set up centers that provide similar services. In addition to assisting existing firms, however, such centers may also assist individuals seeking to start a new company. Transforming an idea or invention into products ready for manufacturing, marketing, and distribution requires a range of business and management skills. To ensure that entrepreneurs are able to commercialize their products, a spectrum of support services can be provided. Entrepreneurial assistance programs often provide technical assistance, limited testing, market evaluation, and general business and management advice.

North Dakota's Center for Innovation and Business Development at the University of North Dakota provides assistance with patent applications, engineering and product testing, and development of a business and marketing plan. Illinois provides similar services through a network of technology commercialization centers at nine universities and two federal laboratories throughout the state. The centers assist entrepreneurs in research assistance, feasibility studies, prototype development, product testing, financing, and production and marketing assistance.

In addition to providing technical assistance, states have set up incubators to provide continuing support for new businesses. Incubator facilities provide low-rent office and laboratory space for entrepreneurs or early startup firms. Additional on-site support services such as office support and computer access are also frequently provided along with on- or off-site management and technical services on a referral basis. While incubators can serve a variety of firms, they are more often targeted to technology-based companies.

In 1983 the North Carolina legislature passed a $2 million High Technology Jobs Act to encourage entrepreneurship among small businesses in the high-tech sector. The Act created the North Carolina Technology Development Authority to implement a seed capital program and establish incubator facilities. The state provides one-time matching grants to local governments to establish incubator facilities.

FINANCIAL ASSISTANCE

A final area in which states have become increasingly active is providing startup and early-stage financing for new, technology-based businesses. An entrepreneur who has developed a new process, product, or service often needs such financing to support activities involved in proving a technology concept from a business point of view; such financing is often referred to as seed capital. Activities to be funded include: development of a working prototype, preparation of a business plan, development of an initial market analysis, and assembly of a management team.

States have taken several approaches to establishing seed capital funds. In some instances the state operates the fund directly, as in the case of Ohio, while in other states, such as Michigan and Pennsylvania, state funds have been used to spur the creation of privately managed funds.

Ohio's Edison Seed Development Fund provides matching funds for research and development leading to the commercialization of new-technology-driven products, processes, and systems. Two types of funding are available under the program: Class I projects can receive funding of up to $50,000 for feasibility studies; under Class II, funding of up to $250,000 is made available for prototype development. Class II funding is structured so that the state receives a payback from its investment. To qualify for funding, the applicant must be an Ohio firm and the research must be conducted in conjunction with an Ohio university. The matching requirement can be met by cash or in-kind contributions in terms of research time, materials, or equipment.

Michigan has taken a somewhat different approach from that of Ohio. Rather than operate a seed capital fund directly, Michigan is capitalizing four privately managed seed capital funds. In July 1986 Michigan issued a Request for Proposals for the establishment of private seed capital companies. An initial capitalization of $2 million per fund was provided by the Michigan Strategic Fund (MSF). The MSF is a state agency created in 1985 to increase the availability of business financing in Michigan. The MSF's programs are funded from oil and gas lease revenues. To qualify for the $2 million initial investment, each fund was required to raise at least $1 million privately. In return for its investment, the MSF will be repaid at 9 percent interest over a ten-year period with all interest and principal due at the end of ten years.

In January 1987 four funds were chosen. Two are in the process of receiving applications, and two are still raising private funds to match the state's investment. Investments by the seed capital companies will be limited to new companies, companies with no prior investment by an institutional investor, and companies with the potential for rapid growth.

Pennsylvania's approach is somewhat similar to Michigan's. Four seed capital funds have been established in conjunction with the state's advanced technology centers. Each center serves as a limited partner in one of the funds. The funds were initially selected in a competitive process. The state provided $750,000 for the initial capitalization of each fund, requiring a 2:1 or 3:1 match from the private sector. The funds operate as private venture capital companies, although they must abide by the following restrictions: investments are limited to Pennsylvania companies; the funds are prohibited from investing in mercantile businesses, i.e., retail and restaurants; and investments are limited to companies with fewer than 50 employees. As of August 1986, a total of $30.4 million is available for investment from Pennsylvania's seed capital funds. Thus the state's appropriation of $4.5 million has been matched by $27 million in private funds.

No comprehensive studies have been undertaken to assess the effectiveness of state commercialization assistance programs. These programs, for the most part, are of use to a very small number of individual businesses. They are predicated on the belief, however, that they will assist the type of firms whose presence within the state will lead to substantial economic growth. Those programs that have been in place for some time, such as the Connecticut Product Development Corporation or the Massachusetts Technology Development Corporation, have proven that the programs can become self-supporting—no longer relying on public subsidies to operate. Once again, the relationship between investments and the economic health of the state remains unknown.

Conclusion: future directions

The foregoing discussion of state initiatives supports the view that states are continuing and expanding their efforts to promote the development and application of new technologies. Thus far, state efforts have focused on creating new institutions to develop and implement science and technology policies, improving university research capacity and encouraging new university–industry partnerships. Having made long-term investments in higher education in general and research in particular, however, states have begun to focus on ways to ensure that the research being supported by the state will actually result in economic gains. Thus, today we find states placing greater emphasis on commercialization, information dissemination, and the general involvement of small businesses in research and development.

Each of these activities is aimed at helping entrepreneurs and small business owners to take the research being developed at both public and private universities and other research facilities located in the state and introduce it into the marketplace. Given that these state programs are designed to address economic development goals, the ability of a state to capture the commercial outcomes of R&D activities will determine the success of these programs.

In a report issued in August 1987, the National Governors' Association's Task Force on Jobs, Growth, and Competitiveness recommended that states "consider creating a comprehensive technology commercialization strategy to address research and development, financing of new technology-based businesses, training, and the application of technology in existing businesses."[12]

More specifically, the governors focused on ways to improve linkages between the business and research communities and ways to increase the rate of technology transfer by disseminating information on research and development, particularly to small and medium-sized companies.

While the governors' recommendations show continued support for state science and technology policies, the real test will be whether these activities can achieve their stated goals and objectives. An important issue facing today's policy makers, therefore, is to determine the effectiveness of these tools in achieving economic development. To date, evaluative data on these efforts have been scarce. This may be changing, however, as the programs mature and program administrators seek to justify their initiatives before state legislators and new administrations.

In April 1987 the National Research Council, the Government/University/Industry Research Roundtable, and the National Governors' Association held a workshop to explore state government strategies for self-assessment of science and technology programs for economic development. The workshop brought together the program managers of approximately a dozen state technology programs to discuss their approaches to assessment.

The workshop participants emphasized that state science and technology programs are long-term initiatives. Many of the programs being undertaken are not expected to yield significant economic growth for as long as 10 to 15 years. Certainly, investment in education would fall into this category. While it might be difficult if not impossible, however, to measure progress toward this ultimate goal, the participants agreed that the programs have near-term goals such as strengthening graduate education and university research or enhancing university–industry collaborative relationships, toward which progress can and should be measured.

The more difficult question is ascertaining the relationship between these goals and the economic health of the state. It was clear from the workshop that although states are beginning to grapple with the issue of assessment, efforts to develop assessment procedures are at a very early stage of development. At present we are still unable to say which initiatives appear to be the most effective.

Notes

1 M. K. Clarke, *Revitalizing state economies* (Washington, D.C.: National Governors' Association, 1986).
2 B. Jones, *State technology programs* (Minnesota Governor's Office of Science and Technology, 1986); and M. K. Clarke, E. P. McGuire & C. Morrison, *The role of science and technology in economic competitiveness* (Washington, D.C.: National Governors' Association and the Conference Board, 1987).
3 M. K. Clarke, *The structure and function of state science and technology offices: preliminary findings* (Washington, D.C.: National Governors' Association, 1987).
4 For a discussion of the program, see *Gubernatorial policymaking through science advice* (Washington, D.C.: National Governors' Association, 1982).
5 Clarke, *Revitalizing state economies.*
6 See C. C. Armington & M. Odle, "Sources of job growth: a new look at the small business role, *Economic Development Commentary*, Fall 1982; C. C. Armington & M. Odle, "Sources of recent employment growth: 1978–1980," prepared for the Second Annual Small Business Research Conference, Bentley College, Waltham, Mass., June 1982; and D. L. Birch, *The job generation process* (Cambridge, Mass.: MIT Program on Neighborhood and Regional Change, 1978).
7 Clarke, McGuire & Morrison, *The role of science and technology in economic competitiveness.*

8 C. Watkins, *State programs to encourage the commercialization of innovative technology and programs for innovative technology research in state economic development strategies* (Washington, D.C.: National Governors' Association, 1985); Clarke, *Revitalizing state economies*.
9 S. Rosenfeld, *The renaissance technician* (Southern Growth Policies Board, 1987).
10 Jones, *State technology programs*.
11 *Progress report* Ben Franklin Partnership Program, Commonwealth of Pennsylvania, August 1987.
12 *Making America work: jobs, growth and competitiveness* (Washington, D.C.: National Governors' Association, 1987), p. 34.

8

State strategies for business assistance

R. SCOTT FOSLER

Introduction

PRIOR TO THE 1970s, relatively few states attempted directly to promote their economies, and those that did focused almost exclusively on the recruitment of business from other states. The southern states in particular mounted aggressive programs of financial incentives and tax abatements in an effort to attract manufacturing branch plants from the North and Midwest. Mississippi's Balance Agriculture with Industry program of the 1930s was one of the first formal industrial recruitment programs, reflecting the agricultural South's desire to catch up with the industrialized regions of the country. Variations of industrial recruitment were introduced in part through short-lived federal programs that encouraged state planning for economic development prior to World War II.

The conventional state approach to business assistance that prevailed through the early 1980s and still weighs heavily in many state programs is rooted in this historical experience with industrial recruitment. Its essential method was to provide a combination of incentives that would sufficiently reduce the cost of doing business to entice a firm to relocate to the state.

Since the 1970s, however, state involvement in economic affairs has changed dramatically. Virtually every state now actively promotes its economy, but the strategies employed have moved far beyond an exclusive, or even predominant, reliance on recruitment. Most states are now concerned broadly with the internal development of the state economy and employ a wide diversity of strategies and a vast array of techniques to that end.

The principal force motivating state experimentation with new approaches to economic development was economic stress. Massachusetts was one of the earliest experimenters, because New England was the first region to feel the sting of the global economic restructuring that has been in evidence since the 1960s. Significantly, the first reaction of Massachusetts leaders in the early 1970s was to fall back on the conventional remedy of business recruitment to replace the jobs lost in dying or relocating industries. But when out-of-state businesses could not be enticed to move to "Taxachusetts," state leaders turned their attention to finding ways of improving the state from within. They learned, in short, that a new, competitive world economy would require a high degree of innovation in all phases of economic activity, including state economic strategy.

As economic hardship visited other regions of the United States during the 1970s and 1980s—the Midwest manufacturing belt, the oil- and mineral-rich states, the agricultural heartland—other states went through much the same process of reaction and learning as Massachusetts. Now virtually all are involved in a new wave of innovation in economic strategy that is reminiscent of the experimentation in social policy that swept the states in the early part of this century.

Business assistance is no longer just a matter of providing financial incentives and tax abatements to lure firms to the state, although both recruitment and the use of cost-reducing incentives are still important components of state programs. Today, states attempt to assist business through a far more complex set of economic strategies.

This chapter discusses seven such strategies. Some of these are compatible with one another, while some are mutually exclusive. Each entails important political choices and requires tailoring to the particular circumstances in each state. All have the potential for both helping and harming individual businesses, industries, and the state economy more generally.

Because both the choice of strategy and the specific means of implementation are so critical to success, the institutional capacity with which states make and implement business assistance decisions is also important. The conventional institutions of state government are

not well suited for this purpose, and one finds an almost frenetic innovation in institutional arrangements for the design and implementation
of economic strategies. Some of these are also discussed as integral to
the strategies themselves.

The economic environment

The first strategy is to improve the general economic or business climate
of the state. It is an outgrowth of the conventional economic principle
that private enterprise requires certain factors for the production
of goods and services, including land, labor, capital, technology,
information, and management. The state's rôle is to facilitate the
development and accessibility, if not, in some cases, actually to provide
these factors. A corollary is for the state to minimize production costs
on which it has some bearing, including those that are directly affected
by government, such as taxes and fees, and costs that may be incurred
by business as a consequence of regulation or deficiencies in public
services.

The underlying assumption here is that the private sector operating
in a free and competitive market is the principal engine of economic
growth, and that it is most likely to flourish in an environment where
specific foundations or generic factors are strong. The task for state
strategy is to determine which are the most important foundations,
especially in light of changing economic forces, and how the state
can assure that they are present at minimal cost.

The Committee for Economic Development (CED) defines the following as key foundations that are both important for the contemporary
economy and factors on which states have some effect:[1]

(a)　a capable and adaptable workforce;
(b)　adequate physical infrastructure;
(c)　well-managed natural resources;
(d)　up-to-date knowledge and technology;
(e)　financing, technical assistance, and regulatory provisions condu-
　　　cive to enterprise development;
(f)　an attractive quality of life;
(g)　a sound fiscal base.

Conventional state economic development programs were rarely concerned with these foundations, since they fell beyond the recruitment
mission of departments of commerce and economic development. State

policy over the years has been involved in all of these foundations, but rarely as part of a consciously designed economic program. Today, however, each of these foundations has become the subject of intense interest on the part of the states, most of whom now recognize their importance to economic vitality.

Virtually every state has mounted a campaign to improve primary and secondary education and to strengthen training programs to upgrade job skills of current workers. The National Governors' Association gave prominence to the education issue in its publication *Time for results: the governors' 1991 report on education*, which many states are using as a guide for education reform.[2] Programs to improve the skill level of the workforce, such as Vermont's Consolidated Council for Employment and Training, which has established 23 basic pre-employment competencies required for young people to obtain a job, have also proliferated throughout the states.

Another priority has been strengthening the states' base in knowledge and technology. A prototype for many states is Pennsylvania's Ben Franklin Partnership, which supports four regional technology centers consisting of consortia of university, business, labor, and government groups interested in the commercial application of science and technology. But every state now has a program that carries the "science and technology" label, such as the Florida High Technology Industry Council or the New Jersey Science and Technology Commission.

The high priority given to human resources and technology as key economic foundations has not lessened the states' interest in more conventional business assistance provisions that are included in the category of "enterprise development." These include providing businesses with information about the state that might be of interest to them as a place for relocation as well as of financial and in-kind (e.g., training assistance, infrastructure improvements) incentives that would help motivate them to relocate.

Information provided to businesses typically includes advertising and promotional literature; general information about the demographic, economic, governmental, and cultural character of the state; and specific information on available sites and buildings. State informational and technical services now range widely into seminars and conferences, management consulting in marketing, strategy and other aspects of business operations, technology transfer, and consulting on personnel and labor relations.

The mainstay of many state economic development programs continues to be financial incentives and tax abatements aimed to reduce the cost of doing business. Direct financial incentives include state loans and loan guarantees, industrial development bonds, grants, and state-supported capital assistance programs. Tax incentives include tax credits for job creation or investment; reductions, delays, or other abatements of property taxes; and deductions or exemptions for inventories, research and development, machinery, equipment, fuels and raw materials, and pollution abatement.[3]

State government regulation has grown so pervasive that modifications in regulation tend to be viewed as forms of "business assistance." States have broad regulatory powers over banking, insurance, telecommunications, professions and trades, land use, the environment, employment, health, occupational safety, labor relations, and consumer affairs. The skill with which regulations protect legitimate public interests without imposing counterproductive costs on business is a factor in determining the general economic climate. Especially important is the extent to which the state regulatory structure establishes competitive markets. Established businesses operating in noncompetitive environments, or those seeking state regulation to protect themselves from competitors, obviously will not perceive state efforts to promote competition as assistance to them. A competitive environment, however, aside from being key to economic efficiency, is the *sine qua non* for businesses seeking entry into the market and a fair chance to operate.

The question of which combination of factors constitutes the strongest foundation for economic development in a state is a topic of long-standing debate. It is reflected in the lively exchange between two organizations that rank states according to standards of economic performance. On one side is the Grant Thornton (formerly Alexander Grant) index, which rates the states (except Hawaii and Alaska) on the basis of their appeal to manufacturing branch plants.[4] On the other side is the Corporation for Enterprise Development, which, in 1987, published its own index that ranks the states according to a different set of measures designed to assess a broader range of factors that affect the economy.[5]

The Corporation for Enterprise Development expressly took issue with the Grant Thornton index, claiming that it reflected too narrow an approach to economic development. In fact, it claimed, states that used that index could well impair their economic performance. Grant Thornton has responded that its index never claimed to be a measure of general economic conditions but explicitly focused on the question of how to attract manufacturing.

States take these rankings quite seriously, since they tend to be highly publicized in the local media and thus reflect publicly on state officials, especially the governor and the director of economic development. Other organizations have also developed indices. *Inc.* magazine ranks states on the basis of their appeal for small and medium-sized businesses.[6] SRI International has developed a set of measures that attempts to assess a state's performance in areas considered to be critical to new economic forces.[7]

Process of economic development

A second strategy is to strengthen the process of economic development. The underlying assumption here, similar to the "foundations" approach, is that the key to economic development is a vigorous private sector driven by a free market. The state's rôle is to identify and correct "market failures" or otherwise to facilitate or encourage enterprise development.

State perspectives on the nature of the economic development process vary according to numerous factors. Since a major political force driving most state economic development programs is the desire to create jobs, the economic development process is frequently equated with the job creation process. That is one reason why conventional economic development programs have been geared toward the recruitment of plants that would generate a large number of jobs. Not only is the single, large influx of new jobs perceived to be beneficial to job seekers (and voters), but it is likely to be reported in the media and thus reflect well on public officials anxious to prove they are "doing something" to improve the economy.

A "job," however, is a variable commodity. It may be low-paying, dead-end, or likely to be terminated if the employer cuts back, fails, or relocates out of the state. The cost of creating jobs, moreover, may be greater than the financial and economic gain they generate.

A contrasting perspective on the economic development process focuses on wealth creation through the entrepreneurial process by which resources are put to more valuable use.[8] As Malecki notes,[9] the process of entrepreneurship is key to regional economic development, more important in fact than the process of technological change.

Higher value, as determined principally by entrepreneurs working in a free market, is the principal goal of the wealth creation strategy. Job creation is not the immediate focus, but is none the less an important by-product of wealth creation. The jobs required in the process of creating higher value, it is alleged, are more likely to pay better, be more enduring, or engender higher skill levels that improve a worker's options in finding other employment. The income, spending power, and ancillary economic growth generated by greater wealth, moreover, are likely to create other jobs.

The types of programs suggested by a focus on the wealth creation process can be sharply at variance with those suggested by focusing on the job creation process. Wealth creation, above all, depends on the existence of vigorous, competitive markets where entrepreneurs have the incentive—both the desire for reward and the fear of failure —to produce innovative, high-quality, low-cost goods and services that meet consumer desires. The wealth creation approach accepts the inevitability of lost jobs, but holds that the resources made available by these losers can be redirected to other more productive pursuits, which in turn will create new jobs. Government has a rôle here in facilitating the transition, helping workers to upgrade their skills and find new employment. Programs that focus primarily on creating and retaining jobs, by contrast, have led states into legislation to forestall plant closures or other measures that risk repelling would-be investors.

The states' interest in the process of economic development has also drawn them more directly into concern with the productivity of business enterprises. They have mounted programs to improve employee productivity through training, improved labor–management relations, worker involvement in decision making, and the management of the workplace. West Virginia, for example, has had a Labor Management Council for over ten years, and many other states have developed similar agencies to improve labor management relations and productivity in individual firms. Some states, such as New York and California, have been shifting their job training programs toward the improvement and more productive use of employee skills in the workplace. In some states such as Kansas, this trend is reflected in the emphasis on updating "customized training programs . . . to meet the needs of new and expanding Kansas employers."[10]

Most states now have programs to assist dislocated workers in finding new employment and to help distressed communities weather economic trauma and replace lost jobs. Most recently, states have adopted legislation to protect home industries against takeovers, such as those that threatened Dayton Hudson in Minnesota and Boeing in Washington State.

Life cycle of the firm

A third strategy is to provide the support appropriate to the variable life-cycle needs of the firm. This is a variation on the more general interest in the process of economic development. It assumes that firms have different needs at different stages of their business lives, and that interventions by state government at key stages in the cycle can facilitate or inhibit development. The principal stages in the life cycle are generally viewed as: startup (including research, development, and production); expansion; maturity; regeneration; decline; and relocation or termination.

The conventional approach to economic development focused on only one stage in the life cycle: relocation. Most states faced with economic difficulty almost instinctively have turned first to this traditional remedy as a way to replace lost jobs. As noted above, Massachusetts, for example, at the depths of its economic slump in the early 1970s, tried to lure firms from other states. But Massachusetts had such a poor reputation that it could not interest serious investors in moving to "Taxachusetts," and so state leaders turned their attention to improving the economic base they already had.

Most states continue to recruit business from outside the state, and many still use traditional financial and tax incentives to attract manufacturing branch plants. Some states continue to provide assistance indiscriminately to businesses in the frantic pursuit of new jobs and investment. Huge and costly packages of financial incentives, tax abatements, and in-kind assistance (such as training and infrastructure provision) are offered without consideration as to whether their costs can be justified by the economic and fiscal returns those businesses are likely to generate.

Other states, however, have attempted to develop a far more selective approach, systematically weighing the costs of assistance programs and packages against the expected return in jobs, income, ancillary business generation, tax base and revenue enhancement, and impact on other businesses. Sophistication in the use of financial incentives, moreover, has also increased.

Many states, however, began to see that while they were out scouring the countryside for new business, they could lose as much as they might gain through the decline or relocation of the business they already had. Initially, this concern was driven by the fear that their home firms would leave, possibly attracted by the incentives that were being offered by competing states. But added to that fear was the growing concern that home companies were in economic difficulty and faced with cutbacks, layoffs, or closure. Thus, business retention joined recruitment as a second stage in a firm's life cycle that was of interest to states.

The thinking went one step further when states realized that some firms inevitably would lose business, relocate, or fail. The question was whether there would be new startups and expanding business to take their place. This realization was heightened by the research of Birch, which stressed the importance of the ratio of business "births" to "deaths" as the key to growth.[11]

Today, one can find state programs that address each of the stages in the life cycle of the firm, a dramatic departure from only a few years ago when the states were preoccupied almost exclusively with recruitment. For the most part, however, these programs were established as isolated and incremental responses to newly reorganized needs or pressures, and not as the result of a clearly thought-out strategy to provide a carefully linked set of programs that corresponds to the changing life-cycle needs of the firm. An important exception is that state officials concerned with providing capital to business have become increasingly aware of the need to tailor programs to the varying needs of firms according to their life-cycle stage.[12]

Research on product life cycles demonstrates that regional economies are affected by changing product as well as firm life cycles, but these relationships as yet are rarely recognized in state policy making.[13]

The size of firms

A fourth strategy is to tailor economic programs to the needs of different-sized firms.

Conventional state programs were geared toward large corporations, especially in so far as they attempted to recruit the branch manufacturing plants of large, national corporations. In the past several years, however, most states have expanded or shifted the emphasis toward small firms, in the belief that smaller firms generate more jobs than larger ones.

Every state now has extensive programs to assist small business. For the most part, these rely on the use of traditional tools of technical, financial, and managerial assistance, tailored to small businesses. For example, industrial development bonds (IDBs) have been modified to extend their tax-exempt advantage to small businesses. These include IDB guarantees that are similar to loan guarantees in protecting the investor and that increase marketability, which is a problem with small issues. States also provide umbrella bonds that aggregate several small issues (generally below $1 million), thereby pooling and reducing credit risks and thus lowering the cost of financing.

Small businesses are thought to have particular difficulty in finding capital in their earliest stages of development. States have attempted to plug this perceived gap with seed capital programs designed specifically for small businesses. States have also established their own venture capital funds or promoted the creation of private venture capital funds through favorable regulatory and tax treatment. The Michigan Strategic Fund, for example, attempts to assure that capital is available to small enterprises, including those requiring seed capital in their earliest stages. It does so through a variety of techniques, viewing itself principally as a "wholesaling" agency whose mission it is to assure that other agencies, both public and private, are "retailing" capital to those enterprises that warrant it in an efficient manner.

Some states have also promoted the creation of business development corporations (in some states known as development credit corporations) to provide capital primarily to small business. The development corporations are privately run banks authorized by state legislation and operated according to state guidelines. They provide working capital and expansion loans generally under $1 million to new and existing business. Such loans may be augmented by assistance from the Small Business Administration.

States also operate a variety of technical and managerial programs to assist small businesses in business planning, marketing strategies, basic operations, record keeping, and financing. Increasing emphasis is now being placed on technology transfer to small businesses. The American Economic Development Council, for example, has been working for the past two years to determine how professional economic developers could promote the transfer of knowledge and technology from available sources to small businesses in their states and communities. A state program in Colorado provides a search service to find experts with the combination of technical knowledge required to solve specific operational problems. In one case, a local economic development specialist was approached for help by a local bakery whose concrete floors were being seriously eroded by spill-over residue from the baking process. The specialist contacted the state technology transfer office, which initiated a search and found specialists familiar with both the chemical reactions associated with baking and the composition of concrete. The knowledge of these experts taken together has been used to define the problem faced by the bakery and propose a range of solutions.

Assistance to small firms is also closely associated with special programs to help women, minorities, and those interested in self-employment become established in business. Such programs use many of the same approaches that are applied to small business assistance in general, but gear them specifically to particular target groups. For example, many states use government procurement as a means of helping small firms generate business, either by helping them learn how to compete for federal government contracts or by creating special programs that set aside a certain proportion of state contracts for small business. Special procurement set-asides are frequently established for such target groups as women and minorities as well.

The means of providing this wide range of assistance varies. Some states simply maintain a series of separate programs that deal with each facet of small business assistance. Others have established offices of small business assistance, usually within the state's principal development agency. And some have attempted to link the state's small business programs with those of local government, community colleges, universities, chambers of commerce, and other entities. In a further effort to integrate small business assistance, many states have established incubators, which combine in a single building or campus low-rent space, pooled business services, accessible transportation, and various technical, managerial, and financial assistance services.

Most small business assistance programs provide assistance directly to individual firms. This contrasts, for example, with a model that has evolved in Italy wherein governmental assistance is channeled through a service center for a given industry (e.g., apparel, machine tools, etc.). Since the service center is under the direction of a board whose members include the client businesses, the assistance is more likely to conform to the real needs of the businesses and be operated aggressively and professionally.[14]

The states' emphasis on small businesses is based in part on a misunderstanding. Research on business startups and expansion has tended to highlight the rôle of small business in job creation and innovation. The tendency to equate "new and expanding business" with "small business" is understandable, since many new and expanding firms are small. Moreover, many people are employed by small business, even if those firms are neither new, nor expanding, nor innovative. And, to be sure, understanding the special needs of small businesses is important in developing successful programs that will assist them or in avoiding policies that could impede them.

However, the key to generating new wealth and jobs is not so much small firms as expanding firms. Over the past five years, 93 percent of new jobs were created by the top 10 percent of companies ranked by growth.[15]

While many expanding firms are relatively new and small, others are of substantial size. Meanwhile, there are many small businesses that are neither new nor likely to expand. In fact, in the normal workings of a competitive market, numerous small businesses fail, contract, or never get off the ground. In some instances this may be due to factors that can be corrected by marginal state assistance, but in many instances it is simply due to the fact that the enterprise was ill-conceived in the first place or managed by people who probably are not likely to operate a successful business no matter what kind of assistance they receive. Of course, the more business startups there are, the more businesses are likely to survive, and the more likely it is that among those will be firms with genuine expansion potential. However, state programs that excessively promote or sustain small businesses which have small chance of surviving on their own are likely to be wasteful or counterproductive.

Strategies geared to the individual needs of different-sized firms also run the risk of failing to recognize the intricate interplay among firms of different sizes. Many small businesses, for example, are dependent on one or a limited number of purchasers, who are likely to be larger businesses. In fact, a potent source of small business development in recent years has been the decision of large firms to purchase by contract goods and services that they previously produced in-house. Thus, many complexes of small firms in reality constitute a *de facto* restructuring of corporate organization, where responsibility is shifted from the large parent company to the smaller legally independent but none the less economically dependent firm.

The importance of this type of relationship has been underscored by the shift of manufacturing from the East and Midwest to the South and West. While basic manufacturing firms and operations have changed location, many of the smaller suppliers of those firms have not. The relocated manufacturing companies, meanwhile, have been finding new suppliers offshore in the Far East, with the consequence that many of their former eastern and midwestern suppliers have declined and been forced to close.

There are also important differences among firms of various size with regard to R&D activities. According to the National Science Foundation, in 1984 companies with 1,000 or more employees spent 94 percent of all funds for business research and development.[16] Much of that R&D effort focuses on improving existing products and processes. Meanwhile, smaller firms have a proportionately better record in developing new products. For example, Apple Computer developed and marketed the personal computer, Xerox document copying, and Federal Express overnight package delivery, each when they were still relatively small corporations.

International competitiveness

A fifth strategy is to strengthen the competitive advantage of the state in the global economy.

The states' first foray into the international field was an extension of their conventional recruitment efforts: they simply expanded their "smokestack chasing" abroad. Tennessee was one of the most successful in persuading foreign firms to locate plants within its borders, having attracted such large Japanese companies as Nissan and Toshiba. Tennessee's leaders paid particular attention to cultivating personal and business relationships with their Japanese counterparts, emphasizing the natural and economic advantages of the state and the presumed similarities in the habits of the workforce. (The Tennesseans reportedly went so far as to point out to the Japanese that they shared in common the experience of having been defeated by the United States in war.) The recruitment of foreign firms involves many of the same issues as the recruitment of domestic firms. For example, is the cost of the subsidy (in loans, grants, tax abatements, and in-kind payments) justified by the benefits the firm brings to the jurisdiction (in jobs, payrolls, expertise, purchases, and tax revenues)?

But the international scope of the competition adds a new dimension, since state and local governments are now providing subsidies to foreign firms. Firms already operating in a state frequently complain that subsidies to attract other firms not only give an advantage to the competition but increase their tax burden to pay the subsidy. Now the complaint is extended to include the fact that the competitor is a foreign company with whom they are trying to compete in global markets.

Foreign investment also raises questions of control, which can be politically charged. Foreign purchase of real estate and domestic business is viewed with concern by some citizens who fear that the new owners will not have the welfare of the state or community at heart. Japanese firms in Hawaii have attempted to alleviate such fears by contributing to local civic and cultural ventures. But the experience of foreign ownership is new for contemporary Americans and the full impact—economic, political, and cultural—remains to be seen.[17]

Attracting foreign investment, however, is but one dimension of state international activities. As the American trade deficit worsened during the early 1980s and jobs were lost to foreign imports, the states became interested in the question of how to promote their exports. In 1983 the New York–New Jersey Port Authority, for example, established the first publicly sponsored export trading company, called Xport, to assist small and medium-sized companies in developing their export markets abroad. Numerous other states have since followed with their own export promotion programs. And virtually every state now has some program to promote exports.

Most state export assistance programs are geared toward small and medium-sized businesses. They provide assistance in determining markets and tradeleads for state products abroad, establishing contacts with foreign importers and distributors, sponsoring trade shows and missions, tailoring products and marketing strategies to foreign markets, and facilitating the use of federal resources for all of these purposes. A few states also provide financial assistance for export promotion.

Many states have established foreign offices, principally in Japan and Europe, to pursue both foreign investment and to promote exports from their states. Governors, other state officials, and state business leaders now make frequent visits abroad for both purposes, as well as to cultivate relationships with the national, regional, local, and private-sector leaders in other countries who are thought to be important to developing effective, long-term economic ties.

The potential for states to increase significantly the exports of their m27home firms remains in question. Nearly 85 percent of American exports are accounted for by large firms, which with few exceptions attend to their own marketing and distribution; many of these firms believe there is little that the states can do for them in this field.

Meanwhile, some American firms perceive the greatest potential for improving their position in the global economy to lie in recapturing the American domestic markets lost to foreign companies in recent years. This, in essence, is "import substitution." As the dollar fell in 1987 approximately to its 1981 level (which preceded the dramatic appreciation from 1981 to 1985 that placed American firms at such a disadvantage in international markets), trade volumes began to shift in favor of domestic firms. By the fall of 1987, it appeared that this shift was finally beginning to make a dent in the U.S. trade deficit. Still, in early 1988 many economists and business executives continued to believe that the dollar would have to fall even further if the United States was to reverse its chronic trade deficit and begin to draw down its huge international debt. This would provide an even greater opportunity for domestic firms to compete against foreign firms not only in foreign markets but in the now "globalized" American market.

In another variation of import substitution, some states encourage in-state firms to purchase from suppliers that are also in-state rather than import them. The State of Washington, for example, has begun a program to identify both imported parts used by firms within the state and Washington firms that produce those same parts, and to promote transactions between the two in-state firms.

Most states have only recently discovered the new "global economy" and continue to perceive their international rôle essentially in terms of attracting business from abroad and promoting state exports in foreign countries. Gradually, however, the states are moving toward a broader international perspective, which recognizes that their economic relationship with the rest of the world is not just a relatively simple calculus of exports versus imports, but a complex dynamic that impacts virtually every aspect of the state economy. Virginia, for example, has embarked on a program of international education that not only intends to improve language, geography, and cultural training in the public schools and universities, but extends as well to increasing the international literacy of officials throughout the state government. The Northern Nevada Language Bank, as another example, provides foreign language services for international business in the state. And the Massachusetts International Coordinating Council, a private organization, concerns itself with a full range of trade, finance, technological, political, language, and cultural issues that affect Massachusetts' future in the world economy.

Some states have also begun to recognize a critical truth that has evaded American economic policy at all levels: much that is innovative and promising in economic development is occurring abroad. The New Jersey–New York Port Authority, for instance, organized a conference in 1986 to expose state and local officials and business leaders in the New York metropolitan area and throughout New York State to the new flexible specialized networks of small firms in northern Italy that are now among the most productive in the world.[18]

In sum, states are learning that their economies are part of an interdependent world economy and that the full range of state economic development strategies and programs must account for that new global reality.

Targeting for growth

A sixth strategy is to identify and promote those industries, firms, or technologies that are thought most likely to offer growth in the future. Favorite targets in recent years have included manufacturing, high-tech, and knowledge-based service industries.

This strategy is most overtly associated with the "picking of winners and losers" identified with national "industrial policy." Its risk lies in presuming that public officials can select emerging industries or firms more accurately than the market despite the limitations of economic theory and analysis. The selection is also subject to political pressures applied by economic interests already within the state that seek favored treatment irrespective of their economic potential.

None the less, most states attempt to steer their economies in the direction of specific industries on the basis of one or more of the following rationales:

(a) First, states already affect their economies in so many ways that a bias of some kind is inescapable. Better to recognize that the bias exists and take action to correct for it or to tilt it in a productive direction than to pretend that it does not exist.

(b) Second, some jurisdictions are too small to develop a diverse economic base that can adjust relatively painlessly and without government assistance to shifting market forces. In an increasingly specialized world economy, smaller regions must find market niches. If they do not attempt to carve out productive niches, they fear they will be driven into dead-end niches, based on low-wage, low-skill industry. Once dependent on such a narrow and unpromising base, they will then be all the more vulnerable to changing market forces.

(c) Third, competing jurisdictions, both within the United States and abroad, are effectively targeting growth and thereby developing a competitive advantage. Taking a similar course of action may simply be a matter of self-defense.

(d) Fourth, it is not necessary to make a definitive choice between a high degree of targeting on the one hand and a total laissez-faire posture on the other. State strategy can foster principal reliance on the market to determine future economic direction, while also taking prudent steps to assure that the state is well positioned to take advantage of emerging growth opportunities. The targets themselves need not be specific firms or industries but generic factors that are likely to undergird a wide variety of future economic activities. Prime among such generic factors is advanced technology.

One recent survey reported that industry and university officials reject state strategies of targeting specific technologies because they do not believe state officials can identify promising technologies.[19] In this view states will be influenced by political considerations and the tendency to "follow the herd" in funding research (thereby missing important breakthroughs in unpopular fields). At the same time, however, they believed that if targeting were to be attempted, it would be preferable at the state rather than the federal level.

Whatever the economic justification for targeting, the fact is that virtually all states are doing it, and technology, "high," "advanced," or otherwise, is a favorite target of all of them. The issue among state economic specialists is not whether to promote technology but how to do it effectively.

Research Triangle Park in North Carolina has served as a model for many states. Research parks have sprung up all over the country in an attempt to lure high-tech firms and research institutions. Most states would like to emulate the high-tech enclaves of Silicon Valley in California or Route 128 in Massachusetts, but they acknowledge that those two areas developed without forethought by state government or other public entities. Research Triangle, on the other hand, was the conscious creation of the State of North Carolina and, hence, would appear to hold great hope for other states that the experience can be replicated.

States are not inclined to acknowledge, however, that Research Triangle involved persistent labor over several decades, that it started early enough to take advantage of the important evolving technologies of recent years, and that the total level of research and development undertaken in the United States would not begin to fill up all the research parks that have been planned by states and localities across the country.

When the technology programs of the states are broken down into their component parts, several common features emerge that demonstrate their broader and more complex composition. They include not only research parks and incubators but, as defined by Plosilla, "policy development, education and training, research and development, entrepreneurship training and assistance, financial assistance to innovative firms, and technology and information transfer."[20] Consequently, what may be perceived as "targeting" of technology from one perspective, in fact, involves numerous programs in diverse areas of state government from another perspective.

A more conventional type of targeting is defined by industrial sector. Both Indiana and Michigan, for example, have determined through formal policy channels that they will work to retain and develop their traditional bases in durable goods manufacturing. Whether they should or will be able to do so depends on one's reading of future economic trends. Some economists, such as Thurow and Dornbusch, predict that American manufacturing jobs will grow substantially in the next few years as a declining dollar improves the terms of trade for American manufacturers, who will be able to recapture domestic markets. There was evidence by early 1988 that this was beginning to occur. Others foresee the inevitable decline not only in manufacturing jobs but in manufacturing output as a proportion of total GNP. The Hudson Institute, for example, predicts that whereas manufacturing accounted for 30 percent of GNP in 1955 and 21 percent in 1985, it will account for only 17 percent in the year 2000.[21]

Some state economic development officials believe that since theory regarding the relationship between policy and economic development is weak, the best strategy is simply to pursue the best opportunity of the moment. Some states simply "follow the herd," or adopt wholesale the economic programs used in other states. There is a certain policy logic and political safety in such an approach, since it would appear to keep a state in the mainstream of development efforts and protect top officials against the charge by political opponents that they are not keeping up with competing states in the aggressiveness of their economic development program. Its weakness lies in the fact that the states are undertaking so many initiatives under the economic rubric, it would be impossible for any one state to manage them all with any degree of proficiency. Besides, many of the new economic programs are highly experimental, so that their wholesale adoption is bound to include some that will fail.

A few states have adopted a general strategic approach that allows wide latitude for taking advantage of opportunities as they may arise. Indiana, for example, has established general strategic goals and an institutional structure, the Indiana Economic Development Council, whose purpose is to coordinate a wide range of public and private economic organizations within the state in the identification and pursuit of more specific objectives that would appear to be compatible with those long-range goals. The Council is seen as an internal "guidance system" that identifies and perpetually seeks out the most opportune targets in keeping with long-term strategic goals.

Fostering synergy

A seventh strategy is to foster synergistic relationships among interdependent but isolated economic resources. The assumption here is that economic development involves more than simply promoting a series of isolated resources, such as trained people, technology, and capital—

it also requires interaction among those interdependent resources. Even a free and vigorous market may not automatically work to assure that the appropriate connections are made and that the necessary critical mass required for dynamic interaction is established.

States have focused particularly on linking education with the workplace, research with business, and training with recruitment programs. However, there is a great deal of experimentation with various groupings of issues and programs. For example, one study of entrepreneurship concluded that five categories of assistance were involved: entrepreneurial networking, managerial and technical assistance, business incubators, entrepreneurial training and education, and venture capital mechanisms.[22]

A 1987 publication of the National Governors' Association, *Making America work*, reflects the trend toward a more comprehensive and integrated treatment of state economic policy by grouping a wide range of issues and recommendations under three major topics: productive workers, efficient workplaces, and responsive communities.[23]

A key to promoting synergy among public and private sectors is to assure that government programs are "market-driven," that is, that they address a real and practical need that will stand up to the test of a competitive private sector. One way to accomplish this is to build market tests into state programs, for example, by requiring firms to identify training needs and share the burden of programs, as does the Massachusetts Bay State Skills Corporation, or to require private lending institutions to participate in ventures funded in part by public capital assistance programs.

State policy is also increasingly interested in the locational dimension of synergy: that is, in assembling and linking the right resources in the same place. Approaches here have taken the form of funding research parks, enterprise zones, centers of excellence, and regional strategies designed to link fragmented state, local, and private programs in the same geographic area. Examples of state programs to focus on substate regional economic development include New York's ten regional development councils, and MASSJOBS Southeast, which links public and private efforts to help firms in southeast Massachusetts.

States also show an increasing interest in broader, interstate regional economies, reflected in the revival of support for interstate organizations. The southern states have worked together for several years through the Southern Growth Policies Board. The northeastern, midwestern, Great Lakes, and western states have also stepped up their support for regional approaches.

Institutions

The scope and complexity of these seven strategies reflect a fundamentally new economic rôle for the states, one for which conventional state institutions are not well suited. Consequently, innovation in institutional arrangements has been as important as—and really inseparable from—the substance of new programs.

New institutions have been developed in the first instance to formulate strategy. States have found that they need a far more sophisticated diagnostic capability to understand state, regional, national, and global economic dynamics and the potential, limits, and actual performance of state programs. Virtually every state has employed cabinet councils and public–private task forces to develop economic strategy. Some have attempted to improve the organization of their analytic and diagnostic capability. Minnesota, for example, has established an Economic Resource Group to coordinate the knowledge of the 110 economic analysts employed in six different state agencies. Most states continue to lack the basic capability to evaluate programs in order to determine what has and has not been working in the past, although some, such as Minnesota, have established serious evaluation efforts.

Another major institutional hurdle is the integration of economically important programs that are functionally organized and hence bureaucratically fragmented: education, training, natural resources, capital availability, technical assistance, land use planning, etc. The organizational challenge is all the greater since even functionally related programs, such as training, may be divided among numerous agencies. Michigan, for example, discovered some 35 agencies involved in training programs alone.

Numerous new institutional forms have been developed to undertake specific tasks associated with the various economic strategies. Many of these are variations of nonprofit, quasi-public organizations established for such purposes as product development, export promotion, training, and venture and seed capital provision.

Other major institutional challenges include coordinating economic policy among the branches of state government (executive, legislative, and judicial), among the levels of government (federal, state, regional, and local), and between the public and private sectors.

These multiple and related needs are reflected in proposals for a major restructuring of institutions involved in economic development. In Oklahoma, for example, a statewide public–private partnership called Oklahoma Futures has been established as part of a proposal that calls for an Economic Development Cabinet, an Economic Innovation System, and a strengthened Department of Commerce.[24]

While the examination of institutional innovation is generally beyond the scope of this chapter, suffice it to say the new institutional arrangements for economic strategy reflect far-reaching changes in the structure and rôle of state and local government.[25]

Conclusion

Taken together, the new strategies and institutional innovations reflect a decidedly new economic rôle for states, one that moves far beyond the relatively simple recruitment focus of just a few years ago. In the context of this volume's principal concern with technology and regional growth, several features of these strategies should be highlighted.

First, assisting businesses involves not only programs that provide direct financial, technical, or other forms of aid to firms but a far more elaborate set of policies that affect the economic vitality of the state. In the past, formal economic development programs were nearly always associated with very specific programs of direct business assistance. Economic development strategies today also involve the development of a range of resources—including technology, labor, and capital—that in turn are key to business success. The development of those resources, moreover, may be carried out through a host of nonbusiness institutions, including government, universities, and nonprofit organizations.

Second, the development and/or use of technology is integral to various aspects of nearly all of the strategies. This is true in the first instance because "technology" is pervasive, if one defines it broadly as the knowledge and capability to employ a variety of means to accomplish productive purposes. In this sense, technology in some form is involved in all business and economic endeavors. "Advanced technology" is essentially a new order of knowledge and capability, which probably requires a higher order of expertise and/or organization. However, yesterday's advanced technology of the internal combustion engine is today's standard technology. Today's advanced technology in computer-assisted manufacturing is likely to be tomorrow's standard technology.

To be sure, states pursue technology-specific strategies geared toward the development and application of new technology or to the sustained and expanded use of sophisticated technology. These include the support of basic and applied research which is believed to lead to the development of commercially valuable technology, the promotion of specific new technologies which are thought to have commercial value, or the general support of higher education and promotion of new technologies in general.

But most of the other nontechnology-specific economic strategies also involve a strong component of technology use or development. The promotion of entrepreneurship, for example, carries a strong implication that new business endeavors will either use or develop new knowledge that is commercially viable. Achieving international competitiveness is regularly believed to require expertise in the most up-to-date technologies. Given the fact that successful business operations today require numerous small changes that reduce cost, add value, or differentiate products and services to meet increasingly segmented market demands, a great deal of new technology is developed very close to, if not at the point of, production or the delivery of service. Consequently, not only do other economic strategies use technology, they may also be involved in the generation of technology.

The preoccupation with technology can lead to the underestimation of the economic potential in businesses that do not involve new or sophisticated technology. This is true of most small businesses, and indeed of most entrepreneurs, both of which are most typically involved in starting, expanding, or sustaining enterprises that employ simple and standard technologies.

Third, a major challenge to state economic strategies is the mismatch between state political boundaries and *de facto* economic regions. States are political institutions whose geographical boundaries frequently bisect economic regions. But over time, the exercise of their political powers has had important economic consequences both in determining the nature and in shaping the contours of those regions. Since technology is integral to economic development and to development strategy, this less than congenial political–economic marriage is of consequence to technology policy as well.

Fourth, all of the above warrant underscoring the point that the nature of institutional arrangements is a key variable in the formulation and implementation of state economic strategy. None of the several generic strategies discussed above could be said to be correct or incorrect in and of itself. In each case, success will depend on how these strategies are conceived, the intelligence with which their formulation accounts for the nature and prevailing forces affecting specific regional economies, and the political and administrative skill with which they are implemented. This applies as well to strategies that are technology-specific and to the way in which technology is considered in the other strategies.

Notes

1 Committee for Economic Development, *Leadership for dynamic state economies* (New York: Committee for Economic Development, 1986).
2 National Governors' Association, *Time for results: the national governors' 1991 report on education* (Washington, D.C.: National Governors' Association, 1986).
3 For an inventory of business assistance programs in each state, see the National Association of State Development Agencies/Urban Institute, *Directory of incentives for business investment and development in the United States* (Washington, D.C.: Urban Institute, 1986).
4 Grant Thornton, *The seventh annual study of general manufacturing climates of the forty-eight contiguous states of America* (Chicago: Grant Thornton, June 1986). The Grant Thornton index uses "22 factors selected by manufacturers as important to business success."
5 Corporation for Enterprise Development, *Making the grade: the development report card for the states* (Washington, D.C.: Corporation for Enterprise Development, March 1987). This index uses broad measures in four areas: economic performance, business vitality, human resource and financial capacity, and government policies.
6 "INC's annual report on the states," *INC.*, October 1987, 76–92.
7 There have been numerous studies surveying state economic initiatives in recent years, including the following: National Governors' Association, *Technology and growth: state incentives in technological innovation* (Washington, D.C.: National Governors' Association, 1983); National Governors' Association, Office of Technology Assessment, U.S. Congress, *Technology, innovation, and regional economic development* (Washington, D.C.: Government Printing Office, 1986); and M. K. Clarke, *Revitalizing state economies: a review of state economic development policies and programs* (Washington, D.C.: National Governors' Association, 1986).
8 R. J. Vaughan, R. Pollard & B. Dyer, *The health of states: policies for a dynamic economy* (Washington, D.C.: Council of State Planning Agencies, 1986).
9 E. Malecki, "Technological innovation and paths to regional economic growth," this volume.
10 "Report of the Legislative Commission on Kansas Economic Development," December 23, 1986, unpublished report, House of Representatives, State of Kansas, Topeka, Kansas.
11 D. L. Birch, *The job generation process* (Cambridge, Mass.: MIT Program on Neighborhood and Regional Change, 1979).
12 See, for example, Wisconsin Legislative Staff Council, "Venture capital: an overview," Madison, Wisconsin, July 21, 1986, p. 3.
13 See A. R. Markusen, *Product cycles, oligopoly and regional development* (Cambridge, Mass.: MIT Press, 1985).
14 C. R. Hatch, "A future that works: manufacturing networks and reindustrialization in U.S. states and cities," a draft report, Center for Urban Reindustrialization Studies, New Jersey Institute of Technology, September 5, 1987.
15 D. L. Birch, "Booming hidden markets," *INC.*, October 1987, p. 15.
16 R. J. Samuelson, "Coping with corporate inefficiency," *Washington Post*, October 7, 1987.
17 It is instructive to consider the issue as it is played out in foreign countries. The

German states, for example, aggressively recruit foreign companies. The state of Baden-Württemberg has established an industrial park specifically for Japanese high-tech firms and offers such services as a Japanese school for the children of Japanese businessmen, as well as a Japanese restaurant. German businesses, in response, claim that such state incentives constitute unfair advantages for their Japanese competitors. The Asia department of the Association of German Industry complains that such subsidies help Japanese undermine German business, especially when combined with perceived Japanese dumping of products in German markets to gain market control (V. Pope, "Japan's investments flood Germany," *Wall Street Journal*, October 7, 1987). As in the United States, foreign investment is not evenly distributed in Germany. The highly industrialized state of North Rhineland Westphalia, for example, contains the headquarters of 400 of the 650 Japanese firms operating in West Germany (including 4,500 business executives). (As a matter of interest, only 3,000 Germans live in Japan, of whom 450 are business executives.)

18 The July/August 1987 edition of *Entrepreneurial Economy* features the European flexible manufacturing networks.

19 National Governors' Association and The Conference Board, *The role of science and technology in economic competitiveness* (Washington, D.C.: National Governors' Association and Conference Board, 1987), p. 19.

20 W. H. Plosilla, "State technical development programs," *Forum for Applied Research and Public Policy* 2, no. 2, Summer 1987, 31.

21 Hudson Institute, *Workforce 2000: work and workers for the twenty-first century* (Indianapolis: Hudson Institute, June 1987), p. xvii.

22 Wisconsin Division of Research and Analysis, *Models of entrepreneurial development programs* (Madison, Wisconsin: Bureau of Research, Department of Development, 1987).

23 National Governors' Association, *Making America work* (Washington, D.C.: National Governors' Association, 1987).

24 Counsel for Community Development, *Oklahoma: tools for a global competitor*, a report to the Joint Fiscal Operations Committee, Oklahoma State Legislature, January 7, 1987.

25 R. S. Fosler, *The new economic role of American states* (New York: Oxford University Press, 1988).

9

An assessment of state technology development programs

JOHN REES & TIM LEWINGTON

OVER THE LAST decade a whole series of technology-based economic development programs have been launched by the states.[1] This chapter deals with the evolution of these programs as well as with the preliminary results of a national survey of companies aimed at assessing their experience with these new state initiatives. To date, there have been some case studies of these emerging programs as well as a few comparative studies between states. But no comprehensive assessment of the impact of these programs has been reported. Before dealing with the programs themselves and their implications, the context of regional economic and political change needs to be addressed in order to explain why a quiet revolution of sorts is taking place.

The regional economic and political context for state policy: a Schumpeterian perspective

In economic terms the 1970s saw the rapid growth of the Sunbelt South, while the 1980s saw a revival of the Northeast. During the 1970s, most states grew in total employment, though in the southern and western states proportions of change were much larger. Although trends for 1980–7 show impressive gains in total employment for both the northeastern and midwestern states, the southern and western states still show very healthy growth trends in total employment. Clearly, regional economic changes are cyclically sensitive, but changes in manufacturing employment reveal that some major structural changes have taken place and continue to take place in the American economy.[2] Much of the economic growth in the United States in the 1970s and 1980s reflects the growth of the service economy in all parts of the country, while changes in manufacturing employment show the impact of deindustrialization, particularly in the states of the Northeast and Midwest. During the 1970s, a clear contrast between Sunbelt and Snowbelt can be detected, in terms of manufacturing, and this trend also comes through into the 1980s.

One factor that looms large behind all these changes is the international context and impact of the dollar on the world market. A strong dollar in the early 1980s meant that American companies could buy production facilities abroad at a lower cost. Once manufacturing goes offshore, however, it is difficult to bring back. This in turn contributes to the trade deficit today, despite a weaker dollar. At the same time that manufacturing suffered during the early 1980s, high interest rates provided a boom in major financial centers across the country, as international financial flows from Tokyo, London, and Zurich enriched the producer service sectors of New York City, Boston, Los Angeles, and other regional financial centers. The revival of the Northeast, then, in the 1980s was influenced to a major degree by international macroeconomics. Many scholars would indeed argue that the impact of state economic development policy pales in comparison with the plight of the dollar and the impact of the federal budget deficit.

Second, the political context of change is also important to the topic of this chapter. The year 1980 was a watershed in American politics, marking for many the end of liberalism and a return to the status quo. Reaganomics represented a "hands-off" approach to the economy, a view that market forces will result in both an efficient and equitable solution for all Americans. The Reagan years also had major implications for intergovernmental relations with the states, resulting in a direct impact on economic development policy. Inactivity at the federal level in terms of spending gave birth to a *de facto* form of New Federalism whereby the second tier of government, the states, became active and innovative players. The states became more concerned about their own destiny, and many took a realistic look at their own comparative advantage. Because of this, a plethora of new programs has emerged at the state level in the 1980s.[3] The experiments launched by individual states have once again made them laboratories for democracy in the American political system, where the seeds of future federal policy may already have been planted. Other policies in the past began as state experiments and were later adopted as federal policy.

Economic development became the rallying point and an umbrella that now embraces new efforts in science and technology policy, human capital policy (i.e., increased expenditure on elementary and high school education, training, and retraining), as well as the more traditional concern with tax incentives. High technology became the panacea for many state policy makers, and Silicon Valley fever spread across the country. The Office of Technology Assessment has documented over 150 new initiatives at the state level alone since 1975, whereas current estimates show the number of new programs to be over 200.[4] Clearly, there is duplication between many states, as neighbors imitate each other. But imitation is not necessarily less successful than innovation. Many programs do not make sense in economic terms, but they are not meant to do so. They make sense in political terms as politicians live and die in the short run.

Given the profound nature of these regional economic and political changes within the United States, one has to ask whether conventional concepts explain all that is taking place. While many may argue that these changes are mere manifestations of conventional neoclassical economic forces at work, it is argued here that Schumpeterian concerns about the evolution of the economy provide a more appropriate interpretive framework.[5] Schumpeter became increasingly concerned with disequilibrium as a dominant theoretical construct in his explanations of economic change, and in 1942 he wrote his powerful passage on "creative destruction," which seems particularly appropriate in understanding the regional economic changes discussed earlier: "The process of industrial mutation . . . incessantly revolutionizes the economic structure from within, incessantly destroying the old one, incessantly creating the new one."[6] In a spatial sense (which Schumpeter did not discuss) deindustrialization, or the loss of manufacturing jobs in the Northeast and Midwest, can be interpreted as the destructive side of the process. Attempts by various levels of government—federal, state, and local as well as the investment activity of industry—can be seen as the creative response to this. But in the United States in the 1980s the most active level of government in this creative process shifted, or indeed evolved, from the federal to the state level. The policies of the federal government have always had a powerful determining effect on regional development, not so much in an explicit regional policy format (like many European governments), but indirectly through agencies such as NASA and the Department of Defense. While the Department of Defense has long been the dominant funder of industrial research and development in the United States, individual states have recently begun to reassess or create their own R&D policies and their own science policies.[7] Most states face considerable fiscal constraints compared with the federal government, not the least being the requirement to balance their budgets. But the last ten years have seen the quiet evolution of state science and technology policy. Most states have been engaged in different and sometimes novel ways of enhancing their potential for economic growth.

A taxonomy of state technology development programs

The types of program introduced by the states have been cataloged by the Office of Technology Assessment as well as by others.[8] Because of the variety of technology-based economic development programs launched by the states, the continued introduction of new programs, and the modification of existing ones, classification itself is not an easy task. In addition, any classification procedure can also introduce bias into any evaluation conducted on these programs. Some programs were designed to achieve long-range objectives, while others were only intended to show short-term benefits. For many of these states, it is difficult to differentiate high-tech development programs from economic development efforts in general. Thus, any attempt at a generic classification makes it difficult to account for a complete description of state initiatives.

Most of the state programs to date fall into three broad categories: new university–industry relationships; direct encouragement of new business startups, with particular focus on entrepreneurial development; and encouragement of upgrading of a state's existing technology base by establishing industrial extension services and other types of technology transfer mechanisms. A more detailed breakdown of these categories is shown in Table 9.1.

Today most states are active in at least one of these areas, while many have adopted more comprehensive approaches. Among the latter, the Ben Franklin Partnership Program of Pennsylvania (initiated in 1982 with a cumulative state appropriation of $30 million and private funding over $90 million) and Ohio's Thomas Edison Program

Table 9.1 Types of state technology development programs.

---

1 University–industry relationships:
  (a) research or science parks;
  (b) technology research centers (ATCs) – usually university-based;
  (c) joint university–industry research (specific projects).
2 Encouraging new business startups:
  (a) increasing financial capital: venture/risk capital for NTBFs;
  (b) entrepreneur training and assistance programs;
  (c) incubators.
3 Technology upgrading:
  (a) dissemination of technical information (e.g., NTIS);
  (b) technology brokering to potential adopters (e.g., NASA);
  (c) industrial extension services: technical assistance, commercialization assistance programs.

Source: Authors' survey of state economic development officials (1987).

(begun in 1983 with state appropriations of over $33 million and nonstate appropriations of $80 million) appear to be among the most comprehensive in the country. While the types of programs involved in these three broad categories have been discussed in this volume and elsewhere,[9] some critical commentary is appropriate on each.

In the area of university–industry relationships, the last ten years have seen the beginning of a new era in the United States.[10] While the majority of R&D funds for the country as a whole have come from the federal government, the rôle of the private sector has increased significantly in recent years—a four-fold increase over the last decade, according to the National Governors' Association.

The research park concept has received much attention as a means of generating new technology, but it is by no means a new phenomenon. We cannot assume that indigenous technology can be developed within the iron walls of a research park any more successfully than within the incubation environment of any major urban agglomeration or any major corporate complex. Bell Lab stands out as one of the more successful but unofficial science parks in American economic history, while one of the more widely publicized science parks in the country, the Research Triangle of North Carolina, still houses many branch plants of large corporations and lacks any significant amount of local venture capital.

Attempts at encouraging new business startups have also taken a variety of forms across the country. These include increasing the availability of financial capital (especially venture capital), encouraging the development of entrepreneurial initiatives, and developing formal incubators.

While much attention is given to the importance of local venture capital as a precondition for new business development, there is much that we do not know about the venture capital industry: how and where it operates and what its real impact is. The geographical sources of formal venture funds are highly concentrated, with over two-thirds coming from three regions of the country: California and the Southwest, the New York/New Jersey area, and New England.[11]

In their efforts to create high-tech complexes in various states, many policy makers have focused either on attracting companies from other states or on conditions that will give birth to new, innovative firms. In many cases this has resulted in the relative neglect of existing industry and the failure to upgrade the technological sophistication of local industry. Yet encouraging the spread and application of the latest available technology, particularly to resource-scarce small firms, can be an important form of economic development policy. While the federal government has a history of involvement in technology transfer programs, technology transfer and the diffusion of innovation is only recently receiving explicit attention from the states. Most of this attention is being focused on the industrial extension service notion, largely due to the relative success of the Cooperative Extension Services of the U.S. Department of Agriculture. While there may be similarities between the type of corn grown in various parts of the country, the greater degree of product specificity in the manufacturing sector makes the agricultural model a questionable one to emulate. Many states have recently implemented technology transfer and commercialization assistance programs, and have been categorized into two types: financial and nonfinancial.[12] While any inventory of state technology development programs would be quickly outdated today, Watkins reminds us that the two most common methods of state sponsorship of research related to economic development are university-affiliated technology research centers and the applied research grant.[13] The technology research center is generally seen as a vehicle for focusing research efforts on the development of specific technologies (e.g., artificial intelligence, biotechnology, microelectronics), whereas the applied grant program usually takes the form of a joint university–industry initiative. Since the benefits derived from such state sponsorship of research ultimately depend on the degree of utilization in the private sector, there is much more to be learned about industrial experience with universities in general and with state-funded technology centers in particular.

Industry's perceptions of such programs plus its experience (or lack of it) with these programs will tell us much about the effectiveness and impact of such efforts. This is one way—but only one way—by which such programs can be evaluated.

Evaluation problems

One theme that underlies many of the chapters in this volume is the need to evaluate the impact of the various technology-based economic development programs that have been introduced at the state and local level. What we know about their impact to date is similar to what Rothwell and Zegveld concluded in their comparative review of innovation policy:

> Having discussed innovation policy in some detail, it must be admitted that we know very little about its effectiveness. ... In view of this it might be said that perhaps the greatest problem of innovation policy is that it has been more an object of faith than of understanding.[14]

The need for impact assessments is even more pressing in the case of the newer technology-based economic development programs where contradictions on evaluation are the result of casual empiricism. In the case of research parks, the General Accounting Office saw them as the most effective model of university–industry cooperation,[15] whereas the National Science Board[16] claims that they have been relatively ineffective. Clearly, such contradictions are to be expected when there is lack of a clearly defined objective for a particular policy. Under such circumstances, Gibbons goes as far as to question "to what extent it is valid to evaluate policy by comparing policy intentions with outcomes."[17] He also points out the importance of distinguishing between policy monitoring as a task separate from policy evaluation, i.e., addressing what happened before asking the more difficult question of whether the policy itself made any difference. It is precisely this last issue which makes policy evaluation a very difficult task.

The objective of evaluation research is to establish whether specific programs have produced their intended effects and to separate these from any unintended effects. Technically, this involves selecting appropriate independent and dependent variables and creating appropriate measures of these variables. With the types of programs discussed in this chapter, however, the lack of appropriate secondary data makes the identification of variables a major problem. As in most cases of evaluation research, the most reliable methods are surveys of decision makers involved with a particular program compared with a sample of decision makers not involved with the same programs. Survey research itself is not without its problems, so that in any policy evaluation effort the use of more than one method is advisable.

At least five different evaluation methods are appropriate in this context, as in others.[18] These include: (a) before and after comparisons, employing either time series analyses or trend analyses of the use of resources spent and the output achieved; (b) control group methods, based on comparisons of the behavior of supported versus nonsupported companies; (c) econometric models, usually involving macroeconomic studies of the relationships between R&D expenditures and productivity; (d) case study methods; and (e) monitoring approaches, which analyze the implementation and administration of programs.

Because of the weaknesses implicit in each of the above methods, the use of more than one method is advocated for evaluating the new economic development policies. While policy evaluation today is a routine exercise for most public agencies, it is always important to consider the political context of evaluation and the way in which state-specific political and institutional conditions affect the design and outcome of various state programs. In reminding us of the inherently political nature of evaluation, Feller suggests that this can have an impact on a number of important issues, including the identification of policy objectives, the selection of appropriate performance measures, and the availability of pertinent data.[19] The evaluation of public-sector programs by public-sector managers becomes inherently suspect; public-sector managers have their own self-interest built into their evaluation.

The short-term nature of political cycles also impacts program evaluation in other ways, usually to the detriment of new programs. The desire to see quick returns can be the death knell for the types of programs discussed here, because most of these programs need a long-term gestation period before any positive result may be evident. As Ahlbrandt and Weaver remind us in their recent description of Pennsylvania's technology development program, "One of the keys to the successful outcome of a region's advanced technology strategy will be the willingness of the partners to commit themselves to a long-term involvement."[20] In this context the use of leveraging ratios (the ratio of industry to state dollars) and the use of job creation measures in particular should be tempered.

Any program evaluation should include the user and potential beneficiary of that program. In the case of university–industry relationships in general, and technology development centers in particular, this should include an assessment from different types of industries and different types of companies. Here size of company also becomes an important variable. Some large companies may choose to become involved in similar technology ventures in a number of different states. The amount of company investment may be relatively small for a large firm, so the risk is spread around a number of state programs in order to maximize the potential return. If a large company has its headquarters and most of its operations outside a particular state, the actual benefit to that state can also be called into question. Because of the different motivations that a company can have for involvement in various state programs, evaluation methodologies that involve the private sector should also be multidimensional. The rest of this chapter deals with the preliminary results of a study designed to assess industry experience with state technology development programs and one type of program in particular.

State technology development centers: a preliminary assessment

Since the goal of this research project was to assess the impact of state technology development programs, the complexities of the states themselves and the variety of programs made it imperative to keep the research design as standardized as possible. Given that the functional specialization of these state programs is also variable, it seemed appropriate to focus on one type of research center: in this case, those involved in microelectronics and computer-aided manufacturing. This is one of the oldest functional areas chosen by many states, which gives some history for assessment purposes.

State technology development centers in microelectronics

A survey of state officials in 1987 allowed us to identify 38 such centers in 20 states. The states are listed in Table 9.2 along with the number of centers per state. The list includes centers that used appropriated state monies for their initiation and excludes research centers (for example, at MIT or Stanford) that were started without state appropriations. Table 9.2 includes advanced technology centers set up at universities as well as those set up adjacent to but independent of university campuses with independent political authority (e.g., the

Table 9.2 States with advanced technology centers in microelectronics and computer-aided technology.

States	Number of centers
Alabama	3
Arizona	1
California	1
Colorado	2
Georgia	2
Illinois	2
Indiana	1
Kansas	2
Massachusetts	1
Michigan	4
Minnesota	1
New Jersey	2
New Mexico	2
New York	4
North Carolina	1
Ohio	2
Pennsylvania	2
Utah	3
Virginia	2
Washington	1

Source: Survey of state science and technology/economic development officials.

Industrial Technology Institute in Michigan and the Microelectronics Research Center in North Carolina). The general pattern seems to be that states appropriate monies for infrastructure (mostly buildings) and some operating costs, while individual research contracts are negotiated between individual centers or universities and industrial companies on a proprietary basis. The diffusion or spread of these centers since 1978 has been fairly rapid. The four earliest funded state research centers in electronics were established in California, Arizona, Minnesota, and North Carolina. Between 1981 and 1984, an additional ten centers were established in a number of states, including a group of states in the industrial Midwest and Northeast that appear to have some of the more comprehensive technology development programs, especially Pennsylvania, Ohio, New York, and Michigan. A further increase in the number of states involved took place between 1985 and 1988 with 12 new centers designated. (We include 1988 because enabling legislation was passed between 1985 and 1987 to allow capital expenditures for the development of these centers.) Clearly, however, appropriations and funding formulae vary considerably from state to state, and the resources of each center also vary.

Because of the relatively short history of these research centers (and indeed other technology development programs), a rigorous comparative assessment does not exist to date. While federally funded centers (mostly the National Science Foundation) have been the subject of some evaluation,[21] most state-funded centers have not been evaluated. One has to be careful in any such evaluation, however, because the goals of such centers and programs differ from state to state, while resources allocated for program implementation also fluctuate widely. But such problems do not make the task of evaluation any less important, particularly if informed decisions are to be made about the continuation or further initiation of such programs.

Research on industry experience with state technology centers

At the inception of this research we expected that center directors would be able to provide names and addresses of companies that had been involved in their center activities so that we could identify a large population of companies to survey. This was unfortunately not the case, despite the use of public monies in these centers. In most cases, public monies were allocated for buildings and some operating costs, while involvement of individual companies took place on a proprietary basis. The protection of confidentiality concerning their research activities is clearly important to companies that become involved with state-funded research centers, and a perceived lack of confidentiality was seen as a reason for many companies not to become involved. While this is understandable among companies on the leading edge of new technology, it does not make the task of assessment or evaluation any easier.

In response to this problem we identified 2,000 companies as *potential clients* of microelectronics and computer-aided manufacturing research centers from several SIC groups and the DUNS file of the Dun and Bradstreet Corporation. The SIC groups targeted were computing equipment manufacturers (357), electronics components manufacturers (367), machine tool companies (3541 and 3542), and aircraft and aircraft engine/component makers (372).

In the rest of this section a preliminary analysis of 100 responding companies out of the first mailout (June 1987) is reported. It cannot be overemphasized that these are *preliminary findings* from a relatively small sample of companies and the characteristics of late respondents may differ from those of early respondents. Clearly there may be a bias among nonrespondents, but this is expected to be minimal and will be addressed in later analyses. The survey questionnaire used was divided into the following four sections: background information on the company; company experience with university–industry programs in general; experiences with particular state-funded research centers; and company experiences with technology development in general.

Of the 100 companies reported on here, 44 were classified as large (with over $10 million in sales in 1986), and 56 were designated as small (with under $10 million in sales). Because of this, we will be able to assess the experiences of small companies with state technology centers and see how they differ from those of large companies, many of which have set up contractual arrangements with a number of universities and state research centers across the country. A good response rate from small businesses is particularly appropriate for this type of assessment because that sector is one that many of these state programs are designed to assist. To date, 42 percent of the responding companies had their headquarters in the Northeast Census region, 26 percent in the North Central region, 12 percent in the South, and 20 percent in the West.

Average funds spent on research and development amounted to 6 percent of total sales among the larger group of companies and 11 percent among the smaller group. Of the larger companies, 64 percent reported that none of their workforce was unionized, compared with 82 percent of the smaller companies. When asked for what government agencies these companies had undertaken work in the past, the federal Department of Defense (DOD) was by far the largest client. For the larger group of companies, 14 percent of total sales went to DOD, while an average of 37 percent of sales went to DOD among the smaller group of companies. Only 18 percent of companies reported that they undertook "basic research," an area targeted by many of the university-based state technology centers.

COMPANY EXPERIENCE WITH UNIVERSITY PROGRAMS

When companies were asked which activities they had been involved in with universities, course enrollment of employees was the most common response (76 percent), followed by the use of faculty as consultants (56 percent), the use of students as research assistants or interns (46 percent), the sale of equipment to a university (42 percent), and specific contractual research projects between universities and the companies (32 percent).

The most important incentives for companies to participate in cooperative research with a university turned out to be access to students as future employees (62 percent), followed by contacts with research faculty (58 percent), and product development issues (50 percent). The use of university computing or other facilities was not a major incentive for companies to engage in cooperative research. The use of university–industry programs to identify "future employees" for a company is an important preliminary finding that should be borne in mind by any government agency, state or federal, involved with employee training and retraining programs.

When asked an open-ended question about what disincentives existed to company participation in university–industry relationships, the rights to data was the most common issue mentioned (i.e., company concerns about public access to the results of university research). This debate over intellectual property rights is receiving more attention from both universities and industry today, but the right-to-privacy issue is seen as a major barrier to further university–industry cooperation by the private sector. This is particularly so for companies on the cutting edge of new technologies, where lack of confidentiality is interpreted as a factor that puts them at a competitive disadvantage. At a time when much effort is being given to the encouragement of cooperative research between universities and industry, the experience of the private sector in this survey still shows that 72 percent of companies see no incentive for this type of activity in the federal tax structure, while 76 percent see no incentive within state tax structures either. If individual states wish to encourage more cooperative ventures between industry and universities, a closer look at their tax structures as an inducement for this activity would seem in order.

Of the 36 companies that documented some form of university–industry cooperative research effort, all but one reported that they were satisfied with their experience. At a time when university–industry activities are growing, if only among a small segment of the private sector, this preliminary finding should be an encouraging one for potential participants, particularly given the disincentives listed earlier by companies responding to the survey. Of the respondents, 58 percent also agreed that the growth of university–industry collaboration had increased personnel mobility between the two sectors, while 46 percent of companies stated that this movement of personnel took the form of university personnel moving to the private sector. If this latter trend continues in the long term and a high proportion of the best researchers end up in industry, such a movement could be detrimental to the university's research mission.

COMPANY EXPERIENCE WITH STATE-FUNDED ADVANCED
TECHNOLOGY CENTERS

In the initial response to our survey, only 10 percent of respondents said that they had been involved with state-funded technology research centers. Therefore, it is premature to generalize from this small number of cases. While two respondents identified themselves as being involved in the Ben Franklin Partnership in Pennsylvania and that program's advanced technology centers (ATCs), they did not identify this as a state-funded ATC program. The general lack of experience among respondents also tells us that they have little information or awareness of these programs. If this trend continues, states need to pay further consideration to information dissemination about their programs.

When asked whether states should continue to participate in technology development programs, 60 percent of companies responded positively. If states do continue to fund technology development programs, 62 percent of companies felt that they should be affiliated to universities, while 23 percent felt that they should not. Such signs of support for state programs and the rôle of universities suggest that the low level of activity reported above may be linked to an information problem. Further clues to the lack of involvement with university-industry technology development programs are provided below.

COMPANY EXPERIENCE WITH TECHNOLOGY DEVELOPMENT IN GENERAL

Of the respondents, 86 percent perceived themselves as leaders in developing new products, while 76 percent also saw decision making in their company as being centralized, with only a few people contributing to the important decisions. Further, 92 percent of the respondents also perceived their labor–management relations as smooth, and marked by a spirit of cooperation.

In a question that asked for the relative importance of various sources of knowledge which was potentially important to the companies in their search for technical knowledge relevant to the development of new products and production processes, interesting patterns emerged among the early responses. Of the respondents, 94 percent saw in-house (company) research and development as an important source of technical knowledge; 88 percent saw trade publications and scientific journals and 86 percent saw customers as important sources. On the other hand, 68 percent of the companies did not perceive government agencies as an important source of technical knowledge, and 66 percent viewed universities as either an unimportant source or as no source at all.

While this part of the survey may be picking up a traditional image in the private sector that government agencies could not possibly be an important source of technical knowledge and that university research is far too removed from reality to be relevant to the more "applied" concerns of industry, these perceptions are real ones and may still have a great deal of impact on the decision of companies not to get involved in collaborative efforts with universities or state technology development programs generally. Again, these early findings suggest that inherent biases among key decision makers together with the lack of information about university and state technology programs need to be addressed by public-sector decision makers before more collaboration between universities and industry can be expected.

Concluding remarks

It is our expectation that this type of survey of industry perceptions and experiences with state technology centers can provide useful feedback to decision makers in both the private and public sectors as to the efficacy of such state programs. The economic gains from such programs can be judged only in the long run, while the short-term concerns of political decision makers may prove to be the death knell of many creative endeavors. According to Merrill, "Measured simply by political acceptance, state governors have in a few years managed to accomplish much more in pursuit of economic development than succeeding national administrations have achieved in the name of industrial innovation and competitiveness."[22] Unless the type of policy evaluation discussed and advocated in this chapter takes place, we will know very little about the impact of these programs and the causal links between technology development and regional economic growth.

Notes

The research support of the Economic Development Administration, U.S. Department of Commerce, is gratefully acknowledged. The views in this chapter, however, are those of the authors and not of the EDA. The authors wish to thank Susan Thomas for her comments on an earlier draft of this chapter.

1   J. Rees (ed.), *Technology, regions and policy* (Totowa, N.J.: Rowman & Littlefield, 1986).
2   B. L. Weinstein, H. Gross & J. Rees, *Regional growth and decline in the United States* (New York: Praeger, 1985).
3   U.S. Congress, Office of Technology Assessment, *Technology, innovation, and regional economic development* (Washington, D.C.: Government Printing Office,

1984); M. K. Clarke, *Revitalizing state economies: a review of state economic development policies and programs* (Washington, D.C.: National Governors' Association, 1986).

4 U.S. Congress, Office of Technology Assessment, *Technology*.

5 For one of the more cogent expositions of this framework, see R. Nelson & S. Winter, *An evolutionary theory of economic change* (Cambridge, Mass.: Harvard University Press, 1982).

6 J. Schumpeter, *Capitalism, socialism, and democracy* (New York: Harper & Row, 1942), p. 83.

7 J. Rees & R. Bradley, "Science policy: the appropriate state and federal roles," in *Knowledge and the state*, ed. J. Sommer (in press).

8 U.S. Congress, Office of Technology Assessment, *Technology*.

9 Rees & Bradley, "Science policy."

10 National Science Board, *University–industry research relationships: selected studies* (Washington, D.C.: Government Printing Office, 1982); D. Dimancescu & J. Botkin, *The new alliance* (Cambridge, Mass.: Ballinger, 1986); D. Gray, T. Solomon & W. Hetzner (eds.), *Technological innovation* (Amsterdam: North-Holland 1986).

11 U.S. Congress, Office of Technology Assessment, *Technology*.

12 C. B. Watkins, *Programs for innovative technology research in state strategies for economic development* (Washington, D.C.: National Governors' Association, 1985).

13 Ibid.

14 R. Rothwell & W. Zegveld, *Industrial innovation and public policy* (Westport, Conn.: Greenwood Press, 1984), p. 153.

15 General Accounting Office, *The federal role in fostering university–industry cooperation*, GAO–PAD 83–22 (Washington, D.C.: Government Printing Office, 1983).

16 National Science Board, *University–industry research relationships*.

17 M. Gibbons, "The evaluation of government policies for innovation," *Policy Studies Review* **3**, 1984, 478.

18 F. Meyer-Krahmer, "Evaluation of industrial innovation policy: concepts, methods, and lessons, *Policy Studies Review* **3**, 1984, 467–75.

19 I. Feller, "Evaluating state advanced technology programs," paper presented at the conference Regions and innovation: comparison of research findings in Europe and the United States, University of Neuchâtel, Switzerland, 1987.

20 R. S. Ahlbrandt & C. Weaver, "Public–private institutions and advanced technology development in southwestern Pennsylvania," *American Planning Association Journal*, 1987, 457.

21 Gray, Solomon & Hetzner, *Technological innovation*.

22 S. A. Merrill, "The politics of micropolicy: innovation and industrial policy in the United States," *Policy Studies Review* **3**, 1984, 451.

10

The impact of elementary and secondary education on state economic development

RAY MARSHALL

The context

Introduction

BECAUSE OF THE presumption that better schools will attract industry and that more schooling will improve income and employment opportunities, education has become an important economic development strategy. And businesses increasingly give the quality of schools very high priority in making their location decisions, not only because of the need to have high-quality workforces, but also because of the importance of quality schools for their employees or their employees' children.[1] Americans have always valued schooling as a means of personal advancement, but many state policy makers believe that the age of high technology makes schooling much more essential to economic growth. This presumption does not go unchallenged, however, since some analysts argue that schooling actually has very little to do with economic development, even in the age of high technology. Indeed, some experts contend that high technology actually "deskills" most jobs, requiring lower, not higher, levels of education.

This chapter examines the relationship between elementary and secondary education and economic development from the state perspective. We should note at the outset, however, that elementary and secondary are pivotal levels of schooling in what should be viewed as a larger learning system with other components. We should, therefore, take note of these other learning systems in order better to understand the rôle of elementary and secondary education in state economic development strategies. More specifically, this chapter seeks to answer the following questions: (a) What are the main functions of education in the age of high technology? (b) How do a state's explicit or implicit development strategies affect its education policies? (c) How do the public elementary and secondary schools relate to other learning systems? (d) What are the implications for education of internationalization, technological innovation, and fundamental demographic changes, all of which combine to revolutionize the context within which economic and education policies must be made? (e) What is the evidence with respect to the relationships between education and economic development? (f) Do the schools really make a difference or does most learning take place outside of (and in spite of) the schools? (g) What can be done to improve elementary and secondary schools? The following sections examine these questions in order.

The functions of education

In developing an education policy, a state must consider the overall importance of schools as well as their rôle in economic development. Although this chapter will stress their vital rôle in human capital formation, schools serve a number of other important functions, not the least of which is as a major employer and one of the largest consumers of a state's revenues. Education is also supposed to improve one's capacity to enjoy life—to build sensitivity and awareness of one's community, humanity, and the world. Schools are, in addition, powerful sorting machines to allocate people to different occupational and social statuses. Schools could, in addition, create cultural and social identity—to give students a common interpretation of a nation's or state's history and a common vision of its future. Closely related is the schools' rôle as a means of indoctrination to a creed, religion, group, or ideology.

In all of these functions, of course, schools can be either positive or negative forces for change. They can cause people to be open-minded and therefore responsive to change or close-minded and resistant; they can cause people to have a sense of community and justice or inculcate a sense of élitism and narrow class, racial, or ethnic self-interest; they can cause people to think rationally or to react blindly; and they can produce large economic returns to states and individuals or they can waste resources. There is substantial evidence that significant changes have to be made if the schools are to realize their full potential as positive forces for change. One leading authority on the relationship between education and development concluded that, in comparison with most other industries, "education is . . . tradition bound. To put it bluntly, the education industry in most societies is big, basic and backward."[2]

Development strategy

The basic assumption of this chapter is that to be effective, a state's elementary and secondary school policies must be related to a coherent economic development strategy. There are, however, a number of choices. One of these, the orthodox economic (OE) approach to economic development, focuses on the accumulation of material wealth, measured by gross or net total or per capita output, but assigns lower priority to reducing unemployment and improving income distribution. It is assumed that even though growth benefits some people and sectors more than others, in the long run these benefits will "trickle down" to less affluent people and places.

An alternative strategy, which I prefer, emphasizes human resource development (HRD). This approach is based on the belief that human resources, not material output, should be the ultimate basis of all wealth. From the HRD perspective, "The goal of development is . . . maximum possible utilization of human resources in more productive activity and the fullest possible development of the skills and knowledge of the labor force which are relevant to such activity."[3] Moreover, the HRD "approaach stresses the reduction of inequality of opportunity. And, in addition to providing more material wealth, it includes better health, better nutrition, and wider involvement in the process of modernization as [the] high priority . . . results of . . . development."[4]

The OE and HRD approaches have similarities as well as differences. They both are essentially economic approaches, and both acknowledge the noneconomic objectives of education. And both consider higher levels of material growth to be desirable. The essential differences are that the orthodox "approach holds that opportunities for employment and learning stem from increased output; the human resource approach maintains that increased output is the result rather than the means of broadening employment opportunities."[5] The HRD approach emphasizes the maximization of learning opportunities as well as the full employment of labor and other resources. Although the orthodox and HRD approaches assign priority to education, both education and educational equity are much more important in an HRD strategy.

Finally, while the OE and HRD approaches have traditionally stressed economic growth, in the internationalized information world of the 1980s and 1990s both must give greater attention to economic competitiveness. Here again, however, definitions and conceptions differ. The orthodox approach gives greater emphasis to reductions in prices, wages, and exchange rates as ways to maintain competitiveness while the HRD approach stresses measures to enable firms or individuals to compete on terms that will make it possible to improve or maintain real incomes.

Whatever development strategy they adopt, state policy makers must place education policy in the broader context of economic development. No serious student of education and the economy would argue that education *alone* will promote development or competitiveness, but almost all would give high priority to education as *part* of a development strategy. Other things must be done to ensure that there is sufficient economic growth and competitiveness. In other words, education is considered to be necessary but not sufficient for economic development and international competitiveness.

Relations between learning systems

Effective education planning must also relate public schools to other learning systems, though this is rarely done systematically, even within the formal public education system. General concepts related to learning and development are often confused. For example, studies showing a high return to *human capital* are sometimes used to justify increased expenditures on *schooling*. However, from an economic development perspective, though schools are pivotal and important, they actually play a relatively small part in human capital formation, which also includes health and attitude formation as well as the acquisition of knowledge and skills. Similarly, there clearly is an important difference between years of schooling and levels of educational achievement. As we shall see, the failure to make this distinction frequently leads to significant inferential errors and policy mistakes.

Formal schooling must therefore be considered in relation to *informal learning systems*. One of the most important of these is the family. Indeed, in the United States and other developed countries, family income is one of the strongest predictors of average educational achievement. There is, moreover, mounting evidence that many children start kindergarten at a disadvantage because they have had inadequate learning opportunities at home. Sometimes these deficiencies are due to inadequate health care and sometimes poor learning environments. The importance of the family as a learning system is one of the reasons that improving mothers' health, education, and nutrition can do much to break the generational aspects of poverty and low incomes. Indeed, since the mother's health at the time of conception and during pregnancy could influence the child's learning ability, interventions like the federal Women's, Infants', and Children's (WIC) program, which provides health and educational services to low-income women and children, yield high personal, fiscal, and social returns. There is strong international evidence that low birth weight is associated with a variety of learning disorders and that high-quality preschool programs could significantly reduce dropouts, crime, welfare dependency, and lagging school performance.[6] The Committee for Economic Development (CED), a policy-oriented business organization, found that the prenatal component of the WIC program returned $3.00 for every $1.00 spent; a quality preschool program returns $4.75 for each $1.00 spent "because of lower costs of special education, public assistance, and crime." Despite these returns, the WIC and Head Start programs serve only about one-third and one-fifth respectively of potential eligibles.[7]

In developing its education policies a state should also consider the relationships between elementary and secondary schools and "second chance" systems for people who either do not complete high school or do not go on to college. Non-college-bound youth constitute a very large group of about 20 million people, or about half of all 16- to 24-year-olds. In fact, the school-to-work process is one of the weakest links in the American labor market system (or "nonsystem") relative to all other industrialized countries. A few young people go into apprenticeship or technical training programs that lead to the skilled trades. And a larger number enter on-the-job or corporate learning programs. The most serious problems are with high school dropouts and those with limited labor market connections who do not qualify for entry into learning systems that lead to better opportunities. This state of affairs is particularly unfortunate because the earnings of young people who do not receive postsecondary education are declining absolutely and relative to those who do.

There are particularly serious problems for young, non-college-bound blacks.

The problems for the non-college-bound are all the more unfortunate in view of the evidence that "second chance" education and training programs yield high returns to the government and to the young people who participate in them. For example, the CED reported that the Job Corps returned $7,400 per participant for each $5,000 invested (in 1977 dollars). Moreover, computerized learning systems originating in the Job Corps have achieved remarkable success in overcoming basic skills deficiencies. One of these, the Comprehensive Competencies Program, can, with 28 hours of instruction, improve average mathematics skills by 1.4 years and reading skills by 1.0 year. Unfortunately, despite great need, by 1987 funding for federal employment and training programs had been reduced to less than one-third of its 1978 level in real terms.

The learning opportunities for these non-college-bound young people raise important equity issues. College students benefit greatly from the $112 billion postsecondary school system (about $10,000 per enrollee), and after they graduate they are the principal beneficiaries of the $210 billion that U.S. companies spend on education and training. By contrast, the federal government spends only $636 million on training and employment services for youths 21 years old and younger under the Job Training Partnership Act (JTPA) and only $656 million on the highly successful Job Corps.

Equity and economic efficiency coonsiderations therefore require at least a doubling of these "second chance" funds for non-college-bound young people. JTPA, passed in 1982, should also provide more funds for supportive services for trainees and for public service jobs for those who are not likely to find private-sector employment. The JTPA should, in addition, change its performance standards to emphasize services to the most seriously disadvantaged; the present main success criteria —cost reductions and placements—encourage program sponsors to "cream off" the most able and therefore do the least for those who need the most help.[8]

Despite its negatives, the JTPA has the positive effect of giving the states more responsibility for federal employment and training programs. The states are logical human resource development agencies and can relate these "second chance" systems to education and other human resource development activities.

State economic policy makers must, in addition, understand the importance of elementary and secondary education for the country's large and growing *on-the-job learning systems*. Although precise information is not available on corporate education programs, what is known suggests that these institutions invest at least as much in education and training as all American colleges and universities combined and have at least as many students.[9] Over 100 corporations provide in-house courses for their employees that can lead to academic degrees. Indeed, about 18 corporate institutions award degrees themselves, and this number will probably grow.

The data in Table 10.1 from the American Society for Training and Development (ASTD) provide the most comprehensive information on the size of the learning enterprise in the United States in the middle of the 1980s, and suggest that expenditures for training and education by the private sector are over twice as large as all postsecondary training in the United States.

Table 10.1 Scale of U.S. education expenditure, mid-1980s.

	Expenditures ($ billions)
Elementary and secondary schools	144
Postsecondary	94
Employee informal training	180
Employee formal training	30
Government training	5
Total	453

Source: A. P. Carnevale, "The learning enterprise," *Training and Development Journal,* January 1986, 18.

The ASTD, like other analysts, reports high returns to education and training. An analysis of 1983 Census data found real productivity returns to corporate learning systems to be 12.6 per cent for college-educated workers and 19 per cent for the non-college-educated. Not surprisingly, the best jobs in terms of lifetime earnings are those with the best on-the-job learning opportunities:

Econometric studies have consistently shown that 15 percent in the variation of income among Americans can be accounted for by formal education. The remaining 85 percent is accounted for by learning in the workplace. Earnings are driven by the ability of working teams to learn together in the context of appropriate technology.[10]

Corporations have a number of reasons for developing their own learning programs. A major factor is the belief that outside educational institutions cannot provide adequate learning opportunities as flexibly or as efficiently as the companies can do it themselves. An important motive for high-tech companies is to provide remedial work, especially in mathematics, science, and technical subjects in order to overcome the public schools' deficiencies in these subjects. In addition, some companies believe that education not only improves their employees' knowledge and skill, but also makes it possible to recruit and retain the most talented workers. Clearly, moreover, intensified competition has provided a major impetus for corporate education programs. Most high-tech companies are particularly concerned about the quality of their workforces relative to their foreign competitors. The director of Motorola's Training and Education Center (M-TEC), for example, believes Motorola has to supplement the education of entry-level employees who "have nowhere near the mathematical competence of our Japanese competition."[11] This had become a big issue, he said, "because we don't think we can gain the competitive edge unless our workers are better educated." Corporations like Bell South established their own accredited education programs because regular colleges did not have the expertise or the equipment to teach telecommunications courses. Many of these corporate schools have been opened to the public and therefore compete directly with public institutions. The corporate need to provide remedial education has also caused many business leaders to become heavily involved in the education reform movement. In 1987, for instance, only 16 percent of the 21,000 applicants for 780 slots passed the New York Telephone Company's basic reading and reasoning skills test. Many companies perceive a deterioration in the quality of applicants at the very time that their education and skill requirements are increasing. David Kearns, chairman of Xerox, believes that "education is a bigger factor in productivity growth than increased capital, economies of scale, or better allocation of resources."[12]

A 1986 study for the U.S. Department of Labor by the Rand Corporation deepens our understanding of the relationships between corporate and public learning systems as well as of the nature and outcomes of company learning systems.[13] The Rand study confirmed some basic assumptions about the effects of education on earnings and employment:

(a) The rate of return to company-sponsored schooling was about 11 percent. Company training had the largest effect on earnings (27 percent); followed by training from "other sources" (13 percent); and on-the-job training (5 percent). The return to schooling was higher when the type of schooling was a significant factor in obtaining a job.

(b) There were positive associations between earnings, technological change, and education, a fact which seems to confirm the so-called "allocative efficiency" of the schooling hypothesis.[14]

(c) The Rand study also underscores the importance of educational equity. Nonwhite men were significantly less likely to get the kind of postschool training that reduces their probability of unemployment and enhances their earnings, even after controlling for levels of schooling and other worker characteristics. There were, however, no significant differences between nonwhite and white women, a finding which confirms other studies. Moreover, a very low proportion of the economically disadvantaged had company training which, as noted earlier, had the highest positive economic results in terms of low unemployment and high earnings gain. Young white men had a significantly higher probability of receiving any training as well as company training.

(d) A major problem with on-the-job training and learning systems is that almost all of it is carried out in large firms, while most of the job growth is in smaller companies. Probably 200 to 300 large companies account for half of the formal training paid for by for-profit companies. Policies therefore need to be developed to make it possible for small companies to meet their education and training needs, probably through associations or learning consortia.

Basic trends

Finally, state education policies must be based on realistic assessments of the major trends affecting economic and human resource development. Three of the most important of these—internationalization, technological change, and certain basic demographic and labor market developments—are "universal imperatives" in the sense that they influence the lives of people everywhere.

INTERNATIONALIZATION

Internationalization increases economic interdependence and therefore makes it much more difficult for countries to pursue independent economic policies. In particular, internationalization breaks the connections between domestic interest rates, consumption, and investment that made macroeconomic policies so effective in the 25 years following World War II. With internationalization, however, an effort to stimulate the U.S. economy when other economies are stagnant will increase imports, thus breaking the connections between increased consumption, investment, and employment in the United States. Similarly, efforts to check inflation by restricting the money supply in order to slow economic expansion will affect exchange rates as well as interest rates. As a consequence, economic activity is stifled because of rising exchange rates (raising the value of the dollar and thus stimulating imports and restricting exports) as well as by higher interest rates. And, following from that, higher levels of unemployment are required to check a given level of inflation.

Internationalization also greatly changes the economics of the firm (or microeconomic policies). Not only has internationalization compelled companies to adopt global strategies, but U.S. companies have also been forced to revamp their internal management and pricing policies. Oligopolies, which dominated basic mass production industries in the United States before the 1970s, attempted to maintain prices and lay off workers during recessions. Changes in demand were therefore absorbed by output and employment and not by wages and prices. Companies in other countries, especially in Japan, developed pricing policies that made oligopoly obsolete. These policies hold employment relatively fixed and adjust to changing demand by flexible price and labor compensation systems. This obviously made it possible for foreign competitors to gain market share from oligopolies in downturns (when foreign competitors reduced prices and held output) and in upturns (when competitors had the capacity to take advantage of increased demand). Flexible labor compensation is achieved through a bonus system that accounts for about a third of the Japanese worker's income. Bonuses depend on company performance. It is obviously much easier not to pay a bonus when sales fall off than it is to cut wages. The firms' adaptability also makes it possible for the entire Japanese economy to adjust more easily to change, greatly enhancing the effectiveness of economic policies to increase employment and output or stabilize prices.

Internationalization makes competitiveness much more important. The United States is a high-wage country, making it difficult to compete through wages alone. Unless greater attention is paid to other ways to compete, American real wages will decline, as they have since the 1970s. Competitiveness requires much more attention to productivity, quality, and flexibility than was the case with traditional U.S. oligopolies. Competing at higher wages puts a premium on technological innovation and better management systems. If the United States loses these advantages, it competes according to wages. The United States has no clear management advantages. *Its basic choice is thus very clear: compete by lowering its standard of living or become more productive and give greater attention to quality and flexibility.*

The requirements of international competition have likewise altered state economic development strategies. Political leaders now realize that a human resource development strategy makes more sense than the prior "growth at any cost" strategies. With greater international corporate mobility, states will lose a development contest based on a strategy of attracting industry by depressing wages and labor standards. Even minimum-wage jobs in the United States are high paying by Third World standards. This is one of the reasons why it no longer makes much sense to attract industry that is on its way to the Third World, as many states have done, especially in the South. This "growth at any price" strategy might have helped a few people, but it consigned most workers to noncompetitive, marginal, low-wage jobs with very limited multiplier effects. It became equally clear that in an internationalized economy what was good for companies was not necessarily good for a state's people. Since people are less mobile than capital and technologies, measures to develop human resources are a much surer way to improve the conditions of people, states, and communities.[15]

TECHNOLOGY

As noted, *technology* is another important universal imperative. We must, however, be very careful about the meaning of technology. To some it means only machinery or equipment, but this definition is far too narrow. Technology really means the way to do things, or more precisely, the use of knowledge, tools, and skills to solve practical problems and extend human capabilities. In a fundamental sense, technology is ideas and knowledge embodied in people, processes, products, management systems, organizational forms, and structures as well as in machinery. Thus, technological innovation and processes are learning systems, though ordinarily taking place outside of school.

Clearly, the skill requirements are greater as one progresses through various stages in the development and use of technology.[16] Much more creativity, problem solving, and experimental skills are required during the developmental and early implementation stages than when maturity is reached and most of the accumulated skill and knowledge has been embodied in the technology and can be easily copied. A major argument of this chapter is that a high-income state has to have more of its workforce involved in the "leading edge" stages before technology is standardized. A major problem for older U.S. industries is the fact that their production systems stressed the use of standardized technologies and of relatively unskilled workers—precisely the kinds of systems most exportable to low-wage places.

Fortunately, both human capital and competitiveness conditions are such that in many areas technology and the quality of workforces will make it possible for wages to be above world market levels. So far, the lowest-wage less developed countries (LDCs) have not been very competitive because of the quality of their workforces, the growing skill requirements for the most advanced technology, and the fact that manufacturing processes are becoming much less labor-intensive and more knowledge- and information-intensive. What is happening is not so much the substitution of physical capital for labor, but the substitution of information for labor and capital.

There is professional disagreement over the *impact* of technology on job skills. Some labor economists have argued that industrialization requires higher skills and higher levels of education because workers must be more mobile, deal with more complicated equipment, and understand more complex processes.[17] Others argue that industrialization and/or capitalism lead to "deskilling" because the technology permits management to fragment and deskill jobs in order to control labor. Indeed, this was the major objective of "scientific management," which has been so influential with U.S. managers.[18]

A June 1987 study by the Hudson Institute disagrees with the "deskilling" hypothesis.[19] Assuming the same skill requirements for occupations in 2000 as in 1984, this study forecasts an average gain in education requirements of 25 percent across all occupational categories, but a growth rate of two to three times faster is expected for the fastest growing fields—lawyers, scientists, and health professionals. In the mid-1980s only 22 percent of jobs required college degrees, but more than half of all the jobs created between 1984 and 2000 are projected to require education beyond high school, "and almost a third will be filled by college graduates."[20]

As noted, some analysts argue that the deskilling hypothesis is supported by the "scientific management" tradition in U.S. companies. Despite evidence of their inappropriateness for modern production systems, the methods and beliefs developed and popularized by

Frederick W. Taylor almost a century ago have left a very strong imprint on U.S. companies and schools.[21]

Nevertheless, there is mounting evidence of continuing resistances and counterforces to Taylorism. One of the most important of these has been the continued and growing importance of traditional skills in automated processes, despite the contrary hopes of authoritarian managers and machine vendors.[22] Brooks and colleagues conclude that:

> Numerous case studies suggest that skilled machinists perform better on computerized systems than those without such experience. Informal interventions, improvisation, and negotiated unsanctioned transactions between workers are much more important to the smooth operation of even the most automated production processes than is often recognized by managers and planners. All of this suggests that the traditional Taylorist management approach may often be creating obstacles to the effective uses of new manufacturing technology in practice.[23]

Despite these disagreements, the following hypotheses are worth exploring:

(a) Emerging technologies will produce rapid changes, placing a premium on adaptable organizations, institutions, individuals, and policies. There probably will not be too much displacement in the short run (i.e., 10 to 15 years), but more in the 1990s and beyond when many of the more sophisticated systems become more widely utilized.

(b) The employment effects of high technology will depend heavily on national policies and private management systems. The critical assumptions behind the optimistic scenario are (i) that national and world economic growth will absorb workers who are displaced by technology; (ii) that markets or other processes will make it possible for resources to be shifted into alternative employment as workers are displaced by technology; and (iii) that cooperative, participatory management systems are developed.

(c) The use of the most productive technology must play an important rôle in the competitiveness of U.S. industry. While it will be possible to perform many tasks in the high-tech workplace with limited education, *the most effective operations* of that workplace will require more, better, and different kinds of education. Workers will have to have much more knowledge than they use at any given time in order to repair equipment, solve problems, communicate with and coordinate parts of worldwide production processes, and participate more effectively in management. Moreover, one of the most important skills in the competitive workforce of the future will require more attention to learning, the analysis of data, the management of responsibility, and the ability to use abstractions. The most competitive workplaces of the future probably will blur the lines between management and workers and there will be more worker ownership and control.[24] Management in the most competitive enterprises will be more concerned about worker security because that strengthens management and worker commitment to quality and productivity, human resource development within the firm (where more and more education and training will take place), and flexibility in human resource use. *There is a direct relationship between employment security and management's willingness to finance the human capital investments required in the most competitive workplaces.* Workers in the most competitive firms will no longer rely exclusively on wages, but will rely increasingly on such nonwage compensation as productivity-based bonuses and ownership dividends. Further, these income systems will compensate workers more for what they know than for what they do. While management will be more concerned about worker security, workers and their organizations will concern themselves more with the economic viability of the enterprises where they work.

There is strong evidence that worker participation can improve the introduction of technology. In this respect robots and automated systems have been much more readily accepted by Japanese than by American workers. American workers not only fear that robots will displace them, but they also are concerned about deskilling and the loss of job control.

One of the most dramatic illustrations of the importance of management systems in international competitiveness is the New United Motor Manufacturing Company Inc. (NUMMI), a joint venture between General Motors (GM) and Toyota in Fremont, California. GM closed this plant in the early 1980s because its management could not make it competitive. It was reopened under Toyota management with the same union (the United Auto Workers), workers, and equipment which GM had used. The main change was a management system that stressed the reduction of job classifications from several hundred to three; the elimination of many of the élitist trappings of management that had been used by GM (i.e., private parking, dining rooms, and a different pay system); much greater worker participation in production systems; a bonus system that makes part of a worker's compensation dependent upon company performance; and greater job security for workers. As a consequence of these changes, NUMMI has become one of the most productive auto plants in the world, much more productive than GM's highly automated operations in Michigan. The lesson from this experience is that a more participatory system that gives workers greater control and direct benefits for their greater contribution can improve quality and productivity.

DEMOGRAPHIC AND LABOR MARKET CHANGES

Some of the most important demographic trends include: the aging of the workforce; and the declining proportion of whites and the increasing proportion of minorities.

An estimated 29 percent of the net increase in the workforce between 1985 and 2000 will be minorities. In 2015 there will be 91 million minority citizens in the U.S. population, with 3 million more hispanics than blacks. Minorities will make up 34 percent of the population (contrasted with 17 percent in 1984) and probably a higher proportion of the workforce. Almost all of the net increase in the workforce will be women and minorities. These changes are mainly because of immigration and the age distribution of each group. According to the 1980 Census, the average white person was 31 years old, the average black 25, and the average Hispanic 22.[25] One of the most important labor market trends is the increased employment of women, which will continue to challenge prevailing employment practices, and the problems of minorities and whites with limited education, which will cause youth unemployment to continue to be a serious problem, despite the declining numbers of young workers. Family structure developments have clear implications for public schools. Often schools have been called upon to compensate for inadequate home environments where there is only one parent, incomes are low, parents have limited education, or parents have to spend so much time making a living that they have limited time for school or to help their children learn. Teachers and school administrators must understand the background of their students if they are to provide effective learning experiences.

There will, moreover, continue to be shortages of some workers due primarily to aging and demographics. For example, about half of the nation's primary and secondary school teachers will retire between 1985 and 1991. These were the teachers of the Baby Boom generation whose children are now in the schools. Since there have been increased job opportunities for women and minorities in other occupations, fewer are entering teaching. Thus, the increased demand and reduced supply will create a very serious shortage of qualified teachers.[26]

Implications for education and learning systems

As noted earlier, the implications of internationalization for workplace skills depend critically on the definition of competitiveness. The fundamental competitiveness question is: How can American companies compete in the U.S. and foreign markets on terms that will make it possible for Americans to maintain or improve their incomes? In technical terms Americans could compete by worsening terms of trade, as they did during the 1970s, even though their trade appeared to be balanced. They were giving up more in real terms to pay for their imports. During the first half of the 1980s, they not only continued to give up more in real terms, but incurred rising net foreign debts as well.[27]

If we assume supportive, or at least neutral, public policies are in place, we can either compete by lowering our standard of living or by paying more attention to the kind of competitiveness that will make it possible for us to maintain or improve our real incomes. These outcomes can be achieved mainly by using leading-edge (not standardized) technology, which, in turn, depends mainly on the quality of the workforce.

There are, unfortunately, no unambiguous measures of workforce quality. One common measure is average years of schooling, where the U.S. ranks higher than any other country. But for a variety of reasons this is not a very good indicator of the quality of a country's workforce. First, not all years of schooling are equal. The U.S. has a relatively short school day and the shortest school year of any major industrial country (175 days versus 249 in Japan). In fact, the typical Japanese high school graduate has the equivalent of at least two more years of actual class time than the typical U.S. high school graduate. Second, time spent in school yields different levels of productivity in terms of educational achievement. Third, as we have seen, only a relatively small part of a person's income-earning knowledge and skill is learned in school.

Some experts argue that the United States has the highest quality upper half of its workforce of any country, but a poorer bottom half than any of its major competitors. This judgment would seem to be confirmed by a number of studies, including the 1986 National Assessment of Educational Progress (NAEP).[28] While this report found that 95 percent of young adults reach or surpass a fourth grade reading level (the standard of literacy adopted by the military almost 50 years ago), this standard was grossly inadequate for modern labor market requirements. For example, only 20 percent of young adults with a high school education or more could write a decent letter, only 12 percent could arrange common fractions in size order, only 4.9 percent could decipher a bus or train schedule, and less than 20 percent could determine the amount of a tip, given the percentage of a bill.

The correlations between behavior and achievement scores have caused widespread concern, not only about the long-run decline in test scores by U.S. students, but also about their low standing on international tests. Analyzing international data, Lerner found the mean scores of U.S. 18-year-old high school seniors to be in the bottom half of rank order scores 13 times and in the top half only 6. American students ranked particularly low in mathematics and some science tests.[29] The latest data confirm these results, with U.S. students ranking near the bottom compared with 24 other countries in the test administered in 1986. U.S. twelfth graders ranked 17th in biology, 22nd in chemistry, and 21st in physics. In a study of 17 countries, American fifth-graders ranked 8th in science achievement (Japan and Korea were tied for the lead), and U.S. ninth graders were about tied with Hong Kong, Thailand, and Singapore for last place.[30]

A good analysis of the kind of higher order thinking skills more workers will be required to have in an internationalized information world is provided by Lauren Resnick, a cognitive psychologist at the University of Pittsburgh. According to Resnick, higher order thinking

(a) is *nonalgorithmic*—the course of action is not fully specified in advance;

(b) is *complex*—the whole process is not mentally "visible" from any single vantage point;

(c) often yields *multiple* rather than single solutions;

(d) involves *nuanced* judgments and interpretations;

(e) involves the application of *multiple* and sometimes *conflicting* criteria;

(f) involves *uncertainty*, because everything related to the task is not known in advance;

(g) involves *self-regulation* of the thinking process rather than control by others;
(h) requires *imposed meanings* by finding patterns or structure in apparent disorder;
(i) requires effort.[31]

Resnick argues that there have been two different traditions in the U.S. school system: one for the masses and the other for the élites. The élite system involves higher order thinking. She argues: "Although it is not new to include thinking, problem solving, and reasoning in someone's curriculum, it is new to include it in everyone's curriculum."[32]

In previous sections I have assumed, along with most policy makers, that there is a positive relationship between education on the one hand and productivity, economic growth, and improved personal incomes and individual welfare on the other. We should emphasize, however, that not all analysts accept this conclusion, and some argue that schools make little difference in student achievement. Although this negative view is a minority position, this is too important an issue to be "solved," as economists frequently do, by assuming it away. Moreover, we must understand the evidence required to settle this issue before we can take measures to improve schools, the need for which is almost universally acknowledged. I therefore now turn to these issues.

The relationship of human resource development to economic development: evidence and issues

This section examines in greater depth the evidence for the impact of education on various economic outcomes. There is little dispute about the facts: there are clear individual and national associations between education and income. But the basic issue is over cause and effect, i.e., whether the higher levels of education *caused* the higher income or whether higher incomes caused higher levels of education.

One important fact discussed above was the dramatic growth during the 1980s in the relative earnings gap between college and high school graduates. We also noted the *assumption* from the Hudson Institute study that future jobs would require higher levels of education, assuming those jobs would require the same levels of education as similar jobs now require. This is an important assumption but is hardly *proof* that those jobs will in fact require more education.

Table 10.2 illustrates the gross impact of education on earnings, which can be seen by comparing the earnings of 20- to 24-year-old out-of-school males in real (1984) dollars by level of education

As these data show, income generally rises with level of education, and the income losses between 1973 and 1984 were less for those young males aged 20 to 24 who had higher levels of education. Except for black male college graduates, the only group to experience higher incomes (16.3 percent) in 1984 than in 1973, the losses were generally higher for blacks and hispanics.

Before exploring the evidence with respect to education and economic performance, we should recall the distinction between *education* (skills and knowledge, or what some analysts use as the measures of the "quality of schooling") and *schooling*. Early studies measuring the relationship between schooling and various social outcomes found very weak relationships, especially when family incomes were controlled for. By contrast, studies that measure the relationship between basic educational skills or competencies, regardless of years of schooling, have found strong positive relationships with various economic and social indices. For example, Berlin and Sum[33] have compiled evidence that individuals with basic skills do better in school work, have higher self-esteem, and are more likely to complete additional years of school, obtain a high school diploma, go on to college, complete college, work more hours, earn higher wages, enter into marriage, and be more productive workers. At the same time, those

Table 10.2 Comparison of the earnings of out-of-school males in real (1984) dollars.

	Real mean earnings ($)		Change in earnings, 1973–4, 20- to 24-year-old males (%)			
	All 20- to 24-year-old males		all	white	black	hispanic
Level of education	1973	1984				
No diploma	11,210	6,552	−41.6	−38.7	−61.3	−38.6
High school graduate	14,342	10,020	−30.1	−26.1	−52.2	−28.1
College graduate	13,443	12,443	−11.0	−12.2	+16.3	−14.9

Source: March 1974 and March 1985 *Current population survey* public use tapes; calculations by Center for Labor Market Studies, Northeastern University; G. Berlin & A. Sum, *Toward a more perfect union* (New York: Ford Foundation, 1988), p. 9.

without good basic skills "will more likely be school dropouts, teenage parents, welfare dependent, or criminally involved."[34]

Education, productivity, and economic development

Just as an individual's income and quality of life improve with added investment in human capital, so too, many have argued, human resource development has a major influence on the income and quality of life of the entire society. Logically, human resource development is important to economic performance and competitiveness because all the keys to competitiveness—efficiency, quality, flexibility, and innovation—depend on well-educated, well-trained people. Countries with limited physical resources, like Germany and Japan, have enjoyed superior economic performance because they have been forced to develop their human resources. Thus, it can be argued that developed people are an almost unlimited asset; undeveloped people can be a serious liability to a society.

What is the evidence for the causal relationship between education and productivity growth? Despite the general preoccupation of many economists with financial affairs and physical capital, a growing body of evidence demonstrates that knowledge, the advancement of technology, and improvements in the quality of human resources are the main sources of economic growth and productivity. On the basis of reviews of several studies, Carnevale concluded that

> People, not machines, are the well-spring of productivity. Since 1929, growth in on-the-job know-how, the reallocation of labor through retraining, and increased labor quality through education, training and health care consistently have accounted for more than three-quarters of productivity improvements and most of our growth in national income. By comparison, over the same period, machine capital has contributed a consistent and disappointing 20 percent or less.[35]

Dennison and others have made the point that human resource development has always been a major determinant of economic development.[36]

Much of the early economic research on education and "human capital" was stimulated by Theodore Schultz's pioneering studies, for which he was awarded the Nobel Prize in economics.[37] Schultz, an agricultural and development economist, believes that much of what really matters about economics would be learned if we could explain why people are poor. In his view, the main causes of human poverty have less to do with availability of land and physical resources than was assumed by most development experts of the 1950s and 1960s, when he was doing his seminal work: "The decisive factors of production in improving the welfare of poor people are not space, energy and cropland; the decisive factors are the improvement in population quality and advances in knowledge."[38] Schultz believes that educated, healthy, motivated people have been able to overcome physical resource constraints. He points to the evidence from agriculture, where research has greatly improved productivity by substituting knowledge for land. Indeed, despite great increases in total output there have been no net additions of physical resources to U.S. agriculture since 1925. "The substitution process is well illustrated by corn: the corn acreage in the United States in 1979, 33 million acres less than in 1932, produced 7.6 billion bushels, three times the amount produced in 1932."[39]

Human capital improvements are particularly important in creating entrepreneurship or improving the ability of people "to perceive, interpret, and respond to new events in a context of risk" and "adjusting to the disequilibrium inherent in the process of modernization."

One of the paradoxes examined by Schultz is the finding that "*the rate of return on investment in human capital has tended to exceed the rate of return on physical capital*" (emphasis added). Most economists not only have calculated returns to education that are large and greater than the return to physical assets, but some believe the calculated rates of return (in terms of *money wages*) actually understate the true returns to education because these calculations ordinarily exclude fringes and a variety of nonmonetary benefits.[40]

International comparisons

International comparisons strengthen our understanding of the individual, fiscal (i.e., where government makes the investment), and social returns to education. In a 1980 report summarizing estimates from 44 countries, the World Bank reached the following general conclusions:

(a) The social and private returns to primary education were higher than for other levels.
(b) Private returns exceed social returns, especially at the university level.
(c) All rates of return to education investments were well above the 10 percent yardstick that developing countries use for the opportunity cost of capital.

(d)   The highest rates of return were in the developing countries.[41]

Table 10.3 shows rates of return to higher and secondary education in the United States. During the 1970s there was a slight decline in the private rate of return to higher education, but relative stability in the return to secondary education.

A technical problem involved in these calculations is the assumption that education improves productivity, which, in turn, causes higher wages. This is a problem because wages may or may not reflect productivity—they could be the result of such factors as monopoly or monopsony power, market imperfections, or custom. To avoid this problem, the World Bank commissioned a study of the relationship between education and physical productivity in agriculture. This study concluded that four years of elementary education improved a farmer's productivity 8.7 percent on the average relative to a farmer with no education.[42] If the complementary relationships of education to factor inputs are included, the productivity of a farmer with four years of education is 13.2 percent higher than for a farmer with no formal education. Complementarity between education and other factors has rather consistently been found to improve performance, whether in such personal outcomes as health and income or in productive functions, as in the agriculture example.

Other World Bank studies have attempted to overcome some of the earlier technical criticisms of studies suggesting linkages between

Table 10.3   Returns to education in the United States (%).

Year	Education level Secondary Higher	
	Social rate of return	
1939	18.2	10.7
1944	14.2	10.6
1959	10.1	11.3
1969	10.7	10.9
	Private rate of return	
1970	11.3	8.8
1971	12.5	8.0
1972	11.3	7.8
1973	12.0	5.5
1974	14.8	4.8
1975	12.8	5.3
1976	11.0	5.3

Source: G. Psacharopoulos, "Returns on education: an updated international comparison," *Comparitive Education* **17**, 1981, 335.

education and output. One such study of the relationships between literacy, life expectancy, and economic growth in 83 developing countries for the period 1960–77 found that the 12 countries with the fastest growth had levels of literacy and life expectancy well above average, which suggests that rapidly growing countries have well-developed human resources.[43]

In order to allow for the interactive relationships between economic development, education, and other aspects of human resource development, Wheeler developed a simultaneous model which was applied to 88 developing countries. This model suggested that education, nutrition, and health all contribute to the growth of output, directly and indirectly, by lowering birth rates and increasing investment. Wheeler found that increasing the literacy rate from 20 to 30 percent increased gross domestic product by 8 to 16 percent.[44] In a similar study published in 1982, Morris not only found a strong relationship between education and economic growth, but also found that physical capital investments have less effect when not supported by educational investments.[45]

Psacharopoulos and Woodhall conclude, on the basis of the World Bank's extensive experience with investments in education, that

> The answer to the question Is it worth investing in education? is ... resoundingly positive. The question Is it more profitable to invest in human skills and capacities or in physical capital? is misguided, however, since it assumes that investment in people and investment in machines are alternatives. Investment choices should be concerned with *how* rather than whether education can contribute to growth. Their proper concern is which particular combination of general and technical education, which subject balance, which teaching methods, and which distribution of resources and opportunities for schooling would allow education to have the maximum impact on development and would best complement investment in physical capital and infrastructure.[46]

Basic competencies

As noted earlier, one problem with some studies of returns to education is the fact that they equate "schooling" with "education" or skills. When these adjustments are made, conclusions often are changed. For example, in calculating returns to education, it is very important to adjust years of schooling for achievement. This can be done by looking at scores on achievement tests like the

NAEP reading, writing, and mathematics tests and the Armed Forces Qualification Test (AFQT), all of which find large achievement gaps for minorities and low-income people, who usually are concentrated in the bottom 25th percentile. On average, minorities' scores were about 70 percent of whites' scores in the mid-1980s, and the average black 17-year-old was reading at about the same level as the average white 13-year-old.

Relating achievement to competence makes it possible to understand better why black high school graduates have lower earnings and employment levels than white high school dropouts. Regardless of the level of schooling, those with higher skills earn more, and this pattern holds regardless of sex, race, or family income.[47] Berlin and Sum also demonstrate the close relationship between basic skills and such pathologies as teenage pregnancy, school dropout, and youth unemployment. These analysts note, in addition, the tendency for education achievement of low-income students to deteriorate more during the summer months than is true for higher income groups. This summer loss phenomenon is very important: according to the evidence from studies by Barbara Heynes, 80 percent of the year-to-year differences in educational achievement between advantaged and disadvantaged students are due to summer loss.[48]

One pilot project, the Summer Training and Education Project (STEP), has demonstrated that the summer loss in mathematics can be completely overcome and the reading loss greatly reduced. STEP is a five-site demonstration project operated jointly by school officials and employment and training staff employed with the federal summer jobs program. STEP provides 14- and 15-year-olds who are behind in school with a half day of work experience (more than 80 hours during the summer) and a half day of intensive remedial education, as well as 18 hours of "life planning instruction." At the end of STEP's first summer, youth who had work experience only (the control group) lost between three-fourths and a full grade equivalent in reading and a half grade in mathematics. STEP participants, by contrast, lost only 0.3 of a grade in reading and actually gained 0.2 of a grade in mathematics. Black and hispanic students did especially well.[49]

Public school efficiency

The evidence reviewed so far makes a fairly compelling case for positive (though not perfect) relationships between human capital, education, productivity, and growth and improvements in personal welfare. This does not mean, however, that these positive relationships are due to *schooling*, a subject to which we now turn.

Many studies have attempted to determine the factors responsible for efficiency in public schools.[50] Although the scope and methods differ in these studies, they generally find substantial differences in the "quality" of schools, measured by performance on standardized tests, but

> differences in quality do not seem to reflect variations in expenditures, class sizes, or other commonly measured attributes of schools and teachers. Instead they appear to result from differences in teacher "skills" that defy detailed description, but that possibly can be measured directly.[51]

One way to gauge performance is in terms of scores on the Scholastic Aptitude Test (SAT).[52] The steady decline in SAT verbal and quantitative scores beginning in 1963 has been a cause of considerable comment. The verbal scores fell about one half of a standard deviation between 1963 and 1979, but increased by less than 0.1 of a standard deviation between 1979 and 1984; the magnitudes were not as large, but the mathematics scores followed the same pattern. Between 1980 and 1987, SAT scores regained only 16 of the 90 points they lost between 1963 and 1980. While scores for white students declined slightly, minority students gained between 1976 and 1987: black students' composite scores increased from 686 to 728, hispanics' from 781 to 803, while white scores declined from 944 to 936. Thus, while there are wide gaps between the scores of minorities and nonminorities, these differences have been narrowing in recent years.[53]

Other recent changes in public school indicators include:

(a) Real expenditure per average daily attendance (ADA) more than doubled between 1950 and 1983, from $1,598 in 1950 to $3,261 in 1983.

(b) Pupil–teacher ratios declined as follows:

	1960	1980
Public schools (total):	25.8	19.0
elementary	28.4	20.5
secondary	21.7	17.1
Private schools (total):	30.7	17.9
elementary	36.1	19.3
secondary	18.6	15.0

(c) Average teachers' salaries rose dramatically during the 1960s, but (like the wages of all workers) fell in real terms in the 1970s, despite the aging (and therefore greater experience) of teachers. In real terms, teachers' salaries were $17,406 in 1960, $23,296 in 1971, and $21,790 in 1983. According to the American Federation of Teachers, average salaries for teachers increased from $23,551 in 1984–5 to $28,085 in 1987–8.[54] As a result of widespread concern about teacher shortages and school reform, teachers' salaries have increased sharply since 1983 while real wages generally have been stagnant. On the basis of these statistics, critics argue that the schools have deteriorated despite increased teachers' salaries and expenditures per ADA. If, they argue, schools were efficient or had much to do with education, how could there be declining SAT scores on the one hand and increasing per-pupil expenditures, declining class sizes, and rising teachers' salaries, on the other?

Economists have tried to answer this question by explaining the factors responsible for school performance through use of production functions (or benefit-cost or cost-quality) studies which relate output (SAT or other scores) or dependent variables to a series of independent (or causal) variables; these ordinarily are such matters as expenditure per ADA or the characteristics of teachers (i.e., education, salaries, experience, or skills).

Most of the early studies failed to show clear and unambiguous relationships between inputs and student performance:

(a) An early production function study was the very controversial 1966 *Coleman report on equality of educational opportunity*, mandated by the Civil Rights Act of 1964. This report appeared to show that family backgrounds and characteristics of students and not differences in schools accounted for most of the differences in student performance.[55]

(b) Some critics argue that schooling does not improve the skills and earnings of students, but merely acts as a screening device to select the most able.[56] Screening rather than skill improvement implies that the social returns to schooling are smaller than the individual returns.

(c) Jencks and colleagues argue that "The characteristics of a school's output depend largely on a single input, namely the characteristics of entering children. Everything else, the school budget, its policies, the characteristics of the teachers—is either secondary or clearly irrelevant."[57]

(d) Bowles and Gintis argue that differences in earnings are caused mainly by capitalist social structure rather than the skill differentials produced by schooling. They also argue that schools adapt to the capitalist social structure rather than being an independent force.[58]

(e) Hanushek, summarizing well over a 100 such studies, concludes:

(i) "of the 112 estimates of the effects of class size [on student performance], only 23 are statistically significant, and only 9 show a statistically significant relationship of the expected positive sign."

(ii) Similarly, most of the 106 studies of the influence of teacher education show no relationship to student performance.

(iii) Teacher experience is one weak, but possible, exception: "a clear majority of estimated coefficients [point] in the right direction, and almost 30 percent are statistically significant."

(iv) Sixty studies of teachers' salaries and 65 of expenditures per student "provide no separate indication of a relationship between expenditures and achievements. Most data do show a strong positive simple correlation between school expenditures and achievement, but the strength of this relationship disappears when differences in family background are controlled for."[59]

(v) Several factors are most strongly correlated with student performance. One such factor is family background: "Virtually regardless of how measured, more educated and more wealthy parents have children who perform better on average."[60] A second factor is the marked quality differences in schools and teachers. Teachers who perform better on verbal ability tests have better classroom performance, though the relationship is not strong.[61] Finally, the skills of teachers as assessed by their supervisors have been found to be highly correlated with their students' adjusted achievement gains.[62]

Effective schools research

One of the main criticisms of early work on the relationship between schooling and incomes was the fact that studies like Coleman's were based on input-output techniques that failed to capture the impact of the kinds of *processes within schools* that might actually have been responsible for improved student achievement. Coleman concluded in his 1966 study that "differences between schools account for only a small fraction of differences in pupil achievement" and that "the school appears unable to exert independent influences to make achievement levels less dependent on the child's background—and this is true within each ethnic group, just as it is between groups."[63] Similarly, Jencks concluded in 1972 that equalizing the quality of elementary or high schools would have only a marginal effect on decreasing cognitive inequality.[64] The main criticism of the Coleman and Jencks input-output studies was their failure to account for the processes by which resources were used in the schools to achieve desired outcomes.[65]

Subsequent studies sought to overcome these defects. Studies that analyzed the allocation of school resources to particular students found positive relationships.[66] Moreover, studies found more positive relationships when they looked at the effects of specific schools rather than at the average effect of all schools. And within these effective schools, a consensus emerged that student achievement could be improved if schools were able to achieve certain characteristics like strong leadership, positive expectations about their students' learning abilities, emphasis on basic skills, allocation of school resources to basic skills goals, an orderly atmosphere, frequent monitoring of performance, and constant feedback to students about their performance.[67]

These "effective schools" studies have been criticized on a number of grounds, including: examining too few schools; inconsistent and sometimes contradictory findings; limited focus; and low standards of effectiveness.

A major criticism of the effective schools studies was their failure to demonstrate *how* the factors associated with effective schools actually increased learning. Moreover, since family backgrounds have usually been found to be strongly associated with achievement, the failure of these studies adequately to control for, or measure the effects of, these background factors on learning weakened their acceptability. We should note, in addition, that even when "effective schools" improved the conditions of disadvantaged students, the standards for success were often far below the national average or the levels in schools attended by higher income students.[68]

Despite these shortcomings, critics acknowledge that the effective schools research has extended the debate and had a more positive effect on public opinion than the pessimism implied by the Coleman and Jencks studies. Moreover, despite methodological shortcomings, critics usually concede that the effective schools conclusions are essentially valid. Purkey and Smith, for example, found a substantive case emerging from the literature. There is a good deal of common sense to the notion that a school is more likely to have relatively high reading or math scores if the staffs agree to emphasize those subjects, are serious and purposeful about the task of teaching, expect students to learn, and create a safe and comfortable environment in which students accurately perceive the school's expectations for academic success and come to share them.[69]

One of the most important conclusions from the effective schools research is that *schools do in fact differ in their effectiveness* and that the *differences are important.* Moreover, as noted, research by economists using production function techniques has demonstrated positive relationships between resources per pupil, achievement scores, and earnings. However, a puzzling outcome of these studies was that while total expenditures per pupil seem to be associated with positive effects, particular expenditures for such things as library books, science laboratories, and the size and age of schools "in general are not statistically powerful determinants of school effectiveness."[70] On the other hand, the character of the human resources used in the schools seems to matter a great deal. These include the teacher's intellectual skills as measured by verbal ability tests, the quality of the college attended by the teacher, and the teacher's experience. Most studies show some teachers to be systematically more effective than others.

A major problem with many of the economic studies of education is the fact that they are based on assumptions from standard production function theory, which assumes that a school is like a factory with certain inputs and outputs (achievement, wages, human capital). The standard production function assumptions are: (a) Decision makers are rational, so that they operate on their production functions, i.e., they choose inputs and techniques rationally from a set of well-defined and well-known possibilities. (b) The relationships between inputs and outputs (i.e., technologies) are fairly well established and generally available. As noted in the discussion of management systems, these standard assumptions of traditional economic theory are highly questionable even when applied to a manufacturing firm. A major defect of both "scientific management" and production function theory is their assumption that there is "one best" way to do a thing. In fact, of course, there is no one best technology for every work situation. Indeed, the objective of effective management systems should be to discover the technology and "production function" that is most suited to them. As Murnane and Nelson emphasize, many techniques used in production are *tacit* and *idiosyncratic*; "tacit" means a capability that is "felt or intuited" rather than well articulated, and "idiosyncratic" means there is no "one best way" to do a particular thing. Murnane and Nelson's basic theme is "that the conventional economic theory of production, based as it is on an implicit assumption that techniques can be largely described, explained, and learned through scrutiny of blueprints does not hold, even approximately, in a field like education."[71]

These analysts suggest an alternative which explains the puzzle of why aggregate expenditures per pupil have positive associations with outcomes—and why the quality of both teachers and fellow students make a difference—while the inputs of particular physical resources do not seem to make much difference, or why certain techniques work in some settings and not others:

> [T]he variation in educational practice is unavoidable and in fact is crucial to effective teaching. The reason is that effective teaching requires information about the skills and personalities of students and about how students interact that can only be obtained during the classroom teaching process. Also, teachers vary greatly in the kinds of interactions they are good at. In other words, effective teaching requires intensive problem solving activity, and creative and personalized responses to frequent unpredicted circumstances. It is clear that this interpretation . . . casts a shadow on the faith that what one teacher or school is doing with success, another can replicate with comparable effect.[72]

The main conclusion I draw from this is that the best approach to educational reform is to bring together good teachers and students and create learning situations where the best techniques can be discovered in each setting. There is no one "best" set that can be discovered through quantitative analysis that would fit all situations. A good teacher has the ability to help learners discover what works for them, understands what is worth learning, and provides *incentives* for students to learn. As noted, moreover, the general requirements found by the effective schools research are useful guides.

Conclusions

This chapter is based on the assumption that changes in technology and the structure of the global economy have altered the rules of international economic competition, to which state human resource development strategies must adjust. Our choices, moreover, have become increasingly clear: we can become competitive by reducing our standard of living or by developing and using leading-edge technologies. The development and use of leading-edge technologies, in turn, require a workforce with very different and higher order thinking and communication skills than traditionally taught by U.S. schools. If the United States wishes to be a high-wage, full-employment economy, the evidence is very strong that the nation must develop very different learning systems. But school reform will not do much to improve competitiveness in the short run. Unless we give greater attention to upgrading the skills and knowledge of people who already are out of school, we are not likely to meet the economic challenges we face in the next 10 to 15 years, when our fate is likely to be determined. Throughout most of America's history, improvements in productivity have been relatively easy. The country has been able to manage with an educated élite, with most workers supplying mainly brawn. If my analysis is correct, Americans will now have to think for a living. Americans historically have valued schooling but not education; they now have to value education and intellectual activity.

In order to meet their new challenge, the states must give much greater attention to improving the productivity of schools and other learning systems. This is so because of the magnitude of the challenge faced: almost all students must be brought up to a level that no more than a third has ever met before. The only way even to approximate this challenge is to make monumental improvements in educational productivity. The required changes are not likely to be achieved by simply adding resources to the present system—fundamental changes must be made in the structure of education institutions.

Some of these fundamental changes are already underway—though they have been small relative to what is required. It is particularly important greatly to improve the status, remuneration, and responsibilities of teachers, the key agents of any reform process. Similarly, world-class schools, like world-class companies, need to develop modern, more participatory management systems. Indeed, we have noted that schools modeled their systems after the obsolete "scientific management" styles developed in the United States during the late 19th and early 20th centuries for a mass production system.

As was the case with companies, some of these Taylorist school practices are giving way to more participatory systems. In part, these changes are dictated by higher levels of education by workers and teachers, but other forces are also at work:

(a) There was always tension between the democratic ideals taught in the schools and the paternalism of the school and the workplace. It was hard for workers or teachers to be treated like adults in the polity and society and like children on the job, though until the 19th Amendment to the U.S. Constitution women often were treated like children in the polity and society, as well as inside the school.

(b) Since a more competitive world economy emphasizes productivity, flexibility, creativity, and quality, participatory work styles have come to be accepted as preconditions for achieving these outcomes. Despite these changes, American classrooms and workplaces still bear heavy Taylorist marks. In fact, because they have not been as directly affected by the more competitive economic environment, schools apparently have changed even less than factories. For example, Gene E. Maeroff, in a recent study for the Rockefeller Foundation,[73] found the relationship between teachers on one side and principals and superintendents on the other typically to be adversarial; he concluded that the principal-teacher relationship was so paternalistic and hierarchical that some principals treat teachers "as though they occupied a niche only slightly above that of the students they teach."[74]

As the Carnegie Foundation for the Advancement of Teaching emphasized in its 1988 report (*Report card on school reform: the teachers speak*), school reforms that merely give teachers more responsibilities without more power are likely to make matters worse, not better. As with worker participation, empowerment does not mean eliminating traditional school leaders, because school reforms are not likely to be effective, or even possible, without the active involvement of enlightened superintendents and principals. But effective reforms also will require more empowerment and active involvement by teachers.

As part of the reform process, we also must change the structure of educational institutions in ways that will significantly alter the *incentives* for students and teachers. The schools must learn the lesson of America's most successful and productive enterprises: they must be client-centered and performance-driven. Effective schools also must establish clear objectives for students and create incentives for educators and administrators to meet those objectives. Effective school systems will, in addition, decentralize decisions to the schools and hold highly qualified professionals accountable for measured student progress. Unfortunately, we do not now have either clear objectives or adequate measures of those outcomes. Considerable attention, therefore, must be given to these matters as the school reform process proceeds. Moreover, efficient systems will specify outcomes, not processes to achieve those outcomes.

School reform should give high priority to educational equity. There can be no doubt that the United States cannot be a world-class economy with an educated élite and the present low levels of education among at least a third of the workforce. Human capital studies make it very clear that people will either be assets or liabilities. Moreover, the demographics make it equally obvious that without educational equity the United States will not have a world-class workforce. As Lester Thurow put it: "Social welfare programs may be a matter of ethics and generosity, but education and training are not. I am willing to pay for, indeed insist upon, the education of my neighbors' children not because I am generous but because I cannot afford to live with them uneducated."[75]

Many successful interventions depend heavily on changing attitudes, especially about expectations and who can and cannot learn. There is clear evidence that children of all social backgrounds, as well as poorly educated adults, can learn as well as anyone and at much higher levels than they do now. Americans must abandon the élitist myth that educational achievement is mainly due to innate ability and not hard work. They also need to get rid of the habit of viewing education as a cost and not an investment, and the equally dangerous ideas that some children cannot learn or that the United States can be a world-class country with an educated élite while most people continue to be trained for "cog" work rather than for higher order thinking skills.

Since the states are mainly responsible for human resource and economic development, they are in a good position to coordinate various parts of the whole learning system. The most serious challenge is to improve elementary and secondary school systems and the school-to-work transition processes for the non-college-bound. While they too need to be modernized, higher educational institutions in the United States are, on the whole, world-class, but the public elementary and secondary schools are not. This is a serious problem because of the pivotal rôle of the elementary and secondary schools in developing the basic and higher-order thinking skills so essential to developing and using leading-edge technologies. Relative to other major industrialized countries, however, the greatest deficiency is probably in the lack of an effective school-to-work transition system for that half of the 16- to 24-year-old population (about 20 million people) who are not college-bound. Most of these young people constitute that part of the workforce that will determine whether or not the United States will become a second-class economic and political power or remain world-class. Meeting the learning deficiencies of this part of the workforce and of adults with educational deficiencies will require strengthening nontraditional learning systems as well as elementary, secondary, and postsecondary institutions, especially the community colleges.

Although states are mainly responsible for their public schools, the federal government also plays a critical rôle, especially for educational equity, "second chance" learning systems, research and development, and the provision of stronger incentives to strengthen on-the-job learning systems (especially for small employers and for minorities). The federal government also could encourage the establishment of national standards for schools, teachers, and other parts of the learning system where appropriate. The problems with the existing learning systems are too serious to be left to the education establishment, any level of government, or the public or private system alone. The extent to which Americans cooperate to improve their learning systems will literally determine what kind of country (or state) they are going to be in the 21st century.

Recommendations

What must the states do better to coordinate elementary and secondary education with economic development? My recommendations for the states would be as follows.

First, states should produce a consensus-based development strategy. Such a strategy should be based on a cognizance of broad international economic trends, but should deal primarily with matters within the states' control and should be designed primarily to improve the incomes of the states' people. As noted, the keys to a world-class economy are technological innovation and high-quality workforces. As David Osborne has observed:

> A quarter century ago, companies looked for cheap labor, cheap power, and good transportation. *Physical* infrastructure was the key. Today, companies look for educated workers, excellent universities, entrepreneurial climates, and an attractive quality of life. Good roads and airports are still important, but *intellectual* infrastructure is the key [emphasis added].[76]

After examining the successful strategies of a number of states, Osborne suggests some guidelines for a successful development strategy that emphasizes encouraging innovative partnerships between state agencies, schools, and businesses to strengthen innovative economic development. This strategy relies on developing a state's indigenous industry rather than "smokestack chasing," which "generally buys a state exactly the wrong kind of industry—those most susceptible to foreign competition." The evidence also suggests that, rather than creating new public programs, states should encourage private institutions to promote the states' developmental objectives. It likewise is clear that states are not likely to produce competitive, high-wage industries by offering low wages, low taxes, or low-interest loans. Finally, successful development strategies are based on creating highly localized public, academic, and business partnerships. Innovative strategies do not chase big companies and they do not target small businesses either; their main objective is to "target innovation, no matter what the size of the company." Finally, while he recommends against interest subsidies, Osborne's studies suggest the importance of making "capital available at market rates to companies that couldn't get it because they are too small, too new, or too risky."[77]

Second, states should also concentrate on improving their school systems. One of the prerequisites for effective reform would be an analysis of public and private, school and nonschool learning systems within a state. Such an understanding will suggest the kind of changes states must make to coordinate better the different components of the system. For example, there is much that states can do to strengthen the relationships between schools and businesses. Businesses, in turn, can provide resources to strengthen schools, including loaned company personnel, contributions of funds to promote innovative school programs, realistic laboratories for field trips, gifts or loans of equipment, and incentives for students to finish school by guaranteeing jobs or scholarships to successful graduates. Businesses also can provide important political support for measures to strengthen the schools. States can, in addition, strengthen the linkages between different components of a state's education system from preschool through graduate school. A state's universities can play an important rôle in research and development work for improved schools and for more effective teacher training. Elementary and secondary schools can, in addition, provide data and resources to facilitate research on learning and ways to improve education. Feedback on the students moving from one level of education to another can be very useful.

States can strengthen education by improving the compensation, education status, and working conditions of teachers, who must be the main actors in any effort to develop world-class learning systems.

The states must, in addition, promote the development of assessment procedures that make it possible to certify to the public that teachers have achieved high standards.

Attracting, developing, and retaining good teachers is necessary, but not enough to create world-class schools. While schools probably are better than they were 30 or 40 years ago, they are not good enough to provide almost all students with the kind of education now provided mainly to the top 20 to 30 percent of students. For one thing, the schools are not organized to make learning either efficient or exciting. While research demonstrates conclusively that students learn in different ways, schools rely almost exclusively on standardized materials and classes. Class lectures are very inefficient teaching techniques; more advanced students grow bored, and those who cannot grasp as quickly as the average, at whom most teachers pitch their lectures, fall further behind. Critics urge teachers to individualize instruction, but the typical school structures and work load make this very difficult. Teachers have very limited choice in selecting texts or deciding what is to be taught and how. What is required, of course, is to relieve teachers of their many nonteaching duties and give them greater time and flexibility in teaching.

A few school districts are beginning to change the traditional structures and procedures designed to run schools like mass production factories turning out standardized students with low-level basic competencies, but not the high-level thinking skills needed for the 21st century.

One of the first school districts to give teachers professional status was Dade County, Florida, which did so in its 1985–6 contract with United Teachers of Dade (UTD). This contract provided a pilot program to introduce School-Based Management/Shared Decision Making (SBM/SDM) systems in 44 Dade County schools. Like many other urban school districts, Dade County had a history of racial tension, labor–management conflict, low teacher morale, high turnover, and very poor student performance. The SBM/SDM system provides for teacher involvement with principals in every aspect of decision making. The schools control their own budgets, and union contract provisions are waived if they stand in the way of education improvements. In exchange for greater responsibilities, salaries were raised 28 percent over a three-year contract, from an average of $33,000 to an average of $40,000 for the 1990–1 school year, when beginning teachers will be paid $26,500 and veteran teachers over $64,000.

The Dade County program provided a number of measures to improve the professional development for teachers, including: expanded professional leave, improved faculty workrooms and lounges, teacher involvement in planning and designing new schools, educational issues forums, teacher involvement in evaluating and selecting principals and assistant principals, career ladders with annual salary increments of up to $8,000, a peer interaction and assistance program, and enhanced responsibility for student discipline.

In another dramatic school reform plan, the Rochester School Board and the local AFT affiliate raised salaries to among the highest in the country—up to $70,000 for lead teachers, a raise of $4,500 for every teacher and an increase of 52 percent for beginning teachers over three years, starting with the 1988–9 school year. In addition to these salary increases, the Rochester contract made dramatic changes in the rôle of teachers. Seniority was modified to make it possible for the most experienced teachers to be assigned to the poorest schools. Rochester also placed teachers on school-based management teams to help decide what should be taught, how the school would operate, and who should fill vacant teaching positions. First-year teachers and teachers who are having difficulties are assigned to work with experienced teachers for several days a year. The local union's president and the superintendent of schools expect to increase the quality of teachers by "counseling out" those who are unsuccessful and by being more selective from the greatly enlarged pool of applicants who have been attracted to Rochester by high salaries and the excitement of the reforms underway there.

The Rochester plan is designed to change a system where dropouts equaled nearly 30 percent, 70 percent of the students were minorities, 40 percent lived in single-parent families, teachers had low status and were underpaid relative to other professionals, morale was low, the most experienced teachers avoided the "worst" schools, and the best teachers tended to leave teaching for other jobs or to become administrators.

One of the most innovative efforts to deal with Rochester's school problems is the home-based guidance system, whereby teachers take responsibility for a small group of about 20 students, not only to monitor their academic progress, but to pay close attention to their personal development and to visit their parents. Rochester teachers have been trained to be alert to the demographic, social, and economic trends affecting students and their families: these changes predispose many students to failure in school as well as in life.

The union president and superintendent of schools stress the experimental nature of the Rochester plan, which is modeled after the recommendations of the Carnegie Task Force on Teaching as a Profession. While there was opposition to the plan from members of the union and the school board, it was approved overwhelmingly by both organizations. There was general consensus that the old system was failing and that with a good faith effort, the new one could work, especially if both the union and the school board continue their cooperative, experimental approach to problem solving. While the contract will cost Rochester $30 million over its three-year term, the school board considers the price worthwhile to give the union a stake in the success of an effort to solve very serious school problems.[78]

School districts in a number of other urban places, mainly where AFT affiliates have bargaining rights, have adopted variants of SBM/SDM and the Rochester plan. These include Prince William County, Virginia; Montgomery County, Maryland; Syracuse, New York; Pittsburgh, Pennsylvania; New York City; Minneapolis; Toledo, Ohio; Hammond, Indiana; and Cincinnati, Ohio.

These experiments are too new to permit evaluation, but the experience in Dade County, one of the earliest of these reforms, is encouraging. Firm data are not yet available, but participants report remarkable improvements. There are waiting lists of teachers who wish to participate in the system. There is not, nor should there be, one measure of school improvement. SAT and other test scores are important indicators, but others include dropout rates, wider course selection, concentration on important courses, and general attitudes and morale. Al Shanker, national AFT president, reports on the remarkable reversal for one Dade County school, Little River Elementary, which was deteriorating physically and

[E]ach year there was a mass exodus of teachers, and each day we were treated like second class citizens and subject to all kinds of distant bureaucracies telling us to do things that didn't work for the kids. The kids knew a lot about drugs, prostitution, and even murder, but they were at the bottom of the heap academically.[79]

Three years after the Dade County pilot was launched,

Little River is a joyous, sparkling school, a beacon of hope in a community that had almost given up. Teachers, paraprofessionals and other support staff are involved in every aspect of decision making, and there's a waiting list for work at the school. Parent participation is high. Unworkable programs have been junked, and new ones designed around the needs of the students and the community. The children want to be in school and "achievement has gone through the ceiling."[80]

As with any experimental program, SBM/SDM will have some failures, but experience suggests that these participatory programs are on the right track. Just as the authoritarian, bureaucratic system at General Motors must give way to more participatory systems like the one at NUMMI—which can be improved—the obsolete mirror image of that management system imposed on the schools early in this century must give way to the more effective SBM/SDM system. Just as Taylor was wrong in his belief that there was one best way to perform a work task, there is no one best way to teach or to organize a school. What SBM/SDM does is to give highly professional teachers the resources and flexibility to develop teaching approaches most suited to their students and to work with administrators in developing the most effective schools. SBM/SDM is a process, not a program; it therefore has the flexibility to adapt and learn from its successes and failures. State governments, therefore, should encourage such experimentation.

Third, and finally, states must work to improve their education system at every level, not just public or elementary and secondary schools. A particularly serious problem, as noted, is with the non-college-bound. States should, therefore, work to provide much better school-to-work transition systems. This can be done by encouraging working partnerships between the schools and employers (public and private) and by encouraging much better coordination between federal employment and training systems, schools, and other human resource development programs, most of which are controlled by the state, but few of which are adequately coordinated to provide a "seamless web" of services to people who need them.

Notes

1 See W. Monague, "Schools rated a key factor in business-site decisions," *Education Week*, September 30, 1987, 1.

2 F. Harbison, *Human resources as the wealth of nations* (New York: Oxford University Press, 1973), p. 56.

3 Ibid. p. 115.

4 Ibid.

5 Ibid. p. 116.

6 J. S. Cotterell, *On the social costs of dropping out of school* (Paolo Alto, Calif.: Stanford University, Education Policy Institute, 1985), p. 17.

7 Committee for Economic Development, Research and Policy Committee, *Children in need* (Washington, D.C.: Committee for Economic Development, 1987), pp. 6–7.

8 For an excellent discussion see William T. Grant Foundation Commission on Work, Family, and Citizenship, "The forgotten half: non-college youth in America," an interim report on the school-to-work transition, January 1988.

9 See N. P. Eurich, *Corporate classrooms* (Washington, D.C.: Carnegie Foundation for the Advancement of Teaching, 1985).

10 A. Carnevale, *Human capital: a high-yield corporate investment* (Washington, D.C.: American Society for Training and Development, 1983), p. 24.

11 C. Mitchell, "Corporate classes: firms broaden scope of their education programs," *Wall Street Journal*, September 28, 1987, 35.

12 J. C. Simpson, "A shallow labor pool spurs business to act to bolster education," *Wall Street Journal*, September 28, 1987, 1.

13 L. A. Lillard & H. W. Ton, *Private sector training: who gets it and what are its effects?* (Santa Monica, Calif.: Rand Corporation, 1986).

14 See F. Welch, "Effects of cohort size on earnings," *Journal of Political Economy*, October 1979, S65–S97.

15 See B. Babbitt, "The states and the reindustrialization of America," *Issues in Science and Technology Policy*, Fall 1984, 84–93; and T. J. Barlik et al., "Saturn and state economic development," *Forum for Applied Research and Public Policy*, Spring 1987, 29–40.

16 W. J. Abernathy, K. B. Clark & A. M. Kantrow, *Industrial renaissance: producing a competitive future for America* (New York: Basic Books, 1983), p. 109.

17 See C. Kerr, J. Dunlop, F. Harbison & C. Myers, *Industrialism and industrial man* (New York: Oxford University Press, 1964).

18 H. Braverman, *Labor and monopoly capital: the degradation of work in the twentieth century* (New York: Monthly Review Press, 1974); P. Kraft, *Programmers and managers: the routinization of computer programming in the United States* (New York: Springer, 1977); J. W. Scott, "The mechanization of women's work," *Scientific American* **247**, September 1982, 166–87; "Required job skills will drop, despite high technology," *Stanford Observer*, May 1983.

19 W. B. Johnston, *Workforce 2000: work and workers in the 21st century* (Indianapolis, Ind.: Hudson Institute, 1987).

20 Ibid., p. 97.

21 D. F. Noble, *Forces of production: a social history of industrial automation* (New York: Knopf, 1984).

22 H. Brooks, L. Schneider & K. Oshima, "Potential impact of new manufacturing technology on employment and work," draft, November 2, 1985, p. 24.

23 Ibid.

24 For a development of this theme see R. Marshall, *Unheard voices: labor and economic policy in a competitive world* (New York: Basic Books, 1987).

25 For a detailed study of the Texas population trends and their political, economic, and labor market implications, see R. Marshall & L. Bouvier, *Population change and the future of Texas* (Washington, D.C.: Population Reference Bureau, 1986).

26 Of course, the concept of labor shortages is relevant only at specified salaries and qualifications. Some observers argue that there will be no teacher shortage in the United States, because in the first half of the 1980s rising teachers' salaries and education reform were attracting more people into teaching. Those who contend that there will be no shortage also argue that the salaries of teachers are not out of line with those of comparable college graduates. However, these arguments assume that marginal changes in the present U.S. education system are adequate. Those of us who believe there need to be radical improvements in the education system in order to make it world-class believe it is not enough just to get warm bodies to stand before classes and "teach." Indeed, we do not believe baccalaureate degrees in education are adequate preparation for teaching. In this latter sense, there will be a serious teacher shortage in the absence of radical changes in teachers' compensation, status, working conditions, and power. For an elaboration of this point, see Carnegie Forum on Education and the Economy, Task Force on Teaching, *A nation prepared* (Washington, D.C.: Carnegie Corporation, 1986).

27 P. G. Peterson, "The morning after," *Atlantic* **260**, October 1987, 47.
28 I. S. Kirsh & A. Jungeblut, *Literacy: a profile of America's young adults* (Princeton, N.J.: Education Testing Service, 1987).
29 B. Lerner, "American education: how are we doing?" *Public Interest*, Fall 1982, 59–82; R. Rothman, "Foreigners outpace American students in science," *Education Week*, January 28, 1987, 1.
30 R. Rothman, "U.S. fares poorly on science test," *Education Week*, March 9, 1988, 4.
31 L. Resnick, *Education and learning to think* (Washington, D.C.: National Academy Press, 1987).
32 Ibid. p. 7.
33 G. Berlin & A. Sum, "American standards of living, family welfare, and the basic skills crisis," speech delivered at a conference of school and employment and training officials, sponsored by the National Governors' Association and the Chief State School Officers, December 1986, p. 2. See also G. Berlin & A. Sum, *Toward a more perfect union* (New York: Ford Foundation, 1987).
34 Berlin & Sum, "American standards of living," p. 2.
35 Carnevale, *Human capital*, pp. 8–9.
36 E. Dennison, *Trends in American economic growth: 1929–1982* (Washington, D.C.: The Brookings Institution, 1985); Harbison, *Human resources as a wealth of nations*; F. Harbison & C. Myers, *Education, manpower, and economic growth* (New York: McGraw-Hill, 1964); T. W. Schultz, *Investing in people: the economics of population quality* (Berkeley: University of California Press, 1981). To some degree, the diverse answers to the impact of education on various economic outcomes depend on the analytical technique used. In his work, Dennison used a growth accounting approach, which is based on the concept of an aggregate production function linking output (Y) to the input of physical capital (K) and labor (L). The simplest production function, assumed in many studies, is linear and homogeneous: $Y = f(K,L)$. Schultz and others, by contrast, used a rate of return on human capital approach. The rate of return requires identification of a rate of interest, or discount, which equates the present value of costs and the present values of expected benefits from education. If the costs of an investment are C_t a year in which the project is expected to yield benefits of B_t a year over n years, then the rate of return (r) is the rate of interest at which the value of present costs, $C_t(Hr)^t$, is exactly equal to the sum of benefits $B_t(Hr)^t$ from year 0 to year n.
37 T. W. Schultz, *Investing in human capital* (New York: The Free Press, 1971); and Schultz, *Investing in people*.
38 Schultz, *Investing in people*, p. 4.
39 Ibid., p. 7.
40 See T. W. Schultz, *The economic value of education* (New York: Columbia University Press, 1963); see also R. Haveman & B. Wolfe, "Education, productivity and wellbeing," in *Education and economic productivity*, ed. E. Dean (Cambridge, Mass.: Ballinger, 1984), pp. 19–55.
41 World Bank, *World development report 1980* (New York: Oxford University Press, 1980).
42 D. T. Jamison & L. J. Lau, *Farmer education and farmer efficiency* (Baltimore: Johns Hopkins University Press, 1982), p. 9.
43 N. Hecks, *Economic growth and human resources*, Staff Working Paper no. 409, (Washington, D.C.: World Bank, 1980).
44 D. Wheeler, *Human resource development and economic growth in developing countries: a simultaneous model*, Staff Working Paper no. 407 (Washington, D.C.: World Bank, 1980).
45 R. Morris, *Economic growth in cross section*, cited by G. Psacharopoulos & M. Woodhall, *Education for development: an analysis of investment choice* (New York: Oxford University Press, for the World Bank, 1985), p. 20.
46 Psacharopoulos & Woodhall, *Education for development*, p. 314.

47 Berlin & Sum, "American standards of living."
48 Ibid., p. 37.
49 Berlin & Sum, *Toward a more perfect union*, pp. 45–46.
50 For a good summary see E. A. Hanushek, "The economics of schooling: production and efficiency in public schools," *Journal of Economic Literature*, September 1986, 1141–71.
51 Ibid., 1142.
52 For a review see Congressional Budget Office, *Educational achievement: explanations and implications of recent trends* (Washington, D.C.: Congressional Budget Office, 1986).
53 W. J. Bennett, *American education: making it work* (Washington, D.C.: U.S. Department of Education, 1988), pp. 9–10.
54 American Federation of Teachers, table of 1988 teachers' salaries, unpublished.
55 J. S. Coleman et al., *Equality of educational opportunity* (Washington, D.C.: U.S. Government Printing Office, 1966).
56 I. Berg, *Education and jobs: the great training robbery* (New York: Praeger 1970); A. Weiss, "A sorting-cum learning model of education," *Journal of Political Economy*, June 1983, 420–42. See also H. Averch et al., *How effective is schooling? A critical review of research* (Englewood Cliffs, N.J.: Educational Technology Publications, 1974).
57 C. Jencks et al., *Inequality: a reassessment of the effects of family and schooling in America* (New York: Basic Books, 1972), p. 256.
58 S. Bowles & H. Gintis, *Schooling in capitalist America* (New York: Basic Books, 1976).
59 Hanushek, "The economics of schooling," 1162.
60 Ibid., p. 1163.
61 E. Hanushek, "Thowing money at schools," *Journal of Policy Analysis Management*, Fall 1981, 19–41.
62 R. J. Murnane, *Impact of school resources on the learning of inner city children* (Cambridge, Mass.: Ballinger, 1975); D. Armor et al., *Analysis of the school preferred reading program in selected Los Angeles schools* (Santa Monica, Calif.: Rand Corporation, 1976).
63 Coleman, *Equality of educational opportunity*, pp. 21, 297.
64 Jencks, *Inequality*, pp. 96, 109.
65 As noted earlier, studies in developing countries challenge the conclusions that educational achievement is due more to family income than to schools. Studies in over 20 developing countries and evaluations of World Bank education projects "all conclude that wealthy school children do not perform better in achievement tests, and thus suggest that socioeconomic background has much less effect on pupil achievement in developing than in developed countries" (Psacharopoulos & Woodhall, *Education for development*, p. 217).
66 See A. A. Summers & B. L. Wolfe, "Do schools make a difference?" *American Economic Review*, September 1977, 639–52.
67 See M. Cohen, "Effective schools: accumulated research findings," *American Education*, January–February 1982, 13–16; L. C. Stedman, "A new look at effective schools literature," *Urban Education*, October 1985, 295–326.
68 See B. Rowan, S. T. Bossert & D. C. Dwyer, "Research on effective schools: a cautionary note," *Educational Researcher*, April 1983, 24–31; W. A. Firestone & R. E. Herriott, "Prescriptions for effective schools don't fit secondary schools," *Educational Leadership*, December 1982, 51–3; S. C. Purkey & M. S. Smith, "Too soon to cheer? Synthesis of research on effective schools," *Educational Leadership*, December 1982, pp. 64–9.
69 Purkey and Smith, "Too soon to cheer?" p. 67.
70 R. J. Murnane & R. R. Nelson, "Production and innovation when techniques are tacit: the case of education," *Journal of Economic Behavior and Organization* **5**, 1984, 357.

71 Ibid., 356.

72 Ibid., 362.

73 G. E. Maeroff, *The empowerment of teachers: overcoming the crisis of confidence* (New York: Teachers College Press, 1988).

74 F. Hechinger, "Closing a destructive gap: bringing teachers and principals together," *New York Times*, May 25, 1988, 22.

75 L. Thurow, *The zero sum solution* (New York: Simon & Schuster, 1986), p. 187.

76 D. Osborne, "The new role models," *INC.*, October, 1987, 78.

77 Ibid.

78 Information about the Rochester Plan comes from personal conversations with Peter McWalters, Rochester Superintendent of Schools, and Rochester Teachers Association President Adam Urbansky.

79 P. Battle, Dade County teacher, quoted by Shanker, "Preparing for the 21st century," in *Where we stand, New York Times*, July 31, 1988, 9.

80 Ibid.

11

Simple faiths, complex facts: vocational education as an economic development strategy

W. NORTON GRUBB

EDUCATION HAS LONG been touted as a mechanism of economic growth. The report of the National Commission on Excellence in Education, *A nation at risk*—a report widely credited with instigating the "excellence" movement in education—promoted educational reform as a way of improving the international competitiveness of the United States. Other purposes of education—the creation of an informed citizenry, the provision of equal opportunity through education, the diffuse benefits of intellectual development—were mentioned but essentially ignored. In headier days when the American economy was booming, during the 1960s, its growth was often attributed to increases in educational attainment. Indeed, Horace Mann's efforts to promote universal public education in the 1830s used rhetoric about the economic effects of education that, except for the style, could have been written during the 1980s. As he declaimed to the Massachusetts Board of Education in 1848:

> The main idea set forth in the creeds of some political reformers, or revolutionizers, is that some people are poor *because* others are rich.

This idea supposes a fixed amount of property in the community, which by fraud or force, or arbitrary law, is unequally divided among men . . . . But the beneficent power of education would not be exhausted, even though it should peaceably abolish all the miseries that spring from the co-existence, side by side, of enormous wealth and squalid want . . . . Beyond the power of diffusing old wealth, it has the prerogative of creating new. It is a thousand times more lucrative than fraud, and adds a thousand-fold more to a nation's resources than the most successful conquests. Knaves and robbers can obtain only what was before possessed by others. But education creates and develops new treasures—treasures not before possessed or dreamed of by any one.[1]

Vocational education in particular has always been promoted for its economic benefits. Since its inception, promoters of vocational education have insisted not only that it benefits individual students, prevents high school dropouts, and creates productive citizens in place of potential liabilities, but also that vocational education could resolve economy-wide problems like unemployment, lagging growth, and declining international competitiveness. Just as American leaders now point to the Japanese economy and its educational system as exemplars, so advocates of vocational education at the turn of the century pointed to Germany's vocational system as the reason for its economic growth.

More recently, the National Commission on Secondary Vocational Education reasserted the economic value of vocational education, especially in a country where 80 percent of jobs do not require a college degree, and the community colleges offered their services to the nation's growth in the task of "putting America back to work."[2] A number of states have promoted their vocational education systems as mechanisms of economic development; the most notable has been North Carolina, which has expanded vocational education in its community colleges as part of an overall educational strategy for economic development. At the local level, community colleges across the country have rushed to expand their offerings in areas related to new technologies, including computer programs, robotics, and energy-related programs.[3]

The popularity of education in general, and vocational education in particular, as mechanisms of economic development is widespread. But there are serious problems in many of these claims. *A nation at risk* quite correctly pointed out the declining economic position of the United States, as well as the declining academic performance of students, but the link between the two was never demonstrated. Indeed, there is no reason at all to think that a mediocre educational system had anything to do with the decline of U.S. steel or of the automobile industry, or with the superiority of the Japanese in engineering and production. The academic literature demonstrating the link between education and economic growth, widely known in bowdlerized forms, also relies on weak logic. Differences in earnings between educated and uneducated workers at one time are applied to changes over time in educational attainments, as if the economic returns to education among individuals apply when educational attainments as a whole increase.[4] More generally, Americans' infatuation with educational attainment and years of education now seems quite misplaced in a period when the *quality* of education is so much under fire.

For vocational education, the "excellence" movement and the recent emphasis on higher academic standards have come as serious blows. Many of the recent National Commission reports criticized vocational education either implicitly or explicitly, and the business community —long a passive supporter—condemned vocational education outright as harmful to the more general preparation and the higher-order skills that business presumably now needs. As the Committee for Economic Development stated,

> Business in general is not interested in narrow vocationalism. In many respects, business believes that the schools in recent years have strayed too far in that direction. For most students, employers would prefer a curriculum that stresses literacy, mathematical skills, and problems-solving skills; one that emphasizes learning how to learn and adapting to change.[5]

Enrollments in vocational programs have declined as graduation requirements have increased, and vocational educators have gone on the defensive to save their vision of education and their jobs. These recent attacks are part of an historically persistent criticism of vocational education for being overly narrow, too concerned with specific job training and not with broader and more flexible preparation. Accumulating evidence about the ineffectiveness of secondary vocational programs has added to the criticism.

There are, then, many problems with the simple faith that education in general and vocational education in particular are effective mechanisms of economic development. Yet it would be as inappropriate to rule out educational approaches as it is to embrace them uncritically. The appeal of educational mechanisms is irresistible: they promise to accomplish so much at relatively low public expense; they offer a mechanism of economic development that, unlike the more centralized planning mechanisms of other advanced capitalist countries, is more consistent with the U.S. version of capitalism and its limited government; and the view that the United States has only its human resources to rely upon, and should develop those resources to their maximum, is a progressive one which individuals of all political backgrounds can support. Above all, in a world where at least some occupations have increasing educational requirements because of technological developments, it would be foolish to abandon education. Education may not be a sufficient condition for economic growth, but it is surely a necessary component.

The problem, then, is to scrutinize more carefully our simple faith in educational mechanisms of economic development and to determine under what conditions they are likely to be effective. Surprisingly, there is almost nothing written on this subject, just as there appears to be very little written about the effectiveness of economic development strategies in general. Most of the writing has come either from advocates or from the human capital tradition, both uncritical of the rôle of education.

In the first section of this chapter, therefore, I will present a series of conditions under which education, and vocational education in particular, would be effective as a mechanism of economic development. The next three sections examine a series of issues that must be faced by states thinking of using their vocational education systems as mechanisms of economic development: the balance between vocational education at the high school level and at the postsecondary level; the development of planning and evaluation mechanisms to keep education and training programs in line with labor market opportunities; and the balance between general and specific training in vocational education.

Vocational education as a mechanism of economic development

The belief in the economic power of education, dating from the early 19th century, has been powerfully reinforced since the turn of this century by the trend for all levels of education to become increasingly vocational. However, many different views about the rôle of education in labor markets have developed, and they show that the rôle of schooling is neither simple nor necessarily direct. It is, therefore, worth being more precise about the ways in which education might lead to economic growth.

Conventional wisdom and human capital theory

The most conventional view about the effectiveness of education in general, and vocational education in particular, assumes that education instills competencies which have value in production, in the sense that they increase the productivity of individuals; then individuals with these competencies earn a premium for them in the labor market. (This view, formally codified in human capital theory, is quite close to Horace Mann's statement and underlies most common statements about the effectiveness of education.) Thus educating an ignorant person replaces a relatively unproductive person (including persons who might be so unproductive that no one will employ them) with one who is more productive. Furthermore, the benefits of such training accrue not only to the individual trained but also to other workers whose productivity is likely to be enhanced, as when the productivity of engineers is increased by having more competent technicians or more intelligent production-line workers; and increased productivity makes it possible either to increase profits or to decrease prices of products and increase sales, or both, benefiting employers as well. The result of education is therefore to create employment for some of those who were previously unemployable, to increase the earnings of the individuals educated, to increase the productivity and earnings of other workers, and to increase profits—a marvelous scenario.

Furthermore, in the human capital mode there is a mechanism to assure equilibrium: as long as there are economic returns to more education, or to a particular type of education (such as vocational education), informed individuals will enter that type of training; but if the market is flooded with individuals of a particular type, then wages in those occupations will fall, fewer students will gain the education necessary for those occupations, and the excess supply will be eliminated. On the other hand, individuals whose training does not increase their productivity—because training is out of date, instructors are inept, methods are out of date, or programs are out of step with labor market demand—will not earn higher returns and no students will apply to these programs. Thus the model implies that poor instruction and bad planning will be eliminated by students "voting with their feet." Economic incentives and disincentives then establish an equilibrium between demand and supply in every occupation, and for every level of education.

However widely accepted, this view has many flaws. An obvious one, of course, is that the corrective mechanisms of the human capital model may not work very well, particularly if students are poorly informed about labor markets; then time in school may not in fact lead to more productive capacities, and vocational programs may develop that train students for declining or obsolete occupations. It is, therefore, important to assure that what is taught in school is consistent with labor market demand. Much of the concern with the content and planning of vocational programs—examined in the three sections—is essentially a search for institutional mechanisms to replace market mechanisms that are likely to be ineffective in assuring the economic productivity of schooling.

For my purpose the most important flaw in the conventional view is that it says nothing about the demand for educated labor: the existence of job opportunities for well-trained workers who are presumably more productive is not usually considered. The convention is simply a supply-side approach to economic development.[6] But a simple thought experiment reveals that this assumption cannot possibly be true. If engineers are more productive than other workers, and Japan is superior because of its relatively large numbers of engineers, it then follows that we should redirect massive numbers of students from business schools (for example) to engineering schools. Even if we had the political will to do this, then many engineering students would not find jobs as engineers because of the manner in which U.S. business is currently organized, and they might end up as very well-trained technicians. Those who did find jobs as engineers would find that engineering salaries had fallen because of the glut of new entrants. For both reasons the expected return to engineering would fall, and another generation of students would resist entering that occupation. There might be benefits to expanding engineering schools, but they would not extend to every graduate, and there might even be some negative consequences from falling salaries.

This simple scenario can be formalized in an elementary economic diagram. In the supply and demand diagrams in Figure 11.1, untrained workers are trained, shifting supply curves in both the markets for educated and uneducated labor. Now the wages of workers trained increase, from w_{u1} to w_{e2}, and employment increases in the market for trained labor. Wages have increased among the educated workers, and employment in more productive occupations has increased, so economic development seems to have occurred.

But, of course, there are many more effects of training, and several conditions are necessary to the realization of these effects. The most obvious is that vocational education in this model acts to increase employment by increasing the supply of trained workers and decreasing wages. Indeed, total wages to trained workers may

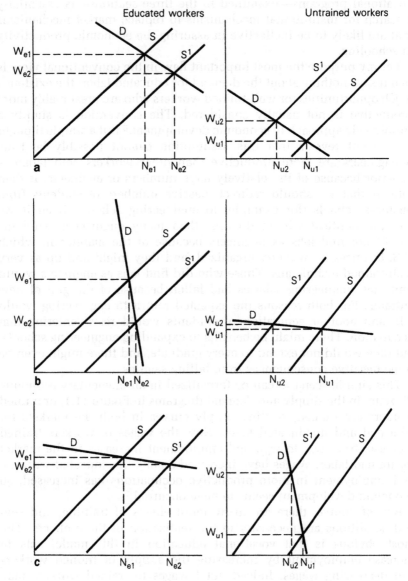

Figure 11.1 Supply of and demand for educated workers.

even fall if the decrease in wages is too great.[7] Furthermore, while there are positive employment effects from the program—because employment increases from N_{e1} to N_{e2}—the increase in employment is not as large as the number of workers newly trained, which is equal to the horizontal displacement of the supply curve. Either some of those newly trained do not find employment in the areas for which they have been trained—a constant problem in vocational education, leading to a concern with placement rates—or some of those formerly working are displaced by newly trained workers, a displacement effect that may be difficult to measure.

In Figure 11.1a, there is an obvious wage advantage of trained workers over untrained workers, and this kind of prediction leads to evaluating vocational programs in terms of their earnings advantages to those who have completed them. However, if access to a training program is unlimited, then supply will continue to shift out of untrained occupations into the training program, so the supply curves S^1 will continue to shift to the right in the market for trained labor and to the left in the market for untrained labor. This can then continue until wages in the two occupations are unequal—that is, until the earnings advantage associated with training has vanished.[8] In this case, evaluating the effects of training by examining earnings differences associated with training will not work; but employment in trained occupations increases, and the real benefits are captured by employers in the form of higher profits (that is, in higher consumers' surplus).

As can easily by seen by rotating the demand curves in Figure 11.1a, the employment effects of vocational education decrease and the fall in wages is greater as demand becomes more inelastic (that is, as the demand curve becomes more vertical)—and vice versa. Figure 11.1b illustrates the effects of a shift in the supply of educated workers because of increased public investment in education in a case where demand is price-inelastic. In this case, wages fall rather drastically, employment in skilled positions is increased only slightly, total wages in skilled positions fall, and overall employment may actually decrease if employment in the unskilled positions declines more than employment increases in skilled positions. Employers benefit enormously from the fall in wages, but several conventional measures of economic development—especially the unemployment rate and total earnings—would not show any improvement. The contrary case exists when demand for trained workers is relatively price-elastic, as in Figure 11.1c, when skilled employment and wages increase.

It follows that vocational education (or any type of education with value in production) is most effective in economic development

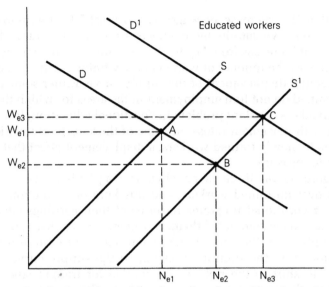

Figure 11.2 Supply of and demand for educated workers, with technological change.

when demand for educated labor is relatively elastic—that is, when employers are willing to increase their employment without decreasing wages very much. Conversely, when demand is almost perfectly inelastic, then the only real effect of training programs is to cause wages to fall. These conclusions are more precise ways of saying that education cannot stimulate employment if positions for educated labor are not available.

What kinds of position are likely to have relatively elastic demand? If there are many possibilities for substituting one kind of labor either for other kinds of employees or for capital or other inputs, then demand will tend to be relatively elastic; limited possibilities for substitution imply inelastic demand. In the case of high-tech employment, many mid-level workers—the technician and technologist level of occupations, which is the usual target of vocational education—may be tied in relatively fixed proportions to capital or computer-driven systems, so possibilities for substitution are limited and the elasticity of demand is low. This raises at least the possibility that high-tech occupations are precisely those for which vocational education is likely to make the smallest impact on employment. While the facts remain murky, this model highlights the importance of knowing a great deal about labor market demand before investing in vocational education.

A rather different scenario recognizes that the economic world is not static, as Figure 11.1 assumes, but that technologies can change and thereby shift demand. In particular, the availability of well-trained workers at lower wages may cause the next generation of technology to use more skilled workers, shifting demand in Figure 11.2 to D^1, resulting in an equilibrium at C rather than B, where both wages and employment in well-trained occupations have increased. Particularly if increasing demand for educated labor is matched with declining demand for untrained workers, this vision of training-led economic development provides benefits to workers and employers alike. Indeed, many of the claims that new technologies will use more highly trained workers, often in conjunction with new technological developments and new ways of organizing work, are implicitly following this model.[9]

This strategy for economic development might be viewed as a labor-oriented component of a rational "industrial policy." Lester Thurow has argued that most governments with industrial policies seek to keep the real costs of capital low as a way to spur investment (including investment in new technologies).[10] Such a policy has the potential for stimulating labor-saving technical change that reduces employment and wages. However, a policy of reducing the wages of skilled workers (but not of unskilled workers) might instead trigger technological change of the sort depicted in Figure 11.2; low-cost capital and low-cost skilled workers in tandem might spur the development of technologies using more capital *and* more skilled workers. The only question is whether and by how much technology will shift to skill-intensive methods if the wages of trained workers fall, a question with no clear answer. However, this approach to "industrial policy" is probably the purview of the federal government, not of the states, whose individual influence on wages and on technological change is likely to be small.

Both Figures 11.1 and 11.2 depend on a relatively conventional model of the labor market, in which wages equilibrate supply and demand. Many alternative theories of labor markets exist, however, and most of them pose even more serious problems for education as a mechanism of economic development. For example, in Thurow's job competition model, the number of jobs is fixed and workers compete for positions in a queue on the basis of their qualifications (rather than on the basis of wages). Then the effect of training some people is to move them higher up in the queue of job applicants and to save employers the costs of training; but since the supply of jobs is fixed, education cannot increase employment directly.[11] In the signaling model developed by Michael Spence and others, schooling is not inherently productive but serves merely to signal which individuals are of greater ability; expanding education at public expense may

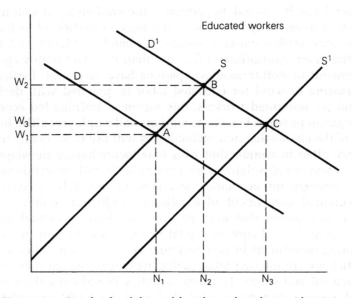

Figure 11.3 Supply of and demand for educated workers, with training.

decrease the cost of signaling one's ability (or may even destroy the value of education as a signal if cost differentials among individuals of different ability levels are eliminated), but cannot expand the amount of employment. Various credentialing models also posit a labor market in which employers employ workers on the basis of educational credentials that have no intrinsic value, so again expanding education may help some individuals over others but cannot contribute to productivity and economic development.[12] Not only is it necessary to examine the nature of demand in order to ascertain what rôle education might play in economic development; it is also necessary to see whether any of these other models explain the use of education in labor markets.

Eliminating shortages

A second commonly mentioned purpose of vocational education is to eliminate shortages of particular types of labor. For example, the Putting America Back to Work project of the American Association of Community and Junior Colleges has emphasized preparation for "skill shortage areas of employment opportunities, particularly in high-technology occupations" such as computer analysis and programing, computer software engineering, and electronic technology. To the extent that shortages of crucial workers develop, entire sectors may be constrained, so this aspect of vocational education may stimulate economic development by unstopping bottlenecks in production.

However, the existence of shortages raises questions about why they develop in the first place and why labor markets cannot eliminate them without public intervention through the usual mechanism of increasing wages. The persistence of shortages of nurses provides an example of an occupation in which low wages have been blamed for shortages, yet wages have not risen relative to other occupations in order to attract more individuals into nursing or to prevent their leaving the profession. In this situation, publicly provided training may in fact be a substitute for the usual wage mechanisms of adjustment. In Figure 11.3, from an initial equilibrium at A an increase in demand from D to D^1 shifts the new equilibrium to B, and—as long as the supply of workers is responsive to wage increases—a wage increase from W_1 to W_2 will restore equilibrium. But if employers maintain wages at the old level W_1, because of an institutional unwillingness to increase them, a shortage will develop. Then increasing vocational education programs to increase the supply of labor in this occupation (from S to S^1) can increase employment at or below W_1, at some new wage like W_3 and a new equilibrium C. This is a scenario in which public education programs meet every increase in demand with an increase in the supply of workers, so that employers need not increase wages. While this response increases employment over the free-market outcome at B, it does so only by lowering wages from W_2 to W_3, and in the process increasing the profits of employers.[13] (Indeed, my interpretation of why employers have so often raised the specter of skill shortages is that any resulting public intervention would prevent their having to increase wages.)

Another reason why shortages might develop is that there are nonprice barriers to increasing the supply of workers; in terms of Figure 11.2, the increase in the supply of workers necessary to move from A to B either cannot take place or does so extremely slowly. One common reason for such supply limitations, in high-tech occupations in particular, is the limited pool of students with enough science and mathematics, and this has led to proposals to increase the teaching of those particular subject areas throughout the elementary and secondary grades. Since this is a long-term solution, efforts to increase enrollments in relatively technical vocational programs may be necessary to eliminate shortages in the short and medium run.

Another reason for supply limitations is the lack of information about job opportunities that would allow new workers to enter the market in which shortages occur. If this is the problem, the appropriate solution is not vocational education itself but information, including adequate vocational counseling at the secondary and postsecondary levels. However, the high-tech field has become glamorous, and it seems implausible that students are unaware of opportunities; indeed, at the postsecondary level students have been flocking into high-tech subjects, perhaps in greater numbers than there are job opportunities available, as discussed below.

The remedy for skill shortages is one of the most attractive and common approaches to the use of education in economic development. However, this tactic requires the identification of labor markets in which demand is shifting and shortages are likely to develop—and existing economic development efforts often neglect to investigate the dynamic nature of demand.

Customized training

An increasingly popular solution to the complaint that firms cannot find the kinds of employee they need has been to establish customized training. Indeed, customized training seems to have become the most popular conception of economic development in community colleges, with the most direct and easily documented effects for workers and firms.[14] In these programs, community colleges and technical institutes provide training in specific occupations for particular companies, often using their equipment and some of their employees as instructors; in this way the content of the programs can be "customized" to the needs of firms. Customized training has been especially attractive in the high-tech area, partly because community colleges and high schools would otherwise have difficulty buying expensive equipment and keeping up to date with changing production technologies.

In examining this rationale for vocational education, the distinction between general training (productive in a wide variety of firms) and firm-specific training (productive in one firm only) is useful. It has long been an article of faith among economists that government might legitimately support general education through subsidies (because of the common benefits or public goods associated with general education) and that students would be willing to pay through tuition for general training that enhances earnings. However, firms will not pay for general training because they cannot capture its benefits as long as workers are free to move to other firms. Conversely, firms should pay for their own firm-specific training since they will be the only ones to benefit.[15] Certainly, government should not support firm-specific training because only the firm and its stockholders (but not its workers) will benefit, at public expense.

In the case of firms complaining about their inability to find particular types of workers, one obvious question is whether the skills they are looking for are firm-specific or relatively general— in which case the previous issue about why shortages might develop is germane. If the skills are firm-specific, it is not surprising that employers cannot find the skills they need in the laborforce, since almost by definition firm-specific skills will not exist unless firms take steps to create them; but then government support of training represents public subsidy of private costs. In this case customized training may be politically popular, since it provides students with employment, community colleges and technical institutes with high placement rates, and firms with cheap training; but there is no reason to think that the publicly subsidized training will increase employment or wages or that it will benefit any of the citizenry except employers.

There might still be a rationale for provision of such training by community colleges, technical institutes, and high schools if there are economies of scale and organization in the provision of training —i.e., if public institutions are better able than firms (especially small firms) to develop training programs quickly. Alternatively, it may be that coordinating general and academic training with firm-specific training is more easily and efficiently done if one institution provides both kinds of training, though this rationale seems weak because most customized training programs appear to be independent of the regular programs of community colleges and do not attempt to integrate general and specific training. In any event, firms should still bear the full costs of the firm-specific component of training, even if it is provided within a public institution.

Still other rationales for customized training exist. One is the promotion of employment for minorities, women, and other disadvantaged groups by targeting these groups for customized training programs. Presumably this approach works by inducing employers through the incentives of subsidized training to hire their new employees from one group (the disadvantaged workers) rather than from another. This strategy may be justified as a way to reduce inequalities among groups of workers and to reduce poverty. However, since disadvantaged groups (especially minorities, women, and youth) often suffer discrimination in labor markets, this approach should be recognized as a form of antidiscrimination policy. In effect, it bribes firms to reduce employment discrimination rather than enforcing equal employment laws against them.

Still another justification of customized training is the attempt to lure firms into underdeveloped regions of a state, including rural areas. While such an approach would be widely accepted, in practice few statewide programs of customized training seem to be concerned with regional imbalances.

Lowering costs to attract business

A major strategy for economic development has been for state and communities to lower costs to businesses in order to attract them from other states and communities. Most often this takes the form of lowering or forgiving taxes or of subsidizing interest costs through tax-free bonds like industrial development revenue bonds. Several states, following the lead of South Carolina, have also established programs of subsidized training for firms moving into the state, presumably to reduce training-related relocation costs. The strategy of increasing the quality of the workforce, articulated most clearly by North Carolina, can be interpreted as reducing the quality-adjusted costs of workers, and the programs to increase vocational education in specific fields may also operate (as in Figure 11.1a) to reduce costs of educated workers and therefore lure firms from other states.

Despite their popularity, many of these inducements, especially tax breaks, have been found to be ineffective, and various groups, including the Advisory Committee on Intergovernmental Relations, have tried to persuade states to abandon their schemes to lure employers.[16] The reason that tax abatements have been so ineffective is that firm location is much more sensitive to markets, labor costs, energy and raw materials costs, and regulatory climate than to taxes, which are small components of total costs. By the same token, these findings suggest that lowering quality-adjusted labor costs through education might be an effective way of attracting employment to a state, and indeed some results have indicated that states with higher spending on education do have higher growth rates.[17] In the battle to attract high-tech employment in particular, the importance of a first-rate university has been a dominant theme; in addition, a survey of high-tech firms by the Joint Economic Committee reported that 96 percent of respondents ranked the availability of technical employees as significant to location and 87 percent felt the availability of professional workers to be crucial. However, statistical analysis has not confirmed the importance of skilled labor to the location of high-tech firms, and has found instead that the location of such firms is more widespread than is commonly thought.[18] It may be, as in so many other aspects of firm location, that the assumption of the importance of skilled technicians to the location of high-tech firms is incorrect.

Although the real effectiveness of educational mechanisms in attracting firms among states is still unclear, a rather different problem is even more crucial. Interstate competition for employment may increase the wellbeing of one state, but only at the expense of another. There are no real economic gains, from a national perspective, in luring a firm from one state to another; indeed, the relocation costs as firms move and as some employees relocate—costs that are disproportionately borne by taxpayers through the favorable tax treatment of depreciation and by employees themselves who bear moving costs—make this kind of shuffling among states inefficient.[19] In fact, if government inducements cause firms to shift from locations which are efficient, considering proximity to markets, raw materials, transportation, and the like, then they may again cause inefficiencies in the economy as a whole, even if some states and firms benefit. Finally, the distribution of the benefits from such inducements is potentially uneven: if a state's education program lowers the wages for trained workers and causes firms to relocate from other states in response, then no real efficiencies have been created; instead firms have been able to use state policy to lower their employment costs (as in Figure 11.1a). Employers gain, but trained workers may not.

There is, to be sure, one case where this kind of "beggar-thy-neighbor" policy may be justified: in providing favorable treatment for a poor region compared with its neighbors. The problem of unequal regions is of course both an interstate problem and an intra-state issue. A state such as Texas, for example, might try to locate employment in the depressed Rio Grande Valley rather than in the Dallas or Austin areas. However, the ability of the federal government to use incentives selectively—to make incentives for employers available to Mississippi but not to Massachusetts—is limited, and most states seem to have been concerned more with development of the state as a whole rather than with balancing substate regions.

However, in other cases policies that attract employment to one state or region at the expense of others should be discouraged. Those writing about economic development strategies should be careful to distinguish those that are effective in stimulating employment across the nation from those that benefit some states at the expense of others.

Retraining

Another attractive strategy is to use vocational education to provide retraining, especially for workers displaced by firms or sectors that are closing down. Analytically, this situation is precisely like that depicted in Figure 11.1a, since we can think of displaced workers as untrained relative to the occupations (including emerging occupations) for which training is required. Therefore all the problems associated with different demand patterns—including possibilities of small employment effects and declining wages when demand is inelastic— are problems in this case as well. In addition, some retraining programs have been customized to particular employers, generating questions about whether such training is really firm-specific and should be paid for by firms rather than governments.

The difference in the case of displaced workers is that they have work experience and presumably have already developed the work habits that employers find so valuable; and if some of their previous job skills are relevant in new occupations, the cost of training them is likely to be lower. Thus there are real economies of training costs in this case.

Equity

Another rationale for vocational education as it relates to economic development is its promise of reducing poverty by integrating various pariah groups into the economy—minorities, women, the handicapped, and other groups with special employment problems. Indeed, the stress of federal legislation since 1963 has been to use federal funds for such special-needs groups. Even if the employment that presumably follows from training comes at the expense of other workers, the fact of women as a group gaining relative to men or minorities relative to women would eliminate some of the most serious inequalities and sources of poverty in the economy.

However, the record of vocational education in improving the employment of these groups has been weak. Segregation by gender within vocational education is powerful, with women dominating secretarial, clerical, and health-related programs while men predominate in trades and technical areas. Segregation by race is less marked and the evidence is sketchy, but minorities—who are adequately represented in vocational education overall—seem to be underrepresented in the most successful programs.[20] Thus it is insufficient simply to call for more enrollments of women, minorities, and other groups in vocational education; it is also necessary to make sure that they are enrolled in *effective* programs.

There are, then, a number of theoretical problems with regard to using vocational education as a mechanism of economic development. Under certain conditions vocational programs can surely increase employment in skilled occupations, increase wages, increase profits, and reduce poverty, but none of these benefits is automatic. They depend not only on the content of programs being appropriate (the subject of the following sections), but also on the nature of demand for skilled occupations. Furthermore, the justification for public subsidy in the case of specific skills is weak, implying that the nature of skills required must be carefully scrutinized. Even in this cursory examination, then, our simple faith in the power of vocational education as a mechanism of economic development is bedeviled by the complexities of labor markets.

The "system" of vocational education: secondary and postsecondary programs

Historically high schools provided vocational education, partly with federal funds, dating back to the Smith-Hughes Act of 1917. However, in the past two decades the vocational enterprise has grown substantially, and a much larger proportion takes place in postsecondary institutions and programs that cater to adults. Within high schools, about 92 percent of students take some vocational education. However, many of these students are taking a single typing, home economics, or auto mechanics course for avocational purposes. National data indicate that there are very few vocational "concentrators" in the high school and a great deal of dabbling in vocational courses; even among those who claim to be in the vocational track, only 41 percent take three or more occupationally specific courses.[21]

Within vocational education, the most important developments are now taking place at the postsecondary level, particularly within community colleges. The change in the community college's rôle in vocational education is itself an arresting development. Over the past two decades community colleges have grown faster than any other level of education; as they have expanded, so their central purpose has changed from that of academic institutions leading to four-year colleges to vocational institutions with final degree and certificate programs. Perhaps three-quarters of students in community colleges are in vocational programs; and the proportion of A.A. degrees in vocational areas has increased markedly, from 51 percent in 1970–1 to 71 percent in 1981–2.[22] Perhaps two-fifths of enrollments in vocational education are now at the postsecondary level,[23] a fraction that has been increasing steadily as community colleges have expanded.

The rise of community college vocational courses has caused a turf battle between the high schools and community colleges; in fact, this is the "squeakiest wheel" in the entire vocational enterprise. The battle is partly over the division of federal funds, since states must divide federal aid through the Carl Perkins Act between their secondary and postsecondary schools. Since federal funds now account for only 7 percent of secondary vocational funding and 4 percent of total postsecondary funding, this battle seems "much ado about nothing." The battle between high schools and community colleges is also over state revenue, of course, and over which level will be given responsibility in state policy.

The real issue confronting state policy on economic development is whether high school or postsecondary vocational programs are more effective, or whether both should coexist. At the national level, the evidence suggests that high school vocational programs are generally *ineffective* in increasing the employment or the earnings of students, except for secretarial and clerical programs for women.[24] At the postsecondary level the findings are at least mixed, with some evidence of effective programs in technical areas.[25]

Even in the absence of conclusive evidence, there are strong reasons for thinking that postsecondary programs can be more effective than high school programs. One involves age: secondary programs send young people into the labor market at age 17 or 18, while many employers are reluctant to hire workers into "adult" jobs—those with stability and possibilities for advancement—until they are in their early twenties. In contrast, community college programs have older students for whom such age discrimination is not an issue. Second, many high school students in vocational programs take introductory courses and general-interest courses such as career exploration. Even among those in the vocational tracks, only about 40 percent take enough occupation-specific courses to have gained job-related skills; many students tend instead to "mill around" in the vocational curriculum, apparently unsure of their goals.[26] At the postsecondary level there is also considerable casual course-taking and exploration of options; but many vocational students are already working and know what they need when they return for additional schooling.

Third, course offerings are much richer and more current at the postsecondary level. For example, one community college in the San Francisco Bay area offered 17 different courses in electronics in 1984–5, ranging from an introductory course called Fundamentals of Electronics to Applied Linear Amplified Analysis. The nearby area vocational school offered only Electronics Design and Manufacturing I and II and Electronics Systems Analysis and Repair I and II. A large comprehensive high school nearby had no course at all in electronics, and the most closely related course a student could take was in machine shop.[27] The charge that high school programs fail to change in response to labor market conditions has been repeated constantly; most high school vocational programs are still dominated by courses in woodworking, metal shop, home economics, clerical skills, and agriculture. Keeping current is also a problem for community colleges, as discussed below, but compared with high schools, community colleges seem to be relatively flexible institutions able to adapt more readily to local needs and labor market conditions.[28]

In particular, community colleges have been able to keep up with the interest in high-tech occupations while high schools are at a serious disadvantage in this area. As evidence, a remarkable shift in curricula in the community colleges has taken place since the 1970s. During the 1970s the highest growth rates in A.A. degrees occurred in relatively conventional fields: in low-tech components of health services (for example, nursing and dental technology); in automotive and construction trades; in agricultural and food services; in public services (fire fighting, police protection, and childcare); and above all in business and commerce. Since 1979 high-tech programs have dominated the growth of community colleges. There has been an upsurge of demand for computer-oriented programs, and enrollments in data processing, in electronics, and in the high-tech components of mechanical/engineering technologies grew much more rapidly than in other areas, while growth in business and commerce and other conventional fields tapered off. Community colleges during this period rushed to develop new programs in such exotic specialties as robotics, laser technology, computer-assisted drafting, and energy-related technologies, amid the more "conventional" courses in computers and electronics.[29] The implication is that community colleges can be responsive in ways that high schools are not.

Finally, because of the "excellence" movement, the view has developed that what high school students need—especially those who have traditionally been the targets of vocational education, such as working class and minority students—is more training in basic academic skills rather than job-related skills. The business community, decrying the lack of basic literacy and simple mathematical abilities among new employees, has encouraged the view that nothing should distract students from the acquisition of such basic abilities. Stiffer graduation requirements have added pressures on students to emphasize more academic course material, and in several quarters high school is seen as the place for more "academic" studies, leaving job-related training to the postsecondary level.

One obvious conclusion, then, is that states interested in vocational education as a mechanism of economic development should give community colleges the principal responsibility for such education.[30] This step would recognize and rationalize the changes that have taken place since 1960. Together with other improvements in planning and evaluation this change would help improve the quality of vocational training and eliminate the ineffective high school programs that distract students from the more general education they should pursue.

This recommendation would not eliminate the rôle of the high school in vocational education, however. Rather, it would give the high schools greater responsibility for academic preparation for postsecondary vocational programs (e.g., the sciences required for technical fields) and for teaching students about the labor market and about the variety of careers available, about which they are often woefully ignorant. Indeed, a more general conception of the high school's rôle in vocational preparation is consistent with calls for more general forms of education and with the conceptions of more general vocational education by the business community. In addition, 2+2 programs retain an important rôle for high schools in preparing students for postsecondary vocational education; other articulation mechanisms, including plans where well-prepared high school students take vocational courses in community colleges, could retain some vocational education at the secondary level.

Planning and evaluation in vocational education

Vocational education is in one sense easier to evaluate than academic education. While there are moral, political, and avocational purposes in vocational education, the goal of preparing students for the labor market is dominant. However, vocational educators operate in a difficult environment: they can never assume (as academic educators sometimes can) that the simple acquisition of more training ("seat time" or "bench time") confers status and enhances employment, and they must respond to a labor market that is ever-changing, unpredictable, and beyond their control. Only effective planning and evaluation can assure that the economic goals of vocational programs are met.

Planning and evaluation encompass various activities. One is the assessment of labor market demand, based on surveys and projections of labor markets and information from employers, to be sure that vocational programs are preparing students for occupations where demand is substantial enough to absorb graduates. (In terms of Figure 11.1a above, this is the nearest equivalent to determining whether demand is relatively elastic or not, or whether it is shifting, as in Figure 11.2). Another is curriculum planning, which ensures that programs teach the capacities and skills required on the job (rather than job skills that are obsolete, trivial, likely to become outmoded, or used by only a few employers). A third is student assessment, which ensures that students have learned the skills taught. A fourth, in some ways the most difficult, is the follow-up of students, which examines the placements, employment patterns, and earnings of students (both completers and noncompleters)—rather than relying on anecdotes and personal stories as evidence of effectiveness. There are many mechanisms of planning and evaluation, including labor market surveys, employer surveys, advisory committees, coordination councils, formal methods of curriculum planning, and student follow-up surveys. A great deal of planning and evaluation must be done at the local level, especially in states that are varied, since few vocational programs operate in a statewide labor market.

Given the centrality of the community colleges to vocational education, the reform of planning and evaluation should probably focus on those functions in the community colleges. Because evaluation and planning are usually local responsibilities, there is great variation around states in the quality of such efforts. Some colleges engage in careful planning and serious follow-up studies in an effort to improve their procedures. Others produce district plans for vocational education that are little more than compliance documents, establish district-wide advisory committees that can provide little information about specific programs, and perform evaluations that are really "self-study" procedures with no independent validation or objective data on program effectiveness.

To be sure, good planning and evaluation can be time-consuming and expensive. They require resources to be set aside specifically for these purposes. Otherwise planning and evaluation requirements become compliance exercises, as they often are in federal programs. The current lack of adequate planning and evaluation and the lack of reliable information are not simple oversights but instead are symptomatic of education and training systems that have emphasized expansion and service delivery over accountability and performance.

As part of any state program for economic development, therefore, it is important to support the development of planning and evaluation procedures for all community college vocational education, emphasizing the articulation of vocational programs with local labor markets. These procedures should be initiated at the state level but carried out locally. There are several important elements, including additional labor market information, models of planning and evaluation, follow-up procedures, more serious program review (including mechanisms for eliminating ineffective programs), technical assistance, and some centralized operations (e.g., data processing).

Specific and general training in vocational education

A consistent criticism of vocational education has been that it provides skill training that is too narrow and too specific to particular occupations.[31] Overly specific training has been faulted for two somewhat different reasons. First, in an economy that is changing rapidly, specific training is likely to become obsolete as the requirements for occupations change and as some occupations decline and others rise. In such a world, the most valuable capacities include the ability to respond to change, the facility to learn quickly, and the basic skills necessary for retraining. Second, many observers have argued that the jobs of the future—particularly in high-tech sectors and in many other jobs that are transformed by new technologies—will require different capacities than the craft and production jobs of conventional manufacturing: greater flexibility; better problem-solving abilities; more independent thought; and the capacity to work in interdependent production processes in which teamwork and employee involvement are crucial. Therefore, narrow conceptions of vocational education seem inadequate to future demands on the education system. The complaint of the Committee for Economic Development about "narrow vocationalism" in the schools is one indication of this view; another is the position of the report of the Panel on Secondary School Education for the Changing Workplace, which concluded that

the need for adaptability and lifelong learning dictates a set of core competencies that are critical to successful careers of high school graduates. The competencies include the ability to read, write, reason, and compute; an understanding of American social and economic life; a knowledge of the basic principles of the physical and biological sciences; experience with cooperation and conflict resolution in groups; and possession of attitudes and personal habits that make for a dependable, responsible, adaptable, and informed worker and citizen . . . . The panel believes that education needed for the workplace does not differ in its essentials from that needed for college or advanced technical training. The central recommendation of this study is that all young Americans, regardless of their career goals, achieve mastery of this core of competencies up to their abilities.[32]

One important cause of overly specific forms of vocational education has been the split between academic and vocational education. This split has allowed vocational programs to develop in isolation from courses in basic cognitive skills. One remedy is to develop more general forms of vocational education by re-integrating academic and vocational education in every way possible. *The unfinished agenda*, a strong defense of high school vocational education, called for "programs and experiences that bridge the gap between the so-called 'academic' and 'vocational' courses."[33] The American Association of Community and Junior Colleges has proposed a "two-tiered education/training package," with the first tier stressing mathematics, science, communications, and analytical and reasoning skills.[34] The 2+2 plan can be interpreted as another effort to broaden vocational education: high school juniors and seniors take science, mathematics, and literacy-related courses oriented around clusters of careers, thereby developing broad competencies, avoiding narrow job training, and leaving technical and specific courses to the postsecondary years.[35] At the same time, other forces continue to push vocational education in the direction of specific training. One is the expansion of short-term job training, employer-based training, and contract education in the community colleges. A second is the tendency of many students in the community colleges—especially many older vocational students—to take a few courses and then return to work, rather than complete a coherent program; indeed, this may be the most serious problem facing the community colleges. Another is the rôle of proprietary schools: when community colleges establish broader programs of education, they can count on competition from proprietary schools offering shorter, more specific programs that seem more "relevant" to jobs. A fourth is the emphasis in JTPA on short, job-specific training and narrow standards of accountability. Yet another is the JTPA model of governance by private industry councils (PICs), dominated by members from private industry; such councils can (though they need not) direct training in more specific directions if they focus too much on the training needs of local businesses.

Above all, the business community is itself divided. While national leaders of leading corporations call for broader education and condemn "narrow vocationalism," local businesses often press for more specific training, and employers do not care much about higher-order thinking when they hire workers for jobs requiring a high school degree or some college certificate.[36] The tension between general and specific forms of vocational education persists, therefore, despite recent efforts to promote more general forms of vocational education.

Developing more general forms of vocational education is difficult under the best of circumstances, though there are positive signs. There is greater recognition now that the old split between academic and vocational education is counterproductive, and schools around the country have experimented with new forms of integration. Integration can probably be neither forced nor required, but it may be possible to nurture it from the state level by supporting experimental programs, disseminating information about model programs, and providing technical assistance and educational leadership.

While it may be difficult to heal the split between academic and vocational education, it is easy to widen this division, particularly by separating academic and vocational education and making the bridge between the two more difficult. Two examples of such separation will suffice. One is the expansion of contract education and other short-term job training in the community colleges. Another is the development of job training in programs like JTPA with only tenuous connections to educational institutions; providing such job training within community colleges promises a partial remedy of this problem. States interested in developing vocational education in general rather than specific directions would do well to avoid any of these mechanisms that widen rather than narrow the gap between the academic and the vocational. More positively, states could support the development of more general forms of vocational education where appropriate, specifically by recommending funding for experimental programs (including two-tier programs, 2+2 models, and other similar efforts) and for dissemination of research and information about model programs. States could also monitor the development of short-term job training, contract education, employer-based training, short-term enrollments, and other forms of specific training in the community colleges, in order to avoid potential excesses.

Conclusions: economic development in a world of complexity

During the last decade, it has dawned on policy analysts that public problems are much more complex than was once thought, with more interacting causes, and therefore require more complicated solutions. In the area of welfare, for example, a new appreciation has developed for the complexity of poverty and for the fact that there are many different kinds of poverty and many causes. As a result the simple, grand solution popular in the 1960s and early 1970s—a negative income tax plan—has passed from public attention, superseded by reform proposals in which many different programs, each aimed at a different strand of poverty, are combined. The need to coordinate the different components of such a policy presents further challenges.

So too in economic development: the causes of high unemployment, slow growth, and lagging incomes are multiple and complex. Lester Thurow has labeled the national problem as "death by a thousand cuts," and at the state and regional level there are at least as many causes. In the area of education alone, a state wanting to improve its system of vocational education and training would have to reform, at a minimum, the relative responsibilities of high schools, community colleges, JTPA and other manpower programs, and the private sector as well as the nature of planning (to keep programs in line with labor markets) and their program content. Indeed, many other issues not even raised here would also have to be addressed. For example, reformers attempting to upgrade the quality of schools have come to realize that any such reforms must be accompanied by changes in teacher training; and so too in vocational education—where shortages of vocational teachers loom as a serious problem, especially in high-tech areas— any serious use of vocational education as an economic development strategy would have to consider ways to improve the supply and quality of teachers.

The most difficult issue is the interaction of educational policy and labor market demand. To be sure, attempts to improve a state's system of vocational education and training—to rationalize the contribution of each component of a state's "system" and to improve planning and responsiveness—would be worthwhile in any event. But the view that education by itself can lead to increased employment, higher earnings, and economic growth is true only under some special (and not particularly realistic) conditions, as the analysis indicated. One implication is that the investigation of the conditions under which such programs are effective must be taken more seriously than in the past.

A further implication is that it is insufficient to rely on a supply-side policy of improving education without simultaneously operating to shift demand. Indeed, the most effective program of economic development should be one that includes both demand-related components and those that improve vocational education and job training in order to respond to demand. This approach should not only be more effective in stimulating economic development; it is also one that allows the real potential of vocational education to be realized.

Notes

The author is a member of the board of the National Center for Research in Vocational Education at the University of California, Berkeley. This chapter has not been supported by the National Center, nor has it been approved as a publication of the National Center.

1 From Horace Mann's twelfth annual report to the Massachusetts Board of Education, in L. Filler (ed.), *Horace Mann on the crisis in education* (Yellow Springs, Ohio: Antioch Press, 1965).

2 National Commission on Secondary Vocational Education, *The unfinished agenda: the role of vocational education in the high school* (Columbus, Ohio: National Center for Research in Vocational Education, 1985); *Putting America back to work: the Kellogg leadership initiative* (Washington, D.C.: American Association of Community and Junior Colleges, 1984).

3 W. N. Grubb, "The bandwagon once more: vocational preparation for high-tech occupations," *Harvard Educational Review* **54**, November 1984, 27–39.

4 For examples of this approach, see D. Jorgenson, "The contribution of education to U.S. economic growth, 1948–73," in *Education and economic productivity*, ed. E. Dean (Cambridge, Mass.: Ballinger, 1984); and E. Denison, *Accounting for slower economic growth: the United States in the 1970s* (Washington, D.C.: Brookings Institution, 1979).

5 *Investing in our children: business and the public schools* (New York: Committee for Economic Development, 1985), p. 15.

6 One of the few individuals writing about economic development to recognize the importance of the demand side has been D. Osborne, *Economic competitiveness: the states take the lead* (Washington, D.C.: Economic Policy Institute, 1987). Osborne recommends, as I do, that education and training programs be demand-driven, rather than focus only on the supply of trained workers.

7 This will happen if the elasticity of demand for trained labor is, in absolute terms, less than one. Of course, there is also a general equilibrium analysis possible, examining the effects on total wages in both the trained and the untrained occupations; then the effect of training depends not only on the elasticity of the demand for trained labor, but also on the elasticity of demand for untrained labor.

8 Of course, this will not occur if places in training programs are limited, or if there are other restrictions—such as high entrance requirements or prerequisites

in mathematics and science that few students have. Many professional and semi-professional groups attempt to limit entry in these and other ways to prevent erosion of their earnings advantages.

9 See, for example, the discussion of the "renaissance technician" in S. Rosenfeld, "The education of the renaissance technician: postsecondary vocational-technical training in the South," *Foresight*, (Southern Growth Policies Board) Fall 1986.

10 L. Thurow, "The case for industrial policies," in *The zero-sum solution: building a world-class American economy*, Ch. 9 (New York: Simon & Schuster, 1985).

11 Education might increase employment indirectly if lower training costs led to lower prices and higher output, but the spirit of Thurow's model is that such price competition does not operate very frequently. See L. Thurow & R. E. B. Lucas, *The American distribution of income: a structural problem* (Washington, D.C.: Joint Economic Committee March 17, 1972).

12 A. M. Spence, *Market signaling: information transfer in hiring and related processes* (Cambridge, Mass.: Harvard University Press, 1974). On credentialing models see V. L. Rawlins & L. Ulman, "The utilization of college-trained manpower in the United States," in *Higher education and the labor market*, ed. M. Gordon (New York: McGraw-Hill, 1974).

13 That is, in shifting from B to C there is an increase in consumer surplus which goes to employers, which presumably takes the form of higher profits. It is unclear whether there is any change in the surplus going to workers. Since the total surplus at C is unambiguously greater than at B, from a societal standpoint we should prefer C to B − except that the distribution of benefits is skewed in favor of employers rather than employees, and the cost of training is not incorporated into this model.

14 S. Rosenfeld, "Vocational education and economic growth," Occasional Paper no. 112 (National Center for Research in Vocational Education, Ohio State University, 1986).

15 G. Becker, *Human capital* (New York: Columbia University Press, 1964).

16 See, for example, R. Vaughn, *State taxation and economic development* (Washington, D.C.: Council of State Planning Agencies, 1979); M. Kieschnick, *Taxes and growth: business incentives and economic development* (Council of State Planning Agencies, 1981); *Regional growth: interstate tax competition* (Washington, D.C.: Advisory Commission on Intergovernmental Relations, March 1981).

17 T. Plaut & J. Pluta, "Business climate, taxes, and state industrial growth in the United States: an empirical analysis," *Southern Economic Journal* 50, July 1983, 99–119.

18 Joint Economic Committee, *Location of high technology firms and regional economic development*, June 1, 1982, pp. 49–56. For statistical evidence, see A. Glasmeier, P. Hall, & A. Markusen, "Recent evidence on high technology spatial tendencies: a preliminary investigation," Working Paper no. 417 (Berkeley: Institute of Urban and Regional Development, University of California, October 1983).

19 Of course, shifts among states in response to real cost differences may still be efficient.

20 C. Benson & E. G. Hoachlander, "A descriptive study of the distribution of federal, state, and local funds for vocational education," project on national vocational education resources (Berkeley: University of California, September 1981); D. Stern, E. G. Hoachlander, S. Choy & C. Benson, *One million hours a day: vocational education in California public secondary schools*, report to the California Policy Seminar. (Berkeley: University of California, June 1986), p. 41.

21 E. G. Hoachlander & S. Choy, *Classifications of secondary vocational education courses and students* (Berkeley: MPR Associates, Nov. 14, 1986).

22 Grubb, "The bandwagon once more," p. 431.

23 This estimate is for 1980–1 and is based on the Vocational Education Data System (VEDS), in National Center for Education Statistics (NCES), "Vocational

education enrollments remain steady," December 1982. However, the VEDs data are widely viewed as incomplete and have since been abandoned, so estimates about enrollments must be interpreted with caution.

24 On the effects of vocational education, see R. Meyer, "An economic analysis of high school education," in The federal role in vocational education: sponsored research, National Commission for Employment Policy, November 1981; J. Grasso & J. Shea, Vocational education and training: impact on youth (Berkeley: Carnegie Council on Policy Studies in Higher Education, 1979); T. Daymont & R. Rumberger, "The impact of high school curriculum on the earnings and employability of youth," in Job training for youth, ed. R. Taylor, H. Rosen & F. Pratzner (Columbus: National Center for Research in Vocational Education, 1982). For results on California, see Stern, Hoachlander, Choy & Benson, One million hours a day.

25 For positive evidence on community college programs, see L. Blair, M. Finn & W. Stevenson, "The returns to the associate degree for technicians," Journal of Human Resources 16, Summer 1981; and H. Heinemann & E. Sussna, "The economic benefits of community college education," Industrial Relations 10, October 1977. Both of these are based on special samples of limited generality. For negative evidence, see D. Breneman & S. Nelson, Financing community colleges: an economic perspective (Washington, D.C.: Brookings Institution, 1981); W. Wilms & S. Hansell, "The dubious promise of post-secondary vocational education: its payoff to drop-outs and graduates in the U.S.A.," International Journal of Economic Development 2, 1982; and F. Pincus, "The false promise of community colleges: class conflict and vocational education," Harvard Educational Review 50, August 1980.

26 Hoachlander & Choy, Classifications of secondary vocational education courses and students, Table 4.

27 Stern, Hoachlander, Choy & Benson, One million hours a day.

28 Berman, Weller Associates, A study of California's community colleges, prepared for the California Roundtable, April 1985, p. 31.

29 Grubb, "The bandwagon once more."

30 My argument is very similar to that made by S. Rosenfeld, both in emphasizing the community colleges rather than high schools and in calling for mechanisms to improve postsecondary vocational programs. See S. Rosenfeld, "Technical and community colleges: catalysts for technology development," in The role of community, technical, and junior colleges in technical education/training and economic development (Washington, D.C.: American Association of Community and Junior Colleges, June 1987).

31 See W. N. Grubb, "The phoenix of vocationalism: implications for evaluation," in The planning papers for the vocational education study (Washington, D.C.: National Institute of Education, 1978); and Stern, Hoachlander, Choy & Benson, One million hours a day. Much of the latter argument has been repeated in D. Stern, "Education for employment over the next twenty-five years," in Berman, Weiler Associates, A study of California's community colleges, vol. 2, Ch. 7.

32 High schools and the changing workplace: The employers' view (Washington, D.C.: National Academy of Sciences, 1984), p. 19.

33 National Commission on Secondary Vocational Education, The unfinished agenda: the role of vocational education in the high school (National Center for Research in Vocational Education, 1984), p. 14.

34 Putting America back to work, p. 29.

35 D. Parnell, The neglected majority (Washington, D.C.: Community College Press, 1985), p. 144.

36 J. McPartland, R. Dawkins & J. Braddock, "The school's role in the transition from education to work: current conditions and future prospects," Report no. 362 (Baltimore: Center for Social Organization of Schools, Johns Hopkins University, April 1986).

12

Engineering regional growth

STUART A. ROSENFELD
& ROBERT D. ATKINSON

Introduction

THE 1980s WILL GO down in history as a decade of educational upheaval and reform. The critiques of elementary and secondary education contained in *A nation at risk* and subsequent reports on all levels of education were framed in terms of human capital formation and highlighted the consequences of poor education for economic development. Among the major forces behind educational reform are new developments in technology and the concerns they raise that American youth is not being adequately prepared to compete successfully in an increasingly technological society and workplace. The President's Commission on Industrial Competitiveness stated this concern clearly: "Our nation's universities and schools have a vital role to play in revitalizing America's competitiveness . . . . Without strong educational institutions, the United States will not be able to capitalize on our key potential strengths in technology and human resources."[1] Perhaps David Nobel expressed the human contribution to technological advance best in *America by design*: "Like every social process, technology is alive. People—particular people in particular places, times, and social contexts—are both the creators of modern technology and the living material of which it is made."[2]

One result of the attention given to schools' rôles in economic development by both political and business leaders has been a rapid expansion of services, which go far beyond teaching and learning. Universities, for example, have become meccas of a high-tech economy, attracting and assisting entrepreneurs and developing and incubating new firms. Technical colleges have added technology development capacity and offer technical assistance programs and a whole host of new and expanded services to support technology-based development. Colleges and universities have gone beyond human resource development, their traditional and most important contribution to growth, and are trying to establish firmly their eminence (and rationales for increased state funding) in the emerging high-tech economy. A second result of the added importance of economic development is that it gives education a regional dimension. The competition for jobs places educational institutions in the box of development tools used to create, support, and attract new businesses at or to a specific site.

Despite the proliferation of new services and programs to promote technological growth, the capacity and capability to provide the scientific and technical knowledge and skills needed to increase the productivity and competitiveness of American business ranks as one of the most vital. That capacity remains the heart of the postsecondary education/economic development nexus. Economic capacity requires a scientific and technical workforce proficient in generating, implementing, and using new technologies. The acquisition of knowledge and skill begins in the public schools; it is fully developed in postsecondary institutions. This chapter will examine the importance of science, engineering, and technical education to economic capacity and development from national and regional perspectives. It will review the demand, supply, and quality of the national and regional scientific and technical workforces and then examine the effects of educational institutions on business investment decisions.

A technical laborforce and economic development

The scientists, engineers, technicians, and managers who matriculate from and continue their education in colleges and universities constitute the most traditional link to economic development. Despite the expanding economic development activities of institutions of higher education, their most important technological function is still to develop the human resources that will concoct, implement, and productively use inventions and innovations and that will prepare the next generation's human resources. The National Science Board clearly states the importance of technical human resource development to the economy: "The only way that we can continue to stay ahead of other countries is to keep ideas flowing through research; to have the best technically trained, most inventive and adaptable workforce of any nation; and to have a citizenry able to make intelligent decisions about technically based issues."[3] Although the demand for technical staff is frequently linked to growth of high-tech industries, traditional industries will have to adopt new technologies to remain competitive, and these industries are equally in need of technically competent human resources.

The importance of scientific and technical human resources was demonstrated in a recent national survey of leaders of business, higher education, and state government.[4] Each was asked to estimate the relative strategic impact of a large number of factors on both business and national economic competitiveness. The single factor that most frequently was rated "critical" was "developing and maintaining adequate supply of science, engineering, and technical personnel." The issue was ranked as critical to national competitiveness by 90 percent of business respondents, 97 percent of university respondents, and 86 percent of state government respondents. In addition, 77 percent of business respondents ranked it critical to the competitiveness of their own companies—also higher than any other single issue ranked by business leaders. Meeting demand, however, is a necessary but not sufficient expectation of scientific, engineering, and technical personnel. They must be well enough prepared to contribute to innovation, discovery, and the improvement of productivity, which comprise the supply side of their economic development capacity.

Thus, the challenge facing education in America is to provide the supply of high-quality scientists, engineers, and technicians necessary to keep up with demand from industry, government, and education. There is growing doubt about the nation's ability to meet the expected demand. Opinions differ over the magnitude and nature of the demand, the expected supply of technically educated and trained workers, and the quality and relevance of available education and training. What is known and what is assumed about the supply, demand, and quality of scientific and technical human resources and human resource development?

The anticipated demand for technically trained personnel

The need for technically educated and trained people will almost certainly increase faster than the demand for all other occupations between now and the year 2000. The only question is at what rate, and which scientific needs will grow fastest. The latest projections of occupational demand for the year 2000 from the U.S. Bureau of Labor Statistics show a 36 percent increase for engineers and a 40 percent for engineering technicians between the years 1986 and 2000—despite a projected 5 percent overall decline in manufacturing employment for the same period.[5] Expected employment in the year 2000, current forecasts for rates of growth, and previous forecasts for rates of growth are shown in Table 12.1.[6]

Two opposing forces influence the demand for technical workers: the aggregate demand for manufacturing, which employs a relatively large share of scientists, engineers, and technicians; and the needs within the manufacturing sector. While an overall decline in employment is projected for the manufacturing sector, changes within that sector suggest relatively greater employment of technically trained people. The fact that all technical occupations are projected to grow in the face of industrial employment decline implies that the occupational mix within manufacturing is changing. In the robotics manufacturing industry in 1982, for example, 23[7] percent of employees were

Table 12.1 Expected employment in scientific and technical occupations, 2000, and annual growth rates, 1984–95 and 1986–2000.

Occupation	Employment (1,000s) 2000	Predicted* growth rate 1984–1995 (%)	Predicted** growth rate 1986–2000 (%)
All manufacturing	18,160	0.60	−0.32
All occupations	133,030	1.27	1.26
Engineers	1,815	2.84	2.02
Electrical/electronics engineers	592	3.95	2.82
Industrial engineers	152	2.39	1.89
Mechanical engineers	309	2.68	0.81
Natural scientists	375	1.12	1.14
Computer & math scientists	702	4.51	3.77
Engineering technicians	933	3.11	2.19
Science & math technicians	262	1.42	1.03
Computer programmers	813	5.05	3.85

  * As forecast in *Monthly Labor Review* **108**, November 1985.
 ** As forecast in *Monthly Labor Review* **110**, September 1987.

engineers and 15.7 percent were engineering technicians. The comparable percentages for all of manufacturing in 1982 were 2.8 percent and 2.2 percent, respectively.

There has been at least one attempt to disaggregate the change in employment of scientists, technicians, and engineers due to the two factors, growth and technology. The results of the study of changes between 1972 and 1982 (Table 12.2) show that 54 percent of the increased demand could be attributed to changes in technology and 46 percent to economic growth.[8] Differences among occupations, however, were quite large. There were, in fact, a number of technical occupations that were reduced by technological advances: metallurgical engineering, drafting, and agricultural and biological technology. Others were increased by technology less than the national average for all occupations: chemistry, geology, civil engineering, physics, and space science. It appears that some professional as well as low-skill occupations are being displaced by technicians.

It is not only the manufacturing sector that employs relatively more technically skilled people. The changing work environment of many service industries, too, requires more technical skills. In fact, the largest increases in occupational demand are in occupations that are concentrated in rapidly growing service industries, such as computer and mathematical sciences and computer programming. It is important to bear in mind, however, that many of these service industries that employ scientific and technical workers are linked directly to manufacturing. It

Table 12.2 Disaggregation of changes in science and engineering employment, 1972–82.

Occupation	Change due to growth (%)	Change due to technology (%)
All occupations	46	54
Computer specialists	25	75
Engineers	41	59
Electrical & electronics	33	67
Industrial	28	72
Mechanical	57	43
Math scientists	47	53
Life & physical scientists	50	50
Operations research	24	76
Science & engineering technicians	55	45
Electrical/engineering	21	79
Industrial	8	92

Source: R. H. Beznek, E. M. Zampelli & J. D. Jones, "Do scientists always benefit?" *Issues in Science and Technology* **4**, Fall 1987, 28–35.

has been estimated that about 25 percent of those employed in service industries are directly linked to manufacturing production.[9]

Although the Department of Labor's projections are national, there are regional patterns to demand, and these roughly follow industrial location patterns. The needs for scientists and engineers tend to aggregate around research universities, defense industries, and corporate research centers, which are more likely to be in urban centers and in the Northeast and Pacific Coast regions. Projected jobs for technicians, however, are more evenly dispersed among both traditional and emerging manufacturing industries, particularly as traditional manufacturers invest more and more in new process technologies. Thus, demand for technicians is likely to be high in the rural South and urban Midwest, which are home to a disproportionate share of older, traditional industries.

The education of future scientists and engineers implies a certain level of doctoral graduates to fill university faculty positions. Supply of such graduates for the next ten years seems secure, since college enrollments are expected to continue to fall and retirement rates to remain low. By the end of the century, however, the demand for doctoral graduates will increase substantially and remain high. The annual number of science and engineering faculty who will be hired between 1998 and 2003 is projected by the U.S. Office of Technology Assessment to be roughly 8,000 to 12,000, which is about double the 3,000 to 7,000 per year projected for the next five years.[10] The ranges represent the extremes, the high and low projections based on the most optimistic and pessimistic assumptions about enrollments, faculty retirements, and resignations.[11]

If private-sector demand for Ph.D. scientists and engineers is high, there may be a serious strain on labor markets and constraint on the ability of the universities to provide the technical resources to support technological growth. And if the past decade is any indication, demand will grow. Over the past ten years, the number of Ph.D. scientists and engineers undertaking research for industry doubled, and the number in consulting, sales, and other professional services more than quadrupled. That would raise the demand for Ph.D.s, conservatively, to about 18,000 per year in the year 2000. Still another source of demand for Ph.D. graduates, not considered in the projections, may come from the community and technical colleges. If the educational curricula for technicians place more emphasis on theory and the colleges become more heavily involved in research and development and technical support for new process technologies, as recommended,[12] they will seek more qualified faculty.

The supply of engineers, scientists, and technicians

The ability to meet the industrial and academic demands for scientists and engineers, and particularly those with advanced degrees, is a critical concern of regions and of the nation and represents one measure of states' capacities for economic growth. The National Academy of Sciences states in its report on science and engineering talent, "Human resources are key to advancing science and technology, yet the U.S. is losing its edge in the cultivation of scientific and engineering personnel."[13] In a survey of 1,719 leaders in New England conducted in 1987 to rank the importance of 12 ways in which colleges and universities can best prepare the workforce for a global economy, "expand the supply of scientifically and technically trained men and women" was second.[14]

While there is general agreement about the need for an increased supply of technical personnel, there is little consensus about the nation's ability to graduate sufficient quantity or adequate quality of technically trained people. Supply of technical human resources is determined by the size and composition of the population, educational resources (e.g., faculty, facilities, and equipment), and the educational and career choices people make. While the first is known with near certainty, the other two are at least in part controllable and subject to public policies.

The most certain component of the projection of supply is the total number of 22-year-olds in the population who will be making career choices. Since that cohort is already born, we know that the number of 22-year-olds will decline—by more than 25 percent by the year 2000. Further, larger proportions of the 22-year-old population will be black and hispanic. In 1985, 17 percent of all 22-year olds were members of racial minorities; in 1995, the figure will rise to 19 percent. This has major implications for technological growth since minorities (other than Asians) have entered engineering and science at less than one-third as high a rate as young white adults, and the difference is even greater in advanced degree programs. That pattern does not seem to be changing significantly. Unless the current pattern does change, the declining entry-level age of this group will seriously impede the nation's ability to respond to increases in demand for a technically trained workforce. The other logical source of labor is women, but they too have participated at much lower levels than white males in the past.[15] Female enrollment in science and engineering in the 1970s has risen, but the most recent evidence cited by the Commission on Professionals in Science and Technology indicates that the gains have leveled—in part because economic opportunities for women in science and engineering remain fewer than for men (Table 12.3).

One response to the declining pool of available scientific and technical personnel is to try to increase the proportion of youth who enter technical fields. However, interest and proficiency in mathematics and science are established long before college, and thus efforts must begin early. According to a study cited by the National Academy of Sciences, "by 10th grade, four-fifths of students are already lost to the S/E talent pool judging from expressions of interest in mathematics, science, and engineering careers."[16] The losses continue through high school and college. By the time a student is a senior, only 1 in 12 high school seniors is taking any science course at all. Based on a survey of the high school class of 1972, 35 percent of all seniors (and 25 percent of all black seniors) who plan to study mathematics, science, or engineering in college change their plans before completing college. In 1983, 12 percent of all people with science or engineering degrees were employed in nonscientific occupations. The other important factor in estimating future supply based on college enrollments is the relative numbers of foreign nationals. At higher levels of education, the influx of foreign nationals into U.S. science programs is very large—often with financial assistance from federal and state governments. In 1985, for example, 46.6 percent of all master's-level students in science and technology and 53.1 percent of all doctoral-level students were foreign citizens. Since 1981 more than half of the doctorates in engineering awarded by U.S. schools have gone to foreign citizens, of whom more than 80 percent were from Asia or the

Table 12.3 Employed women and blacks in science and engineering careers as percentage of total employment, 1976 and 1986.

Field	Percentage			
	Women		Blacks	
	1976	1986	1976	1986
Engineers	1.6	4.0	1.2	1.7
Physical scientists	8.6	13.3	1.7	2.1
Mathematical scientists	23.7	25.9	5.3	5.2
Life scientists	15.9	25.0	2.3	2.1
Environmental scientists	7.1	11.6	3.6	0.9
Computer specialists	17.3	28.9	1.3	3.4

Source: National Science Foundation, *Women and minorities in science* (Washington, D.C.: U.S. Government Printing Office, 1988).

Middle East. In 1988, for the first time, more than half of the doctorates in mathematics were awarded to foreign nationals.

Since the main sources of science and engineering faculty are doctoral programs, and since many foreign nationals return to their homeland, the trend points to serious future shortages of faculty. In fact, 59.2 percent of all engineering department chairpersons reported shortages of faculty during the past four years.[17] As a result, almost half of all engineering teaching assistants were foreign nationals. Could higher education, however, meet its teaching needs without some reliance on foreign nationals? The evidence indicates that current faculty shortages would be exacerbated. For example, in 1982, 18 percent of all full-time engineering faculty and 21 percent of all computer science faculty earned their undergraduate degrees outside of the United States.

The difference in pre-collegiate preparation of U.S. and foreign students in science and engineering apparently results in differences in competencies. In the opinion of the engineering department chairpersons, U.S. students were considered superior on applications, such as designing equipment and running experiments, but foreign students were considered more skilled at developing models. The implication of this is that foreign nationals may be better prepared and better qualified for research. Although many American businesses are wary of sharing information with potential foreign competitors, there is no evidence that businesses are unwilling to use foreign nationals on R&D projects, except on classified or otherwise sensitive projects. However, overreliance on foreign nationals may be perceived as a problem as global competitiveness increases.

From a regional perspective, one more source of supply is from other parts of the country, and geographic mobility of professionals is frequently cited to assuage regional concern about potential shortages. For example, there are significant variations in the numbers of doctoral graduates among regions, as shown in Table 12.4. Even though scientists and engineers are more geographically mobile than the general public, there is a tendency to remain within a region of residency, either for cultural reasons or family, friendship, and school ties. As a result, geographic mobility is somewhat limited, and proximity to supply becomes an advantage to any research or technology-oriented business. Locating near a source of scientific talent, both for access to graduate students and a chance to pre-select new employees, can give a company a competitive edge.

Technicians, who are less likely to have left home to go to school, tend to be less mobile than professionals. Thus, proximity to sources of technical training also influences expansion and location decisions.

Table 12.4 Science and engineering Ph.D. graduates per 1,000 residents, by region for 1982.

Region	Ph.D. graduates/1,000
United States	0.16
New England	0.31
Mid Atlantic	0.17
Midwest	0.17
West North Central	0.15
East South Central	0.06
South Atlantic	0.12
West South Central	0.12
Mountain	0.15
Pacific	0.21

Source: SRI International, *Indicators of economic capacity* (Cleveland, OH: Ameri-Trust Corporation, December 1986).

The preparation of technicians, however, is not as tightly linked to public institutions. A recent analysis by the Department of Labor, for example, of where those employed in various occupations received their education to qualify for their positions shows the range of sources. Two categories, electronic technicians and computer operators, show the scope of the human resource development enterprise (see Table 12.5).

One other response to high demand and insufficient supply is occupational mobility. In theory, market conditions will raise prices of

Table 12.5 Sources of training for qualification for employment for two technical occupations, percentage of total employment, 1984.

Source of training	Electric & electronic technician	Computer operator	All occupations
Four-year college	11.2	7.4	16.5
Junior/community/tech. college	25.3	14.8	5.1
High school	5.7	11.4	4.8
Private post-high school	8.7	4.0	2.2
Public post-high school	2.6	1.7	1.6
Informal on-the-job training	39.1	43.9	27.8
Formal company training	18.5	15.4	9.7
Armed Forces	17.2	1.6	2.0
Correspondence	6.7	0.0	0.8
Other (families, friends)	1.8	1.4	3.3

Note: Numbers do not add to 100 per cent since respondents could list multiple sources of training and all employed did not report they had to qualify. *Source:* U.S. Bureau of Labor Statistics, *Occupational projections and training data*, 1986 edn. (Washington, D.C.: U.S. Department of Labor, April 1986).

occupations in short supply and induce people to shift to high demand occupations. The ability to change fields of technical specialization, however, is quite limited. Some members of the technical laborforce who work in production may be able to react to labor market demands. But those who have developed expertise in narrowly specialized fields, such as within defense industries, are less able to shift into new technical fields. This also means that technical skills are in danger of obsolescence without continuing education. Even less specialized technical work is not very flexible. It would be quite difficult, for example, for an industrial engineer to perform the work of a chemical engineer.

The quality of scientific and technical education

A growing number of critiques of scientific education in the United States suggest that the programs are not practical enough to respond to the needs of industry, are not international enough to cope with the changing structure of industry, and are educating and training with inadequate and outmoded equipment.

The first charge is aimed primarily at engineering schools—specifically that they do not prepare engineers adequately for positions in manufacturing. As Lester Thurow notes, "While America has as many research scientists and engineers as the rest of the world, when one steps beyond research, one discovers that America is an underengineered society. It graduates fewer engineers and scientists than its competitors, puts more into defense, and as a consequence is left with many fewer production engineers than its competitors."[18] Large federal defense contracts entice engineers away from the factories and into the "rarified realms" of space and defense programs and into research,[19] and instruction tends to reflect research for which faculty members are able to secure funding rather than the problems of industry. Engineering design has been relegated to a low priority in the engineering curriculum, while theory is given more weight. Manufacturing engineering has become a title used within industry or in the two-year college, but not in the top engineering schools. Employers report that new engineering graduates often are unable to contribute to design efforts and the company must invest in considerable retraining.[20] In contrast, in West Germany's universities, to obtain an engineering degree a candidate must work for six months in industry, and all engineering professors must have industrial experience.

The second criticism may be more difficult to rectify but is ultimately more important. A recent report by the National Research Council captures the problem, describing the parochialism of U.S. science and engineering curricula: "The educational background of American-born engineers rarely includes exposure to other cultures, and foreign-language skills are minimal."[21] Yet reverse investment, i.e., foreign corporations building and operating facilities in the United States, is growing rapidly, U.S. companies are investing off-shore, and an increasing number of technological innovations and patents are from foreign sources. At some point in their careers many engineers are going to find themselves working for foreign management or moving overseas to work for foreign or U.S. corporations. And nearly all those working in U.S. firms are going to have to monitor and understand foreign innovations, products, and markets, and this will require understanding of and adaptability to other cultures and languages. The report makes a number of recommendations aimed at internationalizing the engineering curricula and warns that "although improvements in the competitive status of the United States will not come about solely as a result of our becoming aware of technological progress made outside the United States, technological isolation will surely undermine the future of our industries and educational institutions."[22]

The last concern is the deteriorating quality of the universities' equipment and laboratories for science and engineering education and research. A study of the nation's science and engineering base by the U.S. General Accounting Office (GAO) in 1987 stated that "In recent years . . . [due to] indicators such as deterioration in university research instrumentation and facilities . . . concern has grown about the health of our science and engineering base."[23] Both the National Science Foundation (NSF) and the National Academy of Sciences (NAS) have released reports since 1985 that addressed the critical capital requirements for research and education. The NSF estimated the need in 1985 at $10 billion.[24] The cost of modernizing engineering laboratories alone was $1.2 billion in 1982. The NAS estimates that "the unmet needs for new construction and renovation vary in the range of $5 to $20 billion in the next 10 to 20 years."[25]

Education and industrial location

As technical skills and innovation become more important to industrial competitiveness, the education and training functions of higher education play a larger rôle in business location decisions. The attraction of business and industry to good education is a relatively new phenomenon. Even in the early 1980s, traditional business climate rankings did not assign high priorities to schools, colleges, or universities. The skills of the workforce were linked to the availability of vocational education and training programs, not to strengths of higher education or qualities of the local schools. College towns such as Madison, Wisconsin, Amherst, Massachusetts, Ann Arbor, Michigan, and Boulder, Colorado, were known for their pristine beauty, and they attracted self-employed professionals—lawyers, physicians, and consultants—but not large-scale employers. If anything, the presence of a college or university raised average local wages, and the aspirations of faculty members for good education for their children led to higher local school taxes.

Today, however, schools are being viewed in a new light. Universities are becoming meccas for economic growth, particularly if they have strong research or technical education programs. It is no longer just states' flagship universities that attract businesses. A second tier of colleges with expanding technical programs, including two-year community colleges and technical institutes, is adding programs and services to attract economic development to their states. The two-year technical colleges, in fact, may be best suited to support technology-based development because their mission is more explicitly and narrowly economic. Finally, there is a connection between business location decisions and the quality of elementary and secondary education. Many businesses have some demand for high school graduates with entry-level skills, including computer literacy and basic skills, and they therefore are concerned with the quality and content of local education. But, equally important, businesses' managers and workers with rising educational aspirations want to send their children to the best schools and will not be satisfied with a mediocre system.

These expanded visions of the rôles of educational institutions in economic development, particularly where advanced technologies are used or produced, have led to new attitudes toward spending on schools. From a local, state, and regional perspective, the new investment dollars that are attracted have become an important rationale for educational spending and a measure of a system's success. Increased spending on education is expected not only to create a more informed and more skilled populace, but to bring more jobs.

Studies on the impact of universities on site location, however, have not been able to isolate the education function of higher education. High skill levels of the occupants of an area can result from either the universities in the area or the in-migration of skilled workers. Similarly, linking universities with industrial location does not automatically suggest that the reason for the location is the training function of the university. Universities provide a wide array of services, such as research and cultural amenities, which may be a more important factor for firm location. As a result, examining the relation between either skill levels and location or universities and location directly addresses the question being considered: does production of skilled workers by community colleges and universities affect the location of industries, especially high-tech industries?

The remainder of this chapter will summarize the status of education in the new business climate indices; review some of the research on both the location patterns of high-tech firms and high-tech workers; and examine existing studies of the factors important to industrial location. Finally, conclusions will be made regarding the importance of the training component of higher education in determining the location of high-tech firms.

The rankings

The latest state economic climate indicators include a variety of measures of the quality of the states' education systems, including expenditures per pupil, R&D expenditures per capita, advanced degrees in science and engineering per capita, and professional publications. The shift away from factors that reflect only quantity, such as size of laborforce, wage rates, and financial incentives, to factors that imply quality, such as R&D dollars and local public schools, represents a significant change from the past. The indicators of economic capacity developed by SRI International and AmeriTrust[26] include a subindex called Accessible Technology, which includes nine different measures for a state's ability to support science and technology. *Making the grade*[27] includes a subindex for Technological Innovation and the Pool of Innovators that consists of measures of university performance.

These new factors are not criteria that the expanding or relocating textile firm, machine tool plant, or fabricator would have considered important a decade ago. On the contrary, low expenditures for public schools and accompanying low tax rates were an attraction to business, regardless of the implications for educational quality. Today businesses increasingly are aware of the importance of education and are willing to pay for better education, if they can be convinced that more money will result in better education. In 1987, according to the executive director of South Carolina's Development Board, businesses considering sites in the state asked about the quality of the schools, and many even asked to see average standardized test scores.

The changes in factors that indicate business climate imply a change in the type of business growth occurring around and about colleges. At one time, the university was perceived as an incubator for new businesses based on innovations developed by university faculty. Much of the growth that occurred was home-grown. Research Triangle Park was an early exception, actively recruiting companies from all over the world to North Carolina. Today, most states are adopting the techniques of yesterday's industrial recruiters: offering incentives and promoting the states' resources to attract businesses as well as encouraging expansion of existing businesses. Scientists and technicians often accompany state industrial recruiters seeking new employers, especially on overseas excursions. Companies that actually conduct research or desire working relationships with colleges or universities are locating in physical proximity to institutions of higher education. The changes in location decision criteria and models represent changes in products and production methods and new perspectives about the rôles of skill and knowledge in productivity and profitability.

Higher education and location decisions: new perspectives

Up until the 1970s firms making location changes were often those that employed mature technologies and long-run, standardized production processes. Physical inputs were more important than informational ones. As a result, the most important factors for the location of these firms were related to labor and material expenses. In contrast, today many of the highest growth firms occupy an earlier place on the product cycle and rely on flexible, often knowledge-driven production. These new firms are equally or more concerned with factors such as quality of life, the skills of the laborforce, and access to services.

Findings of industrial location studies conducted over time and on different types of firms reflect the changes in location factors. Before the 1980s most studies that ranked factors in industrial site decision found that access to markets was among the most important. Access to raw materials and labor supply were ranked second or third, depending on whether the firm was market-oriented or resource-oriented. Costs of transportation, facilities, labor, and utilities also ranked high.[28] These factors indicated an attempt on the part of firms to find the site that yielded the lowest measurable costs. Quality of life and other intangible factors generally were not listed in early locational studies.[29]

Recent studies have found that new location factors, including skill levels of workers, quality of life, and proximity to universities, have been added to and weigh heavily in investment decisions.[30] This is particularly true of high-tech companies. In one survey of high-tech firms, Premus found that their locational factors were significantly different from those normally reported for more traditional firms.[31] He discovered that although access to markets and transportation and energy costs remained high priorities, their importance was less than for other types of industries. Other factors, such as the presence of skilled labor, and factors that make it easy to attract and keep skilled labor, appear more important to high-tech firms than to other firms (Table 12.6).[32]

A number of other surveys of the location factors important to high-tech firms echo these findings. Schmenner's findings confirmed that high-tech firms value locational factors differently than do traditional firms.[33] For example, the importance placed on proximity to a college depended heavily on the type of firm. Only 11 percent of agriculture-related firms, and 14 percent of the specialty chemicals/metals firms felt that the presence of a university nearby would tip the balance in favor of locating at a site. More than 51 percent of the high-tech firms indicated that it would.[34] There also is evidence that location factors differ by the type of corporate function. A survey of corporate planners from Fortune 500 firms found that the importance of quality-of-life factors, such as climate, educational facilities, and culture, varied with the type of facility considered.[35] Quality of life was considered very important or critically important for locating headquarters and R&D functions in

Table 12.6 Factors that influence the regional locations of high-tech companies.

Attribute	Percentage designated significant or very significant
Labor skills/availability	89.3
Labor costs	72.2
Tax climate within region	67.2
Academic institutions	58.7
Cost of living	58.5
Transportation	58.4
Access to markets	58.1
Regional regulatory practices	49.0
Energy costs/availability	41.4
Cultural amenities	36.8
Climate	35.8
Access to raw materials	27.6

Source: R. Premus, *Location of high-tech firms in regional economic development* (Washington, D.C.: Joint Economic Committee of the Congress, 1982), p. 23.

83 percent and 82 percent of the responses, respectively. However, for locating branch plants and distribution centers, quality of life ranked in these categories in only 34 percent and 12 percent of the responses.

Although most industrial location surveys point to the increased importance of access to both skilled labor and universities in the location process, this does not automatically suggest that the location of firms is driven by the training function of higher education. Rather, firms may be drawn to higher education for other reasons. For example, firms may choose to locate near universities for easier access to researchers and research results. A survey of the research needs of Iowa industry found that "most of the manufacturers favored research facilities near research universities, although only 36 percent anticipated an immediate benefit to their firm."[36] Another survey, of high-tech companies across the nation that located their facilities in nonmetropolitan university cities, found that "opportunities for consultation with university people" and "availability of technical personnel with adequate skills" were the two factors that the largest number of respondents marked "absolutely critical."[37] A survey conducted for the Joint Economic Committee of the U.S. Congress in 1982 found that school factors ranked seventh out of 14 factors in importance to high-tech firms.

Another reason for the strong attraction of high-tech industries to institutions of higher education is the range of educational opportunities they offer in addition to technical education and training: continuing and adult education, lecture series, and precollegiate exposure for youth. These constitute important ingredients of the quality of life. Markusen, Hall, and Glasmeier found that educational options were significantly positively correlated with high-tech plant location.[38] Similarly, Herzog and Schlottman found that high-tech workers are significantly less likely to relocate if they live in an area with high-quality education (including higher education).[39] Both of these studies assumed that the quality and availability of higher education increased an area's quality of life and that this subsequently affected both business and worker location choices.

Still another advantage of locating in the vicinity of a university is that students can be employed part-time and during summers, thereby giving the business an opportunity to develop a relationship with the individual that may provide an edge in recruiting as well as a chance to evaluate the capabilities of the individual. A study conducted for the National Science Foundation found that the principal reason industry collaborates with universities in research is to gain early and close contact with students. This ensures a continual supply of skilled part-time employees and faculty consultants and a source of potential employees.[40] Irwin Feller, in his contribution to this book,[41] agrees that industries' primary benefits include access to graduate students as potential employees and access to competent scientists in lieu of expanded external staff commitments.

Locational patterns of technology-based industries and their workforces

There is significant evidence that although high-tech industries are popularly perceived as "footloose," their locational choices actually are quite limited. As Malecki suggests in this volume, despite policy efforts to disperse new technology and innovative economic activities, they display a persistent tendency toward agglomeration and concentration.[42] As evidence of this tendency, another study found that the location of high-tech firms is highly concentrated in particular areas of the nation. In 1977, 71 percent of the total employment in high-tech industries was concentrated in 13 states.[43] Even within these states, the growth of high-tech businesses in rural areas is much less than in metropolitan areas.[44]

In addition, it appears that the mobility of high-tech firms varies according to the stage of the product cycle they are in.[45] Glasmeier found that industrial sectors involved in the early phases of the product cycle migrated less than sectors in later stages;[46] the tendency is to remain close to corporate headquarters. Further, innovative firms appear to be tied to a small number of urban areas. The importance of concentration to firms in the early stages of a production cycle cannot be underestimated. By locating in close proximity to competitors, the firms have increased communication and innovation potential and access to more technical services and suppliers.[47] As they mature, the more routine functions disperse to more distant locations, but often still within the same region. These findings suggest that corporate functions involving the most skilled workers are the ones least likely to move, while those functions employing fewer skilled workers (e.g., branch plants) may be more mobile.

There is some evidence that the areas that attract high-tech firms also attract highly skilled workers and that an environment that will attract these workers is more important than the initial availability of a highly skilled workforce. As Markusen, Hall, and Glasmeier suggest, our reading of the literature on high-tech location and our own previous case studies suggest that high-tech labor pools have been created anew in locations like Silicon Valley, rather than drawing high-tech activity to a previously existing labor force. More relevant, then, are the amenities which are hypothesized to attract high-tech personnel to an area.[48]

If labor is drawn to high technology and not the other way around, studies of labor mobility ought to suggest what kinds of workers are most likely to move. Evidence does suggest that geographic mobility of all workers increases with education, skill, and occupation levels. According to one study, white-collar workers were almost twice as likely to leave their state of birth as were blue-collar workers.[49] Even among white-collar workers, professional salaried workers were 1.6 times as likely to leave their state of birth as were managerial salaried workers, and three times more likely to emigrate than blue-collar craft workers. Education and mobility are also positively correlated for professional and technical workers as a group. As these workers receive more education, their geographic mobility increases.

Mobility patterns also differ among workers in high-tech industries. One study examined the mobility of workers in high-tech industries in six occupational classes: computer specialists, engineers, mathematical specialists, life or physical scientists, operations or systems analysts, and engineering and scientific technicians.[50] It found that life or physical scientists were 3.5 times more likely to move than technicians and that computer specialists were over four times more likely to move than technicians. This difference in mobility among different high-tech occupations may explain Premus's finding relating to the type of labor skills executives deemed essential in location. While labor skills were ranked very high in determining location of high-tech firms in a region, when broken down by occupation, the presence of technical labor was valued most highly (Table 12.7).

Premus hypothesizes that one of the reasons for the differences in this ranking for technical workers may be the difference in "mobility rates of machinists, welders, and computer programers on the one hand, and engineers and scientists on the other. While the data are scarce, engineers and scientists appear to be a highly mobile population."[51]

The evidence that high-tech firms are relatively constrained in their location and that highly skilled personnel are in fact highly mobile suggests that the training of scientists is not as important as

Table 12.7 Influence of availability of workers on the location of high-tech companies within regions.

	Responding "significant" or "very significant" (%)
Technical	96.1
Skilled labor	88.1
Professional labor	87.3
Unskilled labor	52.4

Source: R. Premus, *Location of high-tech firms in regional economic development* (Washington, D.C.: Joint Economic Committee of the Congress, 1982), p. 25.

previously thought in affecting the location of high-tech firms. This is particularly true of those firms located in the early stages of the product cycle. In fact, there appears to be an inverse relationship between firm mobility and worker mobility. The earlier high-tech firms are on the product cycle, the more they are locationally constrained. Yet it is at this period that they hire a greater proportion of highly skilled and more geographically mobile labor. This suggests that highly skilled labor will tend to migrate to areas containing high-tech firms, especially those firms early in the product cycle.

Funding the training function of university education implies an investment in a factor of production that is highly mobile. Universities train scientists and engineers, but unless they are needed and stay where they are trained, the economic impact to the state is reduced. Markusen states that

> while high-tech jobs do coexist with highly skilled labor, the evidence suggests that these pools have been created by high-tech dynamism, rather than vice versa. Engineers and technicians have been recruited to new high-tech centers from other areas of the country. The brain drain from the industrial Midwest, which hosts many of the nation's top engineering schools, is particularly severe.[52]

The evidence presented here suggests that in terms of its training function, the importance of higher education in attracting firms may be overstated. Without other factors, such as metropolitan location, relevant research, and proximity to other similar firms, simply increasing technical educational and training opportunities at universities may not in itself attract firms. Rather, it may produce graduates who subsequently migrate to locations where firms are already situated.

However, where the other factors are present, training can add to an area's locational advantage.

At the two-year colleges, the effect of technical training is more pronounced and the training itself plays a rôle in attracting firms. As firms move down the product cycle they become more mobile, and they need fewer scientists and engineers and more technicians. Technical and community colleges that produce graduates with the types of skill needed by technology-based firms help ensure an area's skilled labor supply. Because technicians are more likely to be residents of the state in which the college is located, have family ties there, and prefer to remain there, firms are under more pressure either to train them themselves or to hire locally trained personnel. Therefore, it appears reasonable to expect that proximity to a first-rate two-year college may assure a continued supply of well-trained technicians, and investments in two-year colleges are likely to pay off locally.

Although additional support for higher education will not automatically translate into increased economic activity being attracted to the state, it is a necessary and important prerequisite. Further, despite these caveats about the independent effects of education on regional growth, a workforce that is more educated is likely to stimulate increased productivity and innovation among existing firms in the state.

Regional implications of technical human resource policies

The effects of any regional imbalances in the distribution of technically trained human resources are not easy to evaluate. Most analyses are made by comparing available demographic statistics. But what does it mean, for example, that North Carolina, considered by many to be a high-tech state, employs less than two-thirds as many scientists and engineers per 1,000 residents as the nation as a whole? Or is the South at a disadvantage because the states in the South Atlantic Census region graduate fewer Ph.D.s in science and engineering than the states in the Midwest? Conversely, do students select a graduate school because of a single recognized faculty member, or do they attend wherever they happen to be accepted, but then graduate and disperse? Professionals already are quite geographically mobile, and technicians are becoming more mobile. An automated plant in Tennessee, according to the manager of human resources, did not hesitate to recruit repair people from the Midwest.[53]

The locational aspects of technical human resources have much more to do with proximity to technical or scientific educational programs, the supplementary services provided, and chances for higher rates of recruitment. If a scientific or technical program is near enough to a school to employ student interns, to use its library, to contract with faculty consultants, to enroll in continuing education classes, the location may be a factor. Those influences generally are more prevalent among firms that are in innovative stages of growth. If, however, a technical resource such as industrial extension casts a statewide net, it may influence some firms' decisions regarding the state, and it may make existing state firms more competitive. Recruitment advantages are linked to a number of other factors, such as range of local opportunities and cultural amenities. Many graduates of MIT and Harvard science and engineering programs, for example, have chosen to remain nearby, in large part because of the concentration of scientific and technical resources in the vicinity. More isolated universities in communities that have less to offer keep few technical graduates. The University of Mississippi, for example, produces engineers for everywhere except Mississippi.

To the extent that states make the policies and provide much of the funding of scientific and technical human resource development, states as geographic entities may influence policy. But, as a result of the greater importance of close proximity of businesses to colleges and universities, differences in the relative availability of technically trained workers within a state or region often are greater than differences in relative availability among states or regions. Areas within a state that are distant from the sources of technical education benefit less from the programs and the state's investments.

Thus, it is our conclusion that the quality and quantity of scientific and technical resources are more strongly related to geographic areas defined by commuting patterns or state boundaries than to regional geographic territories. Regions are artificial groupings, often created by government agencies in order to reduce geographic areas of responsibility into territories of more manageable size, not to signify any rationally aggregated activity. Once data are gathered and displayed by these groupings, however, the regions assume policy significance. Hence, SRI's index of economic capacity is aggregated according to six Census regions, not by states. It is only when states have some political bond—forged by interstate or cooperative agreements, by history, or by similarities in their economies—that the term "region" takes on real significance.

Under conditions where the geographic region is meaningful, there are three arguments for considering regional aggregation of technical human resources. One is where a regionally concentrated industry has unique needs. The textile engineering programs at the North Carolina State University and Clemson University or the robotics programs in Michigan are prime examples of programs that might be considered regional resources. The second argument has to do with that somewhat nebulous term, "business climate." The scientific stature of a region can rise or fall on the quantity and quality of its technical human resources. New England has the reputation of being a high-tech region in large part because of the technical human resources choosing to remain in Massachusetts, but spilling over into southern Maine and New Hampshire. The third is where some political organization binds a region together, such as the Appalachian Regional Commission or the Tennessee Valley Authority. These programs have created some similarities in infrastructure and development strategies that could be rationalized on a regional basis.

Even if one accepts that human resources have regional implications, the policies and programs that shape them are enacted by states and by the federal government. To the extent that states borrow from or emulate their neighboring states, state policies can take on the appearance of regionalization. If the future turns out to be anything like economists and futurists believe it will, the quantity, quality, and distribution of the technical laborforce will be important policy considerations in economic development. Because it takes many years to develop scientific and technical resources, policy decisions made today will determine how well the South meets the challenge. In what directions might states look for policies and programs to enhance their scientific and technical human resources and those of the nation?

State strategies

If states and regions are to be able to keep up with the increasing demand for technically educated and trained workers, innovative public policies will be needed. Among the issues to be considered are: generating a continuing flow of scientists, engineers, and technicians through the educational system and into the workforce in the light of the changing demographic patterns; stabilizing the supply of instructors and professors; making engineering and science curricula more multidisciplinary and responsive to a global economy; and improving the quality and modernity of facilities and equipment. We shall now suggest some possible directions.

Respond to changing composition of the population

Perhaps the most critical issue facing southern policy makers is preparing for the changing composition of the cohort entering college. The approaching "majority minority," the large proportion of minorities and women in the freshman classes, portends problems. At present, there is too little active encouragement of careers in science, engineering, and technical fields. Interventions to keep technical career options open longer for youth must begin long before youth reach college age. It is particularly important to identify minorities and women with interests in and aptitudes for mathematics and science early and prepare them better.

The Southern Growth Policies Board addressed this issue in its report on the 1986 Commission on the Future of the South.[54] It recommended investing in a Top Scholars program at colleges and universities for promising female and minority high school students showing promise in mathematics, science, and technology. To ensure that the investment would have an impact on the state funding it, recipients would be required to work in the state for a specified period of time. Both nationally and regionally, Consortiums for Minorities in Engineering have formed, aimed at increasing minority access and providing model programs to increase minority enrollment.[55]

Take advantage of rising foreign national graduate students

Many foreign graduate students come to study intending to remain and work in the United States. Therefore, instead of viewing the large proportion of foreign nationals as a problem, industry ought to encourage them to work in the region and make plans to utilize their talents. These students represent, in effect, a subsidized resource and a large return on investment, since 90 percent of the foreign national students received their undergraduate educations abroad.

Broaden technical curricula

This is particularly important for engineers and technicians, who will be working in a rapidly changing environment. One issue is the globalization of the economy, which suggests a need to revise curricula. Scientists and engineers receive limited exposure to foreign affairs, while the large influx of foreign nationals into U.S. universities and the small number of Americans studying overseas give other nations a decided advantage. In the absence of increased study abroad, it will take a major change to the American curricula—by adding a large international component—to achieve full participation in international technology transfer and trade. One advantage of having a large number of foreign teaching assistants and professors is that students can be exposed to other cultures and economies.

A related and equally important need is for a more applied and multidisciplinary curricula. It is important, for example, to include enough liberal arts, business, and economics in the curriculum to produce a scientist, engineer, or technician who can adapt to change in technology, in management, and in business. One way to increase the value of engineering to southern industry might be to re-institute cooperative programs. These have a long history in American engineering education, and date back to the 1920s when businesses and university schools of engineering had closer relationships than today. The company gains access to the latest engineering knowledge and the student and the schools gain first-hand knowledge of the needs and problems of industry.

Encourage higher rates of enrollment in graduate programs in science and engineering

Because starting salaries in industry are so high, good students rarely consider pursuing their doctoral studies. This threatens a region's future supply of faculty and researchers. Financial support would have to be increased considerably to compete with industry. West Germany, for example, offers bright graduates stipends of $20,000 to $25,000 with yearly increases to enter graduate school.[56] Financial inducement to enter graduate school is thus one of the recommendations of the recent Task Force on Student Pipeline.[57] One possible alternative to direct stipends is to offer incentives to a company or to a consortium of firms in an industry that would benefit from stronger education to underwrite advanced education under an agreement that the individual would teach for a specified number of years.

Upgrade college instruction and R&D equipment and facilities

There also is persuasive evidence that the facilities and equipment of schools are not keeping pace with advances in technologies. The 1986

Commission on the Future of the South recommended a significant infusion of resources to bring engineering research and graduate programs into a strong, nationally competitive position, and this is one area in which additional funds are needed. Several states have programs targeted to provide scientific and technical equipment for universities.[58] For example New Jersey, in cooperation with the American Electronics Association, recently initiated a 1.6 million dollar program ($400,000 state funds and $1,200,000 in private funds) to increase the support of fellowships in electrical engineering and related disciplines and to purchase additional instructional equipment. In Pennsylvania, the Ben Franklin Partnership Engineering Equipment Grants Program has, with matching funds from the private sector, allocated over 12.5 million dollars since 1982 to engineering departments in the state for the purchase of state-of-the-art instructional equipment. Arizona, spurred by concerns that some high-tech firms were leaving the state for lack of an adequately skilled labor, invested twenty million dollars in Arizona State University's Center for Engineering Excellence to expand and upgrade the engineering instruction.

Moreover, as community and technical colleges develop more technologically sophisticated training programs they will need more advanced, state-of-the-art equipment on which to train students. They, too, are beginning to forge alliances with businesses similar to those established by universities. Tandem Corporation, for example, gave Foothill College in California more than $1 million in computer equipment and various corporations gave Middlesex Community College in New Jersey nearly $4 million to add a new manufacturing technology center. Cuyahoga Community College in Cleveland has corporate resource-sharing agreements with Ohio Bell, Rocketdyne, Xerox, Wang, and other corporations.

Consider "2+2+2" programs in selected technical colleges

The standard definition of "2+2" is combining the last two years of high school with associate degree programs. An extrapolation of that concept is "2+2+2," in which the two-year curriculum is articulated with baccalaureate degree programs. This would give the best graduates of technical education programs opportunities to continue on for engineering degrees. Since 43 percent of all college students in the nation are in two-year institutions, this is a large pool of potential talent. In order to make this a reality, however, the fundamentals taught in the two-year schools would have to be made more rigorous. Calling a course "Physics" or "Calculus" does not ensure that it meets the standards of a university freshman course. Most courses in two-year colleges, in fact, do not because that level of theory is not necessary for their purposes. More advanced courses would have to be added to the curriculum.

Raise the stature of manufacturing engineering

In the early days of engineering, the curriculum focused strongly on improving industrial processes. Engineering today, however, is oriented much more toward theoretical research, which draws more federal research money and academic rewards, than to application. In part as a result of this shift, the status of industrial engineering has become a less prestigious program than, for example, chemical, electrical, or nuclear engineering. Lester Thurow remarks that "While scientists and R&D are admired in the United States, production engineering ranks much lower."[59] States can raise the stature of careers in production in the eyes of high school counselors, students, and college advisors. States might also consider providing scholarships for manufacturing engineering and university chairs for industrial engineering, organizing special in-service training for counselors about the opportunities and needs, providing state R&D grants to applied manufacturing research, or making awards to top industrial engineering students.

Extend outreach for technical education to nonmetropolitan areas

Several states have put in place specific programs to improve their science and engineering programs and increase the supply of technical personnel. Florida and Michigan have established programs to transmit engineering courses by telecommunications from the state universities to firms within the state. In Michigan, for example, General Motors engineers can receive instruction from one of several universities in the state without leaving work. Community colleges have created programs aimed at meeting the demand for technicians across the states. In 1985, Florida established its Centers of Electronics Emphasis program, which includes support of ten vocational schools—five community colleges and five vocational–technical schools—to set up an electronics training curriculum package to meet the needs of the state's growing electronics industries. Incentives, such as forgiving part of student loans or increasing graduate school scholarships, could be designed to encourage engineers to work in depressed areas.

A final word

State governments have not had to concern themselves about science and technical education in the past much beyond footing the bills and allowing the schools and student demand to determine the programs. The crises in science and technology education that occurred, for instance, in the aftermath of Sputnik, have been considered national issues for the federal government to address, not actions for state governments. Now that science and technology are perceived as economic development, however, they have become state and regional policy issues and states now must address the needs of their colleges and universities or risk losing their technological competitiveness in both domestic and world markets.

Notes

1 President's Commision on Industrial Competitiveness, *The higher education–economic development connection* (Washington, D.C.: Government Printing Office, 1984).
2 D. F. Noble, *America by design: science, technology, and the rise of corporate capitalism* (New York: Knopf, 1977).
3 Task Committee on Undergraduate Science and Engineering Education, *Undergraduate science, mathematics, and engineering education* (Washington, D.C.: National Science Board, 1986).
4 Center for Policy Research, *The role of science and technology in economic competitiveness* (Washington, D.C.: National Governors' Association, 1987).
5 G. T. Silvestri & J. M. Lukasiwicz, "A look at occupational employment trends to the year 2000," *Monthly Labor Review* **110**, September 1987,
6 Interestingly, Table 12.1 shows that although the demand for most categories of scientists, engineers, and technicians increased faster than the demand for overall employment, the projected rates of increase were considerably lower than those projected for 1984–95 just two years earlier. The reasons for the decline apparently are based on a change in the projection for manufacturing employment in total. In 1984, DOL projected a net gain for manufacturing employment by 1995, but in a 1986 reversal it projected a net loss over the next 14 years.
7 H. A. Hunt & T. L. Hunt, *Human resource implications of robotics* (Kalamazoo, Mich.: Upjohn Institute, 1983).
8 R. H. Beznek, E. M. Zampelli & J. D. Jones, "Do scientists always benefit?" *Issues in Science and Technology* **4**, Fall 1987, 28–35.
9 S. Cohen & J. Zysman, *Manufacturing matters* (New York: Basic Books, 1987).
10 Office of Technology Assessment, *Demographic trends and the scientific and engineering work force: a technical memorandum* (Washington, D.C.: Government Printing Office, 1985).

11 The projections are based on a model developed by Herring & Sanderson for 191 Report of the President of Princeton University but incorporating OTA's own sets of assumptions.

12 See *National roundtable on economic development: report and recommendations* (Washington, D.C.: American Association of Community and Junior Colleges, 1987).

13 Government/University/Industry Research Roundtable, *Nurturing science and engineering talent: a discussion paper* (Washington, D.C.: National Academy of Sciences, 1987).

14 S. Groennings, "Economic competitiveness and international knowledge," staff paper II (Boston: New England Board of Higher Education, October 1987).

15 National Science Foundation, *Women and minorities in science and engineering* (Washington, D.C.: Government Printing Office, 1986).

16 Government/University/Industry Research Roundtable, *Nurturing science and engineering talent.*

17 E. Barber & R. P. Morgan, "The impact of foreign graduate students on engineering education in the United States," *Science*, April 1987, 33–7.

18 L. C. Thurow, "A Weakness in Process Technology," *Science* **238**, December 1987, 1059.

19 J. Rowe, "Why the engineers left the shop floor," *Washington Monthly*, June 1984, 12–21.

20 A. D. Kerr & R. Byron Pipes, "Why we need hands-on engineering education," *Technology Review* **90**, October 1987, 37–42.

21 Committee on International Cooperation in Engineering, *Strengthening U.S. engineering through international cooperation* (Washington, D.C.: National Academy Press, 1987).

22 Ibid.

23 General Accounting Office, *U.S. Science and engineering base: a synthesis of concerns about budget and policy development* (Washington, D.C.: United States General Accounting Office, March 1987).

24 National Science Foundation, *Infrastructure: The capital requirements for academic research* (Washington, D.C.: Government Printing Office, May 1987).

25 National Science Board, *Academic research facilities: financing strategies* (Washington, D.C.: National Academy Press, 1986).

26 SRI, International, *Indicators of economic capacity* (Cleveland: AmeriTrust Corporation, December 1986).

27 Corporation for Enterprise Development, *Making the grade* (Washington D.C.: Corporation for Enterprise Development, 1987).

28 T. E. McMillan, Jr., "Why manufacturers choose plant location vs. determinants of plant locations," *Land Economics*, August 1965, 239–46.

29 J. P. Blair & R. Premus, "Major factors in industrial location: a review," *Economic Development Quarterly* **1**, 1987, 72–87.

30 For a discussion of this see J. Rees & H. Stafford, "Regional growth and industrial location," in *Technology, regions, and policy* (Totowa, N.J.: Rowman & Littlefield, 1986).

31 R. Premus, *Location of high-tech firms in regional economic development* (Washington, D.C.: Joint Economic Committee of the Congress, 1982), p. 16. One drawback to location studies based on surveys of those firms locating is that responses may be biased in efforts to influence public policy. By listing state and local taxes as an important factor, for example, respondents may hope to influence tax policy. It seems reasonable to assume, however, that responses concerning skilled workers are unlikely to be biased.

32 For example see M. A. Buck, et al., *Feasibility of high-tech company incubation in rural university settings* (Rolla, Missouri: Missouri IncuTech, April 1984); also J. Rees & H. Stafford, "High technology location and regional development: the theoretical base," in *Technology, innovation, and regional economic development* (Washington D.C.: Office of Technology Assessment, 1984).

33 R. W. Schmenner, *Making business location decisions* (Englewood Cliffs, N.J.: Prentice-Hall, 1982), p. 52.

34 J. Lyne, "Site selectors say 'brain power' making quality-of-life factors critical," *Site selection handbook*, August 1987.

35 D. H. Swanson, "Transferring technologies to industry," *Issues in higher education and economic development* (Washington, D.C.: American Association of State Colleges and Universities, 1986).

36 M. A. Buck, et al., *Feasibility of high-tech company incubation.*

37 J. Rees & H. Stafford, "Theories of regional growth and industrial location: their relevance for understanding high-technology complexes," in *Technology, regions, and policy*, p. 44; also E. J. Malecki, *Research and development and the geography of high-technology complexes, in technology, regions and policy*, p. 61.; also K. P. Jarboe, "Location decisions of high technology firms: a case study," *Technovation* **4**, 1986, 117–129.

38 A. Markusen, P. Hall, & A. Glasmeier, *High tech America* (Boston: Allen & Unwin, 1986), p. 155.

39 H. W. Herzog, Jr., & A. M. Schlottmann, *Metropolitan dimensions of high-technology location in the U.S.: worker mobility and residence choice* (unpublished manuscript, 1987).

40 L. Peters & H. I. Fusfeld, "Current U.S. university-industry research connections," in *University-industry research relationships: selected studies* (Washington, D.C., 1982), as cited in Useem, *Low tech education in a high tech world*, p. 181.

41 See Chapter 15.

42 See Chapter 13.

43 A. K. Glasmeier, *High technology industries in the mid-1970's: the distribution of employment*, Working Paper No. 429, University of California, Berkeley, Institute of Urban and Regional Development, 1984.

44 A. K. Glassmeier, *High tech industrialization for whom? the distribution of high tech employment in rural America: a ten year perspective*, Paper presented to the U.S./European Conference on Regional Innovation and Competitiveness, Neuchatel, Switzerland, September 24–5, 1987.

45 See R. M. Ady, "High-technology plants: different criteria for the best location," *Commentary*, Winter 1983.

46 Glasmeier, 1987.

47 N. Dorfman, "Route 128: the development of regional high-tech economy" *Research Policy* **12**, 1983.

48 Markusen, Hall, & Glasmeier, *High tech America*, 1986, p. 146.

49 A. R. Miller, "Interstate migrants in the U.S.: some social and economic differences by type of move," Demography **14**, February 1977, 9.

50 H. W. Herzog, Jr., & A. M. Schlottmann, 1987.

51 Premus, p. 24.

52 A. Markusen, "High-tech plants and jobs," *Commentary*, Fall 1986, 5.

53 S. Rosenfeld, E. Malizia, & M. Dugan, *Reviving the rural factory: automation and work in the South* (Research Triangle Park, Southern Growth Policies Board, May 1988).

54 Commission on the Future of the South, *Halfway home and a long way to go* (Research Triangle Park, NC, 1986).

55 D. Lightman, "Minorities in engineering: a model for success," *Focus* **16**, March 1988.

56 S. Penner, "Tapping the wave of talented immigrants," 1988, p. 79.

57 Engineering Deans Council, *Report of task force on student pipeline*, unpublished paper, American Society for Engineering Education, 1988.

58 E. L. Useem, *Low tech education in a high tech world* (New York: Free Press, 1986).

59 L. C. Thurow, "A weakness in process technology," p. 1661.

13

University–industry R&D relationships

IRWIN FELLER

Introduction

THE REASONS FOR and history of the recent upsurge in university–industry research and development (R&D) relationships in the United States are well known: secular retardation in productivity growth rates, chronic balance of trade deficits—including the waning of trade surpluses in "high-tech" products—and the quest by Rustbelt states to restructure their economies. These trends have led to widespread acceptance of the propositions that the United States has underinvested in domestically oriented research and development and has failed to develop the institutional linkages among sectors of the economy that would accelerate conversion of new scientific advances into commercially applicable technology. The formation of "new alliances" among academia, industry, and government is a widely accepted means of redressing this situation. The benefits to universities and industries of closer collaboration have been extensively described.[1] For industry, the major benefits are access to graduate students as potential employees; access to specialized faculty expertise in lieu of expanded internal staff commitments; and access to new ideas, approaches, and products that enhance the competitive positions of industry groups or individual firms. For universities, the major benefits are research funds for specific projects; acquisition of up-to-date equipment, both for research and instruction; opportunities for faculty to become current with the state of the art in industrial science and technology; an alternative to federal-agency sponsorship of research, which is increasingly perceived as imposing undesirable regulatory constraints on academic behavior; internship and job placement opportunities for students; supplementary income from consulting; and the university's enhanced ability to present itself as contributing to the local, state, or national economy. The "climate" for cooperation is widely seen to have improved and the means to have been found to overcome many, if not all, impediments to university–industry research relationships.[2] University faculty are seen as having been weaned away from exclusive enamoredness with federal or foundation sponsorship of research; industry is seen as having recognized that faculty have findings relevant to their needs; and each group has been found to look more favorably upon the mutual benefits from collaborative undertakings.[3] Clearly issues remain to be worked out by the two sectors, such as the apportionment of intellectual property rights through patent and license agreements or conflicts of interest for faculty if they simultaneously conduct industrially sponsored research and consult with their sponsors in the same specific research area.[4] But, overall, reservations concerning the appropriateness or effectiveness of closer collaboration have been tabled in the present period of "positive-sum" aspirations, specters of long-term economic decline, and programmatic advocacy.

This chapter offers a different perspective on these emergent patterns of collaboration. It focuses less on the generic reasons for collaboration and more on the characteristics of the firms and universities that enter into alliances. The chapter's unifying theme is that of search. The "new alliances" of recent years are frequently described as "experiments" to highlight the perception that the character of these relationships differs in a meaningful manner from the long-standing pattern by which firms contract for performance of faculty research, and also to suggest the problematic and yet-to-be solidified character of recent forms of collaboration.[5] More properly, these undertakings represent searches by firms to adapt their competitive behavior to an economic system characterized by shifts in the importance of a particular production input, "knowledge," and by universities to adapt their internal values, attitudes, and organizational norms to the more transparent status of "science as a commodity."[6] Although necessarily retreading some familiar ground, this perspective facilitates the analysis of the characteristics and boundaries of university–industry alliances for the performance of research and development.

The chapter has two starting points: (a) the economics of technological change, and (b) the organizational missions and norms of universities. It is presented in four parts. The first part offers a general conceptualization of the process of technological innovation, including a critique of the manner in which current treatments of collaborative relationships differentiate between "research" and "technology transfer." The second and third parts describe, respectively, structural trends in the private sector and in universities related to research and development, and examine why and how bilateral arrangements have been entered into from among the multiple options available to each party.[7] The concluding part identifies stresses likely to affect the evolution of stable relationships.

The exploratory nature of this chapter should be noted. University–industry partnerships are emerging amidst a complex and fluid period in which federal, state, regional, and local government, industry, and university rôles and relationships related to research, technology development, and commercialization are being redefined. Positing conceptually discrete categories is a necessary means of comprehending this diversity, but it does not eliminate the jumble now found or the hybrid forms that may emerge. Moreover, although the analysis is couched in terms susceptible to empirical treatment, available data sets are too fragmentary to permit systematic testing of its propositions. Published data on university–industry partnerships, mainly from the National Science Foundation (NSF), are of a highly aggregate character and of limited use to the line of analysis developed here. Several researchers[8] have labored assiduously to compile basic descriptive series and have produced useful typologies, but major data gaps exist concerning aggregate magnitudes; very little information exists at the disaggregated level. Journalistic accounts and more detailed case studies are increasingly plentiful, but these reflect divergent lines of analysis so that any cumulative understanding is limited. Frequently cited models of university participation in processes of technology change (e.g., agricultural research and technology transfer) are poorly understood and are misapplied to contemporary issues.[9] Other facets of university involvement in technology transfer (e.g., technical assistance programs) are also cited widely but have received little systematic study. Moreover, current citations of forms of partnership relate only to successes, not to the substantial body of failures in endeavors closely resembling current initiatives.[10]

Any treatment of university–industry relationships in the context of these multiple changes is, thus, at best, a partial analysis. Impacting on these relationships are policies and actions by the federal government through its promotion of engineering research centers; by state governments through their establishment of advanced technology center programs; and by universities as they seek to develop industrial parks and incubators and to participate in venture capital funds in order to commercialize findings originating from faculty research. These other interventions may reinforce or distort incentives for universities and firms to work together to link academic research and development more effectively with commercially applicable technological innovation.

Research and technology transfer

Embedded in any examination of the relative benefits to industries and universities of collaborative undertakings are the relative competencies of each and of other institutions to perform the several tasks contained within a system of technological change. Indeed, the call for new alliances, in part, represents a statement that traditional assignment of rôles—universities as performers of basic research (science) and firms as performers of applied research and development—is an oversimplified depiction of reality, both past and present.

Any analytical or prescriptive assessment of the content of university–industry R&D alliances is dependent upon a prior employment of a theory (or theories) of technological innovation. More importantly, it is dependent on assumptions made as to the character of linkages between and among stages in any linked set of activities that encompass basic research and technological innovation as nominally polar positions as well as the "characterization" of the knowledge generated and transferred through these stages.

Processes of technological change are treated in an extensive literature. Stage- or process-models (e.g., basic research/applied research/development/commercialization) are widely used analytical devices,[11] although the limitations of the approach are well-known. Critiques of this approach emphasize the nonlinear, multidirectional flows of causation and influence existing between and among stages and the looseness of causal links between "science" and "technology." Given these caveats, process models remain useful depictions of the way decisions are made by the several sectors participating in new collaborative relationships. Firms make decisions between basic, applied, and developmental research, or at least report that they do on

NSF survey forms. Department of Defense laboratories allocate funds among 6.1 (Basic Research), 6.2 (Exploratory Development), and 6.3 (Advanced Development) categories; faculty committees weigh the basic and applied content of published papers in promotion and tenure committees; and state advanced technology programs consider the "applied" or "academic" nature of pending proposals in allocating program funds. The need for some form of process model arises because permeating the discussion of new alliances are implicit theories as to linkages between "research" and "technology transfer." Technology transfer has had and continues to have several different meanings, including improving research utilization, spinoff functions from other R&D activities, and technical assistance.[12] Most generally, it has meant the movement of a particular technique, a specific "hardware," from an original user to a different set of users.

In more current usage concerning university–industry collaboration, technology transfer is defined as "the process through which the results from basic and applied research are communicated to potential users,"[13] or as follows: "University–industry cooperative research is heavily oriented to technology transfer, the movement of ideas and innovations from university laboratories and research centers to industry and on to the marketplace."[14] Rogers' description of the stages of the corporate R&D process and of the way in which university-based knowledge enters into the processes (see Fig. 13.1) is particularly appropriate

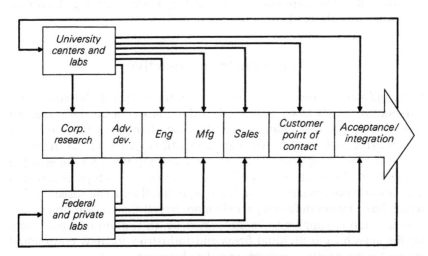

Figure 13.1 Technology transfer continuum. *Source:* D. M. Amidon Rogers, "Building the technology transfer infrastructure: contrast with Japan," 1987 International Symposium of the Technology Transfer Society, June.

here, for it highlights the overlapping set of tasks associated in the transfer of technology between the firm and external sources of research and development, and among activities (and divisions) within a firm. First, university-based R&D activities may relate to several different stages of the firm's research/development/commercialization process. Second, except at the endpoints of sales and consumer point of contact, where typically one does not expect to find university involvement, the contribution of university research and development must still be integrated within the firm into a multidirectional flow of activities and decisions. Finally, the schema highlights a central but widely misunderstood feature of university–industry relationships, namely that the transfer of knowledge occurs at whatever stage of the process of technological innovation universities and firms happen to be forming alliances. What differs is the character of the knowledge and the form in which it is transferred.

A comparable perspective emerges if the worldview is rotated and the university is placed at the center. The type of research and development (knowledge) that universities provide would be arrayed (and labeled) along the following continuum: major advances at the "frontiers of knowledge" in either science or technology (e.g., "basic research"); problem-solving activities that involve some combination of new applications of known principles or of incremental advances in the state of the art (e.g., "applied research"); and specific problem-solving activities, involving applications of existing knowledge (e.g., technical assistance or outreach).

The industry perspective

From industry's perspective, increased interest in collaborating with universities needs to be examined in the context of (a) the increased rôle of technological change as a strategic element in the means by which firms seek to improve their competitive position; (b) increases in private-sector support of research and development; (c) the growing recognition of the importance of strategic research—a type of research that is more proprietary and industry-specific than basic research, but which has a longer deferred period before payoff than development and which is too expensive to be supported by an individual firm;[15] and (d) the search by individual firms and industries for new contractual means for supporting research and development.

Technology, according to competitive strategy theorists such as Porter,[16] provides a unique strategic variable to nullify the advantage of incumbent firms and to create opportunities for newcomers and followers. Technological change is prized not only for its conventional effects (e.g., process innovations that lower production costs or product innovations that serve to create new demands), but because it strengthens the ability of a firm to shape its competitive environment. Technological change may elevate barriers to entry through changed capital requirements; it may enhance or eliminate opportunities for product differentiation; it may alter a firm's relationships with the matrix of supplier, distribution, and user firms with which it is connected.

Technology strategy relates to the options a firm has as to how it employs its scientific and technical resources. The elements of technology strategy include decisions to compete or cooperate; to develop internal or external capabilities; to develop centralized (corporate-level) or decentralized R&D organizations;[17] and to behave "offensively" or "defensively" in initiating or imitating innovative behavior.[18]

Increases in corporate support of industrial research and development for both basic and applied work is another background factor. Industrial funding of R&D projects has increased in constant dollars every year since 1975. Company-funded expenditures rose by 6.6 percent between 1976 and 1980, by 5.5 percent between 1980 and 1984, and by approximately 7 percent between 1984 and 1986.[19] These rates of increase are considerably above those noted for the 1965–76 period, when the slowdown in rates of productivity growth and the deterioration in U.S. international competitiveness, as measured in balance of trade flows in manufactured commodities, first became evident. In current dollars, industry expenditures for research and development in 1985 totaled an estimated $77.5 billion. Two-thirds of this total or $52.4 billion came from company funds.[20] Within the industrial sector, the largest percentage increases in research and development were found in a relatively small number of "high-tech" industrial groupings, such as chemicals and electrical equipment, which in the aggregate increased expenditures from $15.0 billion in constant (1972) dollars in 1976 to $22.0 billion in 1983. R&D expenditures in all other manufacturing industries rose only from $4.7 billion to $6.2 billion. In traditional "smokestack" industries, such as steel, declines in output and employment were matched by decreased levels of R&D expenditures.[21]

Beyond increasing their support of internal R&D units, firms have shown an increased willingness to enter into collaborative R&D relationships with a variety of external sources. These are usually a complex assortment of alliances, with firms variously taking on rôles as prime contractor, subcontractor, and coequal. These alliances include bilateral and multilateral relationships and formal consortia, such as the Microelectronics and Computer Technology Corporation (MCC) and the Semiconductor Research Corporation (SRC). The means by which these rôles are assumed include increased support of corporate R&D laboratories, internal venturings, contracted research (both as performer and sponsor), acquisition of firms, licensee, joint venture, equity participation, and others. These alliances have generally been directed at earlier, "more generic parts of the R&D spectrum" and are seen as supplementary to the firm's principal reliance on internal corporate R&D activities for new technologies.[22]

Given all these developments, the limits to the importance of new alliances to either the university or to industry must be kept in mind. Industry's direct expenditures for research and development at universities and colleges have increased in every year since 1970. In 1985, they totaled an estimated $485 million (current dollars), or 0.009 percent of total industry expenditures of $52.4 billion from internal funds for research and development in that year and about 5 percent of the estimated $9.6 billion expended in academic research and development.[23] More recent estimates for 1986 report a total level of industrial support of $670 million, or about 8 percent of academic expenditure for research and development.[24]

Viewing characteristics of the university–industry alliances in terms of these background conditions suggests that for industry a search process is underway that has three principal components: first, among industries where the underlying sorting mechanisms are the rate at which changes in the scientific and technical knowledge base underlying an industry's product and processes affect intra-firm and interindustry competition; second, by firms within an industry concerning the allocation of resources to different forms of research and development (e.g., basic/applied research); and third, by different-sized firms for means of matching their internal capabilities to assimilate scientific and technological knowledge and their collaboration with external R&D performers. As outlined above, the first of these arrays is evident in the NSF data and the differential rates of R&D expenditure among industries. The second is evident in the increased recourse to external alliances and again in the characteristics of these alliances. The third component, however, has not been adequately treated, and is the focus of the remainder of this chapter.

Firms obviously are interested in having any R&D project produce commercially relevant outcomes. Collaboration with academic scientists through contracting for research projects is one way of securing the scientific expertise of researchers who select the university as the base of their employment. These projects may, of course, generate new products or processes. Several new arrangements appear to have met the expectations of their industrial sponsors for such payoffs. Blumenthal, Gluck, Louis, and Wise's study[25] of biotechnology firms found that such firms which contracted for university research found these contracts to be far more productive of new knowledge for their firms than was in-house research. Research performed at universities produced more than four times as many patent applications per industry dollar invested in R&D projects than did in-house research, as well as producing other forms of trade secrets. Larsen and Wigand report that microelectronics firms were satisfied with collaborative R&D projects produced by faculty at the University of Arizona that stemmed from their support.[26] Journalistic accounts also highlight the tangible products that have flowed from such collaboration.[27] Monsanto has extended its initial contract with Washington University–St. Louis,[28] indicating again a "market demonstration" that the firm has received "value" for its expenditures.

But besides immediately usable scientific or technical advances, firms also are interested in obtaining a "window" into the future as to the economically relevant aspects of science provided by basic research. They also seek lead time over competitors as to which newly uncovered scientific paths are most likely to lead to commercially important end products. Lead time, in contrast to more traditional means of establishing property rights in intellectual knowledge such as patent rights, has taken on new saliency as a means by which firms seek to appropriate the benefits of research.[29] The willingness, for example, of large, high-tech firms to join together to form MCC has been attributed to the fact that

> participation buys lead time through using MCC results. Imitation will not begin until the products using MCC results are marketed or the processes are in commercial use. Then on average it will take imitators two to three years to bring their products or processes into use. A lead time of this duration is very valuable in a rapidly changing industry in which consumers value technical progress highly.[30]

The type of research sought by a firm, and consequently both the type of competencies brought by the academic researchers with whom it seeks to collaborate and the form of the contract it is willing to enter into, are thus influenced by the firm's internal capacity to assimilate differently configured bundles of new knowledge. Following this line of analysis, the key to cooperative university–industry agreements that emphasize basic research or generic applied research is, simultaneously, consistency with a firm's internal capabilities to assimilate new knowledge and with individual faculty/university standards for promotion, tenure and pursuit of academic status. According to the Government/University/Industry Research Roundtable, "The capacity of industry to assimilate advances in research is related to the internal technical capabilities of the industry."[31] The reason for this, according to Mowery, is that there are "significant costs to adopting any solution to firm-specific production settings."[32] The emphasis on windows and lead time carries with it the important implication that the firms who so characterize their collaboration with universities are capable of taking "basic" academic research and working through the applied and developmental R&D necessary to create commercializable products and processes with their own in-house scientific staffs. Not surprisingly, then, one finds that the major long-term contracts for basic research which focused attention on "new alliances," such as those between Monsanto–Washington University of St. Louis and Hoeschst AG–Massachusetts General Hospital–Harvard, have involved firms that have their own internal scientific staffs. This set of characteristics of academic and industrial partners is also evident in the internal logic of SRC's design, in which member companies provide support for what is essentially a decentralized research program conducted at about 30 U.S. universities. The support by individual firms of a basic research program in which publication of findings occurs in the open literature can be explained mainly in terms of the firms' ability to specify research areas and select faculty members to perform this research, and then to be better able to use these findings than nonmembers. As Peck has noted,

> Technology turns out to be more proprietary in its character than economists have thought, at least in the computer and semiconductor industries. For an individual company, access to research can provide a significant competitive advantage, largely in terms of lead time it gives in the marketplace. Old technology may be freely available but a rapid pace of technical advance means that old technology is no substitute for access to current research.[33]

All this suggests the "fit" that has occurred and is likely to continue to hold in the "basic" segment of the R&D continuum, at least between those firms in those industries that are R&D-intensive and those universities whose faculty are regarded as conducting research at the frontiers of knowledge.[34]

These statements of the economic benefits to firms of underwriting university research, however, have important limiting dimensions. Although academic scientists, as Etzkowitz has noted, "have often been eager and willing to direct, or participate in, programs of research and development aiming at commercial application, firms, for their part, do not look to universities for commercial products as such."[35] Instead, they look for new ideas, synergy between their research program and that of the university, and trained students. For example, Robinson notes for the microelectronics industry that "Academic research is not likely to serve as a substitute for research conducted by industrial scientists and engineers who actually develop innovations. Rather, the importance of university research will lie in specialized areas that are only loosely coupled to firms' efforts to define and develop proprietary technologies."[36] Other observers point to the limits of these relationships, albeit in the opposite direction: firms participating in collaborative relationships set the development of patentable and potentially commercial products as important goals, do not consider these developments to be likely outcomes, and yet still report satisfaction with their collaboration.[37]

The university perspective

The generic benefits to universities of closer collaboration with industry have been noted. What needs to be examined are the specific types of knowledge a university is willing (able) to offer to obtain these benefits and the organizational and contractual forms it uses to provide this knowledge.

Universities differ in their capabilities to perform research and in their institutional goals. At the aggregate level, universities can be said to have articulated missions, promulgated internal reward systems, and established organizational counterparts that correspond to the basic/applied developmental stages of the R&D process. Viewed again in the aggregate, performance of the tasks associated with each discrete activity in the continuum can be and is compatible with a wide variety of university criteria for appointment, promotion, tenure, and salary increases. But the aggregate is not a useful guide for determining the sustainability of cooperative undertakings between specific pairs. The need to disaggregate institutional characteristics emerges from the concentrated character of research and graduate education activities within American universities. In 1982, there were 1,457 four-year institutions that offered a baccalaureate degree in at least one science or engineering field. Of this total, 365 institutions offered a master's degree and 295 a doctorate. In 1983, 100 doctorate-granting institutions accounted for 84 per cent of total academic R&D expenditures.[38]

More germane to the formation of new alliances is the extent to which the several possible tasks related to research and development—basic research, applied research—mesh with the objectives of different groupings of universities. Classification systems, such as the widely used Carnegie Foundation typology of doctorate-granting universities and comprehensive universities, capture many but not all of these differences.[39] More accurately, capturing the relevant goal-directed behavior of universities is a hybrid array based on the following three groupings: prestige maximization; market utility; and comprehensiveness.[40] The elements of the first two of these groupings are described by Friedman and Friedman as follows:

> Like all complex organizations, universities have diffuse and sometimes conflicting goals and missions. One goal, however, is paramount and universal among the leading research universities: the maximization of prestige. Prestige is not an abstraction but rather the cornerstone of economically motivated behavior. The preeminent universities attract the renowned scholars, the intellectually outstanding graduate and undergraduate students, and the funding that assures continued supremacy.

> In times of scarce resources, two opposing strategies hold the most economic promise. Institutions can adopt a market utility approach whereby they abandon any serious attempt to be more than a regional or local university, pander to local interests, and actively seek the research grants and contracts that the other camp disdains. The prestige model derives its revenue by sustaining its national and international reputation, catering to a cosmopolitan faculty and student body, and enjoining only those research activities that accentuate its greatness.[41]

The third category reflects the activities of most public colleges and universities, which evolved from teachers' colleges or technical schools into comprehensive colleges or universities. These institutions are characterized as emphasizing undergraduate teaching and applied research rather than graduate work and basic research.[42]

The relationship between this array and various activities related to the performance of research and development is depicted in Figure 13.2. The vertical axis depicts the stages of the R&D process. The horizontal axis denotes the institutional utility accorded to various R&D tasks. As described in the schedules relating these two variables, different types of institutions assign different *a priori* values to providing the type of R&D knowledge associated with different forms of university–industry collaboration. A composite "tenure line" is introduced to operationalize this concept. The intersection of this line with the various institutional schedules highlights a fundamental, if not novel, proposition: that activities deemed worthy of reward and recognition in some institutions are not so received in other institutions. For present purposes, the issue is the segment of R&D activities that corresponds to the point of intersection (and above).

As portrayed, little problem exists with basic research.[43] It is highly esteemed among all institutions, and is compatible with the most exacting "élitist" university criteria for professional performance. Basic

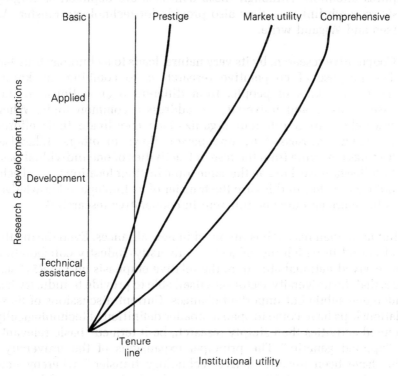

Figure 13.2 Institutional utility received from different R&D activities.

research simultaneously meets the needs of science and technology—of intensive firms for their sought-after "windows" on emerging scientific fields, of each clustering of universities to secure additional funds to pursue research agendas of their own choosing, and of enhanced institutional prestige. (It is useful to note that much of the positive aura surrounding new alliances, particularly as it has affected the shaping of national science policy, in effect, reflects coupling of this type.)[44] Rosenzweig and Turlington's examination of the status of research among member institutions of the Association of American Universities (AAU) likewise fits this mold, as they, too, focus on collaboration between universities and industry principally in terms of the former's need for additional funds for research and upgrading of research facilities in the face of stagnant federal support, and the latter's need to increase its support of basic research in order to become more competitive.[45]

One other reinforcing aspect of the mutuality of interests in alliances that match "high-science" universities and "high-tech" firms requires attention. Although these contracts are depicted as forging basic research linkages, they also provide for technology transfer. As Larsen and Wigand write:

> Cooperative research, by its very nature, leads to technology transfer. The purpose of cooperative research is to combine the knowledge and skills of people, from different organizations, in this case industry and university, to address a common topic. When researchers from different organizations coordinate their efforts, knowledge possessed by one person flows to others. Likewise, findings emerging from the research activities of one individual pass to colleagues working on the same topic in other locations . . . . Technology transfer, in this case the transfer of technological knowledge, is therefore an outcome inherent in cooperative research.[46]

But more than research is involved in new alliances. Even during the brief period in which the subject of university–industry collaboration has received national attention, the relative emphasis on the R&D services that the university sector sees itself able to provide to industry has undergone subtle but important changes. Current discussions of these relationships have come to span a broader definition of technologically oriented activities than simply research, be it termed "basic relevant" or "applied generic." The principal expansions of the university's rôles have been toward "active technology transfer," whereby new university programs (a) "aggressively reach into the research laboratory actively searching for commercializable new applications of technology and then seek to develop the product or process, with an associated business entity, through early-stage commercialization," and (b) seek to accelerate the diffusion of advanced "off-the-shelf" technology to industry,[47] usually by providing some combination of information and extension of field service. The first of these expanded rôles raises a set of issues beyond those that can be addressed here, so only the second form of expanded university involvement in technology transfer is examined.[48] The expansion of university involvement toward more "downstream" involvement in converting research into potentially commercial products has different implications for different types of universities. First, in engineering departments in research-oriented institutions, research directed toward commercialization may still remain close to the "frontiers" of knowledge. As presented above, the successful conversion of technological knowledge into commercial uses revolves about the ability of the corporate sponsor to establish effective means of communication with academic researchers, to learn about the substance of leading-edge research, and then to perform its own further filtering and processing toward commercial ends. Academic scientists may be brought in at some "downstream" R&D stage, but more in the way of consulting than through formal, interinstitutional contracts. Many of the better-known university–industry affiliate programs share this characteristic. For example, MIT's affiliate program in materials processing is described as staying "fairly close to basic research" by working on the microstructure of ceramics.[49]

Second, increased collaboration with industry is a logical expansion of the existing mission and goals of many comprehensive, regional universities. A close congruence exists for these institutions between an enhancement of the professional activities of their faculties, upgrading of instructional programs, and enhancement of institutional resources and regional reputation, on the one hand, and the provision of assistance in solving production-related problems for regionally based firms on the other. As noted by the Association for American State Colleges and Universities (AASCU), "Given the traditional commitment to instruction, research, and public service combined with the responsive nature of the AASCU institutions, economic development should be viewed both as an extension of traditional activities and as an opportunity to adjust rapidly and effectively to new needs."[50] As suggested in Figure 13.2, there is little loss in internal valuation as activity shifts from basic or applied research toward prototype and technical assistance. Thus, included in the ambit of endorsed economic development activities for AASCU members are joint R&D

research programs with industry, technical assistance centers for small businesses, technology transfer, and product development. This set contains elements (e.g., joint research projects) that overlap with those of research-oriented universities but clearly additional elements that would not be as well received. Thus, one would expect that these institutions would establish ties either with a different cluster of corporate partners or with production-oriented divisions within the same research-intensive firms which are entering into collaborative research contracts with more research-oriented universities.

As an example, the University of Hartford's College of Engineering views itself principally as an undergraduate teaching institution. It has developed an Engineering Applications Center to which industrial affiliates contribute $20,000 for five years to support specific research projects. In return, the center provides up to 350 hours of consulting, problem-solving, and technical assistance by center researchers and other faculty and up to 100 hours of time by undergraduate students. The benefits to the university are that the projects constitute "real world" problems that help to augment the quality of instruction (as well as aiding in placement). The projects serve to stretch the skills of faculty by placing them in problem-solving settings where their expertise is being demonstrated. Participation in the Center is also seen as enhancing the morale of faculty as they are able to solve the problems of high-tech firms.[51]

Third, the thrust toward enhanced international competitiveness through technological innovation has served as a strategy by which a select number of private engineering universities have been able to transform themselves from undergraduate instruction and regionally regarded institutions to nationally visible institutions, both in targeted areas of research and for the entrepreneurial qualities of their leadership. Institutions such as Carnegie-Mellon University, Pennsylvania, Rensselaer Polytechnic Institute, New York, Lehigh University, Pennsylvania, and Worcester Polytechnic Institute, Massachusetts, have built upon historic associations to forge even closer links with industry. In the process, these institutions have been able reciprocally to leverage federal, industrial, and state funds to secure a major upgrading of their physical plant and equipment and an upgrading of their educational programs.[52]

The focus to this point has been on types of research and development and, implicitly, on the standard mode of collaboration for research projects, basic or applied, that is, the research grant or contract. An overlapping approach to the matching of university performance of various forms of R&D projects with institutional reward systems relates the organizational forms used to establish partnerships with industry. Three other organizational forms of collaboration have received renewed attention: university-industrial affiliate or consortium programs; university–industry liaison programs; and university-based technical assistance programs. These forms, in many ways, highlight the set of issues raised above concerning an extension of university activities toward commercialization of technology.

Affiliate programs provide for subscription fees from industry to support university-based research undertakings. These programs encompass the spectrum of R&D activities and thus can be (and are) readily incorporated into the activities of each of the three types of universities. MIT's affiliate program, for example, may be viewed as an organizational mechanism for aggregating subscriber fees to support research programs that have both "basic" and "applied" elements. Worcester Polytechnic Institute's Manufacturing Engineering Applications Center (MEAC), by way of contrast, includes contracts for the delivery of finished products to subscribers in as short a period as 6 to 12 months.

According to Dimancescu and Botkin, MEAC provides the quintessential form of technology transfer from a university laboratory as well as serving as an excellent source of graduate students trained to handle modern production techniques. At the same time, MEAC's activities point to potential bounds to the rôle of university–industry collaboration. Some subscribers to MEAC are reported as having complained "that they are not getting the strengths the university has to offer—which is new knowledge that takes longer to create."[53] There also appears to be concern within some subscribing firms that MEAC is being employed to perform tasks that more properly should be assigned to commercial suppliers.

These comments suggest that the closer the university moves toward direct applications, the more likely it is to enter into direct competition as a supplier of knowledge with both in-house engineering development divisions and with capital goods suppliers. Moreover, as a university program moves toward undertaking firm-specific delivery of specific commodities, standard differences in the incentives and track records for on-time and reliable performance of university researchers and either employees or contractees, muted in the surge of enthusiasm over collaborative relations, become important.[54] To the private-sector subscribers of such centers, the more the university seeks to perform services conventionally associated with private-sector organizations, the more the center either is or will be expected to behave like them.

Industrial liaison programs typically provide for visits by subscribing firms to researchers, seminars and workshops on emerging research findings, and publications. The attraction of liaison programs is that they permit a firm to have early insight into scientific and technical advances that may impact upon the firm's lines of business. Tamaribuchi's 1983 survey indicates the increased popularity of these programs. Out of the 40 reporting research universities, 23 had some form of industrial liaison program in 1983. The spread of these programs has quickened: before 1950, there were three; by 1970, eight; by 1980, thirteen; by 1983, eighteen; with another eight universities considering initiating such programs.[55] Tamaribuchi's survey reinforces standard views of the reasons for firms' subscription to these programs. According to university respondents, access to students for purposes of recruitment appears quite prominently as a reason for firms' entrance into these programs; access to faculty ideas relevant to potential innovation by companies did not.

The increase in the number of liaison programs suggests, in economists' parlance, that universities are assuming that they confront an infinitely elastic demand schedule for such services, i.e., that there is an unlimited number of firms seeking to establish new relationships with universities. These programs, however, are competitive with one another, albeit to an undetermined degree. As more universities proffer such programs (or a larger number of research centers within universities already engaged in liaison activities seek to develop their own set of affiliates), firms are beginning to seek to coordinate their externally funded R&D support activities. With tighter (more centralized) internal controls over subscription arrangements, firms may become less willing to subscribe to the numerous liaison programs being initiated, particularly if these programs are clustered in similar fields of technology (e.g., biotechnology). Indeed, nascent selection criteria may be detected. These include technical quality of the institution's research program(s); local or regional proximity, which is mainly a "good neighbor" obligation; and personal (alumni) links between key decision makers and universities.

Liaison programs also may be running afoul of other university/industry-based modes of collaboration. Faculty, for example, who are seeking to promote industrial consortia to support their research have been reported to be less accessible to firms that subscribe to liaison programs but not to the consortia. Moreover, although systematic data are not available on the composition of the firms that subscribe to liaison programs, it appears that the firms that participate in these programs share a relatively common characteristic of being among the larger firms in technologically dynamic fields. Even the most established and formally structured university programs appear to have difficulty in providing the services (and retaining the membership) of small, albeit high-tech, firms. Small firms are held to seek very detailed technical solutions as a return for their membership fees, whereas from the university perspective the program is designed to facilitate faculty research at the frontiers of knowledge.

Technical assistance programs to industry have a long-standing history within many land-grant universities and are increasingly found in other publicly funded institutions. One central issue emerges whenever a university becomes involved in providing technical assistance: are these activities tenurable? As best as one can tell, they are not. Industrial liaison programs and technology transfer/technical assistance programs are predominately staffed by individuals who do not hold academic rank. A review of the personnel complements and program descriptions of the universities belonging to the National Association of Management and Technical Assistance Centers (NAMTAC) indicates that most programs have their own permanent professional staffs to respond to requests for technical assistance, with faculty serving to augment these capabilities.

The logic or necessity of this arrangement follows from the specific, problem-focused character of the service that these programs provide. Technical assistance most generally involves application of existing knowledge to a specific problem; in economic terms, it means assisting a firm to move closer to "best-practice" techniques. This assistance meshes poorly with dominant academic standards for research and scholarly activities, clearly at most AAU institutions, including land-grant universities, and likely at most of the other institutions that offer such services. As a consequence, participation by faculty in these programs is typically on a voluntary basis. Modest rewards in the forms of research or travel funds may be provided to faculty for their participation; but interviews with directors of technical assistance programs at public universities highlight the finding that although "public service" or its equivalent is a category found in promotion and tenure criteria of public universities, faculty, in fact, received little "credit" toward promotion and/or tenure from such participation. The prevailing view for both public and private universities is that faculty find (or have found) their academic careers harmed if their activities in industrial liaison or technology transfer programs detract from the level of research and/or instructional output normally expected of faculty.[56]

Conclusion

The positive-sum aspects of increased university–industry collaborations are apparent: increased support of basic and applied research; increased and improved educational opportunities; upgrading of university facilities; direct and indirect flows of commercially usable knowledge to firms; and improvement of the national and regional economies. Recent events and findings indicate considerable satisfaction and tangible benefits to both parties from more extensive collaboration.

From the perspective of a firm, there is an inherent control device on the character and scope of its commitments to universities. For the most part, again with the exception of major long-term R&D contracts (which are notable mainly for their small numbers and for their concentration in a small number of scientific fields), the commitments made by firms to universities are project-based, modest in expenditure, and short-term. Success produces incentives for continuation of these relationships, shaped at all times by the firm's commitment to research and development and by the competition for these funds from both internal performers of these services and the availability of a (growing) number of nonuniversity external forms for securing scientific and technological knowledge. The failure of a specific contract to produce results creates a search for alternative means of performing research and development. Even success, however, yields problems. Rogers has noted the proliferation of collaborative forms and partnership opportunities—engineering research centers, state economic development initiatives, consortial research arrangements such as the Semiconductor Research Corporation, hundreds of university departmental/institute/research center affiliations, and thousands of specific research projects—offered the Digital Equipment Company (DEC).[57] The profusion of opportunities for alliance has caused firms to scrutinize their aggregate expenditures and to become aware of high degrees of substitutability among modes of collaboration and available partners. DEC and Monsanto have responded to this supply-side phenomenon by establishing administrative positions to monitor and coordinate external R&D programs with universities, and it seems likely that other major firms have corresponding positions or policies, at least with respect to affiliations that exceed some dollar threshold.

Most generally, Friar and Horwitch note that "the recent and current period of experimentation, which has been characterized by the expansion of both external-oriented approaches and a greater variety generally of types of innovation efforts, may be stabilizing."[58] They point to a near-term future consolidation of technology strategy methods and stabilization of the relative rôles of the corporate R&D laboratories and external arrangements. In this context, support available for university alliances can come only in the context of continuing increases in corporate research and development, or in demonstrations of the relatively higher payoffs to corporate ends of academic rather than nonacademic alliances.

The force, both evident and latent, of these new alliances on internal policies, practices, and organizational forms is greater for the university. These relationships, as critics of recent trends have observed, may significantly alter the missions of universities and the behavior of faculty.[59] Potential abuses exist concerning use of graduate student efforts by faculty for their own pecuniary benefits; there may be an internal exodus on campus away from teaching toward research; and academic research agendas may be suborned away from questions related to the betterment of social conditions toward those that improve international competitiveness. These alliances may limit or distort the flow of information among academic scientists and may accelerate turnover of faculty, who, becoming socialized to economic criteria, begin to give increased weight to commercial prospects in choosing among research paths and seek other bases and venues than academic appointments and refereed articles.

Within the more limited ambit of this chapter, the strains that are important in shaping the characteristics of university–industry collaborations are those that arise when the needs of the external sponsors are incompatible with the internal goals of a university and its prevailing standard for evaluating the performance of its personnel. Two principal strains are evident: (a) presence of an incompatibility between the type of R&D activity requested by the external sponsor and that which is compatible with existing institutional norms; and (b) differences relating to technology transfer or, more precisely, firm-specific applications of existing knowledge.

Insight into the different impacts upon the university of different types of contracts is provided by the assessment of Carnegie-Mellon University's participation in collaborative university–industry and university–industry–state government programs by J. C. Williams, Dean of Engineering at Carnegie-Mellon University.[60] Carnegie-Mellon is one of the most enterprising institutions, capitalizing on its long-standing strength as a technically oriented university to achieve new prominence both for its collaboration with industry and its standing as a premier research university. Williams's review covers four centers: the Magnetics Technology Center, the Center for Iron and Steelmaking Research, the Robotics Institute, and the Western Pennsylvania Advanced Technology Center. The first center involves industrial sponsors; the second, industrial sponsors and the National Science Foundation; the third, industrial sponsors and state funds; and the fourth (technically a corporate entity separate from Carnegie-Mellon), industrial sponsors, the University of Pittsburgh, and the Commonwealth of Pennsylvania's Ben Franklin Partnership Program. The character of research agendas differs among these centers, reflecting in large part the orientation of the sponsors. Williams notes the tension inherent in these programs, particularly the tendency for industrial sponsors to encourage university researchers to tackle problems which are too focused or have a very short payoff period. When this happens, the university essentially becomes a surrogate applied-research or problem-solving facility for the sponsor. The difficulty is that universities have no natural advantage in such activities. Moreover, narrowly defined problems restrict the extent to which the creative abilities of faculty and graduate students can be brought to bear on the research topic.[61]

Pressures upon the university for an expanded technology transfer rôle—defined here in terms of the provision of firm-specific information—are likely to arise when firms that lack the internal capabilities to convert research findings into potentially commercial outcomes are induced to enter into contracts with universities.

The technology transfer issue is likely to arise when the intended user is a small rather than a large firm within a given field of technology. If the cases cited above prove to be representative harbingers, it is likely to be yet more of a problem if the pursuit of national or regional economic development induces (or pushes) the university to shift the relative weight it assigns to "prestige" or "market utility." Calls for increased university involvement in technology transfer activities misread the extent to which such transfer already occurs and the processes by which it occurs. Knowledge transfer is an integral component in any university/industry-based R&D activity in which the firm actively seeks to remain abreast of the substance of faculty research, be it through reading research papers, attending technical briefings, visiting laboratories, or directly collaborating in joint projects. Moreover, at question here is neither whether the work is "basic" or "applied," nor whether the university seeks to "transfer" the knowledge. Rather it is whether the intended recipient can "absorb" or "assimilate" research knowledge in the form that such knowledge is customarily provided by the university. Determining the answers to this question are (a) the point (or band) in the R&D continuum at which the firm initially sought the knowledge; and (b) the firm's internal processes for incorporating knowledge generated in this band into its overall business plan and technological capabilities.

Disjuncture (and an early parting of ways) in university–industry alliances are likely when firms enter into alliances based upon misconceptions of the character of the service provided by a university. This parting has been noted in the case of some university–industry liaison programs. Evident, too, are portents of disenchantment by firms with the services they receive upon participating in state-funded advanced technology programs. In one state program, for example, a small robotics firm made in-kind contributions to an advanced technology center and as a member was permitted to sit in on monthly meetings held by a university-based advanced technology center, to view technical reports in various robotics fields. The advanced technology center, however, did not provide services designed to "bring the new technologies into the firm."[62] It was not until after complaints, and, according to Dimancescu and Botkin, "external pressure from influential friends" that the center designated two students to work on CAD technology at the firm.[63] The issue for many universities will be the compatibility between pursuit of basic research and graduate training and research and instructional activities that have a closer link to application, commercialization, and technology transfer. Rosenzweig and Turlington note:

> To risk a tautology . . . what research universities do best – and are almost alone in doing – is fundamental research and the training for research. Their ability to continue to perform these tasks is of crucial importance to the future well-being of industry as a whole although its relevance to the fortunes of any single firm may be difficult to discern at a particular moment.[64]

The lack of congruence between traditional academic reward systems and those contained within the activities associated with liaison and technical assistance activities for most universities is well known. What is striking is not the novelty of the problem but the major push for increased university activities toward aggressive technology transfer (to again use Watkins's term) without comparable attention to its resolution.

Finally, a perspective should be noted that centers on the rôle of universities. This has emerged largely independent of concerns about America's international economic competitiveness but reinforces the call for universities to enter into alliances with firms and state government and to take on an expanded responsibility for a wider range of activities related to technological innovation. There is a rising call within segments of the higher education community for a "revitalization" of the missions of public universities. Land-grant universities, in particular, are held to "have lost their way."[65] The pursuit of disciplinary-based reputation both for individual faculty and for academic units has caused these universities to give inadequate priority to generating and applying knowledge relevant to today's social and economic problems. As faculty have secured external support for their research, they have increasingly moved beyond the control of university administrators, who thus would have difficulty developing a strong mission orientation, even if they wanted to. According to Schuh, a need exists to reinstill a mission orientation in the university, to integrate basic and applied research, and to develop the institutional means of transferring this research to potential users.

Equally forcibly, Lynton and Elman have called for a structural change in the "overarching conception of the university."[66] They start from the proposition that universities are societal institutions charged with the "specific responsibility to create advanced knowledge, interpret it, and disseminate it."[67] Lynton and Elman, however, contend that in recent decades universities have become "astonishingly—and distressingly—uniform"[68] in their internal hierarchy of values, measures of academic responsibility, and faculty reward and incentive systems, all of which emphasizes the creation of advanced knowledge, gives perhaps modest notice to the interpretation of knowledge, but accords passing notice, at best, to the dissemination of knowledge.

Lynton and Elman call for new priorities for the university. To them, as much value should be placed on "interpretation and dissemination of new ideas as on original research."[69] They are also explicit as to what is needed to change priorities: "Basic changes in the existing system of values, incentives and rewards in order to bring about parity of esteem and equality of treatment for the full range of professional activities."[70] Similarly, if less pointedly, Schuh contends that "university administrators need to have discretionary funds, freedom, and responsibility to manage and administer a mission-oriented institution—not a collection of individuals, oriented primarily to their national peers, and who only by chance happen to be at a particular institution."[71]

Converted into the context of this paper, these authors are arguing for a leftward shift in the schedules relating R&D functions and institutional utility and, implicitly too, a rightward shift in institutional tenure lines. The effect of either shift and, *a fortiori*, that of the two taken together would be to expand considerably the legitimized participation of faculty in activities related to the transfer and commercialization of technological innovations.

To yet other observers, a less momentous shift in university norms and organizational forms to accommodate an increased rôle in fostering economic growth through technological innovation may be feasible. Baba has suggested that the "impedance mismatch," the structural and value barriers to university–industry interaction, can be surmounted without damage to the university's core structure and mission when both parties are motivated sufficiently and have some pre-existing knowledge and respect for one another's capabilities. New linkage arrangements, according to Baba, have overcome these barriers while simultaneously preserving the university's "fundamental" academic core

> by peripheralizing and institutionalizing industrial linkage activities away from the core academic structure, and by seizing corporate or institutional control of linkage activities that initially were conducted and controlled at the individual or departmental level. Peripheralization appears to protect the basic disciplinary nature of the academic enterprise, while institutionalization permits centralized control over key resources that hold commercial potential.[72]

Less sanguine views on the stability of boundaries between core and periphery are also now surfacing. As Gibbons has observed, "Both science and the universities have begun to experience a condition of functional overload; of trying to do too many things without altering the form of the institution."[73] If the core or essence of an organization is to be found in the views "held by the dominant group in the organization of what the missions and capabilities should be,"[74] then in fact what Baba is terming the "periphery" has become the core for many institutions, at least to judge by statements of senior academic officials. More accurately, the present setting, at least within research universities, is one of a series of undeclared and unresolved technical, political, and normative skirmishes of the appropriate boundaries of university collaboration with industry.

Williams again suggests the specific character of these skirmishes when he observes, first, that "Universities have so little advantage when conducting tightly structured, goal-oriented research that it is questionable for them to engage in such projects."[75] Then, after noting that state programs heavily focused on economic development produce administrative pressure to do research that is quite pragmatic in scope, he adds that it is "much harder for universities to 'shine' at this type of activity . . . . This does not mean that universities should automatically avoid these projects; it does mean that the faculty and administration involved must pay special attention to avoid pitfalls. With proper care satisfactory results can be achieved."[76] Without proper care, however, the core can shrink and then shrivel.

Notes

This chapter was prepared for the Center for Growth Studies conference entitled "Growth policy in the age of high technology: the rôle of regions and states."

1 D. Praeger & G. Omenn, "Research, innovation and university–industry linkages," *Science* **207**, January 1980, 379–84; D. Baldwin & J. Green, "University–industry relations: a review of the literature," *SRA Journal*, Spring 1984/5, 57–77.

2 D. Fowler, "University–industry research relationships: the research agreement," *Journal of College and University Law* **9**, 1984, 515–31.

3 The willingness of universities to permit greater organizational and policy latitude for collaborative undertakings with industry may also be a countermove needed to keep scientists who perform research in selected areas on their faculty. "Spinoff" is also "spin-away," as faculty become corporate entrepreneurs. Kenney's account of the biotechnology industry highlights the blandishments offered to academic researchers by venture capitalists. In competitive response, universities have sought to make the campus setting more like that of the private sector, in part through adjustment in patent policies, but also in facilitating contractual research with corporations. See M. Kenney, *Biotechnology: the university–industrial complex* (New Haven, Conn.: Yale University Press, 1986). As noted by Richard Cyert, President of Carnegie-Mellon University, his institution's increased involvement in industry and state-funded consortia has permitted the faculty to do "research that is 'relevant' and basic as opposed to basic 'exploratory.' It means that a whole new group of potential faculty, that otherwise would have gone to industry, will stay on campus. Ten years ago they would have moved on" (quoted in D. Dimancescu & J. Botkin, *The new alliance* [Cambridge, Mass.: Ballinger, 1986], p. 46.)

4 R. Varrin & D. Kukich, "Guidelines for industry-sponsored research at universities," *Science* **227**, January 1985, 385–8.

5 According to Samuel Guze, Vice Chancellor for Medical Affairs, Washington University, the Monsanto–Washington University agreement "is an experiment. And like all good experiments, results cannot be guaranteed; we must be prepared for completely unexpected results." S. Guze, "The Monsanto–Washington University Biomedical Research Agreement," in *Partners in the research enterprise*, ed. T. Langfitt, S. Hackney, A. Fishman & A. Glowasky (Philadelphia: University of Pennsylvania Press, 1983), p. 58.

6 M. Gibbons & B. Wittrock (eds.), *Science as a commodity* (London: Longman, 1987).

7 These sections draw freely upon I. Feller, "An evolutionary perspective on emerging university-corporate-state government research and development relationships," a paper presented at the 1986 meeting of the Association for Public Policy Analysis and Management.

8 L. Peters & H. Fusfeld, "Current U.S. university/industry research connections," in National Science Foundation, *University-industry research relationships: selected*

studies (Washington, D.C.: National Science Board, 1983); H. Haller, *Examples of university-industry (government) collaborations* (Ithaca, N.Y.: Cornell University Press, 1984).

9   I. Feller, "Technology transfer, public policy, and the cooperative extension service–OMB imbroglio," *Journal of Policy Analysis and Management* **6**, 1987 307–27.

10 W. H. Lambright & A. Teich, "Using universities: the NASA experience," *Public Policy* **20**, 1972, 61–82; W. Long & I. Feller, "State support of research and development: an uncertain path to economic growth," *Land Economics* **48**, 1972, 220–7; R. Nelson (ed.), *Government and technical progress* (New York: Pergamon, 1982).

11 P. Kelly & M. Kranzberg, *Technological innovation: a critical review of current literature* (San Francisco: San Francisco Press, 1978); N. Rosenberg, "How exogenous is science?" in *Inside the black box* (Cambridge: Cambridge University Press, 1982), pp. 141–59; S. Kline & N. Rosenberg, "An overview of innovation," in *The positive sum strategy*, ed. R. Landau & N. Rosenberg (Washington, D.C.: National Academy Press, 1986).

12 U.S. Congress, House of Representatives, Subcommittee on Science, Research, and Technology, *Domestic technology transfer: issues and options*, 95th Congress, 2nd session, Serial CCC, vol. I (Washington, D.C.: Government Printing Office, 1978).

13 J. Larsen & R. Wigand, "Industry-university technology transfer in microelectronics," *Policy Studies Review* **6**, 1987, 587.

14 Baldwin & Green, "University–industry relations," p. 5.

15 M. Peck, "Joint R&D: the case of Microelectronics and Computer Technology Corporation," *Research Policy* **15**, 1986, 219–31.

16 M. Porter, "The technological dimension of competitive strategy," in *Research on technological innovation, management, and policy*, ed. R. Rosenbloom (Greenwich, Conn.: JAI Press, 1983), vol. 1, pp. 1–33.

17 J. Friar & M. Horwitch, "The emergence of technology strategy," *Technology in Society* **7**, 1985, 151.

18 C. Freeman, *The economics of industrial innovation*, 2nd edn. (Cambridge, Mass.: MIT Press, 1982).

19 National Science Board, *Science indicators: the 1985 report* (Washington D.C.: U.S. Government Printing Office, 1985), pp. 33–4.

20 Ibid., Appendix Table 4–4, p. 252.

21 Ibid., p. 254.

22 H. Fusfeld & C. Haklisch, "Collaborative industrial research in the U.S." *Technovation* **5**, 1987, 305–16; A. Link & G. Tassey, *Strategies for technology-based competition* (Lexington, Mass.: Lexington Books, 1987). This band of the spectrum includes not only "basic relevant" or "strategic research" but also selected forms of "applied research." As Nelson, Peck, and Kalacheck have noted, there are two principal types of applied scientific research, one "aimed at placing the technology of an industry on a stronger scientific footing"; the other involving experimental developments "to test the feasibility and broad attributes of radically new products and process designs" (R. Nelson, M. Peck & E. Kalacheck), *Technology, economic growth, and public policy* [Washington, D.C.: Brookings Institution, 1967], p. 178). Viewed in an evolutionary context, the changed character of relationships between the academic and industrial communities may be seen as a search for the means for closing the gap between the applied research that was too applied for the research-oriented university scientists and too basic for the development- or product-oriented industrial scientist.

23 National Science Board, *Science indicators*, Appendix Table 5–20, p. 279.

24 C. Sims, "Business–campus ventures grow," *New York Times*, December 14, 1987, p. 1.

25 D. Blumenthal, M. Gluck, K. S. Louis & D. Wise, "Industrial support of university research in biotechnology," *Science* **17**, 1986, 242–6.
26 Larsen & Wigand, "Industry-university technology transfer in microelectronics."
27 J. Main, "Business goes to college for a brain gain," *Fortune*, March 16, 1987, 80–6.
28 *Chronicle of Higher Education*, May 5, 1986, 8.
29 Nelson, *Government and technical progress*; R. Levin, W. Cohen & D. Mowery, "R&D appropriability, opportunity market structure: new evidence on some Schumpeterian hypotheses," *American Economic Review Papers and Proceedings* **72**, 1985, 20–4.
30 Peck, "Joint R&D," p. 223.
31 Government/University/Industry Roundtable, *New alliances and partnerships in American science and engineering* (Washington, D.C.: National Academy of Sciences, 1986), p. 7.
32 D. Mowery, "The relationship between intra and contractual forms of research in American manufacturing 1900–1940," *Explorations in Economic History* **20**, October 1980, 367.
33 Peck, "Joint R&D," p. 230.
34 The enhanced prospects it provides of being able to recruit graduate students trained in fields closely linked to a firm's technology is another prominently stated reason for willingness to contribute to university-based consortia. This payoff is "often sufficient to warrant the investment of a firm in such a consortium; the 'first look' or lead time into new knowledge being an added return" (Dimancescu & Botkin, *The new alliance*, p. 95).
35 H. Etzkowitz, "Entrepreneurial scientists and entrepreneurial universities in American academic science," *Minerva* **21**, 1983, 198.
36 F. D. Robinson, "University and industry cooperation in microelectronics research," in *High hopes for high tech*, ed. D. Whittington (Chapel Hill: University of North Carolina Press, 1985), p. 115.
37 D. Gray, E. Johnson & T. Gridley, "University-industry projects and centers," *Evaluation Review* **10**, 1980, 776–93.
38 National Science Board, *Science indicators*, pp. 92–109.
39 Carnegie Council on Policy Studies in Higher Education, *A classification of institutions of higher education* (Princeton, N.J.: Carnegie Foundation for the Advancement of Teaching, 1976).
40 A. Garvin, *The economics of university behaviour* (New York: Academic Press, 1980).
41 R. Friedman & R. Friedman, "Organized research units in academe revisited," in *Managing high technology*, ed. B. W. Mar, W. T. Newell & B. O. Sundberg (Amsterdam: North-Holland, 1985), pp. 82–4.
42 SRI International, *The higher education–economic development connection: emerging roles for public colleges and universities in a changing economy* (Washington, D.C.: American Association of State Colleges and Land Grant Universities, 1986), p. 32.
43 Obviously, it is possible to begin with a wide array of initially postulated conditions. For example, Figure 13.3 illustrates a more polarized set of institutional goals in that for prestige-maximizing universities activities "below" (descriptively not normatively) applied research produce "negative" values for faculty, while for comprehensive institutions the schedule has a backward bending segment, indicating that the institution accords negative values to research that becomes too basic. Also, Figure 13.3 disaggregates market utility institutions into two groups, a more realistic depiction, say, of a bifurcated clustering among land-grant universities. Not drawn, but clearly relevant, is the different positioning along the horizontal axis of the tenure lines appropriate for each class.

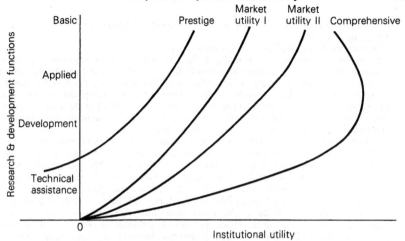

Figure 13.3 Institutional utility received from different R&D activities.

44 National Research Council, *The new engineering research centers* (Washington, D.C.: National Academy Press, 1986).

45 R. Rosenzweig & B. Turlington, *The research universities and their patrons* (Berkeley: University of California Press, 1982).

46 Larsen & Wigand, "Industry–university technology transfer in microelectronics," p. 592.

47 C. Watkins, "Technology transfer from university research in regional development strategies," *Journal of Technology Transfer* **10**, 1985, 61.

48 Also not treated in this chapter is university participation in for-profit and not-for-profit arrangements that seek to secure a share of the economic gains expected from research undertaken by its faculty or otherwise to use the university's resources to promote commercial activity. These topics are discussed in *Trends in technology transfer at universities* (Washington, D.C.: Association of American Universities, 1986).
The Association of American Universities report concludes as follows:

> Whether universities will successfully establish technology transfer entities outside the university structure remains unanswered. The nonprofit model has been challenged by the Internal Revenue Service because of its commercial activities. However, the for-profit entities do not yet have any discernible track record for attracting investors. It remains to be seen whether universities will be able to structure technology transfer and commercial development activities in a manner that maintains the university's academic and research missions and undertake successful commercial activities. (p. 39)

49 Kenney, *Biotechnology*.

50 American Association of State Colleges and Universities, "Economic development: a major responsibility for AASCU institutions," policy statement adopted November 1986.

51 University of Hartford, Engineering Applications Center.

52 G. Dallaire, "RPI's might goal: to help rejuvenate American industry," *Civil Engineering*, 1981, 52-6; P. Abetti, C. LeMaestre & W. Wallace, "The role of technological universities in nurturing innovation," in *Technological*

innovation, ed. D. Gray, T. Solomon & W. Hetzner (Amsterdam: North-Holland, 1986), pp. 251–60.

53 Dimancescu & Botkin, *The new alliance,* p. 90.

54 "A university should never make a firm commitment to achieve a specific research result, or to achieve any result for a fixed or guaranteed amount of funding. Such a commitment is in conflict with the inherently open-ended nature of scientific research. . . . additionally, universities are nonprofit, tax-exempt, financially risk-averse institutions which have no legal right to place institutional funds at financial risk with speculative research commitments" (Fowler, "University–industry research relationships," pp. 518–19).

55 K. Tamaribuchi, "Effectively linking industry with a university resource," in *Proceedings: management of technological innovation: facing the challenge of the 1980s* (Washington, D.C., 1983), pp. 6–9. The scope of liaison programs varies considerably. The range in Tamaribuchi's survey was from those institutions which had six or eight affiliate companies and no separate staff, to the largest programs at Stanford and MIT, which respectively had 330 affiliates and 20 professional staff, and 285 affiliates and 42 professional staff. Seven universities permitted affiliates access to all departments of the university; 19 had programs focused on individual departments, and three had both types of programs. Fees ranged from $1,000 to $50,000, with most universities reporting fees in the $10,000 to $20,000 bracket.

56 For example, the Pennsylvania Technical Assistance Program (PennTAP), the exemplar of a university-based technical assistance program, is a unit within The Pennsylvania State University, a land-grant institution. Still, "Association with PennTAP . . . is not a significant factor in tenure decisions" (J. Schmandt & R. Wilson [eds.], *Promoting high-technology industry* [Boulder, Col.: Westview Press, 1987], p. 213).

57 D. Rogers, "Federally sponsored collaborative research: the industry factor," paper presented at the Midwest Conference on Government Funded Opportunities, Purdue University, May 6, 1986.

58 Friar & Horwitch, "The emergence of technology strategy," p. 169.

59 D. Dickson, *The new politics of science* (New York: Pantheon, 1984).

60 J. C. Williams, "University–industry interactions: finding the balance," *Engineering Education* 77, March 1986, 320–5.

61 Ibid., p. 322.

62 Dimancescu & Botkin, *The new alliance,* p. 71.

63 This type of situation appears to be a latent source of future tension in collaborative university–industry–government R&D programs. Both the federal government and many state governments believe that small high-tech firms are a disproportionate source of new technologies and of job creation. Accordingly, they have designed programs to involve universities with these firms. As described above, these firms may require assistance beyond that comfortably conducted with the scope of a faculty member's accustomed (or academically valued) responsibilities, at least at research-oriented universities.

64 Rosenzweig & Turlington, *The research universities and their patrons,* p. 52.

65 G. E. Schuh, "Revitalizing land grant universities," *Choices,* Spring 1986, 6–10.

66 E. Lynton & S. Elman, *New priorities for the university* (San Francisco: Jossey-Bass, 1987), p. 3.

67 Ibid., p. 1

68 Ibid., p. 11.

69 Ibid., p. 2.

70 Ibid., p. 135.

71 Schuh, "Revitalizing land grant universities."

72 M. Baba, "University innovation to promote economic growth and university/industry relations," in *Promoting economic growth through innovation: proceedings: conference on industrial science and technological innovation,*

ed. P. Abetti, C. LeMaestre & W. Wallace (Amsterdam: North-Holland, 1985), pp. 215, 251–60.

73 Gibbons, 1985, p. xi.
74 M. Halperin, *Bureaucratic politics and foreign policy* (Washington, D.C.: Brookings Institution, 1974), p. 28.
75 Williams, "University–industry interactions," p. 324.
76 Ibid., p. 325.

14

State government–university cooperation

KAREN M. PAGET

Introduction

THE PERCEPTION THAT universities have a key rôle to play in economic development strategies has brought unprecedented attention by state governments to the question of access to university resources. Pressure on universities to help the United States regain and retain its competitive position in the international economy flows from two central conclusions about the rôle of educational institutions in economic development: first, the belief that technological advance stemming from scientific breakthroughs is a primary force in economic growth and, second, the belief that a skilled workforce is critical to future growth and productivity. These beliefs have renewed the search for cooperative links and formal programs between universities and state governments.

Cooperation between universities and state government takes many forms. Individual faculty members contract with state government agencies, advise individual policy makers or policy committees, testify on legislation, and/or serve on task forces and advisory committees. Academic departments and professional schools organize programs in their special areas of expertise that assist state and local policy makers. Specialized institutes and centers within universities offer multidisciplinary views of problems on topics as diverse as transportation, water resources, and ethnic studies.

The focus of this chapter is not on these individual or departmental acts of cooperation, even though these endeavors may represent successful cooperative efforts, tailored as they are to particular agencies or situations. The focus instead is on formal collaborative efforts between governments and universities involving research and its utilization, on issues regarding research agenda determination, and, finally, on the process by which knowledge is transferred and disseminated. This focus is dictated by the fact that knowledge, particularly "new knowledge" (i.e., scientific breakthroughs) is seen as increasingly valuable, both on its own terms and with respect to economic development strategies. Thus the importance of access to knowledge shifts the focus slightly from acts that have been thought of traditionally as comprising the "public service" function of universities to the increasing significance of research.

This chapter argues that contemporary demands for access to university knowledge and research constitute distinctly new pressures on universities, creating changes we are only just beginning to see, let alone understand. Patent offices, technology transfer centers, joint ventures with industry, faculty-owned biotechnology companies, and new political alliances between business and higher education, such as the Council on Research and Technology (CORETECH), are just a few of the manifestations of this new "competitiveness" pressure.

Demands for cooperation are not new, of course. In the postwar period, at least three eras can be distinguished: (a) the federal effort during the 1960s with the war on poverty and the Great Society programs to involve universities in solving urban problems; (b) state-level initiatives in the 1970s to apply university knowledge to the solution of state problems; and (c) current initiatives based on the assumption that research and education are the keys to increased global competitiveness, particularly through the production of new knowledge that can be transferred and commercialized.

While some attention will be paid to university relationships with the federal government during the 1960s, greater emphasis will be placed on relationships with state governments in the 1970s and 1980s. The contrast between the two eras is important: for state governments to seek assistance from their universities to solve public policy problems in areas such as housing, transportation, or land use, as they did in the 1970s, raises fundamentally different questions than when a state government seeks to implement an industrially defined agenda to restore productivity and competitiveness in the world economy, even if economic development goals are viewed as overriding public ones. This is not to suggest that all states view their rôle in this way; it is rather to crystallize the implications of the shift in pressures for cooperation.

Since the literature on university/state government relationships is scanty, particularly with respect to formal programs, this chapter will draw heavily on examples from California to illustrate the relationship. As the director of a collaborative effort between the University of California and state government established in the 1970s to bring the resources of the university to bear on state problems, my experience in carrying out this mandate informs a good deal of the chapter. In addition, because California has long recognized the importance of higher education, science, and technology for a healthy economy, it has experimented with collaborative efforts relatively more than most states. The magnitude of economic activity (if considered separately, California would be the world's seventh largest economy and is predicted to be the fourth largest by the turn of the century), combined with the fact that the higher education enterprise, with premier research universities, was an estimated $15 billion industry in 1987, makes the state fertile ground for exploring the nature of collaboration between the government and the universities.

Scholars are still trying to grasp the nature of the relationships between the production of knowledge, decision-making processes, and public policy outcomes. Such an understanding is difficult due to fundamental differences between the purposes and goals of universities and government. The production of knowledge within universities is driven primarily by issues and problems within particular disciplines, with a tendency toward examining long-range issues. Governments are action-oriented, work on short time lines, and generally need information immediately. Specific programs designed to link the two institutions in order to bring university resources to bear on particular problems have tended to be short-lived and little evaluated. And, given the strong pulls toward academic freedom and autonomy, the nature of such interaction itself—whether with state government or industry—is the subject of substantial controversy within the universities, their commitment to public service notwithstanding.

In this chapter, periods of prior experimentation will be distinguished analytically by (a) the goals of collaboration; (b) the rationales used to forge cooperation; (c) the formal mechanisms established to carry out specific programs; (d) the underlying models and metaphors thought to govern knowledge transfer; and (e) the issues and implications raised in linking two, essentially disparate enterprises.

Disinterested scholarship or active engagement: two traditions

Any discussion of government/university cooperation has to take into account the self-conception of universities, which, for the most part, view with suspicion "too much" involvement with society generally.

Although public service has long been one of the major functions of the American university, along with teaching and research, the boundaries of faculty involvement with constituencies other than students remains ill-defined and controversial. Indeed, conflict has existed throughout the evolution of American universities over their obligations to urban areas, states, the federal government, industrial interests, and the general citizenry.

While there have been many recent efforts to rewrite the guidelines on public service so that such service is seen more as an extension of teaching and research, the legitimacy of such a view still conflicts with an older tradition of the disinterested scholar. As Irwin Feller has noted, sooner or later public service runs up against the reward system of the university—meaning, in essence, that the rewards of tenure and promotion are largely determined by contributions to academic disciplines through peer-reviewed published research in scholarly journals and books, and not through public service.[1] Within the university, public service activity is generally valued less than teaching and research. Historically, the least legitimate form of public service has been interaction with policy makers. One Harvard report, issued in the 1960s when demands for university involvement in urban problems were at their height, concluded that "many of the chief problems confronting our society are not ones that will yield readily, if at all, to the kinds of knowledge university intellectuals can produce."[2] Policy questions were frequently viewed as intimately connected to political questions. The report went on to argue, "We have investigated urban politics, but we have no expert advice to offer a mayor wishing to know how to raise more tax revenue from a reluctant electorate."[3]

The National Association of State Universities and Land Grant Colleges (NASULGC) tackled the low status of public service in a 1985 study that was premised, in part, on a growing recognition of the importance of knowledge and its dissemination. Citing Peter Drucker's contention that knowledge has become "the central resource," the report went on to say:

> The dissemination of knowledge, always viewed as a basic respon-
> sibility of universities, has also acquired new dimensions and new
> meanings. It is no longer enough for American universities to
> focus primarily on the acquisition and scholarly publication of
> new information. There is a growing need for the assimilation
> and synthesis of more and more complex bodies of knowledge.[4]

The authors argue that, when faculty are evaluated by privilege and tenure committees, the rewards of providing consultation and/or conducting applied research should have the same status as teaching or research, since extension of professional service benefits the university by helping it "maintain its role as the principal creator, archivist and transfer agent of knowledge."[5] These service rôles, the authors emphasize, should be played not because of some notion of civic or philanthropic duty or because faculty are publicly funded; rather, they should be played because they draw on "one's academic discipline and professional expertise," which is a legitimate part of the academic enterprise.[6]

One major historical exception (another is the teaching hospital) to the view of the university as insulated from the problems and needs of external constituencies has been, of course, the establishment and evolution of land-grant institutions. This evolution began with the Morrill Act of 1862, which granted public lands to states to "provide colleges for the benefit of agriculture and the mechanic arts."[7] In 1887, Congress also passed the Hatch Act, formally recognizing and funding state-initiated experiment stations, which had been developed as vehicles to apply science to agriculture and to experiment with local conditions.[8] The existence of experiment stations as an intermediary between farmers and researchers, however, did not mean freedom from tensions between scientists wishing to engage in pure or basic research and farmers' needs for useful applications. Yet the creation of county extension agents who could disseminate relevant research and help articulate research projects to academics, along with funding links to the federal Department of Agriculture, makes the agriculture extension an attractive model for linking research with constituency needs.

The agricultural extension service is frequently cited as a model in legislation requesting universities to engage in a new activity or with new constituencies, and its premises have been the basis of program experiments throughout the last 30 years. As we shall see, however, the failure to understand this model, and therefore to apply it properly, has been the cause of much frustration and many abandoned experiments.

The research enterprise itself is a relatively recent phenomenon. The University of California officially established a research function in 1915, when the Regents created a Board of Research.[9] Prior to World War II, there was little government funding of research activity by either the state or federal government, apart from agriculture or public health research. Serious growth in the funding of university research began during World War II when scientists were mobilized for the war effort, conducting weapons research for the Pentagon.

Several forces led to sustained federal interest in research after the war, and kept funds flowing to universities. One report describes the new trend in this way:

> After World War II, things changed. A growing number of Federal government agencies were asking questions of general importance about national defense, health, energy, agriculture, and transportation. Research attracted public interest and there was a new demand for university research from the Federal government.[10]

New federal institutions, such as the National Institutes of Health and the National Science Foundation, were created to reflect this new relationship between the federal government and university research. The Sputnik crisis in 1957 further legitimated the process of setting national goals and enlisting the aid of scientists in various projects. The end of the Eisenhower era brought a whole new set of national priorities to the fore which involved university faculty, including social scientists, in unprecedented ways. By 1963, University of California president Clark Kerr would write about this change in the rôle of American universities by saying, "The university has become a prime instrument of national purpose. This is new. This is the essence of the transformation now engulfing our universities."[11]

The 1960s: the Great Society and the universities

The national goal of putting a man on the moon, articulated by President Kennedy, became a generalized metaphor for applying American technology to other problems. Richard R. Nelson described this enormous faith in American technology:

If we can land a man on the moon, why can't we solve the problems of the ghetto? The question stands as a metaphor for a variety of complaints about the uneven performance of the American political economy. . . why can't we provide medical care at reasonable cost to all who need it, keep the streets, air, and water clean, keep down crime, educate ghetto kids, provide decent and low-cost mass transport, halt the rise in housing and services costs, have reliable television and automobile repair service?[12]

At the federal level, the National Aeronautics and Space Administration (NASA) initiated a program with universities to utilize technology developed primarily for space for "the direct and indirect benefits of such research [which] can contribute to the economic, social and general well-being of the nation."[13] The University of California was one of several universities receiving money under NASA's Sustaining University Program (SUP). The program's objectives were multifold and included funds for buildings, graduate education, and research in the space sciences. However, the provision to utilize "space spinoffs" for community and humanitarian purposes, spelled out in memorandums of understanding with university presidents, went generally unfulfilled despite vigorous efforts on the part of NASA's director, James Webb. In a subsequent review of the program, an evaluator noted that most of the faculty participants in SUP had no knowledge of institutional commitments, made by their university presidents, committing them to community applications.[14] The attempt to develop a multidisciplinary focus on community problems encountered the reluctance of faculty to move away from their own disciplinary work or from basic research, unless it "(1) was of interest to them; (2) did not threaten their intellectual freedom; and (3) did not pose undue time restrictions."[15]

The State of California took "the moon and ghetto" metaphor even more literally: aerospace companies were encouraged to bid on contracts with the State Department of Finance to study problems in criminal justice, waste management, mass transportation, and information storage and retrieval.[16] Work was to be completed within six months. Four projects were selected from 51 bids. The thread that connected the contractor's work on missions such as Mercury, Ranger, Mariner, and Gemini with solving social problems was based on the hope that systems analysis would succeed where traditional approaches had failed.[17] At the end of the contract period, a report to the governor emphasized the experimental nature of the contracts, delineated at length the difference between aerospace corporations and state governments, and concluded that it was up to the legislature to pursue further these "exciting possibilities."[18] The legislature did not choose to pursue additional contracts. One observer claimed that state officials were privately expressing relief that the studies had "not injured them too gravely," and wondered aloud how aerospace engineers would feel about having "the design of an XB-70 . . . entrusted to a group of ornithologists even though some of them may have taken courses in aerodynamics."[19]

The 1960s were also a time of increased faith in social science applications, particularly to urban problems of poverty, race, and unemployment. University administrations were pressured by a variety of constituency groups, both external and internal, to see themselves as part of the urban environment with obligations to the poor. Social scientists conducted studies, planned public policies, designed and evaluated programs of the war on poverty and of the Great Society, and immersed themelves in the problems of cities generally.[20]

One federal program, the Urban Observatories Program, funded by the Department of Housing and Urban Development (HUD) and the Department of Health, Education, and Welfare (HEW), was created to link university research with policy making on urban problems. This program was one of the first to try specific mechanisms to make the connection. Established in ten cities, each observatory's mission was to conduct research and to ensure that the research results were useful to local decision makers. Advisory committees combined representation from academia and local government.[21]

Peter Szanton examined the urban observatories after the five-year funding cycle had been completed and found most of them had not achieved their objectives. He cataloged the problems as follows: (a) time frame—policy makers need information immediately, while faculty require time for data-gathering; (b) different research needs—policy makers need synthesized information drawn from many disciplines, while faculty are generally single-discipline oriented; and (c) the establishment of priorities—what research should be undertaken and by whom. Even though city officials had authority over the research agenda, they lacked "the experience or incentive to exercise it; observatory directors, who might have exercised it on their behalf, were typically underfunded, part-time participants."[22] In addition, Szanton found that giving federal money directly to the universities had created "little incentive to determine what help city agencies wanted or were capable of using." The consequence was that academics conducted research primarily of interest to them.

Szanton reviewed many aspects of the research/policy-maker connection and paid particular attention to the agriculture extension analogy that underlay several of the programs. Szanton argued that trying to apply this nexus in an urban setting was seriously flawed:

> [T]he rural extension analogy was faulty on several grounds. Rural extension developed slowly and experimentally over half a century; it was limited and well specified in purpose; and it was rooted in a congruence of values between the researchers and the whole constituency on which their school depended. None of these conditions held with respect to urban problems.[23]

Urban constituencies were anything but unified. It was difficult to establish a research agenda in instances where frequently there was not even agreement on what the problems were.

By the mid-1970s, academic journals had begun to mirror the debates over university rôles and responsibilities at the local level. Journals in political science and public administration were full of arguments over what, exactly, policy analysis was and what its relationship was to the decision-making or political process.[24] By the end of the decade, if many had become disillusioned by the promise of the social sciences to solve problems, others had decided that the increasing complexity of modern life called for a greater integration of scientific and technological information in public decision making. And, reflecting the change both in Nixon Administration attitudes toward national efforts at problem solving and a cautiousness toward federal government solutions generally, attention shifted to the states. Revenue sharing, in which states received a share of national taxes to apply to state programs, was a primary example.

The 1970s: university and state government interaction

A major impetus toward the creation of state-level programs came from the National Science Foundation (NSF), and focused on increasing the capacity of state decision makers to handle complex, often technologically sophisticated problems such as those found in energy or toxics policies. NSF provided seed funds through its State and Local Intergovernmental Science Policy Planning Program, which may have been the first federal program to focus on strengthening state science and technology capacity.[25] The purpose of the program was to develop mechanisms for greater interaction between scientists and policy makers, or, as one magazine writer put it, NSF's new mandate was "to start a major new effort to have state government go beyond its past dalliance with science advice and really embrace it."[26] That mandate took the form of encouraging the formation of science advisory councils attached to the legislature or the appointment of science advisors to governors' offices, mostly patterned after the federal government.

In California, NSF underwrote, with a three-year $50,000 demonstration grant, an Assembly Science and Technology Advisory Council (attached to the legislature's Assembly Office of Research), which had direct links to Assembly committees and staff.[27] Backed strongly by the Speaker of the Assembly, the Council was able to draw on scientists from throughout California, many of whom had extensive experience at the national level and several of whom were Nobel laureates. The Council's primary purpose was to bring scientific and technological knowledge into the legislative process sufficiently early so that policy decisions would be based on the most current and solid technical information possible. The Council was also to act as an early warning system with respect to emerging technological problems and advancements. NSF hoped that this program would result in explicit and coherent state science policies. Council members, in turn, hoped that states having relationships with their scientific communities would be better positioned to gain federal funds and influence federal policies.[28] Council minutes indicate that members were optimistic about achieving a more comprehensive view of problems than had state officials in the past. They thought the executive branch was too "compartmentalized and self-protective to take a multi-disciplinary approach to problem-solving."[29]

The Council's work was to be carried out through technical panels and studies conducted on energy, health, and employment issues. While the Council was to report its findings to the entire Assembly, acting as a committee of the whole, a specific legislative policy committee was to be formed to guide the Advisory Council in its daily operations. Evaluators gave the experiment generally high marks.[30] They viewed the strengths of the Advisory Council and its technical panels as being high-level, high-quality, and multidisciplinary. The report noted a general enhancement of science and technology in decision making, particularly when there was a high degree of interaction with specific legislative policy committees. Many of the weaknesses related to the failure of the Assembly Speaker to create a policy committee that could give overall guidance to the Council as well as the fact that the Assembly Committee of the Whole rarely met. Without this guidance and interaction with legislative members, the Advisory Council was forced to set most of its own research priorities.

This lack of process affected not only the topics selected but particular approaches to problems since Council members knew very little about how policy makers viewed the problems that research was intended to address. This "missing link," in turn, frequently meant that the research project's relevance to particular problems was unclear. Other problems noted in the evaluation illustrate the barriers that create the gap between original vision and actual implementation:

(a) Lack of interaction with key legislators or staff members of the standing policy committees;
(b) Council members' desire to be responsive to those legislators who did request assistance strained resources;
(c) Advisory Council leaned too heavily on written reports to communicate its findings to the legislature.[31]

Despite these problems, the evaluators' report strongly recommended that the Advisory Council be continued.[32] Before the end of the three-year period, the speakership of the Assembly changed hands and parties. The new speaker went on record as favoring the Advisory Council's continuation. However, when NSF funding ran out, the Council ceased to exist, thus illustrating one of the major problems in any such joint venture: turnover of leadership and lack of sustained commitment at the top.

A problem related to turnover that inhibits learning from programs such as that run by California's Science Advisory Council is that the experience is generally lost, found only in the "fugitive literature of final reports to sponsors."[33] The Council is a perfect example: no one in the current Assembly Office of Research, to which the Council was attached, knew anything about the program, and only an enterprising state librarian was able to complete the detective work to find reports and other research products.

Reading Council reports from the vantage point of 1987, nearly 15 years after they were issued, one is struck by the fact that one report addressing the question of unemployment, particularly in the defense and aerospace industries, raised concerns about the nation's loss of technological leadership in comparison with other countries such as West Germany and Japan. (There was an argument on the panel over how seriously to take these concerns; ultimately, they were adopted as a minority report.) This example raises the problem of how to measure the effectiveness of "early warning" efforts. Frequently, such programs and reports are judged within years or even months of their issuance, before the problems identified become acute. In hindsight, the report appears particularly prescient. Whether or not actions were taken in response to such "alerts" must be treated, of course, as a separate question. It should be noted that the NSF continued to evaluate its state funding and, subsequently, developed a second program—the Science, Engineering, and Technology (SSET) Program—to sustain state efforts.[34]

While Council members included several representatives from the University of California, there was no formal relationship with the university. One of the key members of the Science and Technology Council was Dr. Emil Mrak, chancellor of the University of California at Davis. He repeatedly tried to involve the university more heavily in the effort, particularly in applying continuing research activities to legislative problems. Although the evaluation determined interest among key university officials, "the Council was not able to secure from the university an inventory of research projects or develop other meaningful cooperative activities."[35]

The inability to identify, let alone have access to, university research is a common complaint on the part of state legislators. In 1974, Alan Post, veteran legislative analyst from California, characterized his experience with the University of California as completely *ad hoc*, and pressed for more systematic assistance since the state provided funding for university research. He told university officials that the legislature had no wish to interfere with the basic research function; it simply wanted a "by-product" of that research. Post said the legislature would like to "merely skim the cream off this product in a way that can be used to help us where we need some help."[36]

Echoing the thrust of Post's remarks, a California survey found that most officials (83 percent) wanted more policy-oriented research, but not at the expense of basic research.[37] The survey, part of a larger study by the Rand Corporation entitled "Attitudes of California State government officials toward research utilization," found a growing clientele interested in research, especially the "new breed of political staff" created as a result of the increasing professionalizaton of the legislature. A similar 1974 survey, funded by NSF, of 14 southern states found a pattern of interest in using university services and considerable frustration on the part of state government officials in doing so.[38] Officials contributing to both studies thought the establishment of some kind of coordinating council might help.

Both Post's remarks and the Rand study results were presented to a University of California Conference on Public Service. The discussion focused on basic versus applied research and the preservation of basic research (that "undertaken without reference to immediate practical

goals and [which] seeks to establish general theoretical explanations").
Basic research was also explicitly defined as "clean" in the sense that
time elapses before anyone utilizes the research findings in a
way that creates monetary profit.[39] The biggest danger, the committee
reported, in departing from basic research was that faculty members
could become advocates of particular positions or identify with their
clients:

> In short, the position is frequently taken that a real danger of
> conflict of interest requires special care in selecting service pro-
> jects so that great University interests are not sacrificed to small
> ones.[40]

This discussion between California state officials and faculty was
repeated in many other states during the 1970s. As requests for
assistance increased, stemming from the rationale that the state was a
funder of university research, the debate grew over the appropriate rôle
for faculty. Growing evidence suggested that the relationship between
researcher and policy maker had a better chance of succeeding if there
was a "client" relationship; university officials frequently viewed this
as precisely the danger to be avoided.

State investment in research: the demand for a return

In California, Alan Post's modest request for state government participation in the by-product of university research was replaced by more
aggressive demands from state law makers. State funding of research
at the University of California was substantial ($112.2 million in
1974).[41] Legislators viewed this as a large investment and wanted
some return to the state. Faculty had been granted lower teaching
loads at the University of California, in contrast with the 19-campus
state university system, on the grounds that research was both a
primary function and integral to good teaching. This argument only
heightened the legislators' belief that they should reap some benefits
from the investment in research.[42]

In 1976, a bill was introduced in the California Assembly to establish a public policy think tank within the University of California
to serve state government. The proposed program's philosophy and
intent were outlined in a letter from the bill's author to a University
official:

One outcome of this investment should be information which has significant utility in improving public policy formulation and governmental action. The degree to which the University's research efforts assist public policy decision makers continues to be questioned. There is sufficient concern to warrant experimentation/exploration into ways of strengthening this link betweeen the information needs of state governmental agencies and the research efforts and responsibilities of the University of California.[43]

The bill, however, raised the touchy subject of setting research priorities by stating that the proposed $5 million budget should be reallocated from existing University resources "to accomplish an incremental shift toward a greater investment in policy research. . . . The public dollars are not available to simply increase research; we must shift slightly the state's research priorities."[44] The University did not share the view that legislators should establish research priorities and opposed the bill.

The bill came within two votes of being passed. One of the arguments used by its legislative advocates was the failure of the University to warn law makers of the severe energy shortages in the early 1970s. An offshoot of the investment thesis, some legislators believed that state funding of university research should have resulted in a timely warning, so the effects of the energy crisis could have been cushioned.

With the threatened introduction of the bill again in 1977, negotiations with the University ensued and resulted in a joint program, the California Policy Seminar, a name deliberately chosen to distinguish it from Rand-type think tanks by using the image of a seminar. The Seminar's mission was to "make the research resources of the University of California better known and more accessible to state government officials."[45] The program, although systemwide, was located within the Institute of Governmental Studies on the Berkeley campus, whose historical orientation toward state and local government facilitated the Seminar's development. The legislative antecedents, particularly the example of the energy crisis, shaped the form and nature of the initial research program, which emphasized long-term investigation of issues anticipated to require policy solutions.

While this demand for assistance, using the leverage of state budgets, was repeated in many states throughout the 1970s and resulted in numerous programs designed to help solve state problems, few of the programs then established were incorporated into university structures.[46] Since the California Policy Seminar is an exception to the general pattern, its now decade-long history is worth examining. This history shows, among other things, that even with the sustained interest and commitment of top officials, marrying two disparate structures remains fraught with tensions. The Seminar has also tried to incorporate constant feedback into its program design, allowing for periodic adjustment based upon experience.

A distinguishing characteristic of the Seminar was the joint determination of its activities, including review and selection of research grants, by both university and state decision makers. The governing board included the president of the University; the governor of the State of California; the president *pro tempore* of the California Senate; and the speaker of the California Assembly. Each of these officials appointed additional members to the board.

From 1977 through 1981, the Policy Seminar followed a fairly stable pattern of selecting research. Abstracts of research projects were solicited from all nine campuses and research laboratories, and were in turn narrowed down to a handful of completed proposals from which the board funded four to six projects each year. All abstracts were sent out to legislative committee heads for review. Additionally, both legislative and executive branch officials were encouraged to submit research ideas for policy problems not found in the submitted abstracts. All faculty who were asked to submit full proposals consulted with Sacramento decision makers whose interests were relevant to the proposed research projects. The governing board made final grant decisions. The first four projects, funded for periods of two years at $50,000, were the following:

(a) investigation of environmental chemicals that cause cancer and genetic birth defects and development of a strategy for minimizing human exposure;
(b) design of computerized models of 17 population centers in California that will permit determining the impact on California of fundamental state policy changes;
(c) exploration of social and ecological questions related to agricultural policy in California;
(d) determination of the savings that would result from establishing long-range standards for energy consumption in buildings and by appliances.[47]

President Saxon, in announcing the second round of proposals, said of the Policy Seminar, "I know of no other program similar to it in the nation, where faculty and administrators of the state university have sat down with members of the state government to identify long-range problems facing the state. We have done it in recognition of our responsiblity to help solve the problems of the State of California."[48]

Evaluation and program changes

By 1981, more than 400 faculty had submitted ideas for consideration, and interaction between faculty and governmental decision makers had increased substantially. The Policy Seminar's budget had grown from an initial appropriation of $27,175 to $483,681. Nevertheless, its first director, John Cummins, commissioned a program evaluation that focused primarily on the lengthy timeline for research completion—nearly three years from selection to dissemination of results. The evaluation concluded that commissioning long-term research to meet pressing state needs "was like trying to make apple pie with a Chinese recipe."[49] The chosen recipe had engendered frustration and reduced expectations, which affected the selection process as well as the seriousness with which the University's efforts were regarded. As Cummins assessed the situation, the perception had developed in Sacramento that the time frame was "so unrealistic that it deserved only a modest level of consideration."[50] State leaders were paying less attention to the research projects, and even staff attention was waning.

While Cummins thought some of the research had sparked considerable dialogue among state officials, he concluded that neither the state nor the University had given sufficient thought to the problem of connecting two institutions whose time frames and ways of operating were so fundamentally different. He also addressed the difficulties the state had in defining and setting research priorities:

> The match between knowledge and policy has not been optimal, but it has not been a failure by any means. In this context, it cannot be forgotten that the Legislature in particular has been faulted in many circles for failing to seriously address the major issues confronting the state. Its preoccupation with fundraising and reelection, among other things, has diverted the members' attention to a significant degree. This is only mentioned in this paper to bring to the fore the almost intractable problem which the California Policy Seminar is confronting. Since the Policy Seminar was created as an experiment, we do have an opportunity to continue to grapple with this connection between knowledge and policy in new ways.[51]

In early 1982 the program was restructured to take into account the time constraints under which most decision makers work, while reserving some money for longer-term work. A portion of research funds was allocated to a "short-term initiatives" program for projects initiated by state officials and completed within a single legislative session. This money was allocated internally among the Senate and the Assembly research offices and the Governor's Office.

Concurrently, an attempt was made to connect the "long-term research" projects more closely to state research priorities. An executive committee, comprising mainly senior staff from Sacramento, approved ten specific policy issues to be circulated among the faculty. In addition, the definition of "long-term" was revised to mean research taking a year or more to complete.

Between 1983 and 1986 activity increased generally. While the Seminar had encouraged face-to-face contact between faculty and policy makers from the beginning, most interactions occurred in the context of research submissions. With the more flexible approach and greater responsiveness under the short-term initiatives program, the number and nature of meetings between faculty and state officials increased dramatically. These ranged from traditional academic symposia to workshops, working groups, retreats, and individual meetings between faculty and legislators.

With the advent of a new director in 1986, the Seminar was reshaped to address faculty concerns regarding academic oversight and state officials' concern over the relevance of commissioned research. The Seminar's convenors remain the president of the University, the governor, the Senate president *pro tempore*, and the Assembly speaker. Each convenor appoints three members to serve on a steering committee, which meets once or twice a year. Retaining the principle of joint decision making for research projects, the University also appoints nine members, five of whom are faculty and four systemwide administrators.

Many of the activities previously undertaken under the short-term initiatives rubric have been redesignated as part of a Technical Assistance Program; these projects respond specifically to a client (i.e., a state policy maker from either the legislative or executive branches). A wide range of activities has occurred under the Technical Assistance Program, including visits to a campus by legislators; workshops or seminars on topics as diverse as utility diversification, criminal justice, land use, and vocational education; and a statewide taskforce developing a research agenda for improving water quality. This program recognizes the state's enormous need for information, especially synthesized information and data analysis, in addition to traditional research. For instance, a recent technical assistance project involved analyzing data on California's medically uninsured from larger population surveys.[52] In meetings with governmental representatives from both branches and political parties, it was generally agreed that these data will constitute the basis of future policy discussions. This agreement does not signify consensus on what to do about Californians without medical insurance, and the policy options will vary widely based on ideological and partisan differences; it does mean, however, that one level of argument has been potentially eliminated due to the high quality of the background research. Furthermore, this work was not seen as incompatible with disciplinary demands placed on the researchers, since the results are suitable for publication in other academic forums and the investigators have received additional funds for longitudinal work on the same subject.

The relationship between faculty expertise and policy-maker needs does not always work so smoothly. Two examples highlight the tensions and ambivalences that can occur when faculty are "linked" with policy makers. In one instance, a requested seminar for which faculty needed preparation time was nearly jeopardized by pressure from policy makers who seemed to be fishing for specific legislation and wanted the event to be scheduled immediately. In another instance, a meeting was convened for a senator while a bill was pending; and, although the specific legislation was not mentioned and the topic was placed in an historical overview, some faculty felt the legislative staff were using the session to probe the waters for political opposition and were not seriously interested in exploring the issue.

The Policy Seminar's other activities are conducted under the Policy Research Program. Research proposals on a wide range of policy topics are solicited from faculty on the nine campuses and research laboratories, as abstracts were in earlier years, thus giving faculty the opportunity to initiate projects. Each proposal is reviewed initially to determine whether or not the research addresses an important state issue and whether it is policy-relevant. The proposals are subsequently reviewed by senior state government staff and academics, both for policy relevance and for methodological rigor. Reviews are presented to the Steering Committee for final decisions. The Policy Research Program also provides a forum for the setting of topical research priorities by the Steering Committee *before* the research call goes out to faculty. Examples from the 1987 funding cycle illustrate the range and type of research funded and the rôle the Steering Committee plays in selecting projects. In the most recent Committee deliberations, state officials, while examining a proposal more limited in scope, articulated the greater need for a longitudinal study on high school dropouts. Recognizing that the available grant funds were not sufficient to conduct empirical research of this magnitude, the Committee reserved some money and asked the two faculty investigators whether they would be interested in designing such a study.[53] When the faculty members responded with enthusiasm, a meeting was convened with officials from the Senate and Assembly research offices, the Senate and Assembly education committees, the Governor's Office, and the Department of Education to determine more precisely what type of study would best address the important policy questions. The group described constitutes a kind of policy reference body giving faculty members an enhanced understanding of the policy context of their research while giving policy makers an opportunity to influence the design of such work. Since the legislature and the executive branch are governed by different political parties, reference groups are automatically bipartisan. Increasingly, the Seminar is turning to the creation of these groups either at the outset of research projects or later as a way to inform key policy makers of the results of such research. This technique might be seen as an attempt to create a "client surrogate," since the research projects, unlike the technical assistance activities, are not specifically client-driven. The formation of reference groups responds to findings that research best serves policy makers when they are involved in defining what is relevant.

The California Policy Seminar has not begun to meet all of the demands for assistance. Every year bills are introduced into the state legislature requesting the University of California to devote resources toward the solution of various problems. Those that are passed are seldom accompanied by an appropriation. This omission of additional financial resources seldom alters the expectations associated with such legislation. In the last several years the University has been asked to provide assistance on technology transfer to small businesses, establish a center for cooperatives, and take a lead rôle in finding solutions to the problems facing the state's hispanic population, to name only a few.

Collaborative experiments elsewhere

A comprehensive examination of collaborative experiments has been undertaken by Irwin Feller in his book, *Universities and state governments*, published in 1986.[54] Feller found that few of the programs begun in the 1970s remained in existence, although some states had strong informal networks with their universities. He listed several of the ingredients for a successful program:

> The difficulty in establishing university/state government relationships lies not in formulating linkage arrangements but in having a sufficiently strong appreciation by each partner of the other's unique role, and of the limits to this relationship. This bonding requires a core number of early successes and mutual respect. It necessitates both stable funding and academicians who can serve as brokers between the university and state government. It depends on achieving a position where specific projects and requests for types of assistance can be turned down without rupturing the relationship.[55]

Feller found what previous authors had concluded: there was no consistent pattern to the organizational arrangements linking university resources with state government needs. A late 1970s study of university bureaus, institutes, centers, extension services, and other units had found that each program was "essentially unique."[56] What was important, according to Feller, was the development of an infrastructure within the university that had continuity and stable funding in order to respond quickly when requests came from state government:

> The dilemma repeatedly is that state government's needs arise in the context of specific problems, often with short turnaround times. It is this situation in which the identification and the negotiation of relationships becomes the most frustrating for state officials. Quickness of response depends on the existence of an infrastructure with which state government has a ready contact, of a university inventory, and of policies for communicating advice without acting in an organizational role.[57]

The programs that were successfully instituted in the 1970s shared characteristics that departed from traditional public service outreach programs. They emphasized research, technical responses to legislation, and/or analyses of policy options.[58] Successfully instituted programs also had full-time professional staff who had credibility with both academics and policy makers and who were able to keep faculty interest and autonomy at heart while simultaneously understanding the needs and demands of policy makers.

Thus, a preliminary picture emerges of the barriers that deter successful cooperation as well as the possibilities that encourage continued efforts. Now, however, national economic concerns have shifted the focus from the problem-solving concerns of the 1970s and have generated pressure for new programs and collaborative ventures, with industry often a third partner.

The 1980s: competitive pressures

New pressures to regain productivity and achieve greater competitiveness in the global economy have focused attention on the importance of higher education, often in rhetorical terms not heard since the Soviets launched the Sputnik satellite in the 1950s. As Stanford University president Donald Kennedy said, "It's as though the Japanese orbited a Toyota."[59] Federal and state reports have pointed to two key rôles of higher education in the creation of economic growth: as the generator of new knowledge that might be utilized in the marketplace, and as the producer of a highly skilled workforce needed by the economy. The 1985 President's Commission on Industrial Competitiveness report, *Global competition: the new reality*, defined competitiveness as "the degree to which a nation can, under free and fair market conditions, produce goods and services that meet the test of international markets while simultaneously maintaining or expanding the real incomes of its citizens."[60] Other national goals were seen as derivative of economic goals, obtainable "only if we are competitive in world markets."[61] Innovation and technological advance were viewed as prime drivers of increased productivity and economic growth, which led, in turn, to a renewed interest in scientific research and access to it.

With such emphasis on innovation, contemporary pressures on universities may be characterized by attempts to increase the amount of research and development in science and technology generally, influence the type of research conducted, and ensure its transfer to the marketplace.

Because California is the home of the semiconductor industry, state policy makers felt pressures early to act on behalf of the industry as it began to face increasing Japanese dominance in global markets. In the late 1970s under Governor Jerry Brown, long before the President's Commission report, state officials formed a Commission on Industrial Innovation to explore both the causes of declining R&D expenditures and the state's rôle in reversing these trends. Representatives of the Governor's Office, the legislature, the semiconductor industry, and the University met in early 1981 to discuss Governor Brown's proposals. One result was the formation of the Microelectronics and Computer Research Operations Program (Micro) at the University of

California at Berkeley, supported by both state and industry funds. As the semiconductor industry defined its problems, the Japanese had developed technologies that enabled them to "leapfrog" American companies with new products. This was possible because the Japanese had collaborative arrangements with government to enhance research and ensure the necessary development of future products. However, this type of targeted research was increasingly expensive and too burdensome for individual companies to undertake. This conclusion regarding Japanese competitive advantage created a strong incentive for U.S. industry to forge closer ties to American university researchers, particularly with graduate students, who might work on projects more closely related to industrial needs.[62] California saw its rôle as a catalyst in creating the Micro program, contributing $1 million to the program annually, which, in turn, leveraged matching funds from industry. Faculty and graduate students circulate research proposals among segments of the industry to determine interest. If interest is indicated, proposals compete for funds, with selections made by a board comprising representatives from industry, the University, and the state. The program operates to give industry (the client) a voice in determining what constitutes important research, while allowing researchers to propose and carry out their work in a nonproprietary setting.

In early 1984, the California Senate Office of Research issued a special report entitled *State policies to stimulate research and development*, prepared for the Joint Legislative Committee on Science and Technology.[63] The report reviewed the various options, including state tax incentives, direct state expenditures, joint R&D ventures, capital gains tax reductions, outside investment in California, state "Nobel prizes" for outstanding research work, and a review of patent rights. Basing its conclusions on a sequential model from basic research to development, commercialization, and diffusion, the report concluded that

> basic R&D should be funded through tax subsidies or direct public expenditures, while support of commercialization and diffusion requires private and public investment mechanisms capable of accepting high risk (i.e., royalty financing through R&D limited partnerships). Development, as an intermediate process, could involve elements of both subsidy and investment.[64]

Although the report cited the Micro program at Berkeley as an excellent example of state leadership, no similar programs have been established to date.

In the mid-1980s, state-level commissions took up the broader questions of California's economic future and, in the process, raised the question of university research priorities. A two-volume report was issued by the Senate Select Committee on Long-Range Policy Planning, entitled *California and the 21st century: foundations for a competitive society*.[65] In addition, the Stanford Research Institute (SRI) published a report in conjunction with the Senate Select Committee and the Joint Legislative Committee on Science and Technology called *Meeting California's competitiveness challenge*.[66]

The SRI summary of the two-volume report emphasized "working smarter" in the global economy through "constantly moving to higher value-added products and services."[67] Examples included "specialty agricultural products, design-oriented apparel, specialized printing, enhanced petroleum recovery systems, aerospace, new telecommunications and microelectronics products, and new financial, engineering, business, and research services."[68] The report recommended increased funds to the University of California in fields related to the above examples.

In the Senate Select Committee report, a key policy recommendation to ensure industrial competitiveness was that "the State should establish a research agenda."[69] The most controversial aspect of the recommendation, from the University's perspective, was the creation of a California Research Council charged with establishing a research agenda for the state "by identifying those areas which are vital and most fruitful for research in maintaining the state's competitiveness and promoting health and safety."[70] The report further recommended that the Council "should establish procedures for reviewing, awarding, and monitoring research grants in the identified areas."[71] Since this recommendation was subsequently introduced into the legislative arena, the University has entered a period of prolonged negotiations with the bill's authors, rather than opposing the bill outright. The University argues that it has an internal priority-setting process through the development of the annual budget; consultations on research priorities should be conducted by the University, not the state; and such consultations should be viewed as advisory only. Legislators, meanwhile, argue the need for an independent state body to guide them with respect to priorities. Legislators view the Research Council and the University as institutions that would interact with one another in establishing a state research agenda. The Research Council would prepare a budget reflecting all research in the state, whether by university or state agency or department, and develop a state research agenda. University officials have proceeded with a plan to establish an advisory committee of business, labor, and government officials to advise them of state needs in lieu of the formation of a state research council.

The question of research priorities has been raised by the California Postsecondary Education Commission (CPEC) as well, whose responsibilities include long-range planning and cost containment for all segments of higher education. A recent CPEC report concluded that the legislature could not make informed choices about which research deserves funding support without an overall picture of research.[72] The California Master Plan for Higher Education, adopted in 1960, divides responsibility among three segments of higher education. Under the master plan, the University of California has been the only segment to grant doctorates and receive state funds for research. As part of the 1988 five-year review, however, the legislature is considering a request from the California State University system for research funding as well. A recent hearing focused on research and public service; hence, questions regarding which institutions should conduct research and to what end are being raised in forums separate from those exploring the relationship between research and competitiveness.[73]

In recent years, the University has highlighted certain topics for funding when presenting budget requests to the state. These topical areas are ones that concern the state and are not exclusively linked to competitiveness issues; the University has recommended programs in subjects as diverse as AIDS, toxic substances, Pacific Rim, and biotechnology research. Most of the programs are structured to include interaction with relevant industry and government leaders, mostly through advisory committees. Presentation of the budget in this way, however, has reinforced legislators' arguments that they need to know more about the overall research picture if they are to fund the University's priority choices.

Some federal programs are forcing a further link between universities and state governments, requiring evidence of state financial support when awarding today's "big guy" science projects, such as the superconducting supercollider (SSC).[74] California's incentives package for the SSC was worth $560 million.[75] Big-ticket items, such as the SSC, constitute de facto priority setting for states; projects are not supported as a result of university/state government initiation and decision but because federal funds have been made available for particular projects. Newspaper reports indicate that Governor Deukmejian, upset over losing the supercollider bid, might sue to recover costs of preparing the proposal, adding another irritant to federal/state relationships.[76]

A further example of federal influence on state research priorities is the Sematech competition. Sematech is a consortium of semiconductor firms that have proposed formation of a state-level research institute, funded by both the federal government and the states, in order to keep commercially relevant research flowing to the industry. The rationale for such support was noted in a Department of Defense report that defined the threat of foreign competition as a national security issue:

> The U.S. will depend to a large degree upon foreign sources of microelectronics hardware and technology to meet its defense needs unless measures are taken to help this country recapture and retain leadership in semiconductor manufacturing technology.[77]

California's legislature authorized a $125 million bid, and the state joined with more than 30 others to bid for the Sematech project.[78] The five-year, billion-dollar project was awarded to Texas.

Recent legislative hearings have explored why California is losing major projects to other states. Despite assurances from the chair of the federal site selection committee that the reasons for California's failure to win the SSC project were due to the state's geological problems, legislators are using such failures to launch new initiatives, including science advisors in the Governor's Office, and a reserve account of $25 million to $50 million to solicit federal proposals.[79] Senator John Garamendi argued that the state has not adjusted "to the new system of research contracting, we're not organized, and worst of all we've allowed an aura of complacency to take over believing that our economic destiny is guaranteed."[80] Garamendi made the comments at a press conference where he was flanked by representatives from the biotechnology and engineering industries.

Issues and implications of competitiveness pressures

The pressure on universities to help solve problems concerning loss of economic competitiveness is significantly different from past pressures; it tends to relate, interconnect, and then subsume other goals. Unlike previous demands on universities, these are increasingly backed up by political clout, including the formation of unprecedented coalitions of business and institutions of higher education, such as the Business–Higher Education Forum, the Council on Research and Technology (CORETECH), and the Commission on National Challenges.

In the past, the predominant paradigm of how research breakthroughs become marketable products has been a linear progression from basic research to applied research to technology transfer to product development and commercialization. Since these activities were thought to occur in sequential fashion, often conducted in different institutions, there was a relatively long lead time between the basic research activity and commercialization. The modest levels of private-sector funding of university research, until recently, reflected the fact that industry did not look much to universities for increases in profit margins. The more commercially relevant research took place in industrial laboratories, such as at Bell and IBM. In a penetrating analysis of science in the service of new national goals, former *Science* reporter David Dixon argues that this view has changed; for many companies operating in the global economy, the competitive edge is to be found through basic research:

> What is therefore motivating companies to build close links to universities is not so much the specific results of the research they are sponsoring as the *strategic* advantage that such knowledge provides them in maintaining their competitive position in the international market. The most important information relates not so much to specific products as to broad lines of future product development.[81]

This shift, Dixon argues, helps to explain recent attempts by private industry to increase research funding generally, in addition to influencing particular research agendas.[82] A similar conclusion was advanced by Professor Richard R. Nelson from Columbia University at a recent conference in Washington, D.C. Nelson argued that the old model of a lag between basic science and technological change is "wrong in most instances." Universities were not threatened under this old model, since "academics do what they do." With the realization that the old model is wrong as it applies to many industrial sectors, however, pressure is placed on the research agenda itself.[83]

What are the implications of this shift? The balance of this chapter explores three, somewhat different, sets of issues. In the narrowest sense, one set of issues is associated with the establishment and management of formal collaborative programs, whether for industry, government, or a partnership of all three. The second set, more broadly, consists of public policy questions concerning equity issues: who has access to research? what are the purposes of publicly funded research? is it intended to achieve private or public ends? Finally, the most difficult set of issues with which to grapple concerns paradigms and metaphors underlying policy and program decisions. Our images and beliefs about the nature of knowledge and its transmission, about the process of innovation, or about economic development strategies guide and influence our choices and policies. These metaphors are often implicit in program choices and are adopted without careful examination of their applicability to a particular situation.

Establishing cooperative programs

If the issue is framed narrowly as to how state governments and universities might undertake action to achieve mutual goals, then enough of the "fugitive" literature describing and analyzing previous efforts has been assembled to make some tentative observations about cooperative programs, whether they are aimed at solving public problems or generating commercial applications. To assert that such programs can work, if parameters and expectations are carefully spelled out and understood, should not obscure the fact that establishing and managing them requires grappling with complicated questions. The California Policy Seminar and the Micro program (as well as others) support faculty in their research endeavors, basic and applied, ensuring that the research is salient to particular firms, policy makers, industries, or governments, while protecting faculty from interference with research design or dissemination of findings. For instance, in the Micro program, the distinction between "cutting edge research leading to products in the mid- or long-term" and "product development" preserves the boundary between public and proprietary information, yet allows industry to gain access to basic research findings. In the case of public policy research commissioned by the California Policy Seminar, faculty are protected from undue interference by the grant selection process, since the research proposals are initiated by faculty and reviewed and selected by both policy makers and faculty. Seminar staff buffer faculty during the course of their research by organizing and monitoring interactions with policy makers. At the same time, policy makers are able to select research that has direct relevance to public problems.

In both programs, state policy objectives are viewed as legitimate. For the California Policy Seminar, the policy research funded must be of interest to California officials; the Micro program requires that firms interested in matching funds have either research or manufacturing facilities in California. Constituencies outside the University have a significant voice in the selection process: if a firm or firms do not agree to grant matching funds, no funding is provided by the Micro program. Similarly, if a proposed research project does not meet the test of policy relevance in the California Policy Seminar, it is not funded. Both programs take existing institutional characteristics for granted, and have found mechanisms for linking the University with government or industry, which preserves the norms and values of each institution. Both institutions, the University and state government, are in agreement that the public purposes are legitimate ones.

Public policy questions

While one may argue that sustaining or increasing an overall standard of living is a pre-eminent *public* purpose, research that must be translated into specific products for particular industries or firms favors private interests, not public ones. Demand for such research assistance places cooperative ventures in an entirely different frame of reference than those to which most universities are accustomed, raising new and difficult issues.

While neither the "public realm" nor "private sector" is monolithic in character, the question of who has access and who benefits within the two sectors has become one of the most potent political debates in academia today. As long as the value of information and knowledge is seen as critical to economic survival, the debate is likely to continue. When research was thought to be a benign activity undertaken by professors in ivory towers, the question of economic benefit or loss did not arise.

"Access" questions are not simply theoretical questions. A California court, for example, recently ruled on an "access to research" question, taking it quite out of the philosophical realm. The Agricultural Extension Service at the University of California, which has been intimately involved with the beneficiaries (e.g., farmers) of research over the years, was challenged by the state's farmworkers in a lawsuit filed by the California Rural Legal Assistance (CRLA). The farmworkers, the lawyers argued, had been economically damaged by research activities that contributed to the mechanization of agriculture, which cost them their jobs. Because of the example used, the case has become known as the "Tomato-picker" suit.

Many of the allegations were eventually dropped or decided in favor of the University, including the contention that mechanization research was a "gift of public funds to a private interest," a violation of the state's constitutional prohibition on such gifts.[84] However, in December 1987, a district judge ruled that the Hatch Act did require the University to have a process to ensure that research funded with land grants benefits small or family farmers. The University has appealed against the ruling, arguing that such a process essentially constitutes a social impact statement on proposed research projects, "bringing political pressure to the academic realm, thereby limiting freedom of inquiry."[85] A selection process proposed by CRLA divided research funds into four beneficiary categories: small family farmers, farm laborers, rural residents, and consumers.[86] The entire suit reflects in part the shattering of the value consistency that Peter Szanton found critical to the success of the extension service as a model and the weakness in its use as an analogy for other programs. The extension service could operate effectively, in part, because researchers, the extension agents, and the farmers shared a common commitment to increasing productivity.

It is probably not an accident that this suit arose in a segment of the University in which the broader legitimacy of conducting applied research was largely settled, since once research "in the service of" a particular end or goal becomes accepted, distributional effects become relevant. While the legal controversy in the mechanization case involved the use of federal funds, the concept of subjecting research funded with public monies to project-by-project review for its potential impact on statutorily defined constituencies would revolutionize the way research is conducted.

Increasingly, constituents who do not think the universities are serving their interests have turned to state legislatures for remedies as well as to the courts. In California, for instance, state legislation has requested the University to establish a program in sustainable agriculture, largely regarded as a nontraditional mode of agriculture not well represented in the Division of Agriculture or the Agricultural Extension Service. Another California bill has requested the University of California to assist small businesses with technology transfer, the development and management of businesses themselves, and with job creation in the inner city. Another bill requested the University to establish a curriculum for cooperatives as a separate program, based on claims that there were no existing courses pertinent to establishing and running a cooperative form of business.

It is the question of the relationship between publicly funded research and the potential for private gain, however, that has posed the most serious philosophical questions for universities and government.

Nothing illustrates this dilemma better than the development of biotechnology. Recent discoveries in molecular biology that have unlocked the genetic code are creating a potential for new products and processes similar in impact, some say, to the Industrial Revolution. Most of the controversies over patents and other financial arrangements with industry have concerned the boundaries between business and faculty involvement—the degree of permissible gain for each party. But with attention focused on the tension between carrying out research and making money, questions of purpose have been neglected.

An example regarding vaccine production illustrates the tension over public versus private purposes. Over the last 200 years, approximately 20 vaccines have been produced and marketed by U.S. companies. Estimates of the number of vaccines that could be introduced in the next two decades, through focused research, range from 28 to 42.[87] A congressional hearing revealed that drug companies were not investing in new vaccines, however, for reasons that appeared to have little to do with liability questions or the cost of testing procedures. Analysts concluded that drugs that could be administered in repeated doses were more lucrative financially than vaccines administered only once.[88] Yet the public health implications of new vaccine production are enormous.

At a subsequent conference sponsored by the Institute of Medicine, academic researchers pointed out that market-driven criteria affected basic research as well as product development. The imbalance of virologists to parasitologists was attributed to the "lack of corporate interest in vaccines against parasitic diseases." One researcher had an even more pessimistic view, arguing that there were "no known sources to pay for vaccines for developing countries when the disease does not also exist in industrial countries."[89]

Until recently, most biotechnology research was supported exclusively with public funds, and biotechnology issues received the most attention at the national level. The debate in the 1970s over whether or not applications should be publicly held was resolved in favor of the marketplace. But the vaccine story illustrates the difference that could be made in human lives if research and development were geared toward public ends. In this case, public health professionals and congressional staff identified the gap during hearings on biotechnology and created incentives to produce new vaccines through a national vaccine program. It cannot be assumed, however, that similar "gaps" between potential public purposes and corporate efforts will always be identified. For instance, if the market for products aiding disabled people is not lucrative, who will provide incentives for research and development in that "market segment"? If government does not provide the incentives, they are not likely to exist. If industry defines the research and development agenda and government sees its rôle as helping to carry it out through establishing different research priorities within universities, we will have departed substantially from the relationships of the past.

Problems of paradigms

Beliefs about which R&D strategies to pursue stem mostly from beliefs about how knowledge is transferred. Unlike that available on cooperative experiments, the literature on "knowledge utilization" is voluminous. There are many parallels between literature that addresses public policy decision making and that regarding technology transfer. Both analyses have relied heavily on linear models that posit orderly steps: i.e., production, through transfer, to "consumption." A recent study of actual models of technology transfer found little evidence for the linear, sequential model:

> The traditional assumption was that basic research innovations would be utilized for applied research and product developments and their manufacture would naturally follow. It was expected that all regions of the United States would in time enjoy the benefits of new innovations from research, which were followed by timely developments, commercialization, and diffusion. However, recently it has become evident that the past assumptions about the transfer of technology have been inadequate.[90]

The authors concluded that commercialization was "less of a relay race where players hand off a baton to the next player than it is a basketball game where players pass the ball back and forth as they advance towards the goal."[91] They identified seven different models, most with descriptive names, such as: (a) the information dissemination model; (b) the licensing model; (c) the venture capital model; (d) the large company–joint venture model; (e) the incubator–science park model; (f) the ferret model; and (g) the agriculture extension model.[92] Each model addresses specific barriers in the transfer process. For instance, the licensing model addresses the reluctance of companies to take development risks without exclusive rights to a technology. This problem is overcome by allowing a federal laboratory or a university to determine which industry or firm has the capacity to develop and commercialize the technology, or to determine the award through a competitive bidding process.[93] In the case of the ferret model, currently used in England, individuals who represent business consortiums are permitted to "enter a government laboratory in order to ferret out technology which is useful to the member companies."[94] The authors also conclude that the most natural mode of technology transfer from laboratories and universities is one by which people move and take the knowledge with them, especially graduate students.

Similarly, knowledge utilization literature in public policy has evolved from engineering principles. Acknowledging that university reports and studies seldom find their way directly into a decision-making body, such as a legislature, scholars now talk in terms of knowledge diffusion, knowledge "creep," or percolation processes, terms all designed to describe the indirect and uncertain relationship between knowledge and decision making. Most models, regardless of whether they are drawn from engineering, communications theory, or the now prevalent "enlightenment" paradigm, assume a more or less rational process by which knowledge is transferred. Critics of the knowledge utilization literature have, of course, challenged this assumption, but challenge has not necessarily resulted in better models. A major characteristic of the literature is the lack of analyses focusing on decision makers or other "users" of research findings. Many analyses begin with new research findings or reports and attempt to trace their flow into policy decisions.

The debate over paradigms, models, or metaphors is not one affecting only academicians. For the last decade, states, regions, and single cities have often based economic development strategies on a single metaphor: Silicon Valley. Silicon Valley—the region adjacent to San Jose, California, home of the semiconductor industry and other high-tech companies—has also come to symbolize the important relationships between technology and research universities because of the region's proximity to Stanford University and the University of California at Berkeley. Silicon Valley's phenomenal growth led others to try to duplicate it. The East Coast equivalent, Route 128 in Massachusetts, was injected into the 1988 presidential campaign as the "Massachusetts Miracle," an economic growth model presumably thought replicable despite the ironic choice of words implying precisely the opposite.

None the less, no definitive conclusions have been reached regarding the factors involved in the growth of Silicon Valley. Almost never mentioned in discussions of the Silicon Valley "model" is the rôle of military funding in the early days of the semiconductor industry, which resulted in years of guaranteed markets for computer chips.[95] Even in California, where policy makers are aware of the disparity between the appealing image of Silicon Valley and current worries over unemployment, congestion, sprawl, and the possibility of poisoned aquifers in the Valley, entrepreneurs still talk in terms of creating "Sili-clones."[96] In one instance, a developer was trying to convince the University of California to become a partner in a teleport where the latest research findings from universities, especially those in biotechnology, can be transferred to venture capitalists. The transfer center was seen as "essential . . . if the Bay Area expects to hold its lead in biotech over other U.S. cities and Japan."[97] The vice president of the University of California, Ron Brady, explained that consideration was "happening in the context of demands from state and federal governments for national competitiveness."[98] Brady elaborated on the pressures on universities:

> All the governors from the smokestack states are crying out. The heat is being turned up. Some of the thrust is coming from the enormous success of a much better job of turning out marketable products.[99]

Conclusion

In the same way that documenting changes in the economy has been difficult due to the sheer rapidity with which they have occurred, describing the contemporary research university and its relationships with numerous nonstudent constituencies is virtually impossible. In a decentralized structure—by campus, school, department, institute, and program—changes in these relationships occur in ways that are not particularly visible. It is difficult to have a policy debate about the appropriate rôles between, say, the state government and the university, when the institutional reality being addressed is unclear.

Rosenzweig articulated the changes in the structure of higher education and research activity brought about by the infusion of federal funds in the postwar period.[100] There is as yet little literature describing the flow of monies to faculty whose ability to bypass the university has increased. Some have private consulting firms; others have created nonprofit structures to receive research funds that completely bypass the university. Reporting requirements to track conflicts of interest are largely procedural. The reason most universities cannot provide an overall picture of their research activities is that they simply do not know.

In 1963, a huge controversy greeted Clark Kerr's book *The uses of the university*, which described the contemporary university's many, often contradictory, functions.[101] This description contrasted sharply with images of remote ivory towers. (The controversy raged largely among those who argued that Kerr was not simply describing the "multiversity," but advocating it.) If this chapter has one overriding conclusion, it is that we need contemporary analysis to describe changes that are occurring within large research universities. Such analysis is likely to generate controversy every bit equal to the previous one. However, it seems central to the policy debate of what new rôle relationships *should* be between the university, the state, and other constituencies. It is difficult to debate what one cannot describe.

Notes

1 I. Feller, *Universities and state governments* (New York: Praeger, 1986), pp. 64–83.
2 *The university and the city* (Cambridge, Mass.: Harvard University, Office of the President, 1969), p. 9.
3 Ibid.
4 S. E. Elman & S. Marx Smock, *Professional service and faculty rewards: toward an integrated structure* (Washington, D.C.: National Association of State Universities and Land-Grant Colleges, 1985), p. 6.
5 Ibid., p. 43.
6 Ibid., p. 15.
7 A. H. Depree, *Science in the federal government* (Cambridge, Mass.: Belknap Press of Harvard University Press, 1957), p. 150.
8 Ibid., p. 170.
9 V. A. Stadtman, *The University of California 1868–1968* (New York: McGraw-Hill, 1970), pp. 201–13.
10 National Commission on Research, "Industry and the universities: developing cooperative research relationships in the national interest" (Pasadena, Calif.: California Institute of Technology, 1980).
11 C. Kerr, *The uses of the university* (Cambridge, Mass.: Harvard University Press, 1963), p. 12.
12 R. R. Nelson, *The moon and the ghetto* (New York: Norton, 1977), p. 13.
13 L. L. Henry, "The NASA–university memoranda of understanding" (Syracuse: The Inter-University Case Program, 1969), p. 12. See also W. H. Lambright, "Launching NASA's sustaining university program" (Syracuse: The Inter-University Case Program, 1969).
14 Henry, "The NASA-university memoranda of understanding," p. 85.
15 Ibid., p. 87.
16 State of California, Department of Finance, "The four aerospace contracts: a review of the California experience," xerox copy of report located at the Institute of Governmental Studies Library, University of California, Berkeley, pp. 1–7.
17 Ibid.
18 Ibid., pp. 82–90.
19 I. R. Hoos, "A critique of the application of systems analysis to social problems," internal working paper (Berkeley, Calif.: Space Sciences Laboratory, May 1967), p. 25.
20 See, for instance, H. Aaron, *Politics and the professors* (Washington, D.C.: Brookings Institution, 1978); L. J. Duh (ed.), *The urban condition* (New York: Basic Books, 1963); A. Wildavsky & J. L. Pressman, *Implementation* (Berkeley: University of California Press, 1973).
21 F. W. Heiss, *Urban research and urban policy-making* (Boulder, Colo.: Bureau of Governmental Research and Service, University of Colorado, 1975).

22 P. Szanton, *Not well advised* (New York: Russell Sage Foundation & Ford Foundation, 1981), p. 25.
23 Ibid., p. 10.
24 See, for instance, D. Brobrow, H. Eulau, M. Landau, C. O. Jones & R. Axelrod, "The place of policy analysis," *American Journal of Political Science* **21**, May 1977, 415–33; R. R. Bovbjerg & J. W. Vaupel (eds.), "What is policy analysis?" *Journal of Policy Analysis and Management* **4**, 1985, 419–40; L. E. Lynn, Jr. (ed.), *Knowledge and policy: the uncertain connection*, Study Project on Social Research and Development (Washington, D.C.: National Academy of Sciences, 1978).
25 J. W. Reuss & J. Mack, "State legislatures' response to the state science, engineering, and technology program," National Conference of State Legislatures report to National Science Foundation, Denver, Colorado, August 14, 1978.
26 L. Carter, "State scientific advisors: the effort in Michigan," *Science* **194**, November, 1976, 923.
27 *Newsletter of the California Assembly Science and Technology Council*, Winter 1970, p. 4.
28 Ibid., p. 1.
29 Assembly Science and Technology Council, minutes, January 19, 1970 (available through the California State Library).
30 Assembly Science and Technology Council, "Evaluation and background report," May 1973 (available through the California State Library).
31 Ibid.
32 Ibid.
33 Feller, *Universities and state governments*, p. 2.
34 Reuss & Mack, "State legislatures' response."
35 Assembly Science and Technology Council, "Evaluation and background report," pp. 28–9.
36 "Applied and public service research in the University of California," *Proceedings of the University of California Twenty-Eighth All-University Faculty Conference*, p. 30.
37 A. J. Lipson, "Attitudes of California State government officials toward research utilization," a working note, RAND study, prepared for the California State Science Advisor and Office of Science and Technology, p. 9.
38 J. A. Worthley & J. Apfel, "University assistance to state government," *Journal of Higher Education* **49**, 6, 1978, 49.
39 "Applied and public service research," p. 12.
40 Ibid., p. 14.
41 Letter from Assemblyman John Vasconcellos, Chair of the Assembly Permanent Subcommittee on Postsecondary Education, to John Cummins, Institute of Governmental Studies, University of California at Berkeley, August 7, 1975 (California Policy Seminar files).
42 The Master Plan for Higher Education, adopted in 1960 by the State of California, specified a division of labor between the three segments of higher education in the state—the University of California system, the state university system, and the community colleges—reserving the award of doctoral degrees and research to the University of California system.
43 Vasconcellos to Cummins.
44 Ibid.
45 Early mission statements, 1977–8, California Policy Seminar files.
46 Feller, *University and state governments*, p. 8.
47 California Policy Seminar files.
48 D. Saxon, *University Bulletin*, March 13, 1978.
49 R. Pruger, "Program evaluation," California Policy Seminar files.
50 John Cummins, correspondence in California Policy Seminar files, January 18, 1982.
51 Ibid., p. 3.

52 E. R. Brown, R. B. Valdez, H. Morgenstern, P. Nourjah & C. Hafner, *Californians without health insurance*, California Policy Seminar Technical Assistance Report, 1987.

53 California Policy Seminar Steering Committee Meeting, Sacramento, California, June 22, 1987.

54 Feller, *Universities and state governments*.

55 Ibid., p. 148.

56 R. Sellers & L. Bender, "University public service outreach to state and local government," *State and Local Government Review* 2, 1979, 22.

57 Feller, *University and state governments*, p. 149.

58 Ibid., p. 60.

59 M. Ryan, "Are our universities letting us down?" *Parade*, January 24, 1988, 10.

60 President's Commission on Industrial Competitiveness, *Global competition: the new reality* (Washington, D.C.: Government Printing Office, 1985), p. 5.

61 Ibid., p. 1.

62 Interview with John Griffing, California Senate Office of Research and former member of the Commission on Industrial Innovation, July 22, 1987.

63 *State policies to stimulate research and development* (Sacramento: California Senate Office of Research, 1984).

64 Ibid., p. 3.

65 Senate Select Committee on Long Range Policy Planning, *California and the 21st century: foundations for a competitive society*, 2 vols. (California Senate Select Committee on Long Range Policy Planning, January 1986). See also Stanford Research Institute, *California's economic future*, September 1986.

66 Stanford Research Institute, *Meeting California's competitiveness challenge*, prepared for the Senate Select Committee and the Joint Legislative Committee on Science and Technology, January 1985.

67 Stanford Research Institute, *California's economic future*, p. 3.

68 Ibid.

69 Senate Select Committee on Long Range Policy Planning, *California and the 21st century*, vol. 1, p. 25.

70 Ibid.

71 Ibid.

72 California Postsecondary Education Commission, *Issues related to funding of research at the University of California*, report to the California Legislature, February 1987.

73 Public Hearing, Joint Committee for Review of the Master Plan for Higher Education, Santa Barbara, California, January 29, 1988.

74 See terminology used in S. S. Hall, *Invisible frontiers* (New York: Morgan Entrekin/ Atlantic Monthly Press, 1987).

75 "State offers to build science institute for super collider," *Los Angeles Times*, August 25, 1987.

76 "State may sue for funds spent on the super collider proposal," *San Francisco Examiner*, January 21, 1988.

77 *Los Angeles Times*, September 5, 1987.

78 "California on Sematech finalist list," *San Francisco Examiner*, November 20, 1987.

79 "State effort to sell itself falls short," *San Diego Tribune*, February 25, 1988.

80 "Garamendi: state needs science lead," *Sacramento Bee*, March 3, 1988.

81 D. Dickson, *The new politics of science* (New York: Pantheon, 1984), p. 74.

82 Ibid.

83 Workshop notes, R. R. Nelson, panelist, "Whither U.S. technology policy?" Association of Public Policy Analysis and Management (APPAM), Washington, D.C., October 30, 1987.

84 "Chronological summary and overview of CRLA case," Division of Agriculture memo and attachments, University of California, January 14, 1987.

85 Ibid., p. 6.

86 Ibid., Table 2 attachment.

87 Cited in P. Freeman & T. Robbins's memorandum to Staff Director, U.S. House of Representatives, Committee on Energy and Commerce, September 24, 1985. The Institute of Medicine estimates new vaccine potential as approximately 28; the Department of Defense estimates the higher number.

88 Ibid., p. 3.

89 *Proceedings of a workshop on vaccine innovation and supply*, report prepared by the Institute of Medicine and National Academy of Sciences (Washington, D.C.: U.S. Government Printing Office, August 1986), p. 5.

90 R. C. Dorf & K. K. F. Worthington, "Models for technology transfer from universities and research laboratories," paper distributed at University of California conference Competitiveness and Technology Transfer, June 12, 1987, p. 4.

91 Ibid., p. 2.

92 Ibid., pp. 7–9.

93 Ibid., p. 7.

94 Ibid., p. 8.

95 T. R. Reid, *The chip* (New York: Simon & Schuster, 1985).

96 *Oakland Tribune*, October 11–13, 1987.

97 Ibid., October 11, 1987.

98 Ibid.

99 Ibid.

100 R. Rosenzweig, *The research universities and their patrons* (Berkeley: University of California Press, 1982).

101 Kerr, *The uses of the university*.

15

Creating and sustaining the U.S. technopolis

DAVID V. GIBSON
& RAYMOND W. SMILOR

TWO KEY ASSUMPTIONS are central to this chapter. First, the world is on the threshold of an advanced technological era. The rapid increase in and diversity of new (high) technologies are changing the shape and evolution of societies.[1] Technological advances are dramatically altering the nature of domestic and worldwide economic competition. How U.S. communities and regions anticipate and respond to this new competitive environment will largely determine the health and viability of their economies.[2]

Second, new institutional alliances are altering the strategy and tactics of economic development and diversification. In the United States strategic alliances between the public and private sectors—especially among business, government, and academia—are having far-reaching consequences on the way we think about and take action on economic development.[3]

These two assumptions are captured in the term "technopolis." *Techno* reflects the emphasis on technology, *polis* is the Greek word for "city–state" and reflects the balance between the public and private sectors.[4] The modern technopolis is one that interactively links technology commercialization with public and private sectors to spur economic development and promote technology diversification. As new kinds of institutional developments among business, government, and academia are beginning to promote economic development and technology diversification,[5] a fascinating paradox has emerged—the paradox of competition and cooperation which Ouchi elaborates in his description of the M-Form society:

> The essence of an M-Form society is social integration. An M-Form society represents balance, a balance between the need for government regulation and the need for independent laissez-faire action. A balance between one special interest and another.[6]

Framework and methodology

As an organizing concept, this chapter develops the conceptual framework called the Technopolis Wheel to describe the process of technology development and economic growth in a technopolis (Fig. 15.1). The Technopolis Wheel reflects the interaction of seven major segments in the institutional makeup of a technopolis: the research university; large technology companies; small technology companies; state government; local government; federal government; and support groups. On the one hand, a great deal of competition takes place between a state's universities, companies, and public- and private-sector entities. On the other hand, cooperation is essential for a technopolis to develop and survive over time. Segments of the Technopolis Wheel must find ways to cooperate while competing. This research emphasizes the importance of networking across the seven segments of the Technopolis Wheel—that is, the ability to link public- and private-sector entities, some of which have been traditionally adversarial, to effect change.

The validity and scope for general application of the concept of the Technopolis Wheel have yet to be determined. In the present chapter they are discussed with examples from a mature technopolis (Silicon Valley, California), a developing technopolis (Austin, Texas), and an emerging technopolis (Phoenix, Arizona).[7]

Silicon Valley: overview

Just as Manchester, the Saar Valley, and Pittsburgh were once centers of the industrial society, today's U.S. information society has its heartland in Silicon Valley, a 30-mile by 10-mile strip between San Francisco and San Jose, California. Silicon Valley is the nation's ninth largest

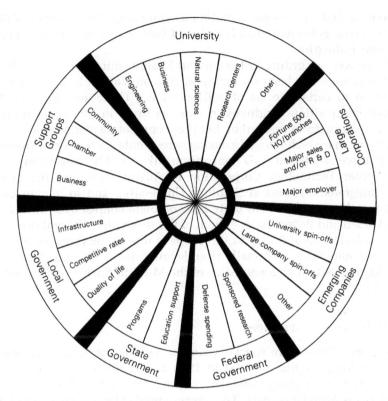

Figure 15.1   The Technopolis Wheel. *Source*: R. W. Smilor, G. Kozmetsky & D. V. Gibson (eds.), *Creating the technopolis: linking technology commercialization and economic development* (Boston, Mass.: Ballinger, 1988).

manufacturing center, with sales of over $40 billion annually. About 40,000 new jobs were created in the Valley each year in the early 1980s. Rogers and Larsen in *Silicon Valley fever* identified the area's economy as among the fastest-growing and wealthiest in the United States.

According to Larsen and Rogers, Silicon Valley is now in its second, more mature phase.[8] The first spurt of growth from 1960 to 1980 is over. The attention generated by the expansion of larger, centralized corporations is shifting to smaller, decentralized companies. Whereas Silicon Valley's childhood years addressed semiconductor and computer manufacturing and the adolescent years saw semiconductor chips and computers being used by other industries, in the late 1980s new subindustries are emerging as a result of innovative microelectronics applications such as medical electronics, communication systems, automotive electronics, telecommunications, and biotechnology. Instead of two main industries—semiconductors and computers—Silicon Valley now serves as headquarters for a broad base of microelectronics applications industries.

Moreover, according to Larsen and Rogers, since the 1980s a basic value change has been occurring in Silicon Valley: from strict competition to certain forms of collaboration.[9] These authors note that much competition continues to exist as firms in the same industry seek to outperform each other, but these competing companies are also likely to share technology licensing agreements, to be co-stockholders in a university-based R&D consortium (like the Microelectronics and Computer Technology Corporation in Austin, Texas, or the Center for Integrated Systems at Stanford University), and to join in other relationships in which no party has complete control over the others. As Larsen and Rogers state, "Much of the stress on collaboration in the microelectronics industry in the 1980s is due to the threat of international competition, especially from Japan. Silicon Valley is beginning to display certain characteristics of the M-Form Society, described by Ouchi."[10]

Austin, Texas: overview

The early 1980s were special years for Texans because of the state's approaching sesquicentennial in 1986 and centennial celebrations at the state's two flagship universities: The University of Texas at Austin and Texas A&M University. The development of the Austin technopolis reached a crescendo in 1983 when the Microelectronics and Computer Technology Corporation (MCC) chose Austin as its headquarters after a major and very public site selection process among some of the most visible high-tech centers in the United States. Austin made headlines in the *New York Times*, the *Wall Street Journal*, and the world press as the next great "Silicon Valley." Nicknamed "Silicon Prairie," "Silicon Gulch" and "Silicon Hills," the area experienced an unprecedented wave of enthusiastic investment along with the perception that it had suddenly become a major technology center.

In 1984 the dramatic and unexpected plunge in oil prices coupled with declining farm and beef prices caused a general economic decline in Texas: a state that previously enjoyed a budget surplus and no corporate or personal income taxes now faced budget deficits. Between 1984 and 1987, Austin began to experience a series of problems revolving around a general economic recession in the state, cutbacks in higher education funding, changes in local governmental attitudes, a speculative development cycle that ended in a plethora of foreclosures and bankruptcies, and a general loss of direction. The development of Austin as a technopolis began to lose momentum.

By 1987 the effects of an economic recession were still quite apparent in Texas and in Austin; however, the state had begun to reverse policy by increasing funding for higher education as well as providing other research support, such as an Advanced Technology and Research Program (ATRP). The ATRP was funded in the amount of $60 million by the 70th Texas Legislature with the expressed purpose of supporting economic development in the state by attracting the best researchers and students to Texas, and by expanding the state's existing technology base. And in early 1988, after a national competition, the main players in the U.S. semiconductor industry chose to locate Sematech, the industry's new research consortium of 13 member companies, in Austin. Austin and Texas were outbid by several other contending states in terms of financial incentives; however, cited as one of the main reasons for choosing Austin was the support and cooperation of state and local public and private agencies.

Phoenix, Arizona: overview

As of 1987, electronics, computers, and aerospace made up the largest portion of manufacturing employment in Arizona. This gave Arizona a much larger share of high-tech employment than the national average. Five of every ten manufacturing jobs in Arizona are in high technology, and 14 large companies account for over three-fourths of the high-tech workforce. Almost 80,000 individuals are employed in high technology, and Phoenix-based Motorola with about 22,000 employees is the state's largest high-tech employer.[11]

According to Wigand, a major key to Arizona's economic success is the state's employment mix.[12] The goods-producing sector (manufacturing, mining, construction) accounts for about 23 percent of total employment. Manufacturing accounts for almost 14 percent of employment, with half of the manufacturing jobs being in high technology. This compares favorably to the national average of only 12 percent of manufacturing employment being related to high technology. Even within Arizona's high-tech component, there is a broad diversity between computers, components, and aerospace. This diversity has allowed the state to do comparatively well economically, even when the semiconductor industry experiences an economic downturn.[13] Arizona's growth rate is consistently among the fastest-growing in the country. With nearly 3 million people, the state's 39 percent growth from 1973 to 1983 placed it fourth nationally in rate of population growth. Nationally the Phoenix metropolitan area is ranked second in population growth in 1986–7. Almost 70 percent of the Arizona population is located in the Phoenix metropolitan area. Phoenix proper is the nation's ninth largest city.

In 1987 a survey was conducted on 150 U.S. cities to assess the number of jobs generated, as well as business startups and other companies enjoying high growth rates. Austin, Texas, was rated first, Orlando, Florida, second, and Phoenix, Arizona, third.[14]

An analysis of the Technopolis Wheel

The university segment

In each technopolis discussed in this chapter, the research university has played a key rôle in the development and maintenance of an area as a technopolis. Stanford University was central to the development of Silicon Valley, and the University continues to contribute to "new subindustries" that are emerging in the area.[15] Technology commercialization in the emerging technopolis of Austin, Texas, is underpinned by The University of Texas at Austin.[16] Finally, Arizona State University is considered key to high-tech development in the Phoenix area.[17]

Dependent as they are on technological innovation, high-tech companies choose to locate in areas where there is strong R&D activity. Much research is conducted by corporations, but the importance of a major research university is well documented.[18] The research university plays a key rôle in the fostering of R&D activities, the attraction of key scholars and talented graduate students, the spinoffs of new companies, the attraction of major technology-based firms, as a magnet for federal and private-sector funding, and as a general source of ideas, employees, and consultants for high technology as well as infrastructure companies.[19]

Universities also team with developers, or become developers themselves, in undertaking projects to provide industrial or commercial space and incubator facilities. Some universities have established affiliates directly or by joint venture to conduct research and to provide specialized services to industry. These may have the effect of accelerating innovation while reducing the cost to companies of supporting the research program. They also create revenues and develop properties adjacent to the universities.[20]

Rogers and Larsen cite the resource of Stanford University, and specifically that of its visionary vice president, Frederick Terman, as critical to the beginning of Silicon Valley.[21] The rise of Stanford to prominence as a nationally recognized research university between 1920 and 1960 implemented the takeoff of the Silicon Valley microelectronics industry. And Silicon Valley helped establish Stanford as a pre-eminent university.[22]

Many of the early Silicon Valley engineers were Stanford graduates who wanted to remain in the Bay area, even though in the mid-1900s there was a feeling of inferiority to the big East Coast electronic firms like RCA.[23] Leede Forest (of the Federal Telegraph Company), who invented the amplifying quality of the vacuum tube, and William Hewlett and David Packard with their entrepreneurial work on a variable-frequency oscillator are prominent examples of the electronics pioneers in the Silicon Valley area who had Stanford University connections.

Larsen and Rogers consider Terman's conception of a university affiliated research park his most important contribution to Silicon Valley and to Stanford.[24] Terman's belief in the value of close university–industry ties led him to suggest leasing a large section of university-owned land to high-tech companies. In 1951 the idea of a university industrial park was completely new, so Terman was a visionary. Hewlett-Packard and Varian Associates were among the first tenants. By 1955, seven companies were in the Park; by 1984, there were 90 tenants and 25,000 employees. Stanford Industrial Park, the first and the most successful of university–industry parks, has served as a model for scores of other high-tech parks in the United States and abroad. The Park also did a great deal for Stanford University, providing cash with which to hire renowned professors and thus improve the academic prestige of the University, which has risen considerably since 1960.

Today there are over 300 research parks in the world, over half of which are located in the United States.[25] Ideally, a park should bring university researchers together with their counterparts in industry, integrating the results produced by both parties. This approach encourages more university research and places the university on the cutting edge of new technological developments.[26]

In Austin the total dollar amount of contracts and grants (both federal and nonfederal) awarded to the University of Texas at Austin (UT) increased steadily each year from 1977 (about $55 million) to 1986 (about $120 million). During this period the University established and organized 18 major research units in the College of Engineering and 32 in the College of Natural Sciences.[27] Most importantly, many of these research units are in areas of cutting-edge technology. A lot of this increased funding could be attributed to the UT Endowed Centennial Program for chairs, professorships, and fellowships in 1983–84. In other words, centennial endowments made a significant difference in attracting researchers who in turn attracted research funds and exceptional graduate students.[28]

An important way to assess the impact of UT in the development of the Austin technopolis is to consider spin-out companies. Of 103 small and medium-sized technology-based companies in existence in Austin in 1986, 53 (or 52 percent) indicated a direct or indirect tie concerning their origin to UT (Fig. 15.2). These companies' founders were UT students, graduates, faculty members, and other UT employees. Their tie to the University enabled many of the companies to start their businesses with a contract that originated while they were involved in University research activities. In addition, the ability to continue their relationship in some capacity with the University was an influential factor in their staying in the area.[29] These firms demonstrate an important requirement for a technopolis—the ability to generate home-grown or indigenous technology-based companies which in turn have a direct impact on job creation and economic diversification.

In a recent National Science Foundation-funded study by Larsen, Wigand, and Rogers,[30] over 70 percent of the respondents within the

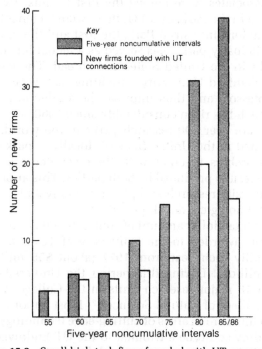

Figure 15.2 Small high-tech firms founded with UT connections.

Phoenix microelectronics industry indicated that the presence or near-ness of Arizona State University (ASU) ranked among the top three reasons to locate in the area. ASU is the nation's sixth largest university with 42,000 students. The engineering program at ASU was favored in 1956 under the guidance of Dean Lee Thompson, who emphasized the development of undergraduate and graduate programs. During the period between 1956 and 1979, 3,198 bachelor's degrees and 1,636 graduate degrees were awarded, including 200 doctoral degrees. Sponsored research funding averaged over $1 million per year.[31]

In 1979, under the current dean, C. Roland Haden, a decision was made to review the status of the School of Engineering and Applied Sciences, partially in response to the growing high-tech industrial base forming in the Phoenix area.[32] A 50-member Advisory Council of Engineering was organized and composed of leaders from high-tech industry in Arizona, representatives of state government, and ASU engineering faculty. The initial goals of this Council were to evaluate the engineering program at ASU and to develop a strategy bringing the College of Engineering and Applied Sciences up to national standards. The eventual goal was to make the College of Engineering and Applied Sciences at ASU one of the top schools in the country in graduate studies and a top research institution.[33]

To support the Engineering Excellence Program a research component composed of four research centers was developed at ASU: the Center for Advanced Research in Transportation, the Center for Solid State Electronics, the Center for Energy Systems, and the Center for Automated Engineering and Robotics. Together these academic and research units emphasize six content areas: solid-state electronics, computers/computer science, computer-aided processes, energy, thermoscience, and transportation.[34]

The major strides accomplished by ASU's College of Engineering and Applied Sciences in a five-year time span are exemplified by the growth of the faculty, students, and physical plant. There are 65 new faculty lines (a 59 percent increase) and 52 new graduate assistant lines (a 33 percent increase).[35] Sponsored research has increased from just over $1 million in 1979 to approximately $9.5 million in 1984 (an 864 percent increase). The undergraduate population has increased from 2,547 in 1979 to 3,351 in 1984 (a 32 percent increase), and graduate enrollments have increased from 712 students in 1979 to 977 in 1984 (a 37 percent increase). Finally, the Engineering Excellence Program has been enhanced with a 120,000 sq. ft. Engineering Research Center which includes a 4,000 sq. ft. class 100 clean room, portions of which are class 10. According to a 1983 National Academy of Sciences study,

ASU's College of Engineering and Applied Sciences was in the top 20 engineering programs in the country.

The growing bond between the restructured engineering program at ASU and industry is seen in the development and implementation of a strong, continuing education component. In 1980 a Center for Professional Development was established as part of the Engineering Excellence Program. The goal of the Center is to meet the increasing demand by engineering and applied science professionals for continuous updating and maintenance of their technical competency and skill. From its inception to 1984, over 160 short courses and institutes were held and attended by more than 5,000 professionals.[36]

The Interactive Instructional Television Program (IITP) began broadcasting courses to off-university sites in 1981. Computer science and engineering courses are directed to the high-tech companies located in the Phoenix area. As of 1986, there were 15 participating sites. Through a sophisticated teleconferencing system, students at the remote sites are able to interact with the faculty member giving the lecture and with students at other remote sites. This method of providing graduate-level courses and special seminars was initiated at the request of local industry so that employees could receive graduate degrees.[37]

Consistent with its emphasis on high-tech research, ASU developed a research park to further university–industry cooperation. The development of the concept for the ASU Research Park was the product of a number of factors. Perhaps most important was pressure placed on ASU by industry to improve the engineering program.[38] The feasibility of the Park was studied by a committee composed of University and business representatives. In 1983 the ASU Board of Regents approved the proposed park, and in the same year the first executive director was hired. In 1984 the Board of Regents approved the master plan and authorized the creation of a separate seven-member nonprofit corporation, Price-Elliot Research Park, Inc. This corporation has as its mission the design, development, marketing, and administration of the Park on behalf of ASU for 99 years.[39]

Most academic and business leaders in the Phoenix area believe that the Park is a very positive asset for ASU.[40] The Park provides a setting in which companies can draw upon the resources and expertise of the University. Since 1987 two buildings have been constructed, and two additional ones, including the International Microelectronics Innovation Center (IMIC), have been started. The Center has its first tenant—VLSI Technology, Inc., from San Jose, California. Several other tenants have signed leases, including four incubator and startup firms. Firms will be able to lease clean room space (class 100, possibly class 10) from IMIC.

The ASU Research Park is still quite young and has yet to mature. However, by comparison it is ahead of other preceding research parks. Research Triangle Park in North Carolina took seven years to acquire its first tenant, and ten years elapsed between Stanford Research Park's first and second building.[41]

Government segments

Federal, state, and local government play vital rôles in the development of a technopolis. However, each level of government affects economic development differently. The federal government impacts a state's economic vitality in two key ways: through the development and operation of military installations and through federal funding for R&D activities.

In his research on Phoenix as an emerging technopolis, Wigand states that industry is included in issue-oriented dialogues with government and that government officials seem aware of, and even sympathetic to, industry's needs. According to Wigand, state government generally cooperates with Arizona's universities to develop projects that will induce desired high-tech developments.[43] Arizona's recent development strategy, formulated in 1983 under the then governor Babbitt, specifically addresses high-tech industry. The report, *Arizona horizons: a strategy for future economic growth*, makes the following general recommendations:

> First, this strategy must put a great deal of emphasis on the high technology future of Arizona . . . . Small business vitalization must be the second major focus . . . ensuring that the optimal economic potential of all areas of the state is recognized and supported . . . .
> Finally, strategies for the promotion of technological innovation, business development and balanced economic growth are incomplete if they do not directly address the critical need for education and manpower training.[44]

While Arizona has a Science and Technology Advisory Board, it has been largely inactive, although according to Wigand it could provide a worthwhile focus for technology transfer programs if it were revived and appropriately constituted.[45] Furthermore, states Wigand, Arizona could take a more aggressive rôle in encouraging the formation of R&D consortia in areas where the state has specialized research capability.[46]

Several studies have been conducted by the Arizona State Office of Economic Planning and Development (OEPAD)—now the Arizona

Department of Commerce—to define the support industry needed by high-tech development. These reports identify opportunities created by high-tech industries, especially for new service and support industry. This office has established a Small Business Development Corporation to assist in funding businesses. By encouraging companies to start up or expand, Arizona not only assists industry already in the state, but also increases the multiplier effect. Thus, high-tech industry may also affect the "low-tech" portions of the state's economy as new products and procedures increase industry efficiency and reduce costs.[47]

Bergstrom Air Force Base is an example of indirect federal government stimulation to the emerging technopolis of Austin, Texas. Bergstrom, established in 1942, has provided fundamental economic stimulation to the Austin region through employment of 1,000 civilian and 6,000 military personnel with an annual payroll of about $167 million. An example of more direct government stimulation to the Austin economy is Balcones Research Park, which was created in the early 1940s when the federal government ceded the land to UT and funded research in strategic resources to support the war effort.

In Texas, as is the case in other regions in the United States, state government is responsible for the major portion of funding for the budgets of public universities. The University of Texas at Austin has benefited tremendously from a Permanent University Fund (PUF), with a 1987 book value at $2.6 billion. This public endowment has been crucial in developing the teaching and research excellence at UT as well as in permitting the acquisition of modern facilities and laboratories. The PUF alone, however, has proven to be insufficient for providing the resources necessary to the development of a world-class university.

For example, in 1984 shortly after MCC decided to locate in Austin—while oil prices were still about $30 a barrel and state revenues increased by $5.4 billion or 17 percent over the previous year—Texas decreased appropriations for higher education by 3 percent. During this period, despite UT's phenomenal growth in endowed chairs, professorships, lectureships and fellowships, despite the location of MCC in Austin, and despite national and international acclaim for UT as a new center of excellence in education, the lack of sustained state support for higher education sent a mixed message to the best scholars and researchers whom the University was trying to attract.[48]

During 1984–6 Texas universities in general were not competitive with other U.S. universities in terms of faculty salary. As of 1987, the gap lessened, but UT System faculty salaries were still below the averages offered in the ten most populous states.[49] And during 1984–6

UT lost some of the outstanding faculty it had previously acquired. As of 1987, many of the University chairs and professorships which had been established in 1983 remained vacant. The few qualified candidates for these endowed positions had been attracted by more substantial offers from universities in other states.

In summary, as Texas state allocations for higher education increased through the late 1970s and the early 1980s, the perception of the development of Austin as a technopolis outside the state increased proportionately as well. On the other hand, as the State of Texas began to cut back its funding to higher education in 1983, the perception of Austin as a developing technopolis declined, and the perception of retrenchment in the University began to emerge.[50]

While state government's primary rôle in creating and sustaining the technopolis is in relation to setting industrial priorities for and funding higher education, local government's primary rôle generally focuses on quality of life, competitive rate structures for such items as utilities, and infrastructure requirements. "Quality of life" carries different meanings given one's perspective and given the subjective attributes of the issues involved. For example, from the developers' perspective high quality of life would consist of a viable business environment, which is considered essential to the attraction, expansion, and retention of high-tech industry. Factors influencing the business environment include taxes and governmental regulations, the availability of appropriate financing, a positive work ethic, and a favorable relationship between business and the community. A realistic and consistent state development strategy, with an understanding of the area's current development status and plans for the future, is also important.[51]

A competitive tax climate is critical to creating and sustaining the technopolis. While tax rates must meet a state's needs, they also must fit a corporation's ability to pay while remaining competitive in its industry. Income and property taxes, unemployment and industrial accident insurance rates, and the procedures of taxing authorities must all be reasonable or else companies will suffer in the face of competition, go out of business, or be driven from the state. Most corporations are well informed about comparative tax rates. Regions that are out of line or that impose additional taxes or requirements, such as unitary taxes, inhibit economic development activities.[52]

Companies are reluctant to locate or to remain in areas with overly complex, burdensome regulations or permit processes. Problems with regulations add to the cost of doing business, increase the time and effort required for business operations, and add to a company's uncertainty.

Examples of regulatory problems include the interpretation and application of environmental regulations, occupational safety and health standards, and municipal standards.[53]

Perceptions vary within any region undergoing the rapid economic growth associated with a developing technopolis, and there is always the possibility that such growth will diminish the very qualities that caused the area to be so attractive to high-tech companies in the first place. This tension between sustained quality of life and sustained economic development has been most visible throughout the development of technopolises.

During the emergence, growth, and maturation of a technopolis, local government tends to move in cycles that favor either the "developers" or the "environmentalists." When local government supports economic growth, then the development of the technopolis is more likely to increase—that is, company relocation seems to be facilitated and obstacles to development seem to diminish. On the other hand, when local government believes quality of life is diminishing, then the development of the technopolis is inhibited—that is, obstacles to development increase (such as high utility rates or slower permit procedures). The issues become quite complex because quality of life and economic development are two sides of the same coin; each has a vital impact on the other.

A community's ability to sustain a high-quality workforce is contingent on the area's perceived desirability as a place to live. Physical setting, natural beauty, and climate are factors that affect such perceptions, along with cultural activities and outdoor recreation opportunities. Because the most talented high-tech employees can find work anywhere, quality-of-life issues are especially important. For example, annual job turnover in Silicon Valley has been about 30 percent. In other words, the average employee would have three different jobs in ten years. Such turnover is encouraged by a shortage of qualified, experienced personnel. To counter such rapid turnover, companies offer their employees short-term benefits and incentives such as stock options, recreational facilities, and training programs.[54] While environmentalists and developers may disagree on what makes for sensible environmental/development policy, most agree that overall quality of life suffers when the people who inhabit the community are out of work and cannot afford to pay the costs associated with infrastructure development, housing, or such factors as expanded park land or recreational opportunities.

Although they admit that it is a factor that is not easily quantifiable, Larsen and Rogers cite factors in the deteriorating quality of life behind the geographical spread of Silicon Valley microelectronics corporations since the early 1980s.[55] Dense development of industry and housing has created urban congestion. Commuter access to an area's high-tech facilities is essential. Large companies have significant employment levels and operate multiple shifts, requiring a good system of surface transportation. Multilane streets, highway, and even freeway access may be required both for workers and for deliveries. Many companies want their facilities to be within a reasonable drive of a major airport. Appropriately developed sites and buildings, therefore, are necessary.

Wigand cites the competitive cost of living as important to attracting people to Arizona.[56] The availability and cost of housing in various price ranges is important, as are food, energy, and transportation costs and personal taxes. Larsen and Rogers cite high land and housing costs as another factor that has influenced large chip makers to leave Silicon Valley.[57] As land prices continue to rise, high-tech companies look for other locations to find cheaper electrical power and less expensive materials. Such a deteriorating quality of life makes it difficult for Silicon Valley to attract workers, especially workers at lower pay levels.

However, in spite of these ominous developments, Larsen and Rogers report that the move of microelectronics manufacturing from Silicon Valley may not be as serious as indicated in popular press reports, which herald the "end" of Silicon Valley.[58] For example, these authors noted that more than 60 semiconductor companies have sprung up in the Valley since 1979, the year the Japanese began making inroads into the U.S. microelectronics industry. Among these newer companies are LSI Logic, Cypress Semiconductor, VLSI Technology, Sierra Semiconductor, and Integrated Device Technology.

While Arizona has a commitment to stimulating further growth in its high-tech sector, this growth has not occurred without negative impact. Wigand[59] notes studies that have focused on the dissatisfaction with various aspects of the deteriorating quality of life in the Phoenix area.[60] Environmental pollution and hazardous emissions associated with the high-tech industry are matters of concern in Phoenix. While state officials contend that Arizona has adequate environmental protection laws covering hazardous wastes and ground and surface waters, the popular press suggests that the funding and staffing necessary to administer those laws adequately are not present.

According to Wigand,[61] Arizona is severely limited in its ability to finance the development of public facilities, especially in advance of their need, because the state constitution places stringent limits on state debt and subsequent limitations have been placed on municipal debt and spending. In rapidly growing areas these limitations make it difficult to construct public facilities until the population they are meant to serve is in place. The resulting inconvenience and increased cost are grudgingly accepted since the "newcomers" are paying their share of needed new facilities. However, in the rush to keep up with growth, adequate maintenance programs for public facilities have been overlooked. As Arizona's development matures, the state will meet the same maintenance, upgrading, and replacement issues faced by eastern states decades ago, and Arizona will pay the price for deferring these expenditures.[62]

Support groups segment (infrastructure)

High-tech companies locate in areas with a concentration of similar companies to take advantage of the available laborforce and infrastructure services. This clustering produces an economy of scale in training and creates opportunities for support industries devoted to laborforce preparation. The availability of a quality workforce is basic to the development of a high-tech industry.

Silicon Valley high-tech companies depend on individuals who can design semiconductor clean rooms, tool delicate fixtures, and design innovative products. Few other places in the world can match the pool of experienced, specialized high-tech brainpower available in Silicon Valley. Companies that need access to such expertise have little choice but to locate where these intellectual resources are concentrated, creating a further agglomeration of microelectronics firms.[63]

Support groups can provide an important networking mechanism for the development of a technopolis. These groups may take a variety of organizational forms representing environmental concerns, labor issues, minority viewpoints, and other community interests. Silicon Valley is a network of networks. Extensive personal contacts facilitate information exchange. News about people changing jobs, about new products, about manufacturing successes and failures—all are instantly common knowledge.[64] Business-based groups relate to the emergence of specific components for high-tech support in the practices of Big Eight accounting firms, law firms, major banks, and other companies. These components provide a source of expertise, even when embryonic, and a reference source for those founding and/or running technology-based enterprises.

High-tech infrastructure requires a significant capital investment as well as commitment to fund continuing operational and maintenance costs. From lending policies that reflect an understanding of industrial conditions and practices to venture capital availability, the financial community must be responsive if it is to capture its share of business.

The growth of venture capital[65] provides a good example of the importance of business-based groups to the development of a technopolis. Venture capital firms serve as intermediaries between investors looking for high returns for their money and entrepreneurs in search of needed capital for their startups. Venture capital firms invest their money largely on the basis of the potential value of an entrepreneur's idea, collateral that conventional bankers consider worthless. Entrepreneurs give up a percentage of the ownership of their new company, often about 50 percent, in exchange for acquiring capital. Silicon Valley is a prime center of venture capital: over one-third of the nation's venture capital companies have an office in Silicon Valley.[66]

In 1980 Austin had virtually no venture capital. However, by 1986 the city had approximately $80 million managed by five firms. The growth was due primarily to two factors, one external and the other internal.[67] Externally, changes in federal tax laws in 1979, 1981, and 1986 pertaining to capital gains encouraged investments in venture capital pools.[68] Internally, the perception of Austin as an emerging technology center encouraged the development of homegrown pools. The sources of the venture capital were a few individuals knowledgeable about the venture capital process as well as the major commercial banks in the area. While funds in these pools increased, most venture capital investments continued to be made outside the state of Texas. Venture capitalists in Austin, while wanting a local window on technology and company development, did not see enough potential for fast-growth companies in the region.[69]

The private sector

Rogers and Larsen have described the main inventions and events in the rise of the microelectronics industry in Silicon Valley (Table 15.1) while emphasizing that companies are constantly starting up, growing, merging, being acquired, or fading away, making it difficult to know exactly how many firms exist at any one time.[70]

In 1982 Rogers and Larsen identified 3,100 electronics manufacturing firms in Silicon Valley.[71] In addition, they emphasized the importance of companies supporting the electronics manufacturers, such as firms engaged in marketing, advertising, research and development, consulting, training, venture capital, and legal and other support services, which brought the total number of firms in the Silicon Valley electronics industry to about 6,000. They noted another

Table 15.1 A chronology of the important inventions, events, and people in the microelectronics high-tech industry.

1912	Lee de Forest discovers the amplification qualities of the vacuum tube in Palo Alto, California, thus making possible radio, television, film, and other communication technologies.
1938	Hewlett-Packard is founded in a garage in Palo Alto by William Hewlett and David Packard, two of the first entrepreneurs in Silicon Valley.
1946	ENIAC, the first mainframe computer, with 18,000 vacuum tubes, is invented at the University of Pennsylvania.
1947	William Shockley, John Bardeen, and Walter Brattain invent the transistor at Bell Labs in Murray Hill, New Jersey. The transistor eventually replaces vacuum tubes.
1955	Shockley leaves Bell Labs to establish Shockley Semiconductor Laboratory in Palo Alto.
1956	Shockley, Bardeen, and Brattain win the Nobel Prize in Physics.
1957	The entrepreneurial spirit of Silicon Valley gets underway when Robert Noyce and seven other brilliant young engineers quit Shockley Semiconductor Laboratory to launch Fairchild Semiconductor. These co-founders later split off to launch over 80 semiconductor firms in Silicon Valley over the next 35 years.
1968	Noyce leaves Fairchild to start Intel.
1971	Invention of microprocessor, a computer control unit on a semiconductor chip, by Ted Hoff of Intel. Silicon Valley is named by the late Don Hoefler, then editor of a local electronics newsletter. Nolan Bushnell designs Pong and launches Atari; the videogame industry is begun.
1976	Steve Jobs and Steve Wozniak build the Apple microcomputer.
1980	Apple goes public: Art Rock, the venture capitalist who had invested $57,000, earns $14 million; Jobs is worth $165 million.
1982	About 3,100 microelectronics firms exist in Silicon Valley; two-thirds have fewer than 10 employees, and only 50 or so have more than 1,000 workers.
1984	Silicon Valley has 15,000 millionaires and 2 billionaires.

Source: E. Rogers & J. K. Larsen, *Silicon Valley fever: growth of high-technology culture* (New York: Basic Books, 1984).

2,000 companies operating in nonelectronics high-tech fields such as chemicals, pharmaceuticals, and biotechnology. Thus, according to their count, the total number of high-tech firms in Silicon Valley was about 8,000 in 1983.

Public attention on Silicon Valley concentrates upon the 54 electronics firms with more than 1,000 employees, companies such as Hewlett-Packard, Intel, and Apple Computer. While the giants constitute about half of the total workforce, the great majority of the firms are very small. Rogers and Larsen state that over two-thirds of Silicon Valley firms have fewer than 10 employees and 85 percent have fewer than 50.[72]

Since the mid-1950s when Motorola established its microelectronics facilities in Phoenix, high-tech manufacturing (computers, electronic components, aerospace, communications, and scientific instrumentation) accounts for almost 50 percent of all manufacturing jobs in Arizona, compared with a 15 percent national average.[73] In 1987 the state had 313 high-tech firms, an increase of 33 percent from 225 firms in 1975. The value of shipments exceeds $5 billion annually.[74]

Arizona has experienced a high-tech growth rate of about 6 percent annually over the past few years, while U.S. high-tech employment has grown by 2.4 percent annually. High-tech employment represents 7 percent of total employment in Arizona, and 3 percent nationally.[75] The largest high-tech employer is Motorola with about 22,000 employees. Between 1975 and 1979 numerous new firms moved to Arizona, including Digital Equipment, IBM, Intel, GTE, and Gould, and many firms made major improvements and expansions within their existing Arizona facilities, including Honeywell, Garrett, and Sperry.

Figure 15.3 shows the incorporation of high-tech companies in

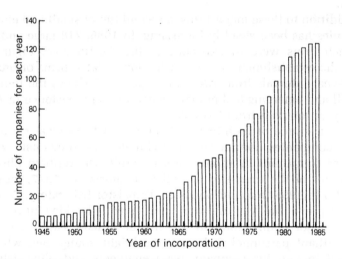

Figure 15.3 Cumulative total of high-tech manufacturing companies in Austin, Texas. *Note:* these companies were defined by the following three-digit codes: 283, 348, 357, 364–7, 369, 376, 379, 381–7. A number of studies have incorporated this definition of high-tech products in analysis of high-tech manufacturing. See Massachusetts Division of Employment Security, Job Market Research Division, *High technology employment: Massachusetts and selected states 1975–9* (Boston: Massachusetts Division of Employment Security, March 1981); P. Doeringer & P. Pannell, "Manpower strategies for New England's high technology sector," paper presented at Conference on Manpower Policy Issues, sponsored by the Commission on Higher Education and the Economy of New England at the Harvard University Graduate School of Business Administration, May 15, 1981; and Joint Economic Committee, U.S. Congress, *Location of high technology firms and regional economic development* (Washington, D.C.: Government Printing Office, June 1981). *Source: Directory of Texas manufacturers* (Austin: Bureau of Business Research, University of Texas, 1986).

Austin from 1945 to 1988. In 1984 growth of these firms leveled off, probably as a result of the general economic recession. These are manufacturing-related technology firms. They do not include service-related technology firms. For Austin, the location and homegrown development of major technology-based companies began in 1955.[76] As shown in the timetable in Figure 15.4, Austin had 32 such major company relocations or foundings as of 1986.

Six of the companies are homegrown, and all six had direct or indirect ties to UT. The location of the other major firms in the area was dependent on two critical elements: the presence of the University and the perception of an affordable high quality of life—that is, a place with high quality-of-life factors where a company could also make a profit. Two four-year clusters are interesting to note: 1965–9 and 1980–4. Major events took place in each of these clusters; during the first, IBM located in Austin, and during the second, MCC located in Austin.

In addition to these major firms, a second tier of small and emerging companies has been steadily increasing. In 1986, 218 large and small high-tech firms were in existence in the Austin area. Figure 15.5 shows the establishment of high technology-related firms or branches in five-year intervals from 1945–85. Figure 15.6 shows the foundings of small and emerging technology-related firms in existence in Austin in five-year intervals from 1945–85.

Another source of high-tech industrial growth is local startups or spinoff companies, founded by individuals who previously worked for other companies in an area. For example, Dr. William Shockley, co-inventor of the transistor at Bell Laboratories in 1947, moved to Palo Alto in 1955 to found Shockley Transistor Laboratory. Although his entrepreneurial venture was short-lived, Shockley nevertheless made a major contribution to the rise of Silicon Valley by identifying brilliant personnel.[77] Among the bright young men whom he recruited to join his company were engineers and physicists who represented the cutting edge of semiconductor technology; most were from the East Coast. A select group of these engineers, called the "Shockley Eight," was imbued with the entrepreneurial spirit that they learned from Shockley. Within a year, all eight left Shockley Transistor Laboratory to start a semiconductor manufacturing company of their own—Fairchild Semiconductor. The Shockley Eight then became the cadre of leaders for the semiconductor industry that sprouted in Silicon Valley. Indeed, Fairchild Semiconductor was the spawning ground for scores of spinoffs.[78] Even with such positive, entrepreneurial rôle models, according to Rogers and Larsen,[79] without the availability

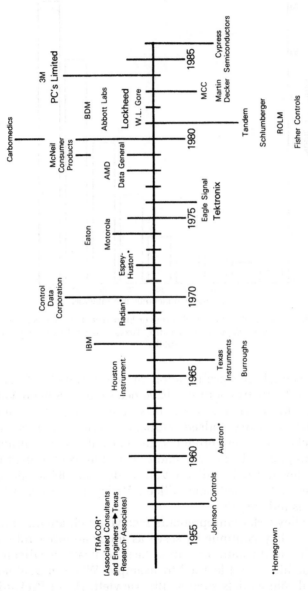

Figure 15.4 Major company relocations or foundings in Austin, Texas, 1955–86. Source: Information from the Austin Chamber of Commerce and survey and interview data.

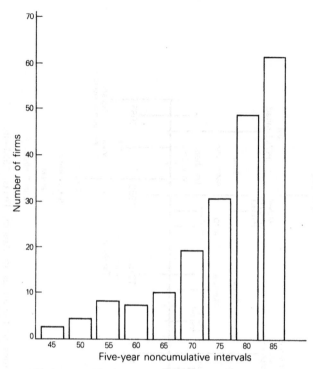

Figure 15.5 Establishment of high-tech firms or branches, 1945–85. *Source: Directory of Austin area high technology firms* (Austin, Texas: Austin Chamber of Commerce, 1986).

of venture capital, the proliferation of semiconductor firms in the 1960s and early 1970s could not have occurred in Silicon Valley. At the time, California venture capitalists believed that semiconductors were a growth industry. Indeed, military customers were standing in line to purchase the new products. In short, all the conditions were right for entrepreneurial growth, and a critical mass of individuals and companies developed in Silicon Valley. By 1983 85 semiconductor firms had been launched, and Silicon Valley had become the U.S. center for this industry.[80]

Silicon Valley's star entrepreneurs receive much attention from the mass media. They continue to serve as much-admired rôle models, adding further to the entrepreneurial head of steam in Silicon Valley. Entrepreneurship is best learned by example. When individuals learn of successful rôle models such as Bill Hewlett, David Packard, Steve Jobs, and Steve Wozniak, they begin to think "If they did it, why can't I?"

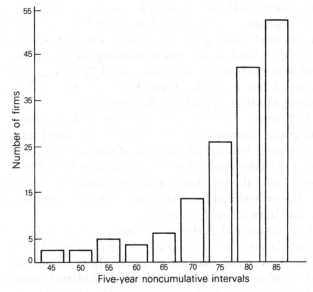

Figure 15.6 Foundings of small and medium-sized technology-related firms, 1945–85. *Source: Directory of Austin area high technology firms* (Austin, Texas: Austin Chamber of Commerce, 1986).

The Tracor case

The centrality of the research university and the importance of entrepreneurial rôle models to the development of a technopolis and subsequent spinoffs from a parent company can be effectively demonstrated through a case study of Tracor, a homegrown company that is the only Fortune 500 company headquartered in Austin. Tracor exemplifies what Kanter calls a "high-innovation" company and what Cooper calls an "incubator organization."[81]

Frank McBee, the founder of Tracor, earned both his bachelor's and master's degrees in mechanical engineering at UT after serving as an Army Air Corps engineer from 1943 to 1946. In the late 1940s, McBee became an instructor and then an assistant professor in the UT Department of Mechanical Engineering. In 1950 he became the supervisor of the mechanical engineering department of UT's Defense Research Laboratory (now called the Applied Research Laboratory) at UT's Balcones Research Park.

In 1955, with funding of $10,000, McBee joined forces with three UT physicists to form Associated Consultants and Engineers, an engineering and consulting firm. Drawing on their UT training and work experience, the four scientists focused their efforts on acoustics research.

They were awarded a $5,000 contract for an industrial noise reduction project. The company's name was changed to Texas Research Associates (TRA) in 1957. During the late 1950s, the four scientists taught and undertook research at UT while working on developing TRA. In 1962 the firm merged with a company called Textran and adopted its present name of Tracor. By this time McBee had left the University to devote himself full-time to building the company.

Figure 15.7 shows that from the College of Engineering and the Defense Research Laboratory at UT came the educated talent to form the entrepreneurial venture of Associated Consultants and Engineers in 1955 that led to the establishment of Tracor in 1962. However, even more impressive is the constant stream of entrepreneurial talent that came from Tracor itself. At least 16 companies have spun out of Tracor since 1962 and have located in Austin.

Figure 15.8 dramatically shows the job creation impact of Tracor and its spinouts on the Austin area. A total of 5,467 persons were employed in these companies as of 1985. These companies are also capable of creating spinouts of their own. Radian Corporation, for example, has spun out four companies. Most importantly, neither Tracor, its spinouts, nor the jobs they created would exist without UT.

Influencers

While each of the institutional segments in the Technopolis Wheel is important to high-tech company development, the ability to link or network the segments is most critical.[82] Indeed, unless the segments are linked in a synergistic way, the development of the technopolis slows or stops. In Austin these segments have been linked by first- and second-level influencers—key individuals who make things happen and who are able to link themselves with other influencers in each of the other segments as well as within each segment.

First-level influencers have a number of criteria in common:[83]

(a) they provide leadership in their specific segment because of their recognized success in that segment;
(b) they maintain extensive personal and professional links to all or almost all the other segments;
(c) they are highly educated;
(d) they move in and out of the other segments with ease;
(e) They are perceived to have credibility by others in the other segments.

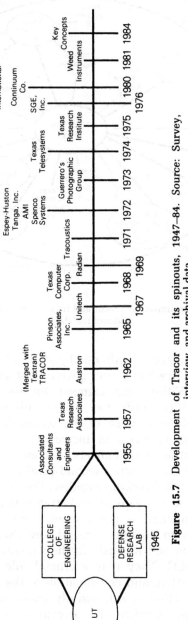

Figure 15.7 Development of Tracor and its spinouts, 1947–84. Source: Survey, interview, and archival data.

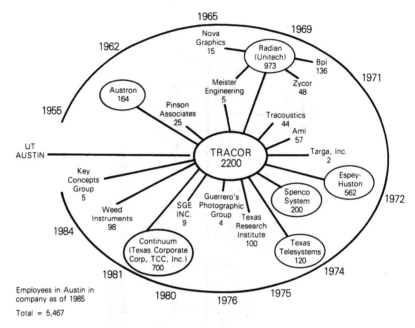

Figure 15.8 Job creation impact of Tracor and its spinouts. *Source:* Survey, interview, and archival data.

Cross-segment linkage is facilitated by second-level influencers who represent business, academia, and government as well as local community interests. Within each segment, the second-level influencer interacts with and generally has the confidence of the first-level influencer. The rôle and scope of the second-level influencer is to act as a gatekeeper in terms of increasing or decreasing flows of information to first-level influencers. Second-level influencers also have their own linkages to other second-level influencers in the other institutional segments. Working together, first-level and second-level influencers initiate new organizational arrangements to make concrete the linkage between business, government, and academia.

Influencers seem to coalesce around key events or activities as described by Gibson and Rogers[84] in their research on the interstate competition for MCC. They play a crucial rôle in conception, initiation, implementation, and coordination of the events or activities. Once an event or action is successfully managed or achieved, they often help to institutionalize the process so that it can function effectively without them. Influencers play a particularly important networking rôle through support groups because these groups can provide convenient opportunities to interact across all segments of the Technopolis Wheel.

In short, an important characteristic of a technopolis is to be able to develop or attract and retain first-level influencers and nurture second-level influencers in all segments of the Technopolis Wheel. Based on the present research and the work of others,[85] it can be argued that the more extensive the networks are across the different segments of the Technopolis Wheel and the higher their level, the more likely cooperative economic (and other) activities are to take place at community and state levels.

Findings

A number of key points emerge about the development and maintenance of technopolies and the framework of the Technopolis Wheel. They are as follows:

(a) The research university plays a pivotal rôle in the development of the technopolis by

  (i)   achieving scientific pre-eminence;
  (ii)   creating, developing, and maintaining new technologies for emerging industries;
  (iii) educating and training the required workforce and professions for economic development through technology;
  (iv)   attracting large technology companies;
  (v)   promoting the development of homegrown technologies; and
  (vi)   contributing to improved quality of life and culture.

(b) Local government can have a significant impact, both positively and negatively, on company formation and relocation, largely from what it chooses to do or not to do in terms of quality of life, competitive rate structures, and infrastructure.

(c) State government can have a significant impact, both positively and negatively, on the development of a technopolis through what it chooses to do or not to do for education, especially in the areas of making and keeping long-term commitments to fund research and development, faculty salaries, student support, and related educational development activities.

(d) Federal government plays an indirect but supportive rôle largely through its allocation of research and development moneys, onsite

R&D programs, and defense-related activities.

(e) Continuity in local, state, and federal government policies has an important impact on maintaining the momentum in the growth of a technopolis.

(f) Large technology companies play a catalytic rôle in the expansion of a technopolis by

  (i)   maintaining relationships with major research universities;
  (ii) becoming a source of talent for the development of new companies; and
  (iii) contributing to job creation and an economic base that can support an affordable quality of life.

(g) Small technology companies facilitate the growth and maintenance of a technopolis by

  (i)   commercializing technologies;
  (ii) diversifying and broadening the economic base of the area;
  (iii) contributing to job creation;
  (iv) spinning companies out of the university and other research institutes; and
  (v)   providing opportunities for venture capital investment.

(h) For a technopolis to prosper, state and local influencers must provide vision, communication, and trust for developing consensus for economic development and technology diversification, especially through networking with other individuals and institutions in other segments of the Technopolis Wheel.

(i) Consensus among and between segments of the Technopolis Wheel is essential for the sustained growth of the technopolis.

The examples discussed in this chapter further emphasize an interesting paradox: the very success of a developing technopolis can lead to greed and many community dissatisfactions. For example, at the local level an affordable quality of life, while subjective and hard to measure, can be a major source of friction between advocates and adversaries of growth. The result can be a shattering of the consensus that originally made the technopolis possible.

In conclusion, this research suggests that the Technopolis Wheel provides a conceptual framework for assessing the relative importance of government, academic, business, and public sectors in the high-tech economic development of a region. By focusing on the interaction among the seven segments of the Wheel, the framework provides a practical perspective on the changing nature of economic development and the importance of new kinds of institutional relationships among the research university, large and emerging corporations, federal, state, and local government, support groups, and key influencers who network these segments in the modern city–state.

Notes

1   P. A. Abetti, C. W. LeMaistre, M. H. Wacholder, "The role of Rensselaer Polytechnic Institute: technopolis development in a mature industrial area," in *Creating the technopolis: linking technology commercialization and economic development*, ed. R. W. Smilor, G. Kozmetsky & D. V. Gibson (Boston, Mass.: Ballinger, 1988), pp. 125–44; E. Rogers & J. K. Larsen, *Silicon Valley fever: growth of high-technology culture* (New York: Basic Books, 1984).

2   M. Castello, *The economic crisis and American society* (Princeton, N.J.: Princeton University Press, 1980); M. Olson, *The rise and decline of nations: economic growth, stagflation, and social rigidities* (New Haven, Conn.: Yale University Press, 1982); R. Bolling & J. Bowles, *America's competitive edge: how to get our country moving again* (New York: McGraw-Hill, 1982); R. B. Reich, *The next American frontier* (New York: Times Books, 1983).

3   F. G. Adams & N. J. Glickman, *Modeling the multiregional economic system* (Lexington, Mass.: Lexington Books, 1980); H. Brooks, L. Liebman & C. Schelling, *Public–private partnership: new opportunities for meeting social needs* (Cambridge, Mass.: Ballinger, 1984); W. G. Ouchi, *The M-Form society: how American teamwork can recapture the competitive edge* (Menlo Park, Calif.: Addison-Wesley, 1984).

4   Adams & Glickman, *Modeling the multiregional economic system*.

5   D. N. Allen & V. Levine, *Nurturing advanced technology enterprises: emerging issues in state and local economic development policy* (New York: Praeger, 1986); J. K. Ryans and W. L. Shanklin, "Implementing a high tech center strategy: the marketing program," in *Creating the technopolis*, ed. Smiler, Kozmetsky & Gibson, pp. 209–20; P. D. Reynolds, "New firms: societal contributions versus survival potential," *Journal of Business Venturing* **2**, Summer 1987, 231–46; B. D. Merrifield, "New business incubators," *Journal of Business Venturing* **2**, Fall 1987, 277–84; D. L. Sexton & R. W. Smilor (eds.), *The art and science of entrepreneurship* (Cambridge, Mass.: Ballinger, 1986).

6   Ouchi, *The M-Form society*, p. 226.

7   H. Aldrich & C. Zimmer, "Entrepreneurship through social networks," in *The art and science of entrepreneurship*," ed. Sexton & Smilor.

8   J. K. Larsen & E. Rogers, "Silicon Valley: the rise and falling off of entrepreneurial fever," in *Creating the technopolis*, ed. Smilor, Kozmetsky & Gibson.

9   Ibid.

10 Ibid.

11 R. T. Wigand, "High technology development in the Phoenix area: taming the desert," in *Creating the technopolis*, ed. Smilor, Kozmetsky & Gibson.

12 Ibid.

13 "Valley National Bank," *Arizona Progress* **41**, September 1986, 2.

14 F. Noyes, "Economic growth dependent on quality of life, officials told," *Arizona Republic*, March 31, 1987, B4, B16.

15 Rogers & Larsen, *Silicon Valley fever*; Larsen & Rogers, "Silicon Valley."

16 Smilor, Kozmetsky & Gibson (eds.) *Creating the technopolis*.

17 Wigand, "High technology development in the Phoenix area."

18   K. Dempsey, "Hi-tech race on for silicon areas in U.S.," *Plant Sites and Parks* **12**, March/April 1985, 1–22; Rogers & Larsen, *Silicon Valley fever*; Abetti, LeMaistre & Wacholder, "The role of Rensselaer Polytechnic Institute: technopolis development in a mature industrial area," in *Creating the technopolis*, ed. Smilor, Kozmetsky & Gibson, pp. 125–44; J. W. Botkin, "Route 128: its history and destiny," in *Creating the technopolis*, ed. Smilor, Kozmetsky & Gibson, pp. 117–23.

19   Sexton & Smilor, *The art and science of entrepreneurship*; J. Doutriaux, "Growth patterns of academic entrepreneurial firms," *Journal of Business Venturing* **2**, Fall 1987, 285–97; Wigand, "High technology development in the Phoenix area."

20   Wigand, "High technology development in the Phoenix area."

21   Rogers & Larsen, *Silicon Valley fever*.

22   Ibid.

23   Ibid., p. 30.

24   Larsen & Rogers, "Silicon Valley."

25   General Accounting Office, *The federal role in fostering university–industry cooperation*, PAD-83–22 (Washington, D.C.: General Accounting Office, 1983); J. M. Gibb, *Science parks and innovative centers: their economic and social impact* (New York: Elsevier, 1985).

26   Wigand, "High technology development in the Phoenix area."

27   *Statistical handbook* (Austin: Office of Statistical Studies, University of Texas 1986-7).

28   Smilor, Kozmetsky & Gibson (eds.), *Creating the technopolis*.

29   Ibid.

30   J. K. Larsen, R. T. Wigand & E. M. Rogers, "Industry–university technology transfer in microelectronics," report submitted to the National Science Foundation, January 1987.

31   G. C. Beakley, C. E. Backus & R. W. Kelly, "Results of the first five-year phase: excellence in engineering for the '80s" report prepared by the Dean's Advisory Council, College of Engineering and Applied Sciences, Arizona State University, Tempe, Arizona, 1985.

32   Wigand, "High technology development in the Phoenix area."

33   Ibid.

34   Ibid.

35   Beakley, Backus & Kelly, "Results of the first five-year phase."

36   Wigand, "High technology development in the Phoenix area."

37   Ibid.

38   Ibid.

39   Ibid.

40   Larsen, Wigand & Rogers, "Industry–university technology transfer in microelectronics."

41   Wigand, "High technology development in the Phoenix area."

42   Ibid.

43   Ibid.

44   *Arizona horizons: a strategy for future economic growth* (Phoenix: Arizona Office of Economic Planning and Development, 1983).

45   Wigand, "High technology development in the Phoenix area."

46   Ibid.

47   Ibid.

48   V. Gibson & E. Rogers, "The MCC comes to Texas," in *Measuring the information society: the Texas studies*, ed. F. Williams (New York: Sage Publications, 1988).

49   *Statistical handbook*.

50   Gibson & Rogers, "The MCC comes to Texas"; Smilor, Kozmetsky & Gibson (eds.), *Creating the technopolis*.

51 Smilor, Kozmetsky & Gibson (eds.), *Creating the technopolis*; Wigand, "High technology development in the Phoenix area"; J. K. Ryans and W. L. Shanklin, "Implementing a high tech center strategy: the marketing program," in *Creating the technopolis*, ed. Smilor, Kozmetsky & Gibson, pp. 209–20.
52 Wigand, "High technology development in the Phoenix area."
53 Ibid.; Smilor, Kozmetsky & Gibson (eds.), *Creating the technopolis*.
54 Rogers & Larsen, *Silicon Valley fever.*
55 Larsen & Rogers, "Silicon Valley."
56 Wigand, "High technology development in the Phoenix area."
57 Larsen & Rogers, "Silicon Valley."
58 Ibid.
59 Wigand, "High technology development in the Phoenix area."
60 K. Price & C. Hodge, "High tech: valley spinning shimmering web of pure silicon," *Arizona Republic*, July 23, 1984, D1; R. Lindsey, "Alarm raised on growth of Phoenix," *New York Times*, March 12, 1987, 15.
61 Wigand, "High technology development in the Phoenix area."
62 Ibid.
63 Larsen & Rogers, "Silicon Valley."
64 Rogers & Larsen, *Silicon Valley fever.*
65 W. E. Wetzel, Jr., "Informal risk capital: knowns and unknowns," in *The art and science of entrepreneurship*, ed. Sexton & Smilor, pp. 85–108; W. E. Wetzel, Jr., "The informal venture capital market: aspects of scale and market efficiency," *Journal of Business Venturing* 2, Fall 1987, 299–313; D. J. Brophy, "Venture capital research," in *The art and science of entrepreneurship*, ed. Sexton & Smilor, pp. 3–23; R. B. Robinson, Jr., "Emerging strategies in the venture capital industry," *Journal of Business Venturing* 2, Winter 1987, 53–77; J. A. Timmons & W. D. Bygrave, "Venture capital's role in financing innovation for economic growth," *Journal of Business Venturing* 1, Spring 1986, 161–76.
66 Larsen & Rogers, "Silicon Valley."
67 G. Kozmetsky, M. D. Gill, Jr. & R. Smilor, *Financing and managing fast-growth companies: the venture capital process* (Lexington, Mass.: Lexington Books, 1986).
68 J. B. Maier & D. A. Walker, "The role of venture capital in financing small business," *Journal of Business Venturing* 2, 1987, 207-14.
69 Kozmetsky, Gill & Smilor, *Financing and managing fast-growth companies.*
70 Rogers & Larsen, *Silicon Valley fever.*
71 Ibid.
72 Ibid.
73 Wigand, "High technology development in the Phoenix area."
74 Arizona Office of Economic Planning and Development, "High technology in Arizona: a market analysis of suppliers in Arizona and the Southwest," Arizona Office of Economic Planning and Development, Phoenix, January 1984, p. 4.
75 Price & Hodge, "High-tech."
76 D. N. Allen, & V. Levine, *Nurturing advanced technology enterprises: emerging issues in state and local economic development policy* (New York: Praeger 1986).
77 Rogers & Larsen, *Silicon Valley fever.*
78 Ibid.
79 Ibid.
80 Ibid.
81 R. Kanter, "Supporting innovation and venture development in established companies," *Journal of Business Venturing* 2, Winter 1985, 47–60; A. C. Cooper, "The role of incubator organizations in the founding of growth-oriented firms," *Journal of Business Venturing* 2, Winter 1985, 75–86.
82 S. Birley, "The role of networks in the entrepreneurial process," *Journal of Business Venturing* 1, Winter 1985, 107–17; H. Aldrich & C. Zimmer, "Entrepre-

neurship through social networks," in *The art and science of entrepreneurship*, ed. Sexton & Smilor, pp. 3–23.

83   Arizona Department of Economic Security, "Arizona education – a statistical overview," *Arizona Labor Market Newsletter*, **8**, June 1984, 21–7.

84   Gibson & Rogers, "The MCC comes to Texas."

85   E. M. Rogers & D. L. Kincaid, *Communication networks: toward a new paradigm for research* (New York: Free Press, 1981); Ouchi, *The M-Form society*; Aldrich & Zimmer, "Entrepreneurship through social networks."

IV
Conclusions

16

Technology and economic development in the states: continuing experiments in growth management

RICHARD P. BARKE

BETWEEN 1981 AND 1985, approximately 2.8 million experienced American workers lost their jobs because their factories were closed. According to the Bureau of Labor Statistics, by January 1986 nearly one-third of those workers was still looking for work, had given up, or had retired. Statistics such as these, coupled with widely-held perceptions that American producers were less technologically progressive than their foreign counterparts, have caused concern about the nation's competitive posture, the availability of jobs, and the "education gap"—in short, the future of economic development. The issue of economic growth is not new to the age of Silicon Valley; innovation, competition, and ambition have always combined with changes in the availability and cost of resources, the advent of new technologies, and social and demographic changes, resulting in unfamiliar opportunities and challenges. However, there are unique aspects—the speed, direction, and characteristics of economic development policy in the last years of this century. New problems—and new forms of old problems—require new solutions.

National industrial policy was rejected in the early 1980s in spite of increasing nervousness about the nation's ability to control its own destiny, because doubts remained about the national government's ability to identify specific industries to assist without making matters worse.[1] Nevertheless, much of the logic and compulsion to act that motivated the industrial policy debate is still very much alive, albeit with major changes in venue and emphasis. The states have emerged as a major arena for action, and "industrial policy" (which refers to equitable responses to structural changes in the economy) has been blended with "innovation policy" (which encourages technological change to enhance industrial productivity and international competitiveness).[2]

Ironically, one legacy of the 1980s (including the Reagan Administration's economic, trade, and "New Federalism" policies) may be a significantly enhanced rôle for the public sector at the state level. The Reagan era saw cutbacks in federal domestic spending programs and regulatory requirements, but the political, economic, and social forces that produced those programs had not disappeared. Those demands found more sympathetic and responsive audiences in state capitals, particularly as bipartisan and cross-ideological coalitions recognized the long-term savings that result from some programs such as prenatal care, educational reform, and economic development. The evolution of the American federal system has not ended, so as the location of decision making shifts, it is important to assess not only current changes but also the potential importance of emerging trends.

To know where we are going and how to improve our ability to shape the future, I will examine the underlying assumptions of state policies for technological growth, the broader context of such policies, and some of the practical implications of succeeding, of failing, and of not trying. We need to assess what the states' experiments have revealed and whether policy learning has occurred. The authors of chapters in this volume have demonstrated the range of issues that is raised by the continuing experiments in state policy making. Questions have been raised about whether the states have become more resourceful and innovative in their approaches and in their use of resources. This chapter is an attempt not only to examine many of those issues from a different perspective, but also to cut across many of the particular problems to find a pattern, a trend, and an agenda for further research.

The perspective to be taken here is one of both hope and caution. The hope derives from an examination of the resourcefulness that many state policy makers have shown. As other authors have demonstrated, technological change has been both a problem and a resource for economic development; that is, not only has technology provided opportunities and challenges for state economic development, but it increasingly has become a tool by which policy makers hope to spur the creation of jobs and wealth. The cautious tone in this chapter derives from an examination of constraints on state policy making that are as real—and often far more immediate—than technology or economics. In particular, I will address the political factors that require policy makers to act, yet often limit their options to short-term, easily justifiable, and simple solutions. I also will discuss the political implications of longer-term and more complex policy options that may be more effective and efficient, but less feasible within the open system of governance to which states are expected to aspire.

A retreat to basic assumptions

American society is fragmented along many dimensions: public and private, national and local, economic and political, and so on. Much of this fragmentation was designed into the American Constitution, or evolved for logical and explicit reasons. For example, some tasks are done best by individuals, while others require collective agreement; some questions can be resolved by empirical investigation, others require a reference to inner values. On the other hand, some aspects of society are fragmented primarily for reasons of convenience or tradition.

To deal with this complexity, conceptual models have been developed that not only allow particular aspects of the world to be analyzed by conveniently reducing them to a few variables, but that also tempt us to believe that we have actually discovered, tested, and proven "truthful" relationships. When we venture into prediction and prescription about social and political phenomena such as the forces of growth and the determinants of policies, the neat analytical categories become somewhat confusing because each solved puzzle is only part of a larger puzzle. Useful assumptions and simple answers can become bridges over reality. Therefore, we must occasionally re-examine the perceptions on which our questions are based.

The depths of changes

The ultimate objective of economic development policy is economic growth, which is generally defined in terms of job creation and wealth. It may result from changes on either the supply or demand side: new resources, new markets, new products, or greater efficiencies in productive technologies. Most probable is economic growth that results from combinations of factors that are mutually reinforcing. Many variables have been investigated and tested against theories of long-term economic growth, such as resource development, an appropriately trained laborforce, and political or economic stability. There are suggestions that firms follow a life cycle of initiation, maturity, regeneration, decline, and termination (see Fosler Ch. 8), and similar metaphors have been used for government agencies, nations, and even civilizations. Joseph Schumpeter's discussion of the "perennial gales of creative destruction" described the essential dynamics of technological change and industrial development, while Rosenberg and Birdzell find the key to economic growth in a combination of the diffusion of authority, the resources and desire to experiment, and diversity in enterprises and markets.[3] Conceptual models encompass the interaction of a large number of factors that manifest themselves as growth and decline.

Because some of the problems at which state economic development actions are aimed are deeply structural, general models such as these can be of practical use. However, other problems are the results of more manipulable difficulties, such as underfunded universities, inadequate highway systems, or misguided antitrust policies. State policies must make assumptions about whether economic problems are fundamental or transient. Karen Paget observed that contemporary pressures inevitably create changes in growth patterns that often cannot be observed or understood immediately. Thus, analysis and prescription of economic development policies should be preceded by the question: are we observing or prescribing only a quantitative increase in rates of development, in the rôles of states, and in linkages between technology and economic growth, or are fundamental qualitative shifts occurring? For example, Bergman pointed out that most state development policies traditionally have been aimed at the transition from agriculture to mass manufacturing or at infrastructural modernization. Neither of these changes was primarily threat-based, however (except in some socialist nations), so if efforts to shift from traditional industrial technologies to advanced technologies are a response to new concerns about foreign competition or American short-sightedness, then deeper underlying causes (as vaporous as national pessimism or higher individual discount rates) should be recognized.

A related caution concerns the operational definition of a "Third Industrial Revolution." Some fundamental changes are certainly occurring, but if the states are expected to respond to those changes, they should be made explicit. Specifically, we should ask whether states are responding primarily to (a) the emergence of markets for microelectronics, biotechnology, and other high technologies, (b) the shift of manufacturing to labor-cheap nations, (c) the decline of manufacturing employment and the increase in service sector jobs, (d) a qualitative change in the dependence of state economic growth on the international economy, or (e) all of these and other factors in complex combination, since they are interrelated. Similarly, why should lower priority be given to ventures that seek new practical applications for existing technology, perhaps in traditional manufacturing industries, than to traditional applications of new technologies?

Each of these definitions of "the problem" suggests different policy responses. It is dangerous to assess state programs on only a few dimensions—particularly those dimensions most convenient for analysts (because of easy operationalization) and elected officials (because of quickly apparent "results").

The rôles of technology

Attempts to define precisely "science" and "technology" for purposes of policy making are common and will not be repeated here (see Marshall, Ch. 10), but it is important to understand that few are advocating an active state rôle in supporting or directing basic scientific research (see Feller, Ch. 13). One of the reasons was summarized by John Sommer:

> science by its nature is the infinite unfolding of questions which defy the construction of priorities and the possibility of funding by public agency, whose allocations are neither characterized by the test of a freely operating market nor a random process which insures "fair" redistribution. A consequence of science policy has been a tableau of non-random distributions.[4]

That is, basic science cannot be planned or evaluated by traditional techniques.

In contrast to basic science, technological change is more commonly used in models or explanations of economic development policy, and is assumed to be more amenable to planning and evaluation. It can be manifested in three ways.[5] First, new technologies create new demands and opportunities as old patterns of production are retired, new patterns emerge, and therefore wealth shifts among categories of producers and workers, and between regions and nations. Thus, technology *sets conditions.*

Second, technological change is a *tool of policy makers.* The implications of new technology for the processes of public policy include
the enhanced detection and identification of problems (such as environmental and health risks), improved collection and analysis of data,
the formulation of more sophisticated models, and the increased
application of expert systems and, perhaps, artificial intelligence to
policy making. The temptation for policy makers to shift more of the
responsibility for decision making to scientists, engineers, and procedural algorithms is likely to accelerate as decision-making technology
becomes more esoteric. Given the relative (albeit shrinking) shortage of
professional policy analysts and policy makers at the state level, this
phenomenon is likely to become more noticeable as decision-making
technologies are diffused among states.

Finally, technological change is often the intended *output* of the
policy process. Technological advance may be only an instrumental
goal in the pursuit of other objectives; modern policy questions are
often operationalized in the form of "how do we maximize our
technological advantages in the area of commerce and trade, defense,
education, and so on, in order to maximize our wealth, security,
health, etc.?" On the other hand, technology itself can be treated as
the policy objective, for several reasons. The processes of research and
development and their application are virtually invisible to policy
makers, which reduces the possibility of effective oversight and allows
specific policy decisions to be delegated to technicians. Failures are
hard to detect and attribute to mistaken decisions, yet successes may
be very visible. Technological change promises impressive indicators
and measures of success such as patents, jobs, and new firms, while
allowing blame for policy failures to be shifted to well-meaning but
anonymous engineers and scientists.

Technology as input and as output dominates most discussions
of state economic development policies, but the pervasiveness of
technology's impact should be a reminder that the key question raised
here (namely, how can the states respond to development challenges
by promoting a particular type of technology?) cannot be modeled as
a well-specified question. Policy makers have reflected the multiple
rôles of technology by eschewing an exclusive focus on high-tech
development in favor of broader strategies that include technological
development in traditional industries and the development of the labor
skills and other human resources that underlie economic growth. The
most comprehensive studies of the relationship between research and
development and economic benefits have concluded that the process

is too complex for correlations to be interpreted as causality, thereby raising serious questions about our capacity to measure the benefits of technology policies.[6]

The proper unit of analysis

The Reagan Administration adopted a set of policies known as "The New Federalism," that attempted to shift many policy responsibilities from national to state and local governments. This book's focus on a larger state rôle in stimulating economic development is based on the perception that the states have moved to fill the vacuum created by Reagan's policies. But why the states, and why now?

Part of the explanation lies in a broad "resurgence of the states," which has been attributed to factors such as lack of confidence in the federal government, state constitutional and institutional reforms, and the strengthening of intergovernmental lobbies. There have been other waves of state government reform, and some have had long-lasting effects (such as innovations in social policies and education), but many other previous bursts of reform have been more sudden, ad hoc (in response to the recommendations of study commissions), and temporary. In contrast, many of the current changes appear to be long-lived and gradual, and they are common to all states. The resurgence falls into three broad categories: the capture of policy fields from the federal government, the seizure of leadership rôles in continuing intergovernmental programs, and policy innovation.[7]

Many state policies lack exact precursors at the federal level, so some state programs cannot be the result of capturing federal policy areas. As Schmandt pointed out, a century ago "a unified national economy required national rather than regional policies," but because the American economy has not undergone a massive fundamental restructuring, many of the policies most relevant to economic growth (such as taxation, antitrust, trade, and macroeconomic policies) remain primarily national. Nevertheless, the states have made significant inroads in traditionally federal policy areas such as workforce training, research, and development. Even if some aspects of the devolution of policy authority are not, strictly speaking, state-level phenomena, the withdrawal of the federal government during the 1980s made the states important arenas of innovation.

The increased activities of the states in development policy also can be partially attributed to changes in intergovernmental programs. Local governments find it difficult to cope with problems that span jurisdictions, such as service delivery, public transportation, and environmental protection. Much of the initiative in assisting cities and counties in intergovernmental policy making began to shift to the federal government during the New Deal and reached a peak during the Johnson and Nixon years, but during the 1980s federal aid to local governments was reduced significantly. The states became more dominant as experience demonstrated the logic of coordinated action in land-use planning, infrastructure development, and redistribution of wealth and opportunities. As a result, there has been a tendency for the geographical jurisdictions of economic development agencies to be enlarged in recognition that city boundaries do not constrain the engines of growth.[8] Other shifts in intergovernmental decision making are illustrated by the increase in formal interstate agreements: by the mid-1980s there were approximately 123 operative interstate compacts, most visibly in areas such as low-level nuclear wastes,[9] but most commonly in water apportionment, bridges and ports, and environmental protection. The willingness of Congress to allow state pre-emption of new or recurrent issues suggests a fundamental alteration of states' powers.

Finally, the states have experienced a burst of creativity in assuming responsibility for some aspects of their own destinies. An array of policy innovations has resulted from new incentives for state governments to compete, and from new patterns of production that have changed some of the determinants of industrial location and job creation. Yet as Malecki demonstrated very clearly, it is not always possible precisely to identify those incentives, freedoms, and patterns and how they might constructively or destructively interact. For example, to what degree do new production patterns influence a firm's decision to locate in a _state_, as opposed to deciding to locate in a region of the nation, a region of a state, or a particular urban area? To what degree are the key factors—infrastructure, entrepreneurial climate, labor characteristics, raw materials, and interaction among producers—most accurately influenced at the state level or most appropriately _aggregated_ at the state level?

State economies are open in the sense that each state has many "economies" (for example, a petrochemical economy, a textile economy, or, more broadly, a manufacturing economy); each is part of a larger context. The high-tech economy of New Hampshire is tied closely to the high-tech economy of Massachusetts (and the regional high-tech economy of New England), but the agricultural economy of Florida is less closely tied to the agricultural economy of Georgia. Separating state, local, and regional policies and effects is conceptually and operationally difficult. For example, although the decisions to locate

MCC and Sematech in Austin or for VLSI Technology to move to Phoenix were attributable in large part to state initiatives, there is a tendency to combine local, regional, and state factors under the rubric of "state policies" without disentangling the factors over which states had exercised control.

Definitions of the problem

State economic development policies are both nourished and constrained by basic motivations. The deepest is individual self-interest: what are the opportunities for entrepreneurs and opportunists to succeed? The logic of cooperation, economies of scale, and positive externalities provide incentives for the pursuit of collective interests as well, not only among firms but also between the private and public sectors. There is also an impetus to bring aboard those who might otherwise be excluded from that collection of interests (such as unorganized consumers, the poor, and unskilled workers), not only for moral reasons, but also as a pragmatic consideration: their deliberate or systematic exclusion could eventually spawn disruptive reactions.

These motivations are not novel to the 1980s, but they may be addressing a new set of problems. Gibson and Smilor (Ch. 15) are correct that "the world is on the threshold of an advanced technological era," but historians of technology have shown that mankind is constantly in that predicament. To determine whether the states have found solutions, it is useful to ask specifically what problems the states are confronting.

NEW JOBS, NEW FIRMS

The primary objective of state economic development policies is to provide jobs. Most other state policies—welfare, health, education, highway construction, and so on—depend on an employed populace and their tax payments. State officials face real incentives to favor certain types of jobs (namely, those that promise prestige, stability, and high long-term multiplier effects).

Policy makers have several general approaches to stimulate economic development. They can attempt to (a) attract jobs that currently exist in other states; (b) attract jobs that have the potential to be created and could be located in many different states; (c) create opportunities for new types of employment by exploiting or mobilizing indigenous resources (human, financial, or physical); or (d) protect existing jobs by supporting traditional bases of employment. A cautious state policy will seek progress on each of these fronts, and the relative emphasis on each will depend on a variety of factors, ranging from the international competitiveness of a state's traditional industries to the political demands of various state interests. Thus, the absence of a particular type of high-tech industrial policy in a state is not necessarily evidence of a lack of a state economic development policy.

In addition, Malecki and Feller have discussed four types of technological change that affect economic development: site-specific, process innovation, product innovation, and ubiquitous. Within each of these categories can be found an array of jobs ranging from the expert engineer and entrepreneur to the low-skilled assembly or maintenance worker. Although policy makers may favor more of the former, they may decide that, because high-tech firms and their skilled workers are more mobile than less-skilled workers, the latter are, in the long run, more important to their goal of providing equitable long-term employment growth. Explanations of state economic development policies must bear in mind that governors or state legislators considering their economic development options may perceive a choice between claiming credit for the creation of 100 eventual high-salary, high-tech jobs or 300 immediate low-salary, traditional manufacturing jobs.

Policy makers' choices are not so clear-cut, of course. Bergman (Ch. 6) showed that employment growth due to the creation of new firms is barely positive over the short run and tends to be very cyclical. Furthermore, most high-tech development occurs in multilocation firms, suggesting that expansion of current facilities plays a more significant rôle in job creation than creation of new firms in new locations. And attempts to put the new jobs in rural areas with high unemployment rates have not been very successful (Glasmeier, Ch. 4). The assumption that employment in rural areas is most in need of policy assistance is not uniformly supported by data; the problem of chronic unemployment is most severe among the residents (especially young minorities) of inner cities and among the laid-off workers in older industrial centers of the Northeast and Midwest. Whether rural areas have first claim to job-creation assistance can also be questioned by referring to contrary statistics: for example, during the 1980s employment in rural areas of Georgia grew faster than employment in most of the state's metropolitan areas. Of course, much of the improvement in traditional manufacturing employment in rural areas during the decade was attributable to international trade factors resulting from the strengthening of the dollar and therefore were temporary. But it is the importance of other factors such as these that poses threats, not only to the analysis of economic development policies, but also to assumptions about the intentions and criteria of the policy makers whose choices are being modeled or prescribed.

BETTER SCHOOLS, SMARTER WORKERS

A common thread in studies of state economic development policies is the rôle of the states in improving the bundle of activities under the general label of "education." Marshall's contribution (Ch. 10) is an eloquent summary of the complexities underlying education as a crucial—perhaps the most crucial—factor in economic growth, and Wilson stated in his chapter, "the human capital needs of the information age. . . are paramount (Ch. 3)." In other words, as more has been learned about the limitations of direct business assistance and as human resource development has ascended the political agenda, development policies appear to have begun a fundamental shift in emphasis.

As an instrument of economic development, education has few negative connotations. Education can be seen as positive-sum; competition among states and universities is seen as traditional, friendly, and beneficial to all. Educational improvement gathers together many warm dimensions (such as a return to basics, discipline, a healthy form of intermural competition, and implications of financial benefits for future generations). Because it emphasizes opportunities rather than guaranteed success, education can be alleged to be generally egalitarian in process, if not in outcome. Finally, although there may be a promise of short-term results, educational programs seem to capture the essence of long-term preparation and stability, since they are an investment in ingenious engineers, efficient managers, and skilled workers.

But is education the key to state-level promotion of technologically-advanced economic development, and if so, what type of education? As Marshall demonstrated, many firms have discovered that employee-training programs, and not necessarily public education, are an important way to improve the supply of relevant labor. He also showed that other factors are vital parts of learning systems (e.g., stable families, good nutrition), and that many economic development plans could bear the risk of slighting large demographic segments of the potential workforce who are best served through social programs. Furthermore, although business leaders may agree that well-trained workers are essential to economic growth, there is weak data on the relationships among educational spending, industrial location, and economic development. Rosenfeld and Atkinson (Ch. 12) demonstrated that demographics, educational resources, and the career choices of future workers may frustrate the plans of policy makers, and Grubb (Ch. 11) showed that vocational education is effective in economic development only when certain conditions apply.

There are several general types of labor required for firms with advancing technology. First, there are *creators*, typically scientists and engineers (roughly, those whom Marshall characterized as having "higher order thinking skills"), who supply ideas for product and process innovations. These ideas may or may not have direct commercial implications, and connections with profitable payoffs may not be discovered immediately. Although the links between creators and job creation may be indirect and lagged, these researchers are perceived as being indispensable to states' futures. Unfortunately, several difficult questions follow directly. In order to share in the rewards of these creators' labors, what types of educational reforms should a state adopt, at what levels, and with how much patience? Would an increased emphasis on science and mathematics in primary grades and high schools have a significant impact on the supply of "creators"? It appears that we do not yet know how to create such minds, so would a state be better served by attempting to raid the creative workforce that may have slowly evolved in another state? If a state invests in the production of native scientists and engineers, how can it prevent other states from capturing the benefits? Until these issues are resolved, no state can base its economic development policies entirely on educational reforms.

After an innovation has been created, another type of labor is required. *Builders* and *managers* are the activators of the system, who must recognize the potential market for the creators' innovations, raise the capital, sign the contracts, rent the space, hire the workers, and so on. Some of these tasks will be assumed by business entrepreneurs, and Malecki has demonstrated that the roots of entrepreneurship are difficult to identify, and, therefore, to foster: "policies cannot create entrepreneurs." Appropriate managerial styles may differ across types and sizes of firms and industries, raising a familiar difficulty for policy makers: is it possible to educate young people, or retrain older workers, to pursue and perfect these skills? Business schools traditionally have neglected entrepreneurial management, which, after all, may be as much a state of mind as an acquired skill. Perhaps profit motives and an aptitude for business are more common than scientific curiosity and engineering skills, so it may be possible for the states to play a smaller state rôle in the education of managers than creators. Until more is known about society's innate supply of these builders and managers, and about the educational system's ability to generate these talents, state policies for economic growth will depend upon a vital yet poorly understood link in the chain of labor.

A third general type of labor consists of the *skilled workers* (both blue-collar and white-collar) who are not sufficiently creative or motivated to be innovators or managers but who nevertheless require substantial education and training. Some of the workers in this category may hold advanced degrees in science, engineering, management, or a professional area, yet they are less compelled to expand frontiers, responding instead primarily to their employers' needs. They are technicians and implementors. In spite of lags in translating needs and opportunities for such workers into specific educational programs, public policies can increase the supply of these skilled workers. In fact, most proposals for using educational reforms to attract advancing-technology industries are aimed at these workers, ranging from engineers with sophisticated graduate training to literate assembly-line workers. However, Grubb has argued that there are several important flaws in the assumption that educational programs aimed at "educated labor" will work quickly enough to satisfy policy makers, or that they can correct for shortages in the supplies of particular types of workers. Marshall showed that although the "deskilling" hypothesis is weakened by empirical evidence, a new type of worker adaptability will be demanded by rapidly changing technologies. In addition, there is some reason to suspect that the adoption of human resource programs may deter state officials from other approaches to economic development: a study of coordination between state employment and training programs and state economic development activities found a negative relationship between (a) the joint administration of physical and human economic development policies and (b) the total number of state tax incentives designed to attract or retain industries.[10]

Finally, there is a very large group of Americans who, to use a harsh yet appropriate term, are irrelevant to high-tech development and for whom high-tech jobs will never be relevant. Some are older, structurally unemployed workers for whom retraining programs are unlikely or inappropriate. Some are the illiterate and functionally illiterate—perhaps as many as one-third of all adult Americans. This group also includes the chronically unemployed with little hope of or interest in developing careers or marketable skills—teenage mothers, undocumented aliens, the "underclass," drug victims, and so on. Understandably, they are rarely mentioned in proposals for the promotion of high-tech industries, and they will benefit only very indirectly from state technology policies. Their presence must be remembered, however, if only because the needs of these workers will compete for the attention and resources of state governments.

If, as Marshall argued convincingly, human resource development is a major determinant of economic growth, and if education programs continue to be central to states' development policies, then schools are likely to become the subject of increasingly intense scrutiny and dispute. Because not all schools are equal, and because they cannot (and should not) produce homogeneous products that compare neatly on a single dimension of skill and achievement, the questions of "what is a 'better' school?" and "what is a 'better' worker?" will be fought largely in the political arena.

IMPROVED INFRASTRUCTURES

Many state economic development policies are intended to strengthen the "labor infrastructure," but it is more common to describe the economic infrastructure: physical capital stock that supports more directly productive capital and supports its activity."[11] For traditional industries, this economic overhead capital generally consists of public utilities (including transportation, electricity and gas production and transmission, and communication networks), along with necessary state services such as fire and police protection, a court system, and so on. These are generally assumed to be necessary but not sufficient conditions for development. Studies of state economic development policy for advanced-technology industries have added two additional types of support to this list: research facilities and "quality of life."

The states are certain to play a rôle in improving the traditional infrastructure, but the differential effects on high-tech industrial growth may be rather small. Most states and localities will continue to have sources of electricity, gas, and water that are adequate for the needs of growing firms; in any case, as Wilson argued, a state-level strategy to gain a competitive advantage in the prices of such services probably would fail in the long run. Innovative programs that have been funded by the states are actively promoted as having implications for other states or even nations. For example, New York's Energy Research and Development Authority has provided $700,000 annually for a Lighting Research Center at Rennselaer Polytechnic Institute to discover ways for homes and offices to use natural and artificial lighting more efficiently; the Center's director stated that "New York's selfish interest in all this is saving energy in the state," but he added that "it makes sense for other states to explore this kind of thing."[12] In addition, for some firms the availability of other services such as disposal of hazardous and toxic wastes may be critical, but state officials' growing awareness of the need for effective waste transportation and treatment policies may reduce states' relative advantages in this area also. Thus, interstate technology transfer will find analogues in the transfer of innovative policies.

State policies to promote technological change in telecommunications systems will be important also, but the tools that are available to state officials to provide an infrastructure of advanced telecommunications are limited. Progressive regulatory policies are vital in the post-divestiture era, particulary as bypass technologies threaten the stability of the overall rate base, but here again a state's differential advantages would be reduced as competitive efforts by one state are copied quickly by other states. It is likely that state efforts such as preferential treatment of innovative systems in rate decisions will have effects too small to be reliably measured (due to the complexity of cost distributions), and direct forms of infrastructural assistance such as subsidies to telecommunications firms are likely to be politically unacceptable. States are making preliminary moves to develop innovative telecommunications networks in their rôle as users of services and purchasers of equipment, but it is too soon to know whether statewide systems of data collection, management, and analysis are significant improvements on private-sector systems such as ISDNs, or whether these innovations will have a measurable impact on state economic growth.

Transportation is another vital component of state economic development. All other things being equal, those locations with better highway and airport service could be expected to draw more of some types of advanced technology firms.[13] As in other aspects of developmental policies, however, the relationships are not simple and easily observable. A study by the Southern Growth Policies Board found that during 1977–82, nonmetropolitan counties in Georgia showed an 11 percent increase in jobs, compared with 21 percent in metropolitan areas; however, rural counties in Georgia (and other southern states) that included interstate highways had *less* job growth than those counties not on the interstate highway system—a pattern opposite to that found by Bergman's examination of counties adjacent to metropolitan areas. Not only are highway improvements only one aspect of employment growth, but simple measures of infrastructural development may be misleading. For example, Bergman found that *reduced* levels of highway construction may be an indication of highway completion—that is, actual, not potential, improvement in transportation. Similarly, access to airports is not insignificant,[14] but policy makers cannot assume that airport industrial parks will guarantee the relocation of advanced-technology firms. Many startup firms, for example, are not likely to have developed a coterie of executive travelers, and they may find it advantageous to use private express delivery services (for which airport proximity is less relevant) for shipments and physical communications.

In addition to familiar economic and labor infrastructures, new types of supportive enterprises are likely to emerge. For example, Gibson and Smilor concluded that "state government's primary rôle in creating and sustaining the technopolis is in relation to setting industrial priorities for and funding of higher education." Malecki has found that "firms locate their R&D facilities in states where universities . . . are competitive in federal R&D programs," but many have sought in vain for the formula for winning such competition. In any case, these new demands mean new problems: it is not clear how support for higher education translates into policy actions. State officials face enormous incentives to use universities to reinforce or redirect particular areas of technology-relevant economic development. Feller has thoroughly investigated the possible relationships among universities and industry and found both logical grounds for cooperation and likely areas of incongruence. Similarly, Marianne Clarke (Ch. 7) argued that new industry–university relationships are also partly a result of changes in the nature of research: increased needs for capital, increasing interdisciplinarity, and looser distinctions between applied and basic research. Coupled with the impetus to strengthen education in general, these incentives have presented state policy makers with both new options and new problems in the treatment of public universities as research infrastructure.

To focus on one example, the rapidly increasing cost of replacing obsolete research equipment has become a significant burden for universities. As a result, suggestions that states could provide assistance to technological development by underwriting laboratory modernization are appealing. State programs could increase subsidies, grants, or matching funds for the purchase of research equipment by universities. However, because the national cost of replacing obsolete equipment is estimated to be over $100 billion, states could have only a marginal effect on the problem in general; to have a significant impact, they would be required to identify particular areas of the research infrastructure to update, and such target selection suggests a new array of problems. In addition, at some universities it is difficult for firms to borrow or rent access to research equipment because of prior demands by faculty and students. As a result, programs such as technology-oriented business incubator facilities are becoming increasingly popular.

A particularly attractive option for some states is the possibility of exploiting federal laboratories for state and local purposes. Tennessee, for example, is working with the Oak Ridge National Laboratory to develop technological industries in the corridor between ORNL and Knoxville. Many national laboratories undertake the full range of R&D activities from basic and applied research to development and application, and a mixture of public and private purposes is familiar to many of these facilities (particularly in aerospace and energy research); these activities have been encouraged by many federal policies.[15] A state such as New Mexico, which is disproportionately blessed with major national laboratories, would be in a position to incorporate national laboratories in its development infrastructure, as the national laboratories could increasingly replace some of the functions of research universities in providing a technological infrastructure for state economic development, such as offering equipment and facilities to firms or by contributing to the education of the state's scientists and engineers.

These attempts will require several important types of obstacles to be overcome. Among these are the requirement that government–industry collaboration be initiated by the private sector, and the need for states to offer national laboratories a balanced set of incentives that are compatible with the laboratories' long-term research programs. As is the case for federal technology programs, it will be important for the states to identify areas of technological development where, for economic or technical reasons, the private sector will not or cannot undertake the risks or investments that state leaders deem likely to provide benefits for the state. Coordination with federal requirements and restrictions will also be required, and experience has revealed the dangers of relying on convoluted, transitory federal policies.[16] Nevertheless, efforts to help technology "over the fence" are being facilitated by the Federal Laboratory Consortium and the 1986 Federal Technology Transfer Act, which encourages federal laboratories to enter cooperative R&D agreements with private industry, universities, and state and local governments.

Another category of infrastructure is subsumed under the phrase "quality of life." It includes characteristics such as favorable climate, access to recreational facilities, environmental quality, medical care, primary and secondary educational systems, and other tangibles and intangibles. Many of these are beyond a state's capacity to affect. Other aspects of these amenities are traditional policy concerns of states, but their leaders already have confronted the expense of making significant improvements in most of these areas. If a state discovered that firm creation or relocation depended *only* on better schools for the children of entrepreneurs and engineers, how many options would they have, particularly over the short term? Furthermore, it would be politically difficult to improve "quality of life" in only specific locations or regions. For example, it may be infeasible for a state to designate one city, county, or region of the state as an "economic development target," since the implications of leaving the citizens of other regions behind raise some significant difficulties. The issue of distribution of state efforts should remain a primary concern to analysts, since it is crucial to policy makers.

"FAIRER" DISTRIBUTION

Technological progress affects the distribution of society's resources: economically, geographically, and, therefore, politically. Schmandt (Ch. 2) observed that until 1950, technological change created incentives for public power to migrate to the center, i.e., the national government, and that more recent technological changes have spawned a tendency toward economic and political decentralization. With this relocation of influence have come questions about new power relationships and the "fairness" of distribution among and within regions and states.

The new loci of centralization are not particularly states or cities, but different types of cities and regions from those that benefited from earlier waves of technological change. Glasmeier clarified some of the reasons for the new dominance of big cities in the high-tech phenomenon, yet many of these reasons are not new. Metropolitan areas originally formed and prospered because of their advantages in infrastructure, educational systems, concentration of business acumen and associates, and so on.[17] The centralization–decentralization debate has always been with us, albeit in different forms. Nevertheless, the distributional aspects of the current wave of urbanized opportunities have several novel features.

Some form of partnership (particularly regarding high-risk, high-cost public works projects) has been acceptable since the earliest days of the Republic. Governments have supported industry through positive regulations, subsidies, tax expenditures, and even macroeconomic tools. However, the distributional implications of development policies may be moving toward the forefront because the nature of that partnership has changed. As the economic optimism of American citizens, business leaders, and elected officials declines, the public sector will be encouraged to take a more active rôle in planning and promotion. Furthermore, the issues of "planning for what?" and "promoting whom?" are now more difficult to deflect because of the greater possibilities for participation by those at whom benefits would not otherwise be directly aimed. In short, when the economic pie was perceived to be growing reliably, there were fewer incentives for the more indirect beneficiaries of economic growth policies to insist on immediate delivery of their shares.

A second factor is a perception shared by many Americans that national priorities have shifted away from helping the most disadvantaged, although actual per capita expenditures by the federal government on need-based social welfare programs declined only slightly during the 1980s. Responsibility for funding many distributional programs has shifted to state governments, in part because federal aid to state and local authorities as a percentage of the federal budget declined by 35 percent between 1973 and 1986. Thus, state programs are likely to be scrutinized for the degree to which they compensate for Washington's alleged shift in priorities.

The distributional implications of urban–rural imbalances in economic development policies have been analyzed extensively. For example, Malecki described the "persistent tendency toward agglomeration and concentration" of innovative economic activities, and he discussed the necessary threshold size for local economies to attract entrepreneurs. Glasmeier wrote that "today's high-tech industries have, for the most part, resisted efforts to spread benefits to less technically adept and less populated areas of the United States," and she demonstrated that the rural areas of the United States have lagged in high-tech manufacturing growth. Of course, the distribution issue turns upon the question of incentives, since if there is no incentive for firms to locate in rural areas, they should not be expected to do so; the mission of the firm is not to spread benefits but to receive them—from customers, from increased productivity and innovation, and, perhaps, from alluring governments. What are the incentives for state officials to provide additional benefits for either traditional or high-tech firms to locate in rural areas?

The most immediate incentives are political. Many state legislatures are dominated by rural interests, and in those state assemblies that are not, the representatives of metropolitan areas cannot consistently exclude rural legislators from voting coalitions. The rural–urban conflict in state capitols has found a new manifestation in disputes over whether metropolitan areas are absorbing an unfair share of states' educational, infrastructural, and economic development resources. The debate has included questions about whether the most disadvantaged—the least skilled urban poor—could ever have any realistic prospects of entering the modern workforce. Even if researchers uncover indisputable evidence concerning the inherent disadvantages facing rural high-tech development (for example, greater returns from encouraging traditional manufacturing or alternative agricultural production in rural areas), such findings will probably have little effect on political pressure to spread the wealth. Indeed, states are likely to face pressure to win high-tech contests with other states before judging themselves on issues of equity.

Apart from politics, why *should* rural areas "climb the ladder of industrial sophistication," in Glasmeier's phrase? Part of the justification is the fear of being left behind as the American economy is transformed into something radically new, yet although there is reason to suspect that high-tech industries will continue to increase in importance to the national and state economies, it is not clear whether, or when, this sector will become dominant. Some state development officers have recognized that the increasing integration of advanced technologies in traditional manufacturing industries (such as chemicals, textiles, and food processing) is making this dispute somewhat irrelevant. In any case, some states have lost new employers because of pressure to locate in an area of a state that offers no particular advantages to the firm.

Another possible spur to rural economic development is wage differentials; employees of more technologically advanced industries earn higher wages, and rural workers generally earn lower wages, so, it is argued, one way to narrow the gap is to merge the two. Of course, one of the desirable features of lower rural wages (namely, lower costs of living) would be lost, especially if a high-wage firm located in a low-wage rural area and sparked a quick and disproportionate boost to housing costs, local educational expenditures, and service delivery. Increased housing and transportation costs in the vicinity of North Carolina's heralded Research Triangle Park, for example, caused an observer to remark, "There is relatively little emerging here for low- to moderate-income people," and the area's attractive quality of life was alleged to be suffering from traffic jams and land speculation.[18]

Another distributional implication of state economic development policies follows from a short-term focus. During the 1980s political candidates and the popular press argued that low-wage areas in the United States had lost large numbers of jobs to foreign competitors, not only because of unfair trade practices, but also because of wage differentials. In policy debates the validity of this argument may be less important than its attractiveness, but even if it were found to be accurate, it is not clear that American decision makers—national, state, local, or private-sector—could counter that trend. Boosting the incomes of rural or low-wage workers would undermine attempts to compete via wages, and policies that would maintain low wages in the name of international competitiveness are unlikely to gain wide support. Attempts to force shifts in production could be not only expensive but also, possibly, eventually self-defeating.

States that pursue economic development through promotion of advanced-technology industries cannot avoid complex distributional questions such as these. Some patterns of distribution are determined by, and can only be corrected by, structural national and international forces, and some distributional issues require tradeoffs that not only may be politically difficult but also logically in conflict.

THE NEED TO TAKE ACTION

Many possible state economic development programs have been discussed, but one phenomenon that straddles all of these proposals may be the most compelling. Put simply, the leaders of state and local governments will be pressed by an assortment of constituents to do *something* about the economic future. These constituents include workers, corporations, academics, and administrators, some of whom are seeking funds for their jobs, plans, projects, and programs. Other stakeholders hope to find fallback justifications for shaky enterprises, and some will expect officials to show their civic concerns in the form of public pronouncements and appropriations.

State economic development policy does not involve an intense ideological battle between an intrusive state and a free market economy. There are some fitting analogies with the American regulatory system, which had its roots in technological transformations of production, economic institutions, and society, and in the resulting rise of trusts, the corporation, natural monopolies, and negative externalities. A century ago the states were the first to respond to these changes. Many of their responses were inappropriate or too vigorous (such as some of the transportation regulations imposed by the Grange states), but there was a widespread perception that public officials should address fundamental new technological and economic challenges. There is a widespread belief that another technological transformation is occurring, just as broad and deep as a century ago, and the American governmental system will respond.

The coherence and consistency of that response will be shaped by how the problem is perceived. First, lagging economic growth may be interpreted as a result of technological trends that cannot be controlled or limited but only chased. In this case, the states' responses will be more reactive than creative. Second, as Americans increasingly see the United States to be falling behind relative to foreign competitors who do not play (or who play *better* than Americans) by American rules, policies will vacillate between competition (for example, through domestic subsidies, "buy American first" programs, or limitations on foreign investment) and friendly cooperation (such as joint ventures and foreign investment incentives). Third, these shifts in economic development frequently will be seen as manifestations of deep-rooted forces that deny equal opportunities to rural or unskilled workers and to the victims of structural economic changes, so the costs of state attempts to "do something" about high-tech industry will be exacerbated by demands to compensate those who are left behind.

The result is likely to be a rather confused disarray of state economic development policies. Bergman wrote of programs that "assume the mantle of technology's fashionable status" and of states that become "policy courtiers" in their efforts to package old programs as high-tech policies. The number of governors mentioning "high technology research" at state universities during their state-of-the-state addresses climbed from two in 1982 to 14 in 1983.[19] Similarly, John Rees and Tim Lewington in Chapter 9 observed that "many programs do not make sense in economic terms, but they are not meant to do so. They make sense in *political terms*," as they must if they are to survive the competition for attention and funds. Nothing could be more American: James Madison prescribed such a system in the *Federalist* (no. 10) in order to provide checks on the powerful through a multiplicity of factions and interests. However, Madison also prescribed a process of "refinement": the passage of public views "through the medium of a chosen body of citizens, whose wisdom may best discern the true interest of their country." Such leadership requires a talent for forging coalitions based on balanced interests.

Will states be able to devise stable coalitions to support steady programs for stimulating economic development over long periods? An official of one state department of industry and trade has described economic development politics as "the politics of inclusion." Ironically, the key to successful policies may be a *failure* to analyze them too closely or too well. For example, studies of tax and fiscal incentives on industrial location decisions have found that they are generally ineffective, yet "a company may find clues about a community's willingness to host industry by its willingness to grant tax and financial incentives.

Industry may find these programs to be mere tokens, insignificant compared with other influences on locations, but they are tokens, nonetheless."[20] In addition, economic development policies can be supported by both conservatives (because the programs often rely on less obtrusive government incentives) and by liberals (because the programs address pressing social and economic problems).[21] In other words, state officials must respond to pressures to act before policy analysts can give them reliable information about the consequences of their actions, and they probably are aware of the inconsistent concepts and justifications used by startup firms, large traditional manufacturers, rural legislators, university presidents, and so on. One key to successful adoption of economic development programs may be to allow these interests mutually to obfuscate their objectives, strategies, and successes.

The contexts of state actions

A question was raised in an earlier section about whether the state is the proper unit of analysis for understanding new patterns of development. For example, if the new activism of the American states was only a result of the decline of the industrial heartland, then we would need to explain why previous economic shifts were not reflected in earlier resurgences of the states' rôle. Among the other novel features of the new state activism in promoting technological change and economic development are not only new industrial technologies, but also changing national and international conditions.

The federal context

Authors frequently disagree over the clarity of the federal system in which state activities have emerged. Wilson wrote that federal and state governments now share powers in most policy areas, in spite of a national Constitution that "defined a federalist system with a fairly clear delineation of responsibilities between the federal and state governments." In contrast, Schmandt found that contests between the national and state governments were anticipated from the beginning of the Republic. Historical analyses have shown that the balance of power in the American federal system was intended to be uneasy as it served two somewhat conflicting purposes: to control the excesses of localism while preserving the rights of individuals to be different.[22]

If the system was designed to be confusing, the designers succeeded. A study published in 1981 found that 326 metaphors and models (such as "dual federalism," "picket fence federalism," "marble cake federalism") to have been used to describe the American federal system.[23] The interconnectedness of federal, state, and local powers is illustrated by Bowman and Kearney's analysis of factors in the revitalization of states including: lack of confidence in the national government, state constitutional reform, court-ordered reapportionment of state legislatures, intergovernmental lobbying, and local government incapacities.

The history of the American federal system reveals the danger in discussing the rôle of the states with the national government in only passive withdrawal. The national government has been active in state and local economic development programs in the past, and given the cyclical nature of power relationships between Washington and the states, the national government probably will reassert itself in this policy area. For example, the rôle of the military sector of the American economy often goes unmentioned in analyses of state economic development, but an effort to reduce the military's growing dependence on foreign producers for technical military supplies (ranging from gallium arsenide to ball bearings) could result in large programs that would overwhelm some states' efforts to plan for their industries' futures.[24] State policy makers cannot know when and in what form (as partner or pre-emptor) Washington's rôle will resurge.

Of course, the national government plays a significant rôle even in comparative retreat. Clarke discussed efforts in the 1960s by the U.S. Department of Commerce to stimulate the states' rôle in technology transfer. Like an aborted attempt by the National Science Foundation in 1977 to assist states in the development of science and technology plans, most initial programs were undercut by a dependence on uncertain federal funds. Cynicism was also justified, at least in some states, by the distribution of federal assistance: during its first four years (fiscal years 1983–6), the Small Business Innovation Research program (which requires 11 government agencies to set aside 1.25 percent of their annual R&D budgets for contracts with small businesses) provided 1,514 contracts to California firms and 996 to companies in Massachusetts, but only three to West Virginia, two to South Dakota, and none to Alaska, North Dakota, and Wyoming.

A result of these experiences during the 1970s and early 1980s was a greater reluctance to rely on direction-setting by the national government and a willingness by entrepreneurial state and local leaders to undertake projects such as St. Paul's Homegrown Economy Project (intended to make the city "self-reliant" by means of local ownership, high interindustry dependence, economic diversification, and so on). The federal government did not withdraw completely, however. For example, the Department of Commerce developed a pilot program for the states by helping Minnesota establish technical assistance projects for finding export opportunities, exploiting automated manufacturing technologies, and commercializing research discoveries at Minnesota's universities.[25]

Another factor in the revitalization of state economic development policy is the burgeoning of effort to define the powers and responsibilities of private developers, state officials, and local governments in so far as land development is related to economic and environmental impacts. The growth of "growth management" was a recognition that many of these problems extended beyond political boundaries. New forms of cooperation between states and localities became more acceptable. Just as important for state development policies, however, was the increasing acquiescence in—and even active support for—growth management policies by the private sector. This has been particularly significant for industries that considered moving or establishing new operations and that shopped for quality-of-life amenities in addition to favorable economic conditions.

Finally, a profound advantage that could accrue to the states as a result of federal tax policy is in the realm of financing. As Wilson discussed (Ch. 3), the states can create innovative methods for funding development policies. The "49 states that have constitutions requiring balanced budgets," are commonly applauded, but there is no mechanism by which the federal government can share the advantages of the off-budget options that states enjoy. Although the 1986 Tax Reform Act required the elimination of tax-exempt, low-interest industrial development bonds by 1989, such instruments have allowed states to invest by borrowing without adding liabilities to the ledger of general state revenues and spending (see Table 16.1). In their continuing search for advantages, by the late 1980s states such as North Carolina

Table 16.1 New issues of long-term state and local government industrial aid securities, 1970–85 (in $ billions).

1970	$0.1	1981	$ 3.4
1975	$0.4	1982	$ 2.9
1978	$0.9	1983	$ 3.6
1979	$1.7	1984	$15.7
1980	$1.7	1985	$14.0

Source: U.S. Department of Commerce, Bureau of the Census, Statistical abstract of the United States 1987 (Washington D.C.: Government Printing Office, 1987), p. 262.

and Georgia were looking for replacements to industrial development bonds (such as a program that would require counties to pledge one mill of their tax revenues to guarantee loans for private manufacturing ventures). The Congressional Budget Office has estimated that in the early 1980s tax-free state and local industrial development bonds were depriving the federal treasury of about $4 billion annually.[26]

The international context

States also have innovated as they have adjusted to the changing international context of their development policies. For example, New York has operated an export promotion program since the 1960s, and by 1988 at least 30 states had such programs. In some cases states have found an advantage in collective action, such as the five southern states that comprise the Mid-South Regional Trade Council. In addition, 23 states have created export finance mechanisms; many are based on Minnesota's Export Finance Authority, which provides pre- and post-export loan guarantees to support business financing through commercial lenders. Some states have been "internationalizing" their college curricula, and Tennessee has provided about $500,000 for a Foreign Language Institute, which opened in 1987, in expectation that the state will attract more foreign industry and tourism as its business leaders, students, and citizens learn more languages.

Competition for foreign sources of economic growth entails both unique and familiar questions about the potential rôle of states and regions. As Fosler pointed out, recruitment of foreign firms and customers raises issues not only about subsidization of foreign competitors, but also about the desirability of extensive foreign investment in American assets. One result has been the "unitary tax" enacted by several states, under which corporations are taxed on a pro rata share of total earnings, including profits earned in other states or nations (raising questions about state encroachment on national powers over treaty-making and regulation of foreign commerce). Another implication of the international context is more familiar: it remains difficult to measure success. Among other problems, evaluations of state policy efforts must disentangle the effects of the international economy; for example, although the seven southeastern states enjoyed a net gain of 54,000 manufacturing jobs during 1980–5, they had lost an estimated 121,000 manufacturing jobs to the high value of the American dollar. In addition, there is still a tendency for policy makers to expect quick results, and to be disappointed. In 1987 Minnesota scaled down its efforts to stimulate trade with Scandinavian countries after less than four years, while a nonprofit export trading company formed by Virginian port cities (VEXTRAC) could claim only a 0.16 percent increase in tonnage shipped after several years of efforts.[27]

The international context also provokes some apparently inconsistent justifications for state economic development policies. Labor-intensive, highly standardized goods, including those produced by both traditional and advanced-technology manufacturing industries, will tend to be produced in low labor-cost markets, and since proximity between producers and consumers is less important, such jobs may be placed wherever production costs are minimized. On the other hand, one of the virtues of high-tech industries is their ability to use flexible manufacturing processes and improved custom designing techniques to provide quick responses to commercial opportunities; the window of profitability in some of these sectors may be shorter than two years. These more sophisticated and complex production techniques require feedback between producers and customers, so to the degree that geographical proximity is necessary for such feedback, production can be regionalized or localized (what Schmandt described as "close interaction between producers and users"). As Malecki argued, the "technology is not fixed in either time or space," and the dispersion of economic benefits from innovations will depend on the rôle of information, labor, and face-to-face contacts along with the availability of productive resources.

Assessing state economic development policies

Because of the range of factors that affect economic development and state policy making, evaluations of options must reduce real complexity to manageable conceptual models. For example, some analyses of the current transformation of industrial society hint of a Ricardian growth perspective in which the scarcity of land as a limit to growth has been replaced by a scarcity of technological advancement. With unclear evidence, however, explanations of economic development are far from completely tested. This is cause for concern, since models such as those of economic change and industrial location are likely to be translated into actual allocations of private money, public money, and opportunity costs. Thus, the recent evolution of state policy away from direct business incentives and toward human resource development has rested at least in part on incremental analyses using models of industrial location and labor markets. The world will not wait for validated theories, but analysts must be sensitive to the distinction between useful models on the one hand, and valid and reliable theories on the other.

Many investigators have been explicit about the uncertainties that persist in each of their areas of inquiry—uncertainties that will grow as states experiment with new policy instruments and face new demands from different constituencies. Paget, for example, has written about the lack of firm causal understanding of how information and knowledge move from universities to private applications, and Grubb found a lack of evidence that education and training programs for workers have succeeded as expected. Bergman's study raised questions such as whether growth of high technology is spurred by highways, by airports, by highways that are built because of airports, or by airports that are built to serve the metropolitan areas that were made possible by highways. And Glasmeier found that states that were already dominant in high technology tended to develop more high-tech jobs than others, and that cannot tell us whether less advantaged states can alter the pattern. An overview of the problems in analyzing state efforts should be helpful in assessing the states' rôle in helping technologically advancing industries.

General state capacities for policy development

The definition, formulation, adoption, and implementation of public policies depend on factors such as the number of decision makers, the number and clarity of objectives, the degree to which core values or instrumental values are agreed upon, the range of possible alternatives, and the uncertainty of outcomes for each possible alternative. It is not yet clear whether the states have inherent advantages in reducing the ill-structuredness of economic development problems in order to make rational and efficient policies.[28]

Fosler found that "conventional state institutions are not well suited" for their new economic rôle, and that although institutional innovations have appeared, the integration of programs is likely to be stymied by the traditional fragmentation of functions. On the other hand, Schmandt found that the states have advantages in bureaucratic flexibility and decentralized drive, in their responsiveness to regional conditions, and in their ability to reform their institutions and procedures. However, there are tradeoffs to be made between central guidance and coordination versus the need for particular types of information and programs to serve narrow locations. Many firms, research needs and activities, and flows of technical information are necessarily national or international. The experience of regulatory policy in the federal system may be relevant: the states have been most effective at discovering needs and implementing programs, but not necessarily at formulating or legitimizing their policies.[29]

Evidence is likely to be found to support any position on the capabilities of the states because they serve as 50 laboratories for experimenting with a variety of innovative policies and policy-making institutions. For example, Rees and Lewington found that "the *goals* of [state-funded research center programs] differ from state to state, while resources allocated for program implementation also fluctuate widely," and Fosler acknowledged that some economic strategies "are compatible with one another, while some are mutually exclusive." Clarke's examination of state science and technology offices found that "while the primary goal of state science and technology policy is economic development, it is also clear that state science and technology policies address a variety of subsidiary goals" that include education, laborforce training, and the formation of working relationships among government, education, and industry. Even without considering the redistributive objectives of economic development policies, they can be broad and complex bundles of programs and policies, and it will be difficult to generalize about the capability of the states.

Fundamental constraints on state actions

Some generalizations about basic constraints on state economic development policies are possible. Nearly all policy processes, both state and federal, suffer from short time horizons. These are usually attributed to the two- or four-year electoral cycle, the short-term incentives and immediate demands provided by the political arena, and high individual discount rates. Yet the focus of state high-tech efforts is usually on quick results.

It is difficult to know how long is long enough. Is a 10- or 15-year time horizon sufficient for building a research infrastructure and an entrepreneurial climate? Some states have budget cycles that are twice as long as the federal government's, but even two-year cycles do not approach the time that is necessary for most development projects to pay off. Ironically, closer ties among government, business, and industry, along with the increased public participation and greater responsiveness that some seek in state activism, may exacerbate the problems of demanding quick results: state governments may be more inclined than the more sluggish federal policy system impatiently to withdraw funds or reorganize university systems.

Other constraints include environmental regulations, such as metropolitan air quality programs that prohibit new major emitters in urban areas.[30] In addition, some state constitutions and statutes prohibit direct business subsidies, for which planners may be grateful in the long run as firms bid up their asking price to locate in one state rather than another; for example, Georgia was able to offer Toyota about $20 million in assistance for a new automobile assembly plant (mainly in training programs and some highway construction), while Kentucky's winning bid of about $120 million included a wide range of incentives and grants. Some of the more generous approaches have backfired; some states, reluctant to appear anti-business by asking for guarantees, have lured firms with millions of dollars in state and local government loans and training grants, only to have a plant close with no early notice. West Virginia filed a $614.6 million suit against Newell, alleging corporate fraud in accepting government-subsidized loans at a time when the firm was planning to close its West Virginia plant.

Other limitations on active state rôles are more structural and not easily overcome. Wilson noted multiple and conflicting state objectives, weak policy instruments, and long-term fiscal pressures that will compete for priority status. Glasmeier discussed fundamental determinants of high-tech industrial growth over which the states can have relatively little influence, and Malecki offered a compelling argument that shaping a favorable entrepreneurial climate is "perhaps the most daunting challenge for policy formation" because of the wide array of factors that affect the location of technological innovation. Some analysts, such as Charles Ferguson, have argued that entrepreneurship can actually damage economic growth by siphoning the greatest talents away from the larger industrial firms that have the resources to develop and market innovative products. In addition, there are clear indications of countereffects that may result from state efforts. Low tax rates imply a low level of infrastructure and quality of life (Glasmeier, Ch. 4), university research parks in the South are inversely related to the conditions that nurture small business (Bergman, Ch. 6), and there is certain to be a point of diminishing returns as states' efforts multiply.

Plausible alternative interpretations of state successes and failures

Even if state economic development policies were uniform there would still be a need to stipulate clearly what constitutes *success*. For example, a low level of funding for a program could reveal a lack of political commitment or a mostly symbolic approach, or it could be evidence of a cautious strategy or a recognition that small programs may be more cost-effective and responsive than large programs. Similarly, a high rate of survival or longevity for small high-tech start-up firms bred in business incubators may be an indication of an unwillingness to underwrite risky ventures—which may be the objective of the program. And how many of these firms would have found financing elsewhere, and would a more intense battle for survival have strengthened these firms for steady growth?

Because this is a new area of endeavor for the states, and thus a new area for inquiry, reliable analyses of states' efforts are still lacking. Wilson cited evidence that state differentials in tax rates probably have a negligible effect on rates of economic growth, and European analysts have reached similar conclusions.[31] Furthermore, there are threats to the validity of purported relationships between state actions and observed outcomes. A state high-tech plan is likely to be both a cause and an effect of technological growth: it may be just as probable that such programs will result from states' attempts to exploit their existing resources and advantages as it is that they will result from attempts to overcome a state's shortcomings. If a state's program appears to be succeeding, will it be possible to distinguish the effects of the program from the effects of the conditions that made the program feasible (which may have had an independent effect on economic growth)? Glasmeier demonstrated that a high ratio of high-tech to low-tech manufacturing in smaller states with little manufacturing history may be the result of a small denominator. Rees and Lewington wrote about a "long-term process of regional convergence in per capita incomes," which could obfuscate the effects of state programs; similar structural convergences are likely to explain at least part of the variance in rates of technological progress across states.

Finally, the political context of state economic development programs reinforces the need for caution in interpreting actions, their purposes, and their consequences. Priorities change, and some "technology development" programs actually may be traditional policies dressed in new clothing. Some state efforts will be primarily defensive and imitative, and these programs should not be assessed by the same standards as truly innovative and energetic programs. An analysis of state programs that ignores political implications trades tractability for validity.

Implications for governance

A shift of policy making to the state level will affect the allocation of the nation's resources, and therefore will be politicized. There are several possible perspectives on the rôle of politics in shaping state policies. First, politics may be seen as a complication, since it introduces criteria other than competitiveness and efficiency to the shaping of economic development. Second, the involvement of the public, either directly or through their representatives, may be viewed as inherently beneficial in so far as it forces society to make adjustments for systemic failures. A third perspective is that the "ascent" of the states by itself promises no greater or lesser politicization of economic development, nor does it automatically mean that the collective wisdom of the public will find a more direct path into the decision-making process.

Politics as a complication

The "Technopolis Wheel" of Gibson and Smilor (Ch.15) provides an interesting starting point. The wheel is based on a conception of a system of government that is divided into seven major conceptual segments whose members "must find ways to cooperate while competing." In essence, this model is a simplified version of a plural society in which power is expressed by interest groups and in which the public interest is promoted through an open struggle among groups who must form moderating coalitions to win majority votes. The most important objective of such a polity is the creation of relatively stable *balances* among interests.[32] Those balances are necessary not only among political parties and candidates but also among social groups, business interests, ideological factions, and so on. The primary objective is *not* high technology, economic development, or job creation, but rather the production of satisfactory solutions that most citizens view as legitimate, if not ideal. (In this sense, the politics of economic development is very similar to the politics of other policy issues.) A form of balancing might also be achieved by a structure known as "corporatism": an "ideal institutional arrangement for linking the associationally organized interests of civil society with the decisional structures of the state."[33] In contrast to the pluralist model, corporatism is not competitive but consensual, entry into the policy process is not free-wheeling but controlled, participants are not numerous but limited in number, lobbying is targeted not at legislators but at a select group of administrators, and decision making is less political and more technocratic. Interests are granted a deliberate representational monopoly within their respective categories in exchange for observing certain controls on their selection of leaders and articulation of demands and supports.

But what are the likely effects of greater state efforts on the participation of groups and individuals in political decision making, and second, what impacts will this participation have on the *substance* of technology development policies? To begin with first principles, we should consider James Madison's defense of the Constitution that the states were being asked to ratify. He wrote in the *Federalist* of the logic of federalism:

> The smaller the society, the fewer probably will be the distinct parties and interests composing it; the fewer the distinct parties and interests, the more frequently will a majority be found of the same party; and the smaller the number of individuals composing a majority, and the smaller the compass within which they are placed, the more easily will they concert and execute their plans of oppression. Extend the sphere, and you take in a greater variety of parties and interests; you make it less probable that a majority of the whole will have a common motive to invade the rights of other citizens; or if such a common motive exists, it will be more difficult for all who feel it to discover their own strength, and to act in unison with each other.

Madison and his associates based the Constitution on this principle—simple in principle but untidy in execution—in order to increase the likelihood that a majority would never be able to deprive any minority of their natural rights and to ensure that a complex, extended society would create enough fragmented interests to prevent any tyranny of the majority. The "great and aggregate interests" would be referred to the national government, while the "local and particular" would be governed by the state legislatures. The object was to be a balance between "the public weal" and "local prejudices." No exact formula was proposed.

An enhanced rôle for the states—whether pluralist or corporatist—offers no inherent subversion or support of the Madisonian concept of federalism except in policy areas excluded by the Constitution, such as fundamental political rights, coinage of money, treaties with other nations, or regulation of interstate and foreign commerce. With these exceptions, the resurgence of the states in making policy for the "local and particular" is consistent with Constitutional principles. In fact, there is room for state activism to increase the protections sought by the Framers *if* the balancing of interests that occurs in the state capitol is more likely, *and* includes more interests, than policy making that occurs in Washington. This outcome often is assumed by advocates of decentralization of political power from the national government to the states, but unfortunately, it is not at all certain.

Public participation

It does not appear that the resurgence of the states was sparked by—or created—an increase in political activism at the state and local level. There was no bottom-up groundswell of support for an expansion of state economic development programs, for an increase in funding for advanced-technology industries, or for a shift of university responsibilities toward the training of skilled workers and entrepreneurs. At best, the general public usually has provided a rather poorly articulated set of broad demands for "better jobs," "more opportunity," and economic growth. Nevertheless, the new and strengthened functions of state government discussed in this book relate directly to public participation in policy making.

Many potential obstacles to "improved" governance at the state level can be discovered either in experience or by conjecture. First, the outcomes of political battles often are determined by the relative concentration of benefits and costs for those who will win or lose from proposed policies, so any tilt toward greater concentration for any interest as a result of a shift to the states will have direct political consequences. If the losers become more likely to lose, then the legitimacy of the system of governance will have suffered. Because the benefits (at least in the short term) of high-tech assistance policies will accrue primarily (or so it is likely to appear) to relatively small, well-educated, affluent groups (who are already more politically active than the more poorly endowed citizens), the process is likely to appear *less* legitimate to many. Whether this tendency will dwindle as policies shift from direct business assistance efforts to broader structural policies (that is, infrastructure development and human resource development) will depend as much on *perceived* fairness as on actual distributions of benefits. In addition, history has shown (particulary during the 1860s and 1950s–60s) that the groups that are the most disenfranchised have tended to fare better when their causes were heard at the national level rather than in the states.

A second implication follows from the proliferation of economic development policies, strategies, and tools at the state and local level. At the national level there are many access points for participation within the legislative, judicial, and bureaucratic processes, and proposed policies usually must fail only once to fail completely; the advantage, then, is for those who wish to block an action. With a devolution of political power away from Washington, however, there will be more arenas in which the winners can win (potentially 50 states, 3,000 counties, and nearly 36,000 cities and towns), but also more in which the losers can lose. For example, a group concerned about the environmental implications of using toxic solvents in semiconductor production techniques would "fail" if only one state or locality embraced a potential employer whom the group perceived to be endangering employees or neighbors, yet the firm would "win" if it found that one hungry location. Thus, the costs of participation (and therefore the odds of success) shift.

Public wisdom and control

Such outcomes are likely because of several characteristics of state policy making. Americans are less likely to know the names of their governors and mayors than the name of the president, and although 46 percent can name their congressman and 39 percent can name both senators from their state, only 28 percent can name their state senator.[34] State politics and policies are usually less salient to the public than national politics and issues, in part because Americans rely on network television news for much of their information. In addition, a mobile population finds it difficult to focus on local issues that may be relevant only until the next household move. Voting turnout for gubernatorial elections is usually smaller than turnout for presidential elections, and other forms of political participation also reflect the rather low esteem in which citizens generally hold their state governments.[35] Direct forms of public participation such as the initiative may appear appealing, but they conflict with the concept of representative democracy and they invite well-financed interests to wage expensive and one-sided media campaigns.[36] In their analysis of federalism and regulation, Mashaw and Rose-Ackerman found that, contrary to popular wisdom, participation is "a 'natural' result of decentralization" and state government "may be optimally designed, not for democratic responsiveness, but for special-interest capture."[37]

Furthermore, state governments are likely to take many of the actions proposed for economic development quietly and unobtrusively. Industrial development bonds fuel neither public passions nor headlines. Few voters will show concern about a $2 million state seed capital fund, and groups will not organize to oppose high-tech business incubators. This lack of attention is not always a result of closed procedures in state government; to the contrary, all states have open meeting laws (although the meaning of "meeting" is stretched creatively sometimes), and states adopted open records laws before the national government. Yet most citizens remain uninvolved by choice, by unawareness of choices, or by opportunity costs. A study by the Advisory Commission on Intergovernmental Relations found that explicit statutory provisions for community involvement in federal revenue sharing laws had little impact on decisions at the state level.[38]

The prospects for expanded participation by decentralization of political action need not be entirely dismal, however. Whether for reasons of conscience or to abort the potential for conflict, state officials may actively recruit the less established interests by offering parallel programs for low-tech industries, farmers, and service workers. Federal incentives to states to promote public participation are likely to infect even those programs that have no direct federal ties. As Paget found in her study of powerful public universities, the producers of what the states want are not always united and dominant. And there are examples like Rhode Island's 1984 "Greenhouse Compact," which the voters of the state rejected by a margin of 4:1. This plan, devised by the Governor's Strategic Development Commission, included industrial subsidies, education and training programs, high-tech incubators, and venture capital incentives. It was developed and endorsed by a broad coalition of business, university leaders, statewide newspapers, the AFL-CIO, both political parties, members of Congress, and the state legislative leadership—a perfect corporatist compact that failed in a public referendum because, according to a public opinion survey, 80 percent of voters believed that "too many special interests" had contrived an élitist boondoggle for banks, politicians, and big business.[39] The Rhode Island experience illustrates Jurgen Schmandt's observation that the close partnership between government and private institutions has been criticized for its diffusion of public and private responsibilities, its lack of political accountability, and its tendency to prefer costly and hardware-oriented solutions in assessing policy alternatives.[40]

Other examples are not reassuring to proponents of decentralization of decision making as a tool of direct democracy. A survey in January 1988 found that 56 percent of the voters in North Carolina knew nothing about the proposed Superconducting Supercollider, which the governor had already spent $1.5 million to promote and for which he had promised $152 million for roads and schools; of those who had heard or read of it, 48 percent favored the project's location in their state, while 36 percent said that it would not be worth the cost.[41] Lack of understanding is hardly the voter's fault in every case; a proposed constitutional amendment on a 1988 Georgia ballot asked voters, "Shall the Constitution be amended so as to allow the owner of property located within a constitutional industrial area located on an island voluntarily to remove the property from such industrial area?" The purpose of the amendment was to allow the city of Savannah to annex Hutchinson Island, site of a proposed $500 million commercial and residential development, but few voters could have known that.

The evidence suggests that the results of increased public awareness and participation in state-level formulation of policies may not be what advocates of those actions intended. From NIMBY ("Not In My Backyard") to IMFY ("In My Front Yard"), the public confounds policy makers' best plans; that is why the public was given a rôle.

Implications of state attempts

A complete analysis of state economic development efforts will take into account the broader implications of successes (however they are defined), of failed attempts, and of failures *to* attempt. A complete list is not possible, but several effects should be considered.

Zero-sum or positive-sum?

The language sometimes used in examinations of state economic development programs suggests that the supply of ingenuity, resources, finances, and jobs is fixed: states wish to *lure* firms away from other states, they *compete*, and they try to counter the *threats* posed by other states or nations. As Wilson observed, the zero-sum assumption underlies the use of incentives, and it is clearly manifested in the increasing attempts by states and universities to attract research funding through "pork-barrel" science appropriations rather than traditional peer-review processes. Illustrations are plentiful; in 1987, for example, the governor of Minnesota responded to a decision by US West to locate a $50 million telecommunications research facility in Colorado by urging the University of Minnesota to increase its contribution to the state's economic development effort (and, perhaps, to find "beer-drinking lobbyists" who might be more successful than professors).[42] Evidence of the zero-sum assumption was also evident in Georgia's efforts to create a Seed Capital Fund for "small, young, entrepreneurial firms engaged in innovative work in the areas of technology, manufacturing, or agriculture": one advocate told the state legislature, "If we do not start soon, it will be too late. I hope that next year you do not receive a report on how well South Carolina or Alabama are doing, and how much further behind we are."[43]

The zero-sum assumption has direct implications for state policy making. Competition among states for the same firms and activities will raise not only the stakes but also the costs of recruitment. As a result, proposals for multistate efforts may increase, helping states to avoid a type of "prisoner's dilemma," in which noncooperation would ultimately damage the interests of all, while cooperation would be mutually beneficial. Irwin Feller's description of the current era as a "period of 'positive-sum' aspirations" referred to collaboration *within* states, but the logic applies more widely as well.

It is important to ask to what degree the zero-sum assumption is widespread and persistent, or whether it has been yielding to a broader perspective, one that sees the interrelatedness of state, national, and international forces in technological change and economic development.[44] Further research is needed to determine whether the causes and effects of the shifts discussed in this book include a shift toward a positive-sum point of view. There is evidence of increasing exploitation of indigenous resources, including human capital, and technological change itself implies increased efficiency and new uses for familiar resources. If the states are able to transcend the narrow, short-term, competitive focus on their own interests in favor of a more integrated, resource-driven perspective, then their potential for a larger rôle in economic development is greatly enhanced.

Duplication of efforts

The degree to which research and development benefit or suffer from independence is as much a question for philosophers of science as it is a subject for economists. Are concepts such as economies of scale and natural monopoly appropriate in investigations of technological innovation? It would be helpful to know whether states are any better than the federal government at fulfilling one of the most important tasks of technology policy: distinguishing those areas of research and development where it is desirable to coordinate public and private efforts from those areas where duplication and even confusion are tolerable or desirable. Coordination of research efforts is advantageous in some realms but not in all.[45] For example, no one insists that only one approach or one institution be employed in cancer research. Like government and business, science is both competitive and collaborative. The challenge is to define "research efficiency" or "scientific productivity." There is no formula for determining when one laboratory, or one state, should be allocated a particular research or development task. To succeed, research and development must be able to pursue what will later be revealed as dead ends, yet some paths must be predicted well enough to rule out some courses of action.

Distribution of benefits

Attempts to stimulate economic development through state technology policies are certain to include two characteristics: increased use of public universities for commercial ends, and redistribution of wealth and opportunities. Writing on the first point, Feller and Paget demonstrated that the exploitation of educational systems is appropriate until the basic task—education—begins to be undermined by drains on resources, secrecy, or other demands. A particular problem for states will be to capture the benefits produced by educational investments.[46] Rosenfeld and Atkinson argued that generalizations about the supply of trained workers are risky since the mobility of skilled workers differs widely by area of specialization, with engineers and scientists being particularly "footloose." In summary, they say that "although additional support for higher education will not automatically translate into increased economic activity being attracted to the state, it is a necessary and important prerequisite." The indirect benefits are likely to be significant yet difficult to prove.

State efforts to encourage technological development will spread benefits unevenly, both geographically and socially. To Rosenfeld and Atkinson, the tendency for technical resources to concentrate in relatively few urban areas is "an especially thorny policy issue"; Fosler discussed the possibility that state officials may feel compelled "simply to pursue the best opportunity of the moment," without being able to aim benefits evenly at regions and groups; Glasmeier showed that for some industries, such as microelectronics and computers, the suburbs win; and Grubb exposed the rationales that will induce states to provide public subsidies for the private costs to firms of supplying themselves with trained workers.

The Research Triangle Park effect ("the poor and less educated are being squeezed out through a kind of high-tech gentrification") will not be an isolated incident.[47] Increasingly, rural counties with traditional manufacturing bases are finding it difficult to maintain wage competitiveness with expanding white-collar suburbs. Policy makers and policy advocates will confront two politically important questions. First, is it possible to offer adequate compensation in the form of alternative benefits to those who perceive themselves, accurately or not, as being completely divorced from the high-tech phenomenon? The answer will be determined by political incentives.

Second, is it possible confidently to assert that the *net* state or national social welfare is enhanced by competition among the states? Wilson argued that "though there is nothing wrong, in principle, with direct competition among states in industrial recruitment, the long-term effectiveness of this strategy for individual states is questionable and certainly does little to improve the national economy." In contrast, Malecki found that efforts to attract R&D facilities are likely to have indirect but significant benefits in general, such as longer-term perspectives and enhanced "intellectual climates."

Failed state efforts should be examined for evidence of gains, and the data base here is not so small. For example, after Atlanta came in second to Austin in the contest for MCC, the state developed the Georgia Research Consortium in order to be prepared for the next opportunity. Georgia provided $75 million to universities during the next four years, and state officials claimed that the framework for productive collaboration among the universities, businesses, and government of the state was a resounding success. It would be difficult to know whether this or other forms of cooperation would have emerged anyway. Similarly, when Sematech chose Austin for its advanced research facility (after three dozen states offered free space at university research parks, low-interest loans, and cash), the other 11 finalists received $50,000 planning grants to help them develop the capacity to be chosen for contractual research projects.

An extreme prospect for the future is suggested by the history of the Economic Development Administration, begun in 1961 to provide small grants and loans for "depressed areas" with high unemployment and poverty levels. The counties that qualified initially included less than 5 percent of the American population, but political forces had their effect: by 1980 the program included 2,500 of the nation's 3,000 counties and nearly 85 percent of the population.[48] A proliferation of state economic development programs may someday lead to the designation of the entire United States as a "technologically depressed area," qualifying for special benefits.

Conclusion

The contributions to this book reflect deep insights into many significant aspects of technology policy and state economic development. Obviously, given the experimental and dynamic nature of American policy making, much work will always remain. Nevertheless, several problems in our current knowledge are particularly pressing. First, there is a great need for more research on past state efforts. Rees and Lewington, Malecki, Feller, Marshall, and other authors have demonstrated that analyses of complex phenomena do not need to simplify away the essence of the issue, whether it is the nature of technological development, the forces that drive entrepreneurship, or the relationships among state institutions. The wide array of policy instruments discussed in this book suggests an ample supply of research topics. Second, it is crucial that researchers develop better data on current problems and policies; state-level science and technology indicators are very difficult to find, and when coupled with data obstacles for state-level economic variables, this gap has the potential to stymie future analysts. Finally, given the multiple objectives, conflicting perspectives, and shift ing priorities discussed in this book, many researchers would benefit from personal involvement in state policy making. The validity threats that result from such participation are smaller than the losses of explana-tory power that result from poorly specified models and experiments.

Of course, states cannot completely determine their own economic destinies. However, we have seen that there are promising new approaches that are already being tested in a variety of states. There also appears to be sufficient political support for state governments to continue developing new strategies for growth, although conflicts are inevitable as new patterns of opportunity and wealth emerge. In their introduction, Schmandt and Wilson indicated that a blurring of the high-tech/traditional manufacturing dichotomy will weaken the political opposition to states' efforts.

States will be experimenting with new policy approaches in a highly unstable arena. They can attempt to protect themselves by providing appropriate tools and opportunities for their citizens, but the states will remain largely reactive as national and international events continually reshape their context. The evidence points to education as the key: it is a necessary but not sufficient condition for technological and economic growth, because its effects are uncertain, uncapturable, and mostly long-term. As Wilson, Grubb, and Paget emphasized, the educational systems of states serve many goals simultaneously, and exploitation of any particular aspect of the educational system for particular purposes will impose costs, many of which will be subtle. Similarly, a favorable business climate is necessary, but the state rôle will be largely limited to encouraging a creative business sector and aiding the formation of networks among creative researchers. There is little evidence that states will find the keys to placing technology or job creation precisely where they want them. Their efforts may be most successful when they aim at creating a sufficient critical mass of the correct combination of intellectual and labor skills, financial resources, and optimism, but it is not yet clear what constitutes a "sufficient" critical mass. What appears to be clear is the salience of Marshall's comment (not only for students and workers but for policy makers and analysts): "we will now have to think for a living."

It is tempting to ask, "Who will be the winners?" Unfortunately, such a question ignores the basic argument of this chapter. No state, industry, group, or region can be named, because there are too many ways to measure success. Perhaps it would be the state with the highest number of high-tech jobs, or perhaps the state with the highest rate of transformation. The most successful state could be the one that excels in isolating itself from the buffeting of federal and international forces, or it could be the one that builds the most extensive ties with external economies. The winner could be defined as the group, industry, program, or political leader that develops the most emulated program (to many in the 1980s, that state was North Carolina), but the winner also could be the quiet, gradual, long-term evolver that builds a strong educational base and infrastructure years before claiming job creation. And, as we have seen, many will measure success in terms of the perceived equity of distribution; the truest form of succeeding might be found in the streets of inner cities rather than in gleaming technology parks. In short, as the state rôle in economic development grows, so will the number of dimensions on which it will be judged.

By definition, growth requires change, and the acceleration of technological change in industry and academia will stymie the best attempts of officials to designate the precise needs, opportunities, and resources of the state. Thus, states will be attempting to fulfill their responsibilities to be cautious and innovative at the same time. They will need to balance risks—not to find the "correct" solutions in a technical sense, but to discover those policies that balance current needs and the long-term welfare of their citizens.[49] The most successful state economic development programs could be those in which control and influence become *futile* because of the inherent dynamism of the technological sector. We should expect to see a variety of policy instruments being developed and tested, in various combinations, as states continue to do what they have done so well for more than a century: to continue the experiments in the politics and economics of progress.

Notes

1 See D. Osborne, *The next agenda: governors and state economic development* (Cambridge, Mass.: Harvard Business School Press, 1988).
2 S. A. Merrill, "The politics of micropolicy: innovation and industrial policy in the United States," in *Government innovation policy: design, implementation, evaluation*, ed. J. D. Roessner (New York: St. Martin's Press, 1988).
3 N. Rosenberg & L. E. Birdzell, Jr., *How the West grew rich: the economic transformation of the industrial world* (New York: Basic Books, 1986).
4 J. W. Sommer, "Distributional character and consequences of the public funding of science," paper prepared for Western Regional Science Association meetings, Kona, Hawaii, 1987, p. 37.
5 In Chapter 5 of this volume Malecki discussed four types of technological change specifically as they affect the location of economic activity. My purpose in this

section is broader: how technology affects the policy process generally. The key conclusion is similar, however. Each type of technological change has differential effects—on groups, over time, across industries and regions, and so on.

6 See U.S. Congress, Office of Technology Assessment, *Research funding as an investment: can we measure the returns?* (Washington, D.C.: Government Printing Office, 1986); and N. Rosenberg, *Inside the black box: technology and economics* (New York: Cambridge University Press, 1982).

7 A. O'M. Bowman & R. C. Kearney, *The resurgence of the states* (Englewood Cliffs, N.J.: Prentice-Hall, 1986) p. 27.

8 D. R. Judd & R. L. Ready, "Entrepreneurial cities and the new policies of economic development," in *Reagan and the cities*, ed. G. E. Peterson and C. W. Lewis (Washington, D.C.: Urban Institute Press, 1986).

9 By 1988, 41 states had joined in eight regional nuclear waste compacts to choose disposal sites under the prodding of the federal government's 1980 Low-Level Radioactive Waste Policy Act, but popular opposition to the agreements had forced Nebraska to hold an initiative on whether to pull out of the five-state Central Interstate compact, and other states were under similar pressure.

10 S. A. MacManus, "Linking state employment and training and economic development programs: a 20-state analysis," *Public Administration Review* 46, November/December 1986, 640–50.

11 B. Herrick & C. P. Kindleberger, *Economic development*, 4th edn. (New York: McGraw-Hill, 1983).

12 "New York funds the light fantastic," *Governing*, April 1988, 13.

13 The central rôle attributed to transportation and other physical infrastructures in making regions attractive to high-tech industries is in odd conflict with some of the assumptions that underlie much of the policy advocacy; many proponents of emphasizing high technology over traditional manufacturing industries probably envision clean, electronic, or cerebral means of production that require no heavy trucking or waste treatment.

14 For example, in assessing the increase in the number of international firms doing business in Georgia (from about 150 in 1976 to nearly 1,200 in 1988), state economic development officials perceive the most important factor to be the advent of direct international flights to and from Atlanta.

15 An example is the Stevenson-Wydler Act, which requires national laboratories to spend 0.5 percent of their budget on the transfer of developed technologies to other users, including industry.

16 See, for example, F. W. Wolek, "Guayule: a case study in civilian technology," *Technology in Society* 7, 1985, 11–23.

17 R. V. Bruce described the factors that created Boston's ascendancy in science during the early 19th Century in *The launching of American science 1846–1876* (Ithaca, N.Y.: Cornell University Press, 1987). These included the city's age, quality of life, natural environment, spirit and values (particularly hard work and devotion to education), élite patronage, and scientific institutions (societies, libraries, and Harvard College).

18 T. C. Hayes, "Triangle Park: North Carolina's high-tech payoff," *New York Times*, April 26, 1987, 12F.

19 E. B. Herzik, "Governors and the issues," *State Government* 56, November 1983, 58–64.

20 R. W. Schmenner, "Industrial location and urban public management," in *The perspective city*, ed. A. P. Solomon (Boston: MIT Press, 1980).

21 Judd & Ready, "Entrepreneurial cities and the new policies of economic development," p. 217.

22 M. Diamond, "The ends of federalism," in *The federal polity*, ed. D. J. Elazar (New Brunswick, N.J.: Transaction Books, 1974). Also see M. Derthick, "American federalism: Madison's middle ground in the 1980s," *Public Administration Review* 47, 1987.

23 W. H. Stewart, "Metaphors, models and the development of federal theory," *Publius* **12**, Spring 1982, 5–24.

24 R. W. Lotchin, *The martial metropolis: U.S. cities in war and peace* (New York: Praeger, 1984).

25 *Governing*, December 1987, pp. 15–16.

26 Congressional Budget Office, *The federal role in state industrial development programs* (Washington, D.C.: Government Printing Office, 1984).

27 K. Sylvester, "Exploring made easy (or how states and cities are selling products overseas)," *Governing* **1**, January 1988, 36–43.

28 R. P. Barke, "State and federal capabilities for structuring scientific and technological information," unpublished manuscript, 1986.

29 J. L. Mashaw & S. Rose-Ackerman, "Federalism and regulation," prepared for the Urban Institute Workshop on "The Reagan Administration's regulatory relief effort: a midterm assessment," Washington, D.C., June 13–14, 1983.

30 One state industrial planner revealed that, after receiving inquiries from firms about industrial locations, his first call is always to the state Department of Natural Resources to find out which areas cannot be considered.

31 See W. B. Stohr, "Toward a framework for evaluating the effects of technology complexes and science parks," *Economia Internazionale* **39**, May/November 1986, 299–311.

32 R. P. Barke, *Science, technology, and public policy* (Washington, D.C.: Congressional Quarterly Press, 1986).

33 P. Schmitter, "Still the century of corporatism?" in *Trends toward corporatist intermediation*, ed. P. Schmitter & G. Lehmbruch (Beverly Hills, Calif.: Sage Publications, 1979), p. 9.

34 R. S. Erikson, N. R. Luttbeg & K. L. Tedin, *American public opinion: its origins, content, and impact*, 3rd edn. (New York: Wiley, 1988) p. 42.

35 Bowman & Kearney, *The resurgence of the states*, pp. 107–9.

36 W. Pound & L. Simon, "A political tide continues to ebb and flow," *State Legislatures* **11**, January 1985, 11–17; and Bowman & Kearney, *The resurgence of the states*, pp. 113–19.

37 Mashaw & Rose-Ackerman, "Federalism and regulation," p. 16.

38 Bowman & Kearney, *The resurgence of the states*, p. 126.

39 J. Carroll, M. Hyde & W. Hudson, "Economic development policy: why Rhode Islanders rejected the Greenhouse Compact," *State Government* **58**, Fall 1985, 110–12.

40 J. Schmandt, "Toward a theory of the modern state: administrative versus scientific state," in *Technology and international affairs*, ed. J. S. Szyliowicz (New York: Praeger, 1981), p. 71.

41 *Atlanta Journal*, January 31, 1988, 25a.

42 *Governing*, February 1988, 10–11.

43 R. G. Schwartz, statement to House Committee on University System of Georgia, Georgia General Assembly, Atlanta, 1988.

44 For a cogent argument against the zero-sum perspective, see R. C. Feiock & M. Dubnick, "The positive effect of state economic development policies on economic growth in the U.S.," paper presented at the annual meeting of the Southern Political Science Association, Atlanta, November 3–5, 1988.

45 Barke, *Science, technology, and public policy*.

46 In at least one state, this imbalance of tasks has led to proposals that university economic development programs (such as technology incubators and applied research consortia) be administered by new allocational and governance institutions that would be free of demands to distribute *educational* resources according to traditional or political formulas.

47 Hayes, "Triangle Park: North Carolina's high-tech payoff."

48 D. S. Wright, *Understanding intergovernmental relations*, 3rd edn. (Pacific Grove, Calif.: Brooks/Cole, 1988).

49 A workshop of the Government/University/Industry Research Roundtable referred
    to this distinction as "proximate goals" and "ultimate goals"; the group recognized
    the methodological difficulties in identifying and measuring each, but particularly
    proximate goals (given the weak understanding of their economic impacts). See
    *State government strategies for self-assessment of science and technology programs
    for economic development* (Washington, D.C.: National Research Council, April 1987).

Index

References in italics are to figures

For Product Safety Concerns and Information please contact our
EU representative GPSR@taylorandfrancis.com Taylor & Francis
Verlag GmbH, Kaufingerstraße 24, 80331 München, Germany